ANALECTA BIBLICA

INVESTIGATIONES SCIENTIFICAE IN RES BIBLICAS

—————————————— 114 ——————————————

JAMES McCAFFREY, O.C.D.

THE HOUSE WITH MANY ROOMS
THE TEMPLE THEME OF Jn. 14,2-3

ROMA
EDITRICE PONTIFICIO ISTITUTO BIBLICO
1988

Vidimus et approbamus ad normam Statutorum

Pontificii Instituti Biblici de Urbe
Romae, die 6 mensis octobris anni 1987

R. P. Albert Vanhoye, S.J.
R. P. Ignace de la Potterie, S.J.

ISBN 88-7653-114-9

© 1987 - E.P.I.B. - ROMA

Editrice Pontificia Università Gregoriana
Editrice Pontificio Istituto Biblico
Piazza della Pilotta, 35 - 00187 Rome, Italy

ACKNOWLEDGEMENTS

This volume contains the somewhat modified text of a doctoral thesis presented at the Biblical Institute in Rome on April, 2nd., 1981. It is now published with the approval of my moderator, A. Vanhoye, S.J. and of the second reader, I. de la Potterie, S.J. It was the latter who first stirred my interest in St. John's Gospel during my years of study at the Biblical Institute; and the former who guided this work to completion with consummate patience and skill. To both of these scholars I am deeply grateful.

However, there are several others who also deserve a word of thanks. I was first encouraged to undertake this work by J. McPolin, S.J. and it was he who also assured me in advance that I had the ability to execute it. Time has indeed vindicated his judgment. Besides, I am indebted to M. McNamara, M.S.C. for many valuable insights into the Targums. I am pleased to record my thanks here also to both of these men for their friendship and support during my years as professor of S. Scripture at Milltown Park, Dublin, and as Dean of the Faculty of Theology there. My thanks must also extend to my tutors and friends in the École Biblique, Jerusalem, where I researched some of the material for this thesis. The final completion of the work was rendered so much easier by the understanding and appreciation of my own Carmelite community here in Ushaw College, Durham. To them also a special word of thanks is due.

There is for me something curiously fitting that I should find myself during the final stages of this work as a lecturer and tutor at Ushaw College, Durham University, which can boast of such distinguished Johannine scholars as B. F. Westcott and C. K. Barrett. I was indeed fortunate to be able to discuss the central insight of this work with the latter.

Finally, I would like to offer this work in gratitude to the Mother of God. I do this in the firm belief that it contains some important insights worth recording. But if not, hopefully it will provide tinder at least to catch the spark of another man's fire.

SUMMARY OF CONTENTS

Part I – **The Jewish Background**

CHAPTER IV. *The Return of Jesus to take the Disciples*

Part II – **Text and Context**

CHAPTER V. *Literary Questions*

CHAPTER VI.   *John 14,2-3: A Second Level of Meaning*

CHAPTER VII. *Complementary Texts*

CHAPTER VIII.   *A Unity of Two Levels*

ABBREVIATIONS

BOOKS OF THE BIBLE

Old Testament			*New Testament*	
Gn	Jdt	Dn	Mt	Phlm
Ex	Est	Hos	Mk	Heb
Lv	Jb	Jl	Lk	Jas
Nm	Ps(s)	Am	Jn	1-2 Pt
Dt	Prv	Ob	Acts	1-3 Jn
Jos	Eccl	Jon	Rom	Jude
Jgs	Ct	Mi	1-2 Cor	Ap
Ru	Wis	Na	Gal	
1-2 Sm	Sir	Hb	Eph	
1-2 Kgs	Is	Zeph	Phil	
1-2 Chr	Jer	Hag	Col	
Ezr	Lam	Ze	1-2 Thes	
Neh	1 Bar	Mal	1-2 Tm	
Tb	Ez	1-2 Mc	Ti	

JEWISH EXTRA-BIBLICAL LITERATURE

Antiq	Antiquitates
Apc Abr	Apocalypse of Abraham
Apc Mos	Apocalypse of Moses
2 Bar	Syrian Apocalypse of Baruch (= II Baruch)
3 Bar	Greek Apocalypse of Baruch (= III Baruch)
Bell	Bellum Iudaicum
CD	Damascus Document
De post Caini	De posteritate Caini
3 Esd	III Esdras (= I Esdras LXX)
4 Esd	IV Esdras
Exsec	De Exsecrationibus
Jos	Flavius Josephus
Jub	Jubilees
Leg All	Legum Allegoriae
3 Mc	III Maccabees
4 Mc	IV Maccabees
Mish	Mishnah

Mos	De Vita Mosis
Phl	Philo
Pss Sol	Psalms of Solomon
Quaest Ex	Quaestiones in Exodum
IQ	Ist Qumran Cave
IQH	Hymns
IQpHab	Habakkuk Commentary
IQM	Rule of War
IQS	Manual of Discipline
IQSa	Additional two columns of IQS
IQSb	Additional columns of IQS (Blessings)
4Q	4th Qumran Cave
4QSl	The Holocaust of the Sabbath
4QFlor	Florilegium
4QTob ar^{a-d}	Fragments of Tobias, 4 Aramaic manuscripts
4QTob hebr^a	Fragments of Tobias, Hebrew manuscript
4QPB	Patriarchal Blessings
4QpIsa^d	Commentary on Isaiah, fourth copy
Sib Or	Sibylline Oracles
Spec	De Specialibus Legibus
Som	De Somniis
Tal	Talmud
Test Mos	Testament of Moses
Test XII Pat	Testament of the XII Patriarchs
Test Levi	Testament of Levi
Test Ben	Testament of Benjamin
Test Sim	Testament of Simeon
Test Judah	Testament of Judah
Test Sol	Testament of Solomon
Tg	Targum

JOURNALS, COLLECTIONS AND SERIES

AASOR	Annual of the American Schools of Oriental Research
AJT	American Journal of Theology
AnBib	Analecta Biblica
Angel	Angelicum
AssSeign	Assemblées du Seigneur
ATANT	Abhandlungen zur Theologie des Alten und Neuen Testaments
ATR	Anglican Theological Review
BA	Biblical Archaeologist
BASOR	Bulletin of the American Schools of Oriental Reaearch
BBB	Bonner Biblische Beiträge
BDF	F. Blass and A. Debrunner (as translated by R. W. Funk). *A Greek Grammar of the New Testament and Other Early Christian Literature*, Chicago, 1969

Bib	Biblica
BibOr	Bibbia e Oriente
BJRL	Bulletin of the John Ryland Library
BLE	Bulletin de Littérature Ecclésiastique
BRes	Biblical Research
BTB	Biblical Theology Bulletin
BuL	Bibel und Leben
BVC	Bible et Vie Chrétienne
BZ	Biblische Zeitschrift
BZAW	Beihefte zur Zeitschrift für die Alttestamentliche Wissenschaft
BZNW	Beihefte zur Zeitschrift für die Neutestamentliche Wissenschaft
CahRB	Cahiers Revue Biblique
CBQ	Catholic Biblical Quarterly
CCL	Corpus Christianorum. Series Latina
ChQR	Church Quarterly Review
CivCat	La Civiltà Cattolica
Conc	Concilium
ConiNT	Coniectanea Neotestamentica
CSCO	Corpus Scriptorum Christianorum Orientalium
CSEL	Corpus Scriptorum Ecclesiasticorum Latinorum
CultBibl	Cultura Biblica
DBS	Dictionnaire de la Bible, Supplément
DictSpir	Dictionnaire de Spiritualité
DivThom	Divus Thomas (Freiburg)
DThom	Divus Thomas (Piacenza)
EphCarm	Ephemerides Carmeliticae
EstBíbl	Estudios Bíblicos
ÉBib	Études Bibliques
EsprVie	Esprit et Vie
ETL	Ephemerides Theologicae Lovanienses
EvTh	Evangelische Theologie
Exp	Expositor
ExpT	Expository Times
FRLANT	Forschungen zur Religion und Literatur des Alten und Neuen Testaments, Göttingen
GL	Geist und Leben
Greg	Gregorianum
HeyJ	Heythrop Journal
HTKNT	Herders Theologischer Kommentar zum Neuen Testament
HTR	Harvard Theological Review
IBS	Irish Biblical Studies
ICC	The International Critical Commentary
Interp	Interpretation
Irén	Irénikon
ITQ	Irish Theological Quarterly
JBL	Journal of Biblical Literature
JNES	Journal of Near Eastern Studies
JSOT	Journal for the Study of the Old Testament

JTS	Journal of Theological Studies
LumV	Lumière et Vie
MelSRel	Mélanges de Science Religieuse
MillSt	Milltown Studies
MTZ	Münchener Theologische Zeitschrift
NovT	Novum Testamentum
NovTSup	Novum Testamentum, Supplements
NRT	Nouvelle Revue Théologique
NTA	New Testament Abstracts
NTS	New Testament Studies
PG	Patrologia Graeca
PL	Patrologia Latina
PO	Patrologia Orientalis
RB	Revue Biblique
RBibIT	Rivista Biblica
RechBibl	Recherches Bibliques
RecSR	Recherches de Science Religieuse
RHPR	Revue d'Histoire et de Philosophie Religieuse
RQ	Revue de Qumran
RSPT	Revue des Sciences Philosophiques et Théologiques
RT	Revue Thomiste
RThPh	Revue de Théologie et de Philosophie
SacrPag	Sacra Pagina. Miscellanea biblica Congressus internationalis catholici de re biblica, Paris-Gembloux, 1959
Sal	Salesianum
SBT	Studies in Biblical Theology
ScEcc	Sciences Ecclésiastiques
SC	Sources Chrétiennes
Script	Scripture
StANT	Studien zum Alten und Neuen Testament
StB	Strack-Billerbeck, *Kommentar zum Neuen Testament aus Talmud und Midrash*
StudEvang I	Studia Evangelica. Papers presented to the International Congress on "The Four Gospels in 1957", Oxford, 1957 (TU 73), Berlin, 1959
StudEvang II	Studia Evangelica, vol. II. Papers presented to the Second International Congress on New Testament Studies. Part I: The New Testament Scriptures, Oxford, 1961 (TU 87), Berlin, 1964
SymbOs	Symbolae Osloenses
TD	Theology Digest
TDNT	Theological Dictionary of the New Testament
ThBl	Theologische Blätter
TLZ	Theologische Literaturzeitung
TR	Theologische Rundschau
TS	Theological Studies
TÜTQ	Tübinger Theologische Quartalschrift
TWAT	Theologisches Wörterbuch zum Alten Testament
TWNT	Theologisches Wörterbuch zum Neuen Testament

TZ	Theologische Zeitschrift
VD	Verbum Domini
VetTSup	Vetus Testamentum, Supplements
VieSP	Vie Spirituelle
VTB	Vocabulaire de Théologie Biblique
ZAW	Zeitschrift für die Alttestamentliche Wissenschaft
ZKT	Zeitschrift für Katholische Theologie
ZNW	Zeitschrift für die Neutestamentliche Wissenschaft und die Kunde der Älteren Kirche
ZTK	Zeitschrift für Theologie und Kirche

OTHER ABBREVIATIONS

BJ	Bible de Jérusalem (French edition)
GNT	The Greek New Testament, ed. by K. Aland, M. Black, B.-M. Metzger, A. Wikgren, Stuttgart, 1966
JB	Jerusalem Bible (English edition)
KJ	The Authorised Version of 1611, or the King James Bible
L.S.	Liddell, H. G.-Scott, R., *A Greek-English Lexicon*
LXX	The Septuagint
MT	Masoretic Text
NCB	New Clarendon Bible
NEB	New English Bible
NT	New Testament
OL	Old Latin (Vetus Latina)
OT	Old Testament
RSV	Revised Standard Version
SB	La Sainte Bible — "Bible de Jérusalem" — traduite en français. D. Mollat, *L'Évangile selon saint Jean*, Paris, ³1973
TOB	Traduction Oecuménique de la Bible
Vulg	Vulgate

The translations of biblical texts are taken from the *Revised Standard Version: Catholic Edition* unless otherwise indicated, or unless the argument demands a more literal rendering. Manuscript evidence for the text of the New Testament is cited according to the sigla of *The Greek New Testament*, ed. by K. Aland, M. Black, B.-M. Metzger, A. Wikgren, Stuttgart, 1966.

Commentators mentioned in the bibliography are cited by name, with *op. cit.* In citing other works, the full reference is given in the notes of each chapter and each subsequent reference to these same works in the chapter is given as *op. cit.*, with a reference to the note of the first citation in brackets, e.g. *op. cit.* (n. 7).

INTRODUCTION

A. ARGUMENT

The argument of this thesis may be stated briefly. It is concerned with the text of Jn 14,2-3. We find this text at the centre of the farewell discourses in the fourth gospel (13,1-17,26). The text describes the redemptive work of Christ in terms which pertain to the family and its intimate personal relationships.

But it is our contention that here there are also temple implications which are significant for a correct understanding of the text. In our view this text states in equivalent Johannine terms that the New Temple of the risen Jesus is the way of access to the heavenly temple of the Father's house.

More precisely we have interpreted the term τόπος (twice repeated) to mean "temple" or "sanctuary" (comp. 4,20: 11,48). Some scholars have intimated this.[1] But no one has provided extensive arguments in support of this meaning. Neither has anyone, to our knowledge, developed fully its implications for an understanding of Jn 14,2-3 as a whole. Such, hopefully, will be the contribution of this thesis.

B. PROBLEMS OF THE TEXT

The text bristles with difficulties. R. E. Brown observes laconically: "these two verses are extraordinarily difficult".[2] Here we find a strange blend of what is static and dynamic. There is something permanent and fixed about the text; and yet at the same time it has a perpetual movement of "going" and "coming". It is definite and at the same time

---

[1] See, A. M. SERRA, *Contributi dell'antica letteratura giudaica per l'esegesi di Giovanni, 2,1-12 e 19,25-27* (ROMA, 1977), 380; also J. MARSH, *op. cit.* 502. W. D. DAVIES expresses the same thought in more general terms. See, *The Gospel and the Land* (London, 1974), 318.

[2] See, *op. cit.* 625.

indefinite.[3] It is even cumbersome, with two apparent contradictions.[4] In it two different perspectives, the past and the future, seem to fuse. What is explicit can hardly be distinguished from what is implicit. Besides, it is difficult to know in what precise literary milieu we should search for the background to our text.[5]

So, too, the style is a subtle blend of spatial metaphors and existential language stripped of all imagery.[6] There is little comparable to it in the fourth gospel for sheer subtlety and richness of language.

The difficulties of the text are also clear from the inability of Thomas to understand the words of Jesus (14,5).[7] His hesitation alone suggests that the text is open to several possible interpretations none of which would seem to impose itself necessarily.

Besides, the text itself seems to be curiously incomplete. The immediate context is full of the activity of Jesus and that of the disciples. But our text refers only to the activity of Jesus, with no reference whatever to the response of the disciples.

Finally, there is no general agreement on whether the phrase εἰ δὲ μή (14,2b) is a statement or a question.[8] Even the accepted reading of Merk is by no means certain.[9]

---

[3] This indefinite aspect of the text has not passed unnoticed by the exegetes. R. Brêchet writes: "Le présent de venir laisse une certaine indétermination". See, "Du Christ à l'Eglise", *DivThom* 56 (1953) 89.

[4] Jesus apparently asserts that he is going to the Father's house (πορεύομαι) and that he is at the same time already there before the journey (ὅπου εἰμι ἐγώ); and he also promises to take the disciples "along with himself" (παραλήμψομαι) "to himself" (πρὸς ἐμαυτόν). Here A. L. Humphries argues strongly for the translation: "Take along with me to my home". See "A Note on πρὸς ἐμαυτόν (John xiv,3) and εἰς τα ἴδια (John 1,11)", *ExpT* 53 (1941) 356.

[5] C. H. Dodd outlines the various possibilities of background for the fourth gospel in general. See, *The Interpretation of the Fourth Gospel* (Cambridge, 1960) 10-130. G. Fischer provides a general outline of the background to Jn 14,2-3 in Gnostic and Mandean literature, in the OT, in Jewish Apocalyptic literature, and in later Jewish and Rabbinical literature. See, *Die himmlischen Wohnungen. Untersuchungen zu Joh 14,2f.* (Frankfurt/Main, 1975) 105-290. See also C. K. Barrett, *The Gospel of John and Judaism* (London, 1957).

[6] The phrase "where I am you also may be" of John 14,3c is no longer on the level of metaphor.

[7] On the Johannine technique of misunderstanding, see J. Leroy, *Rätsel und Missverständnis. Ein Beitrag zur Formgeschichte des Johannesevangeliums*, BBB 30 (Bonn, 1968); also O. Cullmann, "Der johanneische Gebrauch doppeldeutiger Ausdrücke als Schlüssel zum Verständnis des vierten Evangeliums", *TZ* 4 (1948) 360-372.

[8] G. Fischer has treated admirably of the text under this aspect. See *op. cit.* (n. 5) 35-56.

[9] There is considerable patristic evidence for reading "with my Father" (μαρὰ τῷ ματρί). See M.-E. Boismard, "Critique textuelle et citations patristiques", *RB* 57 (1950) 388-391.

C. USEFULNESS OF OUR STUDY

The text itself is supremely important. We may aptly apply to it the words of C. H. Dodd: "This is the climax towards which everything has been moving from the moment when Christ, in full consciousness of his unique relation to the Father, washed his disciples' feet that they might have part with Him. It is also the climax of the thought of the whole Gospel".[10]

There are indeed several factors which suggest that a more nuanced appraisal of the text may be useful. There is in the first place the dearth of bibliography, dealing directly with our text.[11] Articles are few.[12] The one brief and perceptive article which has appeared recently by R. H. Gundry entitled, "'In my Father's House are many Moναί' (John 14.2)" (1967), makes no mention of the temple theme in Jn 14,2-3.[13] Besides, there is a recent book devoted entirely to our text by G. Fischer, *Die himmlischen Wohnungen: Untersuchungen zu Joh 14,2f* (1975). This author explicitly rejects any reference to the temple in our text.[14] Apart from the commentators on the fourth gospel in general, very little work has been done on our text, and in particular practically nothing under the aspect of the temple theme.

Finally, we add as a motive for reassessment the confusion of the commentators.[15] The "Father's house" has been variously explained as

---

[10] See C. H. Dodd, *op. cit.* (n. 5) 419.

[11] Books on the temple in general are by no means lacking. Several more recent books treat admirably of the temple in general terms. See R. E. Clements, *God and Temple* (Oxford, 1965); R. J. McKelvey, *The New Temple. The Church in the New Testament.* (Oxford, 1969); Y. Congar, *The Mystery of the Temple* (London, 1962). Th. A. Busink, *Tempel von Jerusalem von Solomo bis Herodes. Eine archäologisch-historische Studie unter Berücksichtigung des westsemitischen Tempelbaus*, 2. Band: *Von Ezechiel bis Middot*, (Leiden, 1980). Clements, concerned almost exclusively with the OT treatment of the theme, never cites our text. Congar refers to it only once in a note (*op. cit.* 230, n. 6). McKelvey provides a brief, but very inadequate study of our text (*op. cit.* 140-141).

[12] We have discovered only seven articles which treat directly of our text. R. H. Gundry, "'In my Father's House are many Moναί' (John 14,2)", *ZNW* 58 (1967) 68-72; T. S. Berry, "Critical Note on St. John xiv,2", *Exp (2nd series)* 3 (1882) 397-400; J. Courtenay James, "Mansiones Multae", *ExpT* 27 (1915-1916) 427-428; A. L. Humphries, "A Note on πρὸς ἐμαυτόν (John xiv,3) and εἰς τα ἴδια (John 1,11)", *ExpT* 53 (1941) 356; O. Schaefer, "Der Sinn der Rede Jesu von den vielen Wohnungen in seines Vaters Hause und von dem Weg zu ihm (Joh. 14,1-2)", *ZNW* 32 (1933) 200-217; W. B. Bacon, "In my Father's house are many mansions (Jn 14,2)", *ExpT* 43 (1931-1932) 477-478; G. Widengren, "En la maison de mon Père sont demeures nombreuses", *Svensk Exegetisk Årsbok* 37-38 (1972-1973) 9-15.

[13] See, *op. cit.* (n. 12).

[14] see, *op. cit.* (n. 5) 68. 124. R. J. McKelvey also rejects any reference to the temple in our text. See *op. cit.* (n. 11) 141.

[15] The interpretations of the various commentators will be considered again later in more detail.

heaven, the heavenly temple, the messianic kingdom, even the universe. So, too, the μοναί or "dwelling-places" have been explained respectively as rooms, temple-rooms by analogy with the rooms in the Jerusalem temple, even as spiritual positions in Christ and different degrees of spiritual indwelling, and degrees of beatitude. The τόπος to be prepared has been variously explained as the disciples themselves, the upper room, the real and true passover, the temple of the body of Jesus, while the actual process of "preparation" has been explained with reference to the passion-death of Jesus. So, too, the "coming" of Jesus has been interpreted now as the final coming of the risen Jesus at the Parousia, now as his coming at the Easter apparitions, or at the moment of death, or even more specifically of martyrdom, and even with reference to a repeated coming of the risen Jesus in anticipation of his final coming.

It is reasonable to expect that a serious attempt to clarify this confusion would prove useful. This, however, will only be achieved if strict attention is given to method. We believe that we can achieve this clarification by the use of a rigorous method that suits the Johannine perspectives of the fourth gospel. Hence the importance of explaining our method.

D.   METHOD

We distinguish two levels of meaning in the text. In our use of this distinction we stand firmly in the company of Léon-Dufour, and several other distinguished commentators.[16] However, no author to our knowledge has applied the distinction of two levels to our text.

We would like to suggest an alternative designation to that of Léon-Dufour for this double meaning.[17] It seems preferable to us, because it is more faithful (in our view) to the Johannine perspectives of the fourth gospel. The first level of meaning would correspond to the meaning of the text understood as the gospel gradually unfolds, that is, prior to the passion-resurrection of Jesus; the second level of meaning would correspond to the meaning of the text understood in the light of the end of the gospel, that is, after the passion-resurrection of Jesus. Hence, we prefer to designate the two levels of meaning, the first level pre-Paschal; and the second level, post-Paschal, respectively.

This pre-Paschal or first level of understanding would correspond to the understanding, however imperfect, which the disciples had gained of

---

[16] See, D. W. WEAD, *The Literary Devices in the Fourth Gospel* (Basel, 1970) 1-11; O. CULLMANN, *Early Christian Worship* (London, 1953) passim; X. LÉON-DUFOUR, "Le signe du temple selon saint Jean", *RecSR* 39 (1951-1952) 155-175.

[17] X. LÉON-DUFOUR distinguishes the understanding of Jesus' audience and the understanding of the readers of the gospel. See, *op. cit.* (n. 16) 155-157. 159.

the person of Jesus through years of continual contact with him in his ministry. The failure of the disciples to understand Jesus fully is stated expressly by John in his gospel (comp. 13,7; 16,29-30). The first level would also correspond to the imperfect or incipient faith of the disciples prior to the passion-resurrection of Jesus (comp. 1,50; 2,11; 11,40).

The post-Paschal or second level of understanding would correspond to the deeper and fuller and more perfect understanding of the mystery of the person of Jesus after his passion-resurrection (8,28; 13,19; 14,29). This future deeper understanding of the disciples is again indicated expressly by John in his gospel (2,22; 12,16; 13,7). The second level would also correspond to the perfect faith of the disciples after the passion-resurrection under the action of the promised Paraclete (14,26; 16,13). It is nothing else than a deeper understanding of the words and actions of Jesus due to the working of the Spirit in the early Johannine church.

Several examples of explicit Johannine reinterpretation can be found in the fourth gospel (2,21; 11,51; 12,33).[18] We note with a view to our interpretation of 14,2-3 that all of these three explicit reinterpretations have a link with the temple theme, explicit (2,21) or implicit (11,51; cf. τόπος, 11,48; and 12,33; cf. ὑψόω, 12,32 and Is. 2,2). This would seem to indicate some preoccupation on the part of the evangelist to reinterpret the revelation of Jesus concerning his own person in the light of the temple theme.

Clearly, the text of the fourth gospel itself provides us with a solid basis for our method of interpretation. So much so that O. Cullmann can write: "the Gospel of John indicates in so many places the necessity of a double meaning, that enquiry into the deeper unexpressed sense is to be raised, in this gospel, to the status of a principle of interpretation."[19]

However, some further precision would appear to be necessary in order to avoid any possible ambiguity in the application of this principle of interpretation to our text. The text of Jn 14,2-3 forms part of a large discourse (13,31-17,26), which depends on an extended use of figurative language. John calls it a "paroimia" (16,25(2x).29; comp. 10,6). This is a general term for a figurative use of language. John is also explicit that such a figurative use of language will not be necessary later, when Jesus will no longer speak in figures (16,25). However, it is necessary for the moment to convey the deeper post-Paschal level of meaning.

Here in the discourse we also find a Johannine use of misunderstanding. We must be careful to distinguish between this misunderstanding and our two levels of meaning in the text. There is a

---

[18] We should distinguish these texts from Jn 7,39. This text is not strictly speaking a reinterpretation. It is only intelligible in a post-Paschal perspective.
[19] See, op. cit. (n. 16) 57.

misunderstanding of the text, because the disciples fail to see that Jesus is using metaphorical language. But the misunderstanding disappears, once it is understood that the language of the text is not to be taken in a material sense, but in a spiritual sense. However, the double level of meaning still remains. We know that the text is not to be taken in a material sense, but the spiritual sense cannot yet be defined precisely at a first level of meaning. This spiritual sense can only be defined at a second level of meaning in the light of the passion-resurrection.

It is important for our interpretation of Jn 14,2-3 to establish at the outset a first level of meaning. We can then proceed to investigate the meaning which the language of our text can also have in John, when we interpret it in a figurative sense at a second deeper post-Paschal level of meaning. This figurative sense of the language used by John cannot be entirely separated from the literal sense.[20] The language itself remains the same. The figurative use of it transfers the literal sense to a higher plane, or level of meaning. It does not contradict it.

We stress that there is a close and indissoluble unity between our two levels of understanding. This is basic to our method. There can be no dichotomy in the text. The second level of understanding, the post-Paschal, is merely a deeper understanding of the first level, the pre-Paschal: there is development from the first level of understanding to the second, not in the words and not in the actions of Jesus, but in our understanding of them, under the light of the Spirit.

E.   DIVISION

I.   Part I: **Jewish Background to Jn 14,2-3**

The first part of our thesis deals with the Jewish background to our text. This is preceded by a general chapter in which we provide an interpretation of our text at the first level of meaning; and at the same time open up the possibilities in the text for a deeper level of understanding. A study of the Jewish background will help us to establish, even more convincingly, this first level of meaning in our text.

The influence of the Jewish tradition on the formation of the fourth gospel in general is already widely accepted. We will explore this same

---

[20] The understanding of Jn 14,2-3 by the disciples in a literal sense, or the first level of meaning in our text, is not what is generally referred to as the sensus litteralis, or the literal sense of S. Scripture, which is the sense the human author directly intended and which his words convey. In our distinction of levels it is only the second level of meaning in the text that is directly intended by the sacred author.

tradition with reference to our text, and compare the vocabulary and perspectives of Jn 14,2-3 with it. Our approach is through the vocabulary to the themes which it evokes. In this way we hope to show how Jn 14,2-3 may be interpreted in continuity with that tradition, and at the same time to highlight the difference and show how we pass to a highter plane in John. Similarities, differences, and superiority are the three relationships which we will note in regard to the Johannine text when studied within the Jewish tradition.

Thus we hope to point out at least a possible way towards an understanding of Jn 14,2-3; and by stressing the complementary aspect of Christian revelation in John to show also in what way our text bears the stamp of Johannine originality. Only in this way can the Christian fulfilment in John be defined. We accept that fidelity to our method may prove somewhat tedious and repetitive at times, especially when it is sustained at length. But we hope that clarity and consistency will result and compensate somewhat for any uneasy flow of style.

Our method of procedure in this treatment of the background to our text cannot ignore the hesitation of Thomas expressed in 14,5. This indicates that there may be several interpretations of our text possible in line with the Jewish tradition. No single interpretation would necessarily exclude any other possible one, at least not at the first level of understanding. Our method will respect this openness of the text, and our conclusions will also be necessarily influenced by it; that is, they will be tentative.

2. Part II: **Text and Context of Jn 14,2-3**

This second part of our thesis deals directly with our text and its context, immediate and general. Here we will concentrate on the second deeper level of meaning in the text. However, some preliminary questions must first be resolved and the structure of the immediate context and of the text itself must be determined. Only then can we provide our complete interpretation of the text itself.

Here we will also provide a study of our text within the more general context of the fourth gospel. We will compare the perspectives of Jn 14,2-3 with those of other Johannine texts. These perspectives do not necessarily agree; there may be tension between them. By this comparison of texts we will try to isolate the similarities, the differences and those aspects which are complementary to our understanding of Jn 14,2-3. In this way we hope to clarify, support and complement our understanding of Jn 14,2-3 by what the rest of the gospel reveals to us of the Johannine perspectives. The evangelist is his own best commentator.

By way of conclusion to this second section, and to our thesis as a whole, we hope to show the close unity between our interpretation of the text at a first and second level of understanding.

Thus it is hoped that a comparison of Jn 14,2-3 with the literary milieu of the Jewish tradition which provides the background to it (Part I), and a precise analysis of the text itself within the immediate context, together with an examination of its links with other temple texts within the more general context of the fourth gospel (Part II) will yield a more nuanced interpretation of this central text of the fourth gospel.

CHAPTER I

JN 14,2-3: A FIRST LEVEL OF MEANING –
SOME DEEPER POSSIBILITIES OF THE TEXT?

A. TEXT [1]

In this thesis we are dealing directly with the following text:

14,2a ἐν τῇ οἰκίᾳ τοῦ πατρός μου μοναὶ πολλαί εἰσιν·
  2b εἰ δὲ μή, εἶπον ἂν ὑμῖν ὅτι πορεύομαι ἑτοιμάσαι τόπον ὑμῖν;
  3a καὶ ἐὰν πορευθῶ καὶ ἑτοιμάσω τόπον ὑμῖν,
  3b πάλιν ἔρχομαι καὶ παραλήμψομαι ὑμᾶς πρὸς ἐμαυτόν,
  3c ἵνα ὅπου εἰμὶ ἐγὼ καὶ ὑμεῖς ἦτε.

We translate as follows:

14,2a In my Father's house there are many rooms.
  2b If it were not so, would I have told you that I am going to prepare a place for you?
  3a And if I go and prepare a place for you,
  3b I will come again and I will take you to myself,
  3c in order that where I am you may be also.

B. INTERPRETATION

1. The goal of Jesus' Journey: the Father's house with the many rooms

(a) THE FATHER'S HOUSE. Here we offer at the outset an interpretation of our text at the first level of meaning, with some of the possibilities which it opens up in line with Johannine perspectives for a still deeper level of understanding. The first member states explicitly: "In my Father's house there are many rooms" (14,2a). Literally, the term

---

[1] We accept the text as we find it in the critical editions. See, A. MERK, *Novum Testamentum Graece et Latine* (Rome, 1957); D. E. NESTLE, *Novum Testamentum Graece et Latine* (Stuttgart, 1930); K. ALAND/M. BLACK/B. M. METZGER/A. WIKGREN, *The Greek New Testament* (Stuttgart, 1966).

οἰκία means "house".[2] In a material (or spatial) sense it refers to a building where one dwells. It is used in this sense in the fourth gospel (11,31; 12,3).[3] We find the term used in 14,2a in a metaphorical sense. It is a spatial metaphor to indicate the place where God, the Father of Jesus, dwells: his temple. However, the question of Thomas in 14,5 indicates some misunderstanding about the location of this Father's house. The text of the fourth gospel provides ample evidence to justify this confusion in the minds of the disciples about what precisely is intended by Jesus.

(i) *The Jerusalem Temple.* We find the same phrase "my Father's house" in almost identical terms in 2,16.[4] There is a clear verbal link between the two phrases:

2,16   τὸν οἶκον τοῦ πατρός μου-comp. τοῦ οἴκου σου (2,17).
14,2 ἐν τῇ οἰκίᾳ τοῦ πατρός μου.

The phrase is peculiar to John as a designation of the Jerusalem temple.[5] Besides, these are the only two explicit references to "the Father's house" in the fourth gospel. The definite article (τῇ), the possessive adjective (μου) and the possessive genitive (τοῦ πατρός) all designate this house of 14,2a as one which should be identifiable by the disciples. Moreover, the important and striking verbal link seems to indicate rather that the evangelist designedly repeats the phrase in 14,2-3 in order to recall the first reference to it in 2,16 (comp. 2,17);[6] and so deliberately describes the goal of Jesus' journey in order to evoke the idea of the Jerusalem temple with the phrase "in my Father's house". This is all the more likely against the OT and Jewish background where the Jerusalem temple is "the house of God" par excellence.[7] But Thomas confesses ignorance about where this Father's house is located in space (14,5). No such ignorance would be possible with reference to the Jerusalem temple alone. An alternative meaning for the phrase "my Father's house" would also seem to be required, then, in accordance with Johannine perspectives. Only in this way can we justify the misunderstanding and confusion of 14,5.

---

[2] See, O. MICHEL, *TDNT* V 131; also *L.S.* 120.

[3] The term οἰκία is found five times in the fourth gospel (4,53; 8,35; 11,31; 12,3; 14,2).

[4] The importance of this text for an understanding of 14,2-3 has been noted. See, O. SCHAEFER, "Der Sinn der Rede Jesu von den vielen Wohnungen in seines Vaters Hause und von dem Weg zu ihm (Joh. 14,2-3)", *ZNW* 32 (1933) 212; also R. E. BROWN, *op. cit.* 627; B. F. WESTCOTT 200. The sole difference between the two phrases is the use of οἶκος in 2,16 (also in 2,17) as distinct from οἰκία in 14,2. The reason for this change will be treated at length later.

[5] The phrase does not occur elsewhere in the NT. The closest parallel is Lk 2,49.

[6] O. MICHEL observes that the two expressions cannot be seen in isolation. See, *TDNT* V 132.

[7] The phrase οἶκος (τοῦ) Θεοῦ was the fixed and common one for the Jerusalem temple in the Jewish tradition.

(ii) *The Heavenly Temple.* Such an alternative meaning of the phrase is indeed possible. The Father's house might also be understood with reference to the heavenly temple. The Father's house is the goal of Jesus' journey. However, this same journey is explicitly designated in 16,28 as a departure of Jesus out of this world: "I am leaving this world again and I am journeying to the Father" (πάλιν ἀφίημι τὸν κόσμον καὶ πορεύομαι πρὸς τὸν πατέρα) (cf. also 17,11.12.13; comp. 13,1). The "world" (κόσμος) in this sense is the sphere of men, the disciples (cf. 17,11.13.15; comp. 13,1). But this is the negative aspect of Jesus' journey, the terminus a quo. Moreover, this is not explicit in 14,2-3. However, it is implied at least in 13,33, if the Father's house is understood as the heavenly goal of Jesus' journey: Jesus will be with his disciples only yet a little while (comp. 14,25).

The positive aspect of this journey, or the terminus ad quem, the goal, is the Father's house itself or the place where God, the Father of Jesus, dwells (cf. πρὸς τὸν πατέρα, 16,28; comp. 17,11.13). In the fourth gospel "heaven" is conceived as the place where the Father dwells. At prayer Jesus raises his eyes "upwards" to his Father in 11,41 (ἄνω ... Πάτερ). This is specified more precisely in 17,1 as to "heaven" to his Father (εἰς τὸν οὐρανόν... Πάτερ). In 12,28 the voice of the Father is heard from "heaven" (ἐκ τοῦ οὐρανοῦ). The Father's house, then, where Jesus journeys in 14,2-3, may be rightly understood in accord with Johannine perspectives as a reference to "heaven" (οὐρανός), the transcendent sphere of God, where the Father of Jesus dwells.

However, the term οἰκία is also open to interpretation in the more personal and spiritual sense of a "family" or "household".[8] In fact, John also employs the term οἰκία in this transferred sense of a "family" or "household" (cf. 4,53; 8,35). The figure of a "house" (οἰκία and cognates) is one of the most frequent metaphors in the NT for the believer's place in the domestic domain of God.[9] So, too, the use of the term τεκνία in 13,33 seems to suggest something of a filial relationship already existing in the disciples.[10] Moreover, a future filial relationship would also seem to be implied in the promise of Jesus not to leave his disciples ὀρφανοί in 14,18. Besides, the οἰκία is the place where Jesus dwells with his Father (ὅπου εἰμὶ ἐγώ) in the filial relationship of a Son (πατρός μου).

---

[8] See, *L.S.* 1203.

[9] On this aspect of NT thought, see A. Vanhoye, "La maison spirituelle (I P 2,1-10)", *AssSeign* 43 (1964) 16-29.

[10] The term τεκνία is used only here in the fourth gospel. However, it is common in the other Johannine writings (cf. I Jn 2,1.12.28; 3,7.18; 4,4; 5,21; comp. Gal 4,19). It is the diminutive form of the term τέκνον used three times in the fourth gospel (cf. 1,12; 8,39; 11,52).

The term οἰκία is clearly open to interpretation in the sense of "family" or "household" in 14,2-3. In fact, this is the sole meaning given to the term by R. H. Gundry.[11] However, this cannot be its sole meaning. Such a meaning would certainly be possible if the disciples were actually reunited personally with Jesus in his filial relationship with his Father in the house, or if the disciples actually occupied the house as members of a unified family. But for this the return of Jesus to take the disciples into such a unity in the Father's house would be necessary. Besides, to interpret in 14,2-3 as "family" or "household" is to go beyond the spatial imagery of the text to a deeper personal and spiritual reality which the term may signify (comp. 4,53; 8,35). Before the departure of Jesus the minds of the disciples are closed to any such possible deeper meaning of the text. The first level of meaning is entirely in spatial terms.

It would seem, then, that the minds of the disciples as expressed in 14,5 are wavering between two possible Johannine understandings in a spatial sense of the phrase "my Father's house", either with reference to the Jerusalem temple or with reference to the heavenly temple; or with reference to both at the same time.

(b) THE MANY ROOMS.

(i) *Rooms.* In the Father's house there are many μοναί. Literally, the term μονή means a permanent abode, or dwelling-place.[12] In a material (or spatial) sense it refers here to the place, or "spatial area", within the house where one dwells: a room.[13] The term is used only twice in the NT; both instances are in John (cf. 14,2.23).[14] It seems to derive from the preferred Johannine verb μένω.[15] Hence the idea of permanence and stability is duly stressed.[16] But the term is used here in a metaphorical sense. It is used as a spatial metaphor to indicate a possibility of accommodation, or of dwelling in the house. The Father's house of 14,2 has many possibilities for others to dwell in it. Thus it is capable of admitting the disciples. As yet these "rooms" are not occupied by the

---

[11] This exegete writes: "The Father's house is no longer heaven, but God's household or family". See, "'In my Father's house are many Μοναί' (John 14,2)", *ZNW* 58 (1967) 70.

[12] See, *L.S.* 1143.

[13] The widespread English rendering of 14,2 "In my Father's house are many mansions" derives originally from TYNDALE (1526).

[14] The term occurs only once besides in the OT (I Mc 7,38).

[15] It is clear from NT usage that this is a preferred Johannine verb:

Syn	Jn	I.II.III. Jn	Ap	Total Jn	Total NT
12	40	27	I	68	118

[16] The verb expresses the permanency of a relationship in John (12,34; 1,32; 6,27; 15,16; I Jn 2,17).

disciples. The text merely states the possibility of such. Whether some of these "rooms" are already inhabited by others or not (for example, by celestial beings such as angels) [17] before the disciples are taken to dwell there cannot be determined from the text.

However, the term μονή is also open to interpretation in a more spiritual sense as a noun of action in the sense of an "abiding" or "dwelling". [18] Such seems to be the meaning of the term in 14,23. [19] There it describes an inner enduring personal relationship of Jesus (with the Father) dwelling, or abiding, spiritually in the believer. The verb μένω from which the noun μονή derives, is frequent besides in the farewell discourses with ἐν to describe such a deep spiritual relationship of in-dwelling (cf. 15,3.4(2x).5.6.7(2x).9.10(2x)). So, too, the larger context of the fourth gospel and the Johannine literature abundantly confirms this (comp. 6,56; 1 Jn 2,6.10.14.24.27.28; 3,6.9.17.24; 4,12.13.15.16). In all of these passages μένω ἐν denotes a deep spiritual relationship. In fact, this is the sole meaning given to the term μονή by R. H. Gundry. [20] However, this cannot be its sole meaning. [21] Such a meaning would certainly be possible, if the Father's house were a family of actual dwellers abiding, or dwelling, spiritually in union with Jesus in the Father. But for this the return of Jesus to take the disciples into this unity in the house would be necessary. Besides, to interpret μονή in 14,2-3 as a spiritual "space" where one might dwell spiritually would be to go beyond the spatial imagery to the deeper spiritual meaning which the term may signify. But this meaning is still closed to the disciples.

(ii) *Many.* These "rooms" in the Father's house are "many" (πολλαί). This term πολλαί is to be taken quantitatively, not qualitatively. [22] It

---

[17] In the OT the heavenly temple is inhabited by immortal beings (cf. I Kgs 22,19f; Jb 1,6-12; 2,1-7; Is 6,1f; Ze 3,1-7; Dn 7,9f).

[18] The term μονή can be used as a noun of action to signify the action of dwelling (or abiding). See, *L.S.* 1143. So, too, the term may designate a "mode of being". See, C. K. BARRETT, *op. cit.* 456.

[19] In 14,2-3 the author is clearly thinking of compartments or dwelling-places, since the μοναί are explicitly designated as existing permanently in (ἐν) a building (οἰκία). The use of the spatial metaphor in 14,2-3 requires a local sense. However, the use of the term μονή with the verb ποιεῖσθαι in 14,23 is different. There the use of μονή as a noun of action would not be out of place in the context, meaning, "permanent abiding".

[20] See, *op. cit.* (n. 11) 70.

[21] To our knowledge D. W. WEAD is the only exegete who has underlined the possibility of a double meaning for the term μονή: "In 14,2 a spiritual meaning forms the basis for the double meaning of the noun, μοναί. Μοναί refers not only to the dwelling places we can expect with God but also that we can look forward to dwelling with Christ spiritually". See, *The Literary Devices in John's Gospel (Basel, 1970) 32.*

[22] J. COURTENAY JAMES rightly observes: "The adjective denotes number not degree". See, "Mansiones Multae", *ExpT* 27 (1915-16) 428.

designates number, not variety nor degree. The general use of the term πολύς in the fourth gospel suggests this. It is also suggested by our text itself and its immediate context.

The term (οἱ)πολλοί, without further qualification, is used invariably in the fourth gospel to designate a great number (cf. 2,23; 4,39; 6,60.66; 7,31; 8,30; 10,20.41.42; 11,19.45.55; 12,11.42; 19,20). Besides, when it qualifies a noun, it often indicates an abundance or great quantity of something, whether in the singular (χόρτος, 6,10; γογγυσμός, 7,12; καρπός, 12,24; 15,5,8; χρόνος, 5,6; ὄχλος, 6,2,4; 12,9.12) or in the plural (ὕδατα, 3,23; ἡμέραι 2,12; ἔργα, 10,32; σημεῖα, 11,47; 20,30; 21,25).

However, in several of these uses of the term the connotation of diversity, or variety, can by no means be excluded. This is so with the triple use of the neuter πολλά (8,26; 14,30; 16,12). The neuter plural of its very nature is more indefinite. So, too, it may indicate variety, or diversity, with reference to "fruit" (12,24; 15,5.8), "works" (10,32), and "signs" (11,47; 20,30; 21,25). However, even in these cases it is the quantity that is directly stressed. It is the evidence of the gospel elsewhere that points to the possibility also of a diversity and variety of these things. So, too, the additional ἄλλα should be noted with reference to the "many signs" (20,30; 21,25).

Besides, there is nothing in the text itself to indicate that a variety, or diversity, of rooms is intended. On the contrary. The disciples as a group are addressed in 14,2-3 (ὑμῖν... ὑμᾶς... ὑμεῖς). There is no distinction. It is for the disciples as such a group that Jesus is about to prepare a place in the Father's house with the many rooms. The imagery is that of a spacious house with rooms enough, and more than enough, for all of them to dwell there. There is nothing in the text itself to indicate diversity, or a higher degree or level of dwelling-places for one disciple rather than the other.[23]

Such an interpretation would also be completely foreign to the immediate context. The promise of access to the Father's house with these many "rooms" (μοναί) in 14,2-3 is designed to provide all the disciples indiscriminately with a basis for security and confidence in time of fear and distress (cf. 14,1.27). It is the connotation of permanency (or stability) in the term μονή which makes it admirably fitted to ensure this. The promise of diverse "rooms", or in varying degrees of excellence, as dwelling-places for the disciples is hardly well suited to this purpose.

---

[23] IRENAEUS testifies that such was indeed the interpretation of the presbyters. See, *Adv. haer. V, 36, I.* The different dwelling-places of Jn 14,2-3 represented different degrees of future happiness and the vision of God. See, A. ORBE, "Las Tres Moradas de la Casa Paterna de S. Ireneo a Gregorio de Elvira" in *Miscellanea J. A. de Aldama*, (Granada, 1969) 69-92.

Neither can there be any question of the μοναί signifying stations on a journey or stopping-places.[24] The "many rooms" qualify the Father's house as the goal of the journey; they do not refer in any way to the journey itself. Besides, such stopping-places, or stations, would be necessarily temporary. Again such an interpretation would be clearly out of context. The transience of a temporary sojourn would not provide a stable and secure basis for the confidence to which Jesus encourages his disciples in 14,1.

Finally, we note that these "rooms" (μοναί) "are" in the Father's house. It is present tense (εἰσιν). Here and now they exist permanently. The preposition "in" (ἐν) should be taken in a simple local sense. It indicates the place where the many possibilities for dwelling exist permanently for the disciples, namely, in the Jerusalem temple, or in the heavenly temple where God, the Father of Jesus, dwells.

In the first member of the text, then, we have a simple and direct statement of fact. It would seem to indicate to the disciples before the departure of Jesus that there are at all times sufficient, and more than sufficient, possibilities for others to dwell permanently in this Father's house, although as yet it is not quite clear whether it is the Jerusalem temple or the heavenly temple which is intended.

2. The Way to the Father's House

(a) THE JOURNEY TO PREPARE A PLACE.

(i) *The Journey of Jesus.*   In the second member of our text Jesus states explicitly: "I am going to prepare a place for you". Literally, the term πορεύομαι means "to journey".[25] In a material (or spatial) sense it designates a journey of Jesus, by a physical movement in space. We find the verb in this sense in the fourth gospel (4,50(2x); (7,53); (8,1.11); 8,59; 10,4; 11,11; 20,17). Here it indicates a movement of access to the Father's house (positive aspect) (comp. 14,12.28; 16,28), which also implies departure from the disciples (negative aspect) (comp. 13,33; 16,28). It

---

[24] The term μονή is found in this sense in Pausanias (x,41) and is also used in this sense by ORIGEN (*de Princip.* ii. xi. 6). It is also accepted by B. F. WESTCOTT, *op. cit.* 200. This interpretation has a modern champion in R. A. EDWARDS, *The Gospel according to St. John — its Criticism and Interpretation* (London, 1954) 106. However, it has been adequately refuted by T. S. BERRY, "Critical note on St. John, xiv,2", *Exp* (2nd series) 3 (1882) 397-400. J. B. PHILLIPS sums up the refutation of any such interpretation admirably. See, *The Gospels in Modern English*, (London, 1958), Appendix, note, 6.

[25] See, *L.S.* 1449.

refers to some kind of physical movement in space to the goal of the Father's house, such as a journey on pilgrimage to the Jerusalem temple (if the Father's house designates the earthly temple), or a bodily ascension (if the Father's house designates the heavenly temple).

Such an interpretation of πορεύομαι is quite in accord with Johannine perspectives. The verb itself is never used with reference to a journey to the temple in Jerusalem. However, the movement on pilgrimage to the Jerusalem temple is repeatedly designated in John as an ascending movement by means of the verb ἀναβαίνω (2,13; 5,1; 7,8(2x).10(2x).14; 11,55; 12,20).[26] This is the technical term for a pilgrimage to the Jerusalem temple. The verb πορεύομαι is used with reference to the journey of Jesus to his heavenly Father, both implicitly (16,7) and explicitly (14,12.28; 16,28). We have a perfect parallel to this use of the verb in Acts when it describes Jesus "journeying into heaven" (αὐτὸν πορευόμενον εἰς τὸν οὐρανόν) (1,11; comp. 1,10). By means of this journey in 14,2-3 Jesus traverses the distance which separates the world of the disciples, or the sphere of men, from the transcendent heavenly sphere of God.

The verb πορεύομαι itself is a futuristic present. It describes a journey already (in some sense) in the process of being realised, and at the same time still in the future.[27] The context of 14,2-3 specifies that this journey will take place in the immediate future (ἔτι μικρόν, 13,33). There is no precise indication of the manner, or how, of this journey. The verb in itself is open to interpretation with reference to any specific kind of journey of Jesus. The assertion by Peter of his readiness to "lay down his life" for Jesus (13,37b) would seem to intimate his understanding of this journey of Jesus as a journey fraught with difficulties and dangers, even the possibility of physical death (comp. 8,22; 11,16). But as yet there is nothing to show that this journey of Jesus may be understood, not as physical movement in space such as a bodily ascension to heaven, nor as the physical act of dying; but in a far deeper sense of a spiritual movement of Jesus into communion with his heavenly Father through his passion-resurrection.[28] The text in itself is certainly open to such an interpretation. But again this is to move beyond the spatial imagery to the deeper spiritual reality which the term πορεύομαι may signify in the

---

[26] This same verb is also used in the fourth gospel to indicate a journey to heaven (cf. 3,13; 6,62; 20,17(2x); comp. 1,51).

[27] See, *BDF 323.*

[28] Both the material sense and the possible deeper spiritual sense of the verb πορεύομαι have been well explained by O. DA SPINETOLI. See, "Il ritorno di Gesù al Padre nella soteriologia giovannea" in *San Giovanni* (Brescia, 1964) 145.

fourth gospel.[29] Neither is there anything as yet to indicate the deeper possible sacrificial aspect of this journey of Jesus opened up by the use of the phrase ψυχὴν τίθημι in the immediate context (13,37.38).[30] The minds of the disciples are still closed to this possible deeper level of meaning.

(ii) *The Preparation of a Place.* The purpose of Jesus' journey is designated explicitly as "to prepare a place for you" (ἑτοιμάσαι τόπον ὑμῖν). Literally, the term ἑτοιμάζω means "to make ready", or "to put something in order".[31] In a material (or spatial) sense, it means to prepare something or to put it in order physically. The term τόπος in a material (or spatial) sense means literally "place", some kind of physical "space" or spatial area.[32] We find the term in this sense in the fourth gospel (4,13; 6,10.23; 10,40; 11,6.30; 18,2; 19,13.17.20.41; 20,7.25). The verb ἑτοιμάζω is found nowhere else in the fourth gospel. But here it is used with the noun τόπος in a spatial sense. It indicates that the purpose of Jesus' journey is to render the Father's house with the many rooms accessible to the disciples, or to prepare it for their admission. We have an equivalent in the English phrase "to make room" for someone, meaning to make some place capable of being occupied by someone, or to render it accessible to them.

This is the meaning also suggested by the immediate context. The temporary inability of the disciples to follow Jesus on this journey to the Father's house is stressed in the preceding verses (13,36bc). However, we find in 14,2-3 that after the preparation the Father's house becomes accessible. On the condition of his departure to prepare a place, Jesus will return to take the disciples with him to the Father's house. Thus the goal of the Father's house, inaccessible to the disciples previously, now becomes accessible to them after the preparation. Nothing but the journey of preparation could have rendered it so.

However, the fourth gospel also provides us with a highly technical use of the term τόπος to designate the Jerusalem temple (4,20; 11,48). The term τόπος in our text is indefinite, without the article. As such it is open

---

[29] A variety of verbs may be found in John to designate this deeper spiritual sense of a movement of Jesus out of the world into communion with the Father through the passion-resurrection, e.g. μεταβαίνω (13,1), ὑπάγω (7,33; 8,14.21; 13,3.33.36; 14,4.28; 16,5.10.17), πορεύομαι (14,12.28; 16,7,28), ἔρχομαι (17,11.13), ἀφίημι (16,28), ἀναβαίνω (3,13; 6,62; 20,17), ἀπέρχομαι (16,7). It is for John this same deep spiritual reality which is designated by the use of the verb ὑψόω (3,14; 8,28; 12,32.34), and the verb δοξάζω (12,23.29; 13,31-32; 17,15).

[30] The sacrificial aspect of this phrase has been well explained by A. VANHOYE. See, "L'œuvre du Christ, don dù Père (Jn. 5,36 et 17,4)", *RecSR* 48 (1960) 401-402, also n. 40.

[31] See, *L.S.* 903.

[32] See, *L.S.* 1806.

to interpretation with reference to any specific τόπος whatever, like a "sanctuary" or "temple". Besides, it is not stated directly (nor explicitly) that Jesus goes to the Father's house to prepare a place for the disciples there. The text says so only indirectly (or implicitly). It is stated directly (and explicitly) only that Jesus goes to prepare a "place". Clearly, we cannot exclude the interpretation of τόπος as "sanctuary" or "temple" intimated by some exegetes.[33]

Moreover, it is highly significant in this regard that the body of Jesus is explicitly designated in 2,21 as a "temple" (ναός). But as yet there is nothing to show how this journey of Jesus through his passion- resurrection might possibly prepare a τόπος in this highly technical sense of "sanctuary" or "temple". Indeed to understand 14,2-3 in this sense would be to go beyond the spatial imagery of the text to the deeper reality of a spiritual "temple", or "sanctuary", like the risen body of Jesus. Besides, the minds of the disciples are still closed to any such possible transformation of the temple of the body of Jesus through his passion-resurrection.

Finally, we note that a "place" is to be prepared for the disciples. There is no question whatever of anything being prepared by Jesus for himself. He enters the Father's house with the full right of a Son who already in some sense dwells there perpetually and permanently (ὅπου εἰμὶ ἐγώ).[34] The Father's house with the many rooms is to be prepared for the disciples alone.[35] The ὑμῖν is dative of advantage.

Furthermore, there is evidence elsewhere in the gospel to show that John invests his disciples with a wider significance as representatives of all future believers (comp. 1,35-51).[36] Besides, the phrase ὁ πιστεύων of 14,12 also seems to point to some kind of wider application of the words of Jesus in the discourse (comp. 3,15).[37] The reference to the disciples in 14,2-3 is certainly open to such a wider possibility of meaning. However, there is nothing in the text itself to show that such is its wider application, and the minds of the disciples before the departure of Jesus would be closed to any such possible deeper meaning of the text.

---

[33] See, Introduction, n. I.

[34] Several exegetes have noted this entrance by Jesus into his Father's house by right as a Son. See, B. F. WESTCOTT, *op. cit.* 200; also O. SCHAEFER, *op. cit.* (n. 4), 212-213; and O. MICHEL, *TDNT* V 122.

[35] The object of the process of preparation is directly "place" and indirectly "the Father's house with the many rooms". The whole process of preparation is for the disciples; but it is not the disciples themselves that are prepared either directly or indirectly. Even the clever comment of Augustine on Jn 14,2-3 does not seem to have avoided some confusion: "parat autem quodammodo mansiones, mansionibus parando mansores". See, *In Jo* LXVIII, 2, PL 35: 1814.

[36] See, B. F. WESTCOTT, *op. cit.* 23-24.

[37] Compare also the phrase ὁ ἀγαπῶν (14,21(2x).24). This aspect of the discourse and of our text will be developed at length later (ch. V).

(b) RETURN OF JESUS TO TAKE THE DISCIPLES TO HIMSELF.

(i) *Return.* The text goes on to say explicitly: "I am coming again" (πάλιν ἔρχομαι). This is conditional on the departure of Jesus (ἐὰν πορευθῶ). The conjunction retains its full weight as a condition.[38] It is implicit in the text that Jesus comes from the Father's house, his temple. So, too, it is implicit that he returns to the disciples (comp. ἔρχομαι with, πρὸς ὑμᾶς, 14,18,28). Literally, the term ἔρχομαι means "to come".[39] In a material (or spatial) sense ἔρχομαι designates the coming of Jesus, by a physical movement in space. We find the verb repeatedly in this sense in the fourth gospel (1,29; 3,2.22.26; 4,5.7.16.27.43). Here in 14,2-3, then, it indicates a spatial movement of Jesus intervening in favour of his disciples.

An interpretation of the verb ἔρχομαι with reference to an intervention of Jesus from heaven would be in accord with Johannine perspectives. The term "heaven" (οὐρανός) is inseparable in the fourth gospel from the place of Jesus' origin.[40] The phrase "from heaven" (ἐκ τοῦ οὐρανοῦ) almost invariably indicates the divine and transcendent origin of Jesus.[41] In this regard the synonymous parallelism of 3,31 is highly significant: ὁ ἄνωθεν/ὁ ἐκ τοῦ οὐρανοῦ ἐρχόμενος ἐπάνω πάντων ἐστίν.

The parallel terms ἄνωθεν and ἐκ τοῦ οὐρανοῦ have an identical meaning here with reference to the place of Jesus' origin. Again, we find repeated assertions with identically the same meaning to the effect that Jesus has "come out from God" (8,42; 13,3; 16,27.30), "from the Father" (16,28; 17,8), and that he has "descended from heaven" (6,33.38.41.42.50.51.58) and "come into the world" (1,9; 3,19; 6,14; 9,39; 11,27; 12,46; 16,28; 18,37). Considered in this light, Jesus would be "coming" to the sphere of the disciples from the heavenly abode of God, his Father, as from his own transcendent and divine source, or place of origin.

We have a similar kind of intervention from heaven in the Pauline description of the Second Coming with the verb καταβαίνω: "The Lord will descend from heaven (καταβήσεται ἀπ' οὐρανοῦ)". I Thes 4,16.[42]

---

[38] R. BULTMANN would soften this ἐὰν of 14,2-3 to the equivalent of ὅταν. See, *op. cit.* 600, n. 3.

[39] See, *L.S.* 694.

[40] On this term οὐρανός and its use in John, see H. TRAUB, *TDNT* V 497-536; also A. SERRA, *Contributi dell'antica letteratura giudaica per l'esegesi di Giovanni 2,1-12 e 19,25-27* (Roma, 1977) 294-301.

[41] The text of 12,28 is the sole exception.

[42] Several exegetes note this link between I Thes 4,13-18 and our text of Jn 14,2-3. See, C. H. DODD, *The Interpretation of the Fourth Gospel*, (Cambridge, 1960) 404; also M.-E. BOISMARD, "L'évolution du thème eschatologique dans les traditions johanniques", *RB* 68 (1961) 522. However, the limitations of this parallel should also be carefully noted. In I Thes 4,13-18 it is not Jesus who will take Christians to himself as in Jn 14,2-3, but God who will do so through Jesus.

However, the use of the verb ἔρχομαι is part of NT usage to designate the final eschatological intervention of Jesus at the Parousia (Acts 1,11; Ap 1,7; 22,12.17.20).[43] There is also an example of this usage in the fourth gospel (21,22.23). Even the questions of the disciples after the announcement of 14,2-3 seem to indicate an understanding of this promised future "coming" with reference to the eschatological intervention of Jesus. The words of reproach to Philip in 14,9 direct him away from any kind of spectacular intervention of Jesus visible to man. So, too, the question of 14,22 reveals a similar expectation of a glorious manifestation in line with Jewish eschatological expectations (comp. Acts 10,40-41). Moreover, the vocabulary of the discourse itself is rich with echoes of the OT eschatological vocabulary (ἔτι μικρόν[44] ... ἐν ἐκείνῃ τῇ ἡμέρᾳ).[45]

The verb ἔρχομαι itself is a futuristic present.[46] It describes a "coming" of Jesus already in the process of being realised, and at the same time still in the future. There is no indication in the text itself in what manner this eschatological intervention of Jesus will actually take place, nor when it will take place — in the immediate future or in the still far distant future. Apart from the "coming" of Jesus at the Parousia (21,22.23), there are also several interventions of the risen Jesus designated explicitly with the verb ἔρχομαι in the fourth gospel. Such an intervention is described in the immediate context of 14,2-3 with reference to the resurrection in 14,18 (comp. 20,19.24.26; also 21,13), and with reference to the indwelling of Jesus (with the Father) in 14,23. In 16,8 the verb ἔρχομαι also designates the intervention of the risen Jesus through the Spirit. The verb ἔρχομαι itself is open to interpretation with reference to every possible kind of intervention by the risen Jesus, after the Father's house has been rendered accessible to the disciples. No possible intervention after his departure can be excluded. However, there is nothing to show that this "coming" of Jesus in 14,2-3 takes on any of these possible deeper meanings. Again, this would be to move beyond the spatial imagery to the deeper level of meaning.

---

[43] See, J. SCHNEIDER, *TDNT* II 672-675.

[44] The phrase is found as an eschatological formula in the OT. In the LXX it is generally found in this shortened form ἔτι μικρόν. There it is used to underline the imminence of the eschatological events (cf. Is 10,25; 29,17; Jer 28(31), 33; Hos 1,4; comp. Hag 2,6; Ps 37(36),10). It is this OT eschatological formula which lies behind the ἔτι χρόνον μικρόν of Jn 7,33 and 12,35. G. FISCHER explains the import of the formula. See, *Die himmlischen Wohnungen: Untersuchungen zu Joh 14,2* (Frankfurt/Main, 1975) 314.

[45] This phrase is also found as an eschatological formula repeatedly in the OT. We find simple ἡμέρα (Ze 14,1 (in plural)) and ἐν τῇ ἡμέρᾳ ἐκείνῃ (Ze 14,6.8.13; comp. 12,11; 13,1.21). G. FISCHER again explains well. See, *op. cit.* (n. 44) 318-319.

[46] See, n. 27.

There is no parallel example of ἔρχομαι with πάλιν to describe the eschatological intervention in John, nor indeed anywhere else in the NT. This gives additional force to this Johannine use of πάλιν in 14,2-3. The adverb πάλιν when used of place signifies in general "back" or "backwards", and when used of time "again" or "once more".[47] Both of these meanings are relevant here. Jesus will come again, or return. The phrase indicates that the future "coming" of Jesus will be a return to the disciples. As such the phrase fits admirably into the setting of Jesus' departure as a motive of consolation for the disciples in their bereavement (cf. 14,1.27; comp. 16,6). This meaning implies the departure of Jesus (πορεύομαι) and links closely both aspects of our text, namely, going (πορεύομαι) and coming (ἔρχομαι). But Jesus will also come "again" or "once more". His first intervention at the Incarnation is designated in the fourth gospel by the verb ἔρχομαι (1,9.11). The use of ἔρχομαι, then, with πάλιν in 14,2-3 may also evoke (at least implicitly) this first intervention of Jesus.

(ii) *Journey of the disciples with Jesus.* The effect of Jesus' return is explicitly stated: "and I will take you with me" (καὶ παραλήψομαι ὑμᾶς). The καί may best be taken as a καί of consequence.[48] Literally, the term παραλαμβάνω means "to take along with".[49] In a material (or spatial) sense it designates a journey of the disciples with Jesus by a physical movement in space. The simple form of the verb is common in John.[50] However, the compound form with παρά is comparatively rare. Apart from 14,3 it occurs only twice (cf. 1,11; 19,16). In both cases it means "to receive". Moreover, it is used in a passive sense as complementary to something offered. In 14,2-3, however, the use of the verb is active, with no complementary activity of the disciples directly indicated. Hence, there is no exact parallel in the fourth gospel to the usage of 14,2-3. Here the verb refers to a personal attitude of Jesus and indicates the effect on the disciples of his future intervention. This will be a movement of access by the disciples with Jesus to the Father's house. This is at least implicit in the text of 14,2-3, although explicitly the text merely states that Jesus will return to take the disciples, not to the Father's house (εἰς τὴν οἰκίαν τοῦ πατρός μου) but "to himself" (πρὸς ἐμαυτόν). The verb παραλαμβάνω

---

[47] This adverb πάλιν is explained "of time, again, once more" and "of place, back, backwards (the usual sense in early EP), mostly joined with verbs of going and coming". *L.S.* 1292.

[48] See, *BDF* 323. 442.

[49] See, Introduction, n. 4.

[50] I. DE LA POTTERIE provides us with a concise survey of all possible Johannine uses of the verb λαμβάνω in its simple form. See, "La Parole de Jésus 'Voici ta Mère' et l'accueil du disciple (Jn 19,27b)", *Marianum* 36 (1974) 32-33.

refers then in a material sense to some kind of physical movement of the disciples with Jesus in space to the goal of the Father's house, as a result of the intervention of Jesus, such as a pilgrimage to the Jerusalem temple (if the Father's house designates the earthly temple), or a bodily assumption to the divine and transcendent sphere of God (if the Father's house designates the heavenly temple). By this latter kind of journey the disciples would traverse the distance which separates their world from the sphere of God. It would thus imply a departure of the disciples from the sphere of men.

This journey of the disciples with Jesus, as a result of his intervention, is parallel to the journey of Jesus alone (prior to the preparation). Moreover, the use of the compound verb παραλαμβάνω, rather than the simple form, indicates an important identity between the movement of Jesus (prior to the preparation) and that of the disciples with Jesus through his intervention (after the preparation). The disciples travel with Jesus, because of his intervention (after the preparation), along the same way traversed by Jesus (before the preparation). So, too, as a result of this same intervention they traverse with Jesus the same distance which separates them from the Father's house. This journey with Jesus through his intervention gives the disciples actual access to the Father's house, after it has been rendered accessible to them by the preparation of a place. In a word, what Jesus accomplishes alone (before the preparation) is accomplished by the disciples with him as a result of his intervention (after the preparation).

The bodily assumption of Jesus himself is described with the compound form of the verb λαμβάνω in Acts: "a cloud took him out of their sight" (ὑπέλαβεν) (1,9), and again "this Jesus who was taken up from you into heaven" (ἀναλημφθεὶς ἀφ' ὑμῶν εἰς τὸν οὐρανόν) (1,11; comp. also ἀναλαμβάνω, Acts 1,2.22; Mk 16,19; I Tm 3,16; ἀνάλημψις, Lk 9,51). The verb λαμβάνω with its compounds seems to acquire a special religious significance in the early tradition to describe the bodily assumption of Jesus into heaven.

There is no further indication in the text of 14,2-3 itself in what manner this movement of the disciples with Jesus will actually take place. Nor is there any indication of when it will take place. All the text says explicitly is "I will take you with me". The text simply describes the effect of the "coming" of Jesus whenever and however that "coming" will take place. The verb παραλαμβάνω itself is open to interpretation with reference to every possible way in which Jesus can take the disciples to himself when he comes again, after the journey of preparation is complete.

3. The Goal of the Disciples' Journey: Reunion with Jesus in the Father's House

(a) JESUS HIMSELF. The phrase πρὸς ἐμαυτόν designates Jesus himself explicitly and directly as the goal of his own future intervention in favour of his disciples. This means that Jesus will take the disciples to be personally reunited with himself, or take them into his own company or fellowship with himself.[51] A comparison with the parallel text of Jn 17,24c illustrates the meaning well:

παραλήμψομαι ὑμ. πρὸς ἐμαυτόν ἵν. ὅπ. ἐι. ἐγ. κ. ὑμεῖς ἦτε.
θέλω   ἵν. ὅπ. ἐι. ἐγ. κἀκεῖνοι ὦσιν μετ'ἐμοῦ.

The presence of μετ'ἐμοῦ in 17,24c is not an addition with respect to our text.[52] It corresponds to the πρὸς ἐμαυτόν of 14,3b. We find the phrase μετ'ἐμοῦ elsewhere in the fourth gospel to describe the fellowship of the disciples with Jesus (cf. 13,8; comp. 13,33; 14,16; 17,12), and even that of the Father with Jesus (8,29;[53] 16,32). However, the Johannine use of the preposition πρός stresses the dynamic aspect of this movement of the disciples into fellowship with Jesus.[54] The movement of the text, then, is from plurality (ὑμᾶς) into the unity of a fellowship with Jesus (πρὸς ἐμαυτόν) in the Father's house (ὅπου εἰμὶ ἐγώ). Some kind of at-one-ment with Jesus is clearly promised.

However, there appears to be something cumbersome about this interpretation of the text, almost tautological. Jesus has already said that he will take the disciples "along with himself" (παραλήψομαι), or in his company. If the compound form of the verb with παρά be given its full weight — and it should be[55] — then the disciples are already in the

---

[51] A. L. HUMPHRIES suggests that the phrase πρὸς ἐμαυτόν means "to my home". He thus translates: "I will come again and take you with me to my home". See, "A Note on πρὸς ἐμαυτόν (John xiv,3) and εἰς τὰ ἴδια (John 1,11)", *ExpT* 53 (1941) 356. However, to designate this as the sole meaning of the text without further distinction is to impoverish it. John says directly and explicitly that Jesus will take the disciples "to himself" (πρὸς ἐμαυτόν), and only indirectly and implicitly that he will take them to "the Father's house", or "to my home".

[52] P. GRELOT explains well the import of the phrase μετ'ἐμοῦ in his comment on Lk 23,43: "La préposition employée en grec (μετά) n'exprime pas seulement l'accompagnement (comme σύν dans les cas ordinaires), mais l'association étroite, la vie partagée, la communion au même destin". See, *De la mort à la vie éternelle* (Paris, 1971) 213.

[53] W. BAUER links Jn 8,29 with the passion of Jesus. See, *op. cit.* 124.

[54] The prepositions πρός and εἰς have the same dynamic connotation in John. See, I. DE LA POTTERIE, "L'emploi dynamique de εἰς dans Saint Jean et ses incidences théologiques", *Bib* 43 (1962) 366-387.

[55] It is inconceivable that an adroit writer like John would use the compound form of the verb loosely in preference to the simple form. Elsewhere John is careful to distinguish the compound from the simple form, even in the same verse (cf. 1,11). See, n. 51.

company of Jesus, or in fellowship with him. How, then, can Jesus say that he will take them into fellowship, or communion, with himself (πρὸς ἐμαυτόν); or even why should he have to do so, if they are already in fellowship with him? There does not seem to be any adequate solution — at least at this first level of meaning — to this apparently strange precision of the text, which insists on the personal relationship of the disciples with Jesus through the phrase πρὸς ἐμαυτόν and by means of it also indicates Jesus as the goal of the disciples (comp. Mk 14,33; Mt 12,45; 18,16).

(b) THE FATHER'S HOUSE WHERE JESUS DWELLS. Jesus does not say directly (nor explicitly) that he will take the disciples to the Father's house. But he does say so indirectly (or implicitly). This is implicit in the phrase "in order that where I am you may be also" (ἵνα ὅπου εἰμὶ ἐγὼ καὶ ὑμεῖς ἦτε). The ἵνα is final. It designates the purpose of the intervention of Jesus. This phrase "where I am" (ὅπου εἰμι ἐγώ) is part of John's spatial vocabulary.[56] It qualifies the goal of the Father's house still further. Here it designates the Father's house as the place where Jesus as Son dwells (or is) permanently.[57] The Father's house with the many rooms is already here and now, even before the preparation, the permanent dwelling-place of Jesus. Jesus is already where he promises to take the disciples later (παραλήμψομαι ἵνα... καὶ ὑμεῖς). The verb εἰμί must be given its full value as a present (εἰσιν, 14,2a).[58] Jesus promises to take the disciples in the future to his Father's house to be with him there in that place where he himself is at all times, permanently and continually, in fellowship with the Father.

But here again we find something cumbersome in our interpretation of the text. There is an apparent contradiction of perspectives. The perspective of the phrase "I am going" (πορεύομαι) is future. It is the same goal of Jesus' future journey which is designated by the phrase "where I am" (ὅπου εἰμὶ εγώ) of 14,2-3 (comp. 7,34.36; 17,24), and the phrase "where I am going" (ὅπου ἐγὼ ὑπάγω) of 13,33 (comp. 14,4;

---

[56] D. MOLLAT designates it explicitly as such. See, "Remarques sur le vocabulaire spatial du quatrième évangile", StudEvang I (TU 73) 326.

[57] Here we have the suggestion of a community of life, or family life, in the Father's house. However, there is no question of the disciples being already in the Father's house before the preparation and return of Jesus. If they were, then why return to take them to it? In no way can we accept without further qualification the interpretation of R. H. GUNDRY: "The reception of believers by Jesus at his coming will not be for the purpose of taking them to their abiding-places; it is consequent on their being in those abiding-places before he comes". See, op. cit. (n. 11) 70.

[58] R. BULTMANN wrongly interprets the present tense as the equivalent of a future. See, op. cit. 307, n. 6. It should be noted that the present tense of the verb "to be" is in contrast with a future in 12,26, and so can in no way be the equivalent of a future.

8,21.22). Jesus has not yet gone to the Father's house (πορεύομαι), and must still go there. For this reason he is at a distance from his Father's house and so belongs to the sphere of men. Yet in some sense he is perpetually and continually in the Father's house, or with the Father (comp. παρὰ τῷ πατρί, 8,38). He belongs at all times to the heavenly and transcendent sphere of God. How, then, can Jesus already belong to the heavenly sphere of God and at the same time belong to the sphere of men? There does not seem to be any adequate solution to this apparent conflict of perspectives in the text — at least at the first level of meaning.

However, the use of the phrase ὅπου εἰμὶ ἐγώ in 14,2-3 is also an indirect reference to the divine name (comp. 7,34.36; 17,24).[59] The use of εἰμί is open to a much deeper level of meaning. It may indicate the present of the divine mode of being which transcends the human mode of being-in-the-world (cf. 1,1). This present εἰμί of the phrase ὅπου εἰμὶ ἐγώ is a-temporal. It is neatly distinguished in 7,34.36 from the future which immediately precedes it; the future is appropriate to the human condition of the Jews, their mode of being-in-the-world, while the present εἰμί expresses by contrast the heavenly and eternal condition of Jesus, his mode of being-in-God. But this divine mode of being is referred to in the immediate context of 14,2-3 as a deep spiritual relationship of in-being between Jesus and the Father (14,10-11.20), and the sharing of the disciples in it as a deep spiritual relationship of in-being between the disciples and Jesus in the Father (14,20). Jesus would thus be promising in 14,2-3 that the disciples in the Father's house would become (after the journey of preparation) a family of dwellers reunited in Jesus himself with the Father by a deep spiritual bond of in-being. But any such positive effect of deep spiritual union, or communion with God, would necessarily imply in Johannine terms the complementary negative effect of taking the disciples out of the Johannine world of "sin", or unbelief, which is totally opposed to God and Jesus.

There is nothing in the text, however, to show that the promise of 14.2-3 takes on this deeper spiritual meaning. The second member of our text would seem to convey to the disciples before the departure of Jesus that Jesus is about to leave them in order to make the Father's house, with its many possibilities for others to dwell there, accessible to them; and that afterwards he will come again at the Second Coming to take the disciples along with him to the Father's house so that they may be reunited with him there.

---

[59] See, R. H. GUNDRY, op. cit. (n. 11) 72, n. 11. There can be no question of direct reference to the divine name. The order of the phrase is reversed from ἐγώ εἰμι to εἰμὶ ἐγώ. Besides, it is not an absolute use of the phrase, since it is qualified by ὅπου. So, too, the chiastic structure of the phrase εἰμὶ .... ἐγώ .... ὑμεῖς .... ἦτε .... puts the stress on the sharing of the disciples with Jesus in his destiny, and not on his transcendence and remoteness from his disciples.

CONCLUSION

We now have an interpretation of our text at the first level of meaning. The first member (14,2a) would seem to indicate that already before the departure of Jesus there are at all times sufficient, and more than sufficient, possibilities for others to dwell permanently in the Father's house, although as yet it is not quite clear whether it is the Jerusalem temple or the heavenly temple which is intended. The second member (14,2b-3) would seem to indicate before this same departure that Jesus is about to leave the disciples in order to make this Father's house, with its many possibilities for others to dwell there, accessible to the disciples; and that afterwards Jesus himself will come again at the Second Coming to take the disciples along with him to the Father's house so that they may be reunited with him there.

Nevertheless, there still appears to be something cumbersome about our interpretation. Jesus at one and the same time shares in the human condition of the disciples (πορεύομαι) and in the heavenly condition of God (ὅπου εἰμὶ ἐγώ) on two entirely distinct planes at a distance one from the other. So, too, Jesus promises to take the disciples who are already in his company (παραλήμψομαι) into his company (πρὸς ἐμαυτόν). There does not seem to be any adequate solution to these baffling features of the text — at least at this first level of meaning.

However, the text is rich in possibilities for an interpretation at a second level of meaning. But this deeper spiritual understanding is only possible after the passion-resurrection of Jesus in the light of the gift of the Spirit.

Before we explore these deeper possibilities of meaning more in detail, however, we must first study the Jewish background in order to establish more convincingly the first level of meaning in the text. To this Jewish background we now turn our attention.

PART I: JEWISH BACKGROUND

CHAPTER II

THE HOUSE WITH MANY ROOMS

A. THE HOUSE

1. Vocabulary: House

(a) IN GENERAL.

(i) *Temple.* In the LXX οἰκία and οἶκος are not distinguished in certain cases.[1] The literal meaning is "house" or "dwelling".[2] However, the use of οἶκος is much more frequent than οἰκία.[3] The former is a favourite LXX term. Both terms οἶκος[4] and οἰκία[5] are found in a transferred sense. So, it is perfectly intelligible that the term οἶκος should be used in a metaphorical sense to designate the house of God: his temple. The use of οἰκία to designate an ordinary house-building does occur.[6] But it is never used to designate the temple.[7] On the other hand, the phrase οἶκος(τοῦ)Θεοῦ becomes a fixed term for the sanctuary or temple.[8] The phrase also designates the eschatological temple.[9] Besides, the temple is explicitly designated in relation to God as "my house" (ὁ οἶκος μου).[10]

---

[1] See, O. MICHEL, *TDNT*, V, 131.

[2] See, *L S.* 1204.

[3] The former is found some 2034x, and the latter 272x.

[4] See, Jb 17,13; Eccl 12,3; Hos 8,1; 9,15; Ze 9,8.

[5] See, Jb 4,19; Eccl 12,3; Ps 119(118), 54; comp. Jb 30,2-3.

[6] The two terms οἶκος and οἰκία are used alternatively in this sense (Jer 22,13-14; Jgs 19,18; comp. Jos 2,18-19).

[7] Ze 5,11 is only an apparent exception. The term does not refer here to a dwelling-place of God in the strict sense, or a temple.

[8] See, Gn 28,17.19; Ex 23,19; Is 65,5; Ze 14,21. The term οἶκος itself is also used as a designation of the temple without any further modifications (cf. I Kgs 6-8 (passim)). It is also used of the eschatological temple (Ez 43,5.10). We might compare the use of the phrase οἶκος Κυρίου (cf. I Chr 9,23; I Kgs 5,14; Ze 6,12.14).

[9] See, Is 2,2/Mi 4,2; Is 56,5; Ze 14,21; comp. Tb 15,4-5.

[10] See, Hag 1,9; Ze 1,15; Is 56,5 (eschatological temple); comp. Is 56,7; 60,7. God sometimes designates the land of Israel as "my house". It is thus considered as a sanctuary of God, a kind of extension of the temple (cf. Ex 15,17; Jer 12,7; Hos 9,15; Ze 9,8). The people are frequently referred to as the house of Israel; but they are never called

So, too, in later Judaism οἶκος τοῦ Θεοῦ remained in use to designate the Jerusalem temple.[11] We find the term οἶκος in the LXX for the heavenly temple,[12] as we find it in later Judaism to designate the same.[13]

(ii) *Family*. The term in the LXX designates a "family", either in the ordinary sense of a family, meaning those who belong to the same household,[14] or in a wider sense with reference to a family of descendants.[15] There is a highly significant use of the term οἶκος, meaning family, in the oft-recurring phrase "the house of my Father":

> "Now then, swear to me by the Lord that as I have dealt kindly with you, you also will deal kindly with my Father's house (καὶ ποιήσετε καὶ ὑμεῖς ἔλεος ἐν τῷ οἴκῳ τοῦ πατρός μου), and save the house of my Father (καὶ ζωγρήσετε τὸν οἶκον τοῦ πατρός μου) and my mother and brothers and my whole house and all that belongs to them" (Jos 2,12-13).

So, too, in extra-biblical literature we find the phrase "the house of my Father". But it is never used of the temple. Occasionally, it would seem to refer to the family.[16]

---

the house of God, as some exegetes appear to suggest. See, O. MICHEL, *TDNT*, V, 124; also, B. GÄRTNER, *The Temple and the Community in Qumran and the New Testament* (Cambridge, 1965) 21. The text of Nm 12,7 is no exception (comp. Heb 3,2). The reference to the temple is dominant here also. The Targum Onkelos, however, does explain the τῷ οἴκῳ μου (LXX) = ביתי (MT) of Nm 12,7 as "my people". See, S. AALEN, "'Reign' and 'House' in the Kingdom of God in the Gospels", *NTS* 8 (1962) 236.

[11] See, JOSEPHUS *Bell.* 4,281.

[12] See, Mi 1,2: Is 63,15; Dt 26,15.

[13] Enoch (Greek Ethiopian version), 14,10.13.15; 25,4. See, *Apocalypsis Henochi Graece*, ed. M. BLACK (Fragmenta Pseudepigraphorum quae supersunt Graece) (Leiden, 1970).

[14] See, Gn 7,1; 12,1.17; Ex 12,4 (οἰκία); Lv 16,6; Nm 16,32: Jos 22,15.

[15] See, Gn 18,19; Dt 25,9; I Sm 2,35; I Kgs 2,24; I Chr 17,10.25.

[16] The phrase "my father's house" (בית אבי, in Phoenician) occurs in the Kilamuwa inscription (ANET 500): "My father's house was in the midst of mighty kings. Everybody stretched forth his hand to eat it". Here "the father's house" probably means royal power, kingdom, or such like. See, Z. S. HARRIS, *A Grammar of the Phoenician Language* (New Haven, 1936). Harris renders here as "dynasty" (p. 86). Moreover, Hadad reads (line 8): "Moreover, I sat on my father's throne and Hadah (the god) gave into my hands (line 9) the sceptre of authority, (he cut off) sword and slander from my father's house". This inscription is by Panammu I, whose father QRL was possibly a usurper. The phrase "father's house" here more probably means family, or such like. The translation is from J. C. L. GIBSON, *Textbook of Syrian Semitic Inscriptions*, Vol. II, *Aramaic Inscriptions* (Oxford, 1975). Finally, Barrakab, line 12 (ANET 501) reads: "I took over the house of my father". See, H. DONNER-W. ROLLIG, *Kanaanäische und Aramäische Inschriften*. Band II. DONNER/ROLLIG says: "Warscheinlicher aber handelt es sich um einen bautechnischen Ausdruck, vg I Reg. 6,6.10; Ezech 41,6)" (p. 233). However, it is difficult to see that the palace can be intended. The term is used in connection with throne and is synonymous with "house" further down. "House" is used at the end of the text in the sense of palace. Since there was no good palace in his father's times, Barrakab built "this house"; hence "house of his father", which he says he took over, scarsely means palace as suggested.

Finally, it should be noted that the Israelite "house" is a patriarchal family, and its unity is founded on blood-ties.[17]

(b) IN PARTICULAR.

(i) *Nathan Oracle.*[18] The Nathan oracle contains a curious play on the term "house" (2 Sm 7,5-17; 1 Chr 17,4-15).[19] The prophecy is built around a contrast: David is not to build a house (meaning temple) for God (2 Sm 7,5; 1 Chr 17,4), but God is to build a house (meaning dynasty) for him (2 Sm 7,11; 1 Chr 17,10). The substance of the prophecy is the perpetuity of the Davidic dynasty (2 Sm 7,12-16). David himself understood it in this way (2 Sm 7,19.25.27.29; 23,5). So it was also understood in the general OT tradition (Pss 89(88),29-37; 132(131),11-12), where it becomes the first in a series relating to the Davidic Messiah (comp. Is 7,14; Mi 4,14ff: Hag 2,23ff).[20]

It should be noted that there are significant modifications in the parallel accounts of this oracle. 1 Chr 17,11 expresses a more personal aspect than 2 Sm 7,12:

2 Sm 7,12	*1 Chr 17,11*
I will raise up after you	I will raise up after you
your offspring (τὸ σπέρμα σου)	your offspring (τὸ σπέρμα σου)
who shall come forth	who will be *one of your*
from *your body*	*sons*
LXX ὅς ἔσται ἐκ τῆς κοιλίας	ὅς ἔσται ἐκ τῆς κοιλίας
σου	σου
MT אשר יצא ממעיך	אשר יהיה מבניך

---

[17] See, R. DE VAUX, *Ancient Israel. Its Life and Institutions* (London, 1961) 20.

[18] It is generally agreed that the Nathan oracle has a complex literary history. See, A. CAQUOT, "La prophétie de Nathan et ses échos lyriques", *VetTSup* 9, 213-224; R. E. CLEMENTS, *God and Temple* (Oxford, 1965) 55f; T.N.D. Mettinger, *King and Messiah. The Civil and Sacral Legitimation of the Israelite Kings* (London, 1976) 42-61. This oracle is basic to an understanding of the theology of the temple and its later developments within the main stream of the Jewish temple tradition.

[19] See, *JB* ad loc., n. "a".

[20] J. BECKER observes that messianism, in the sense of the expectation of a royal son of David, appears no earlier than the second century, B.C. See, *Messiaserwartung im Alten Testament* (Stuttgart, 1977) 74. We know from Qumran (4QFlor) that the oracle of Nathan was interpreted to refer to the Messiah (comp. Lk 1,32-33; Jn 7,42; Acts 2,30; Heb 1,5). See, D. JUEL, *Messiah and Temple* (Missoula, 1977) 185.

The modification of 2 Sm 7,16 in the parallel text of I Chr 17,14 is also significant:

2 Sm 7,16	*LXX*
And *his house* and his kingdom *shall be made sure forever* before me and his throne shall be established forever.	καὶ πιστωθήσεται ὁ οἶκος αὐτοῦ (ונאמן ביתך) καὶ ἡ βασιλεία αὐτοῦ ἕως αἰῶνος ἐνώπιον ἐμοῦ, καὶ ὁ θρόνος αὐτοῦ ἔσται ἀνωρθωμένος εἰς τὸν αἰῶνα.

I Chr 17,14	
And *I will maintain him in my house*	καὶ πιστώσω αὐτὸν ἐν οἴκῳ μου (והעמדתיהו בביתי) [21]
and his throne shall be established forever.	καὶ ἐν βασιλείᾳ αὐτοῦ ἕως αἰῶνος, καὶ ὁ θρόνος αὐτοῦ ἔσται ἀν. ἕω. αἰ.

Thus in I Chr 17,14 the son who will build a house for God (I Chr 17,12) will abide permanently "in my house" (ἐν οἴκῳ μου).

Moreover, there is a further significant modification in Targum I Chr 17,14. Here the son, who is to be the Messiah,[22] will abide faithfully in the temple:

> "And I will maintain him faithful (or sure or steadfast) (מהימן) in my people, in my house (i.e. God's house) of holiness (בבית מקדשי) and in my kingdom forever, and the throne of his kingdom shall be established forever".

The phrase "my house of holiness" is an unambiguous reference to the sanctuary, God's house.[23]

Finally, we note the significant father/son relationship between this descendant of David and Yahweh himself:

> "I will be his father (εἰς πατέρα) and he will be my son (εἰς υἱόν) (2 Sm 7,14/I Chr 17,13)".

---

[21] The MT has עמד, in the hiphil. It means "to take one's stand, stand". This verb is often rendered by μένω in the LXX. See, F. HAUCK, *TDNT*, IV, 575.

[22] The sensitivity of the Targumist in his translation suggests that his text is messianic in the mind of the author. See, D. JUEL, *op. cit.* (n. 20) 169-197.

[23] On the phrase בית מקדש of the Targum to I Chr 17,14, S. AALEN says: "The house of God is unambiguously designated as the temple". See, *op. cit.* (n. 10) 234. D. JUEL makes a similar observation on the Targums to Isaiah and Zechariah. See, *op. cit.* (n. 20) 188, with a full list of examples in note, 47.

The Targums, however, are at pains to qualify this relationship as purely symbolic.

Thus we have evidence for an expectation within the Jewish tradition where the Davidic Messiah, who is to have some kind of father/son relationship with Yahweh himself, will abide permanently in the earthly temple.

(ii) *Qumran.* In the text of Qumran the term "house" takes on a meaning in line with the OT sense of "family". It is also inseparably linked with the idea of "temple". We find the term "house" as a characterisation for the community in IQS. The "house" in 9,6 ("a holy house for Aaron" = בית קודש לאהרן) would seem to be the clearest use of "house" for the temple: it is parallel to the "dwelling of infinite holiness" (מעון קודש קודשים) in 8,8 and probably parallel to the "most holy foundation for Aaron" (יסוד קודש קודשים לאהרן). Even in 8,5 the phrase "the holy house" in Israel (בית קודש) would seem to be a reference to the temple. But the "house of perfection and truth in Israel" (בית תמים ואמת בישראל) in 8,9, the "house of community for Israel" (בית יחד לישראל) in 9,6, and "house of truth in Israel" (בית האמת בישראל) in 5,6 are by no means unambiguous references to the temple.

In addition to IQS the text of CD 3,18-4,10 also deserves special attention. The text speaks about a "sure house in Israel" (בית נאמן בישראל) that God has built. Again, it is not immediately apparent that "sure house", as a designation for community, means "temple". S. Aalen has argued that the "sure house" built by God is a reference to 2 Sm 3,35 (the prophecy to Samuel), and that echoes of Nathan's oracle are also present, especially in the form of the prophecy in I Chr 17,10, where the verb בנה is used with the בית God is to build for David.[24] But whatever the origin of the terminology, in the present context "sure house" must refer to the temple.[25]

In the Manual of Discipline, we see that the community is a cohesive unit and functions as God's house:

> "At that time the members of the community shall be set apart as a house of holiness (בית קודש) for Aaron, in order to be united as a holy of holies and a house of community for Israel (להוחד קודש קודשים ובית יחד לישדאל) for those who walk in perfection" (9,5-6).

Finally, a brief reference should be made to IQpHab 12,3f, in which the council of the community עצת היחד is identified with "Lebanon" in Hb 2,17. According to a widespread tradition of interpretation, Lebanon

---

[24] See, *op. cit.* (n. 10) 235.
[25] See, G. KLINZING, *Die Umdeutung des Kultus in der Qumrangemeinde und im Neuen Testament* (Göttingen, 1971) 78.

= temple.[26] Among the sectarians at Qumran, the belief is held that the community = temple. Based on the belief of the sect and the traditional interpretation of "Lebanon", the Qumran exegete is thus able to make the equation Lebanon = community (here council of the community).

Thus we find convincing evidence which precedes Christianity for a use of the term "house" as temple imagery to designate a religious community, where the spiritual relationship replaces the physical. In the Damascus document the community calls itself "the house of Peleg" (בית פלג)[27] because it has left the holy city and separated itself from ungodly leaders (4,2). The physical descent is no longer sufficient for membership in the "house"; the religious conviction and membership in a group are decisive.[28]

2. Themes

(a) HEAVENLY TEMPLE.   In the OT heaven is represented as God's temple:[29]

> "The Lord shall be a witness against you, the Lord from his holy temple (ἐξ οἴκου ἁγίου αὐτοῦ). For behold the Lord is coming forth out of his place (ἐκ τοῦ τόπου αὐτοῦ), and will come down and tread upon the high places of the earth" (Mi 1,2-3; cf. also Is 63,15; Dt 26,15).

Besides, the OT clearly represents the earthly sanctuary as modelled on a heavenly exemplar:

> "And you shall erect the tabernacle according to the plan (κατὰ τὸ εἶδος) for it which has been shown you on the mountain" (Ex 26,30; cf. also Ex 25,9(2x); Ex 25,40; comp. Jer 17,12; Wisd 9,10).

It is clear from Philo that later Judaism was also familiar with the archetypal sanctuary:

> "He (Moses) saw with the soul's eye the immaterial forms of the immaterial objects about to be made, and these forms had to be reproduced in copies (μιμήματα) perceived by the senses, taken from the original draught (ἀρχέτυπος), so to speak, and from patterns conceived in the mind ... So the shape of the model (παράδειγμα) was stamped upon the mind of the prophet". (Mos ii. 74-6; cf. also i.158; Quaest Ex ii.52.82).[30]

---

[26] See, G. VERMES, *Scripture and Tradition in Judaism* (Leiden, 1961) 26-39.

[27] See, Gn 10,25.

[28] Consequently, the new "house" belongs no more to the "house" of Juda (CD 4,2).

[29] In the OT three-tiered world-view, heaven is the abode proper to God, remote from men and inaccessible to them (cf. Is 14,12-15). See, P. GRELOT, *De la mort à la vie éternelle* (Paris, 1971) 107.206; also H. TRAUB, *TDNT* V 507. Thus heaven in the OT is represented in general as God's dwelling-place (e.g. Pss 2,4; 11(10),4; Is 63,15; 64,1-2; Eccl 5,2).

[30] The translation is from the Loeb Classical Library edition. We note that this archetypal temple is created by God.

However, the problem of God's transcendence (dwelling in heaven) and his immanence (dwelling in an earthly temple) is never fully resolved in the OT (cf. Is 66,1-2; comp. Is 57,15; 2 Sm 7,5.7; I Kgs 8,27; comp. I Chr 17,4-6; 2 Chr 6,7ff). Still, these two temples, the earthly and the heavenly, share a mysterious identity in the OT. In the cultic act the celestial world and the terrestrial meet (comp. Ps 57(56),3). This same idea of a heavenly worship, and therefore of a heavenly temple, is also present in Qumran. Here again the celestial and terrestrial meet in the cultic act:

> "He (God) has granted them a share in the lot of the Saints (i.e. the angels) and has united their assembly, the Council of the Community, with the Sons of heaven" (IQS ii,7f; comp. IQH 3,21f).

All this indicates that by the beginning of the Christian era the heavenly temple and worship, and some kind of access to the heavenly world, and union with it, were familiar to Palestinian Judaism. However, this heavenly temple as such has no eschatological connotations in the OT.[31]

(b) PARADISE OF THE JUST.[32]

(i) *Paradise and the Promised Land.*   The earliest biblical representation of paradise is a concrete picture of earthly happiness (Gn 2,8-9). There man's life of intimacy and familiarity with God is vividly portrayed (Gn 3,8; comp. 2,3-9). But even after the fall God's promise of happiness directs man, not to heaven, but to a promised land which bears the distinctive marks of earthly bliss (Ex 20,12; 23,22-26; Dt 8,4-10; comp. 6,2-3). This promised land already has a savour of paradise (Ex 3,8; Dt 8,4-10).

The experience of Israel in the promised land becomes later for the prophets a true prefiguring of eschatological happiness. Salvation history advances towards a kind of paradise regained (Hos 2,14-23; Is 11,6-9; 51,3; 65,25; Ez 36,35; 47,7-12; Jl 3,18(4,18)). Just as a life of intimacy and familiarity with God was essential to the happiness of the first paradise, so too the joy of life-with-God will constitute the eschatological

---

[31] Wisd 3,14 is no exception (comp. Is 56,4-5).

[32] On the various aspects of the theme discussed here, see, P. GRELOT, *op. cit.* (n. 29); P. BEAUCHAMP, "Le salut corporel des justes et la conclusion du livre de la sagesse", *Bib* 45 (1964) 491-526; B. J. ALFRINK, "L'idée de résurrection d'après Daniel, XII, 1-2", *Bib* 40 (1959) 355-371; R. E. MURPHY, "'To know your might is the root of immortality' (Wisd 15,3)", CBQ 25 (1963) 88-93; E. COTHENET, "Paradis", DBS, VI, 1178-1219; R. MARTIN-ACHARD, *De la mort à la résurrection d'après l'Ancien Testament*, (Neuchâtel-Paris, 1956); K. SCHUBERT, "Die Entwicklung der Auferstehungslehre von der nachexilischen bis zur frührabbinischen Zeit", BZ 6 (1962) 177-214.

happiness finally to be regained. This transformation reaches even to the universe (Is 65,17; 66,22; comp. 43,19). Effectively, these texts suggest a radical transformation of the human condition and a transfiguration of the universe.

(ii) *Afterlife.* This same image of paradise lies behind yet another tradition which has a special importance in the Jewish concept of the afterlife. By way of exception to the common law of death (or equivalently descent into hell) Enoch (Gn 5,24; comp. Sir 44,16; 49,14-16) and Elijah (2 Kgs 2,9f; comp. Sir 48,9-10; cf. also Mal 3,22-23 (LXX)) are transported out of this world. God reserves a super-terrestrial happiness for both of these men. At the end of their earthly life they continue a life-with-God. Both of these figures, Enoch (I En 70) and Elijah (I En 89) again have a special significance for the Jewish representation of the afterlife in the Book of Enoch.[33]

Even without any explicit speculation on the afterlife, the psalms already bear witness to a spiritual longing (Pss 42(41)-43(42); 63(62); 84(83); 137(136); 143(142)). It is not the joy of earthly gifts that is desired. In some mysterious way man's beatitude is here linked with a spiritual longing for a life-with-God. Some of the psalms even seem to imply belief in the afterlife (Pss 16(15),10-11; 73(72),23-24; 49(48),15). The redemption of the just is conceived after the fashion of transference to a life-with-God.

These first glimpses of the psalmist already prepare the way for the doctrine of retribution in the Book of Wisdom.[34] Here the hope of the just "is full of immortality" (3,4); they are "in the hand of God" (3,1), "at peace" (3,3); "at rest" (4,7); death is only an appearance for them (3,2). We find tableaux of external happiness scattered with classical metaphors: the just will shine (3,7; comp. Dn 12,3), they shall reign (3,8; 5,16; comp. Dn 7,27; Is 62,3). But behind these metaphors we discover the essential of a promised happiness in a life-with-God: those who are faithful in love will dwell with him (οἱ πιστοὶ ἐν ἀγάπῃ προσμενοῦσιν αὐτῷ, 3,9); they will share the life of the divine lot among the saints (5,5). It is all well summed up in Wisdom, 5,15: "the righteous live forever" (Δίκαιοι δὲ εἰς τὸν αἰῶνα ζῶσιν).

All these pregnant expressions look primarily to the afterlife. However, we find no mention of the resurrection of the just in the Book

---

[33] See, P. Grelot, "La légende d'Hénoch dans les Apocryphes et dans la Bible. Origine et signification", *RecSR* 46 (1958) 205.

[34] Job had already provided a criticism of the current theory of happiness proposed by his friends (Jb 4,6-9; 8,8-22) with a contradiction provided by the facts (Jb 21; 24,1-12; 23).

of Wisdom.[35] It is worthy of note that here the concrete tableaux of eternal happiness are all related to the Visitation and the Judgment of God as in the eschatology of the prophets and of the Apocalypses (Wis 3,7.13; 4,15; 4,20-5,1). However, it is surely difficult to accept that all these expressions of Wisdom are merely a euphemism for sheol. Be that as it may, there is nothing to indicate that access to eternal life took place immediately after death, or departure from the world.

(iii) *Resurrection.* The doctrine of the resurrection is a relatively late acquisition of OT eschatological hope. Isaiah speaks of "the remnant" to be saved at the final crisis (Is 4,2-3; comp. Jer 3,17f). And the most ancient prophetic texts represent the eschatological work of God in the image of a resurrection from the dead (Ez 37,1-4; Is 26,19). The Book of Daniel takes up this perspective of collective eschatology (12,1).[36] But here we find in addition a new perspective of individual eschatology (12,2).[37] Daniel applies the resurrection to the individual martyrs. This in turn is inseparable from the problem of individual retribution.[38]

The text of Dn 12,1-4 is clearly eschatological[39] and deals explicitly with the resurrection (ἀναστήσονται, 12,2). It first predicts the final deliverance of God's people (σωθήσεται), all of those whose name is written in the Book of Life (12,1). Many should rise from the dead (ἀναστήσονται), with some of these to everlasting life (εἰς ζωὴν αἰώνιον, 12,2) and some to shame and everlasting disgrace (εἰς ὀνειδισμὸν καὶ εἰς αἰσχύνην αἰώνιον, 12,2). The resurrection of Dn 12,2-4 refers both to the just and unjust alike,[40] although it is directly ordained to eternal life for the just alone. These will become assimilated to, or join, the heavenly host, and enter into a transfigured universe: "and those who are wise shall shine like the brightness of the firmament; and those who turn many to righteousness, like the stars for ever and ever" (Dn 12,3; comp. Is 25,8).[41]

---

[35] See, P. BEAUCHAMP, *op. cit.* (n. 32) 491.

[36] J. J. COLLINS explains the conceptual framework of the text. See, *The Apocalyptic Vision of the Book of Daniel* (Missoula, 1977), 138.

[37] On this text of Daniel, 12,1-3, see G. W. E. NICKELSBURG, Jr., *Resurrection, Immortality, and Eternal Life in Intertestamental Judaism* (London, 1972) 11-27.

[38] See, note, 34.

[39] This is clear from the beginning of ch. 12 which begins with "at that time" (ובעת ההיא). This in turn corresponds to the terminology "at the time of the end" (ובעת קץ), which introduces the preceding passage (11,40-45). The eschatological character of our text is also clear from the apocalyptic expression "and there shall be a time of trouble, such as never has been since there was a nation till that time" (v.1), meaning, till the time of the end (comp. Mt 24,21; Mk 12,19).

[40] B. J. ALFRINK erroneously (in our view) refers the "resurrection" of Dn 12,2 solely to the just and not to sinners. See, *op. cit.* (n. 32) 365-366.

[41] J. J. COLLINS explains that "to shine like the stars" means "to join the angelic host", and provides ample evidence in support of this meaning. See, *op. cit.* (n. 36) 137.

Here the happiness promised is de-materialised somewhat. It is literally the happiness of "eternal life" in a kind of paradise regained, as the just will awake to "everlasting life" (εἰς ζωὴν αἰώνιον, Dn 12,2; comp. Gn 3,22, ζήσεται εἰς τὸν αἰῶνα) in the company of the heavenly host. However, the nature of this afterlife is not made any more precise, although the final destiny of the just is at least assured. It is firmly linked with a collective eschatology: "your people" (MT) = "all the people" (LXX) will be saved" (v. 1).[42]

The Book of Maccabees reiterates this Jewish faith in the resurrection (2 Mc 7,1.11.14.23.28.36; 12,38-45; 14,46). It is a question of bodily resurrection (2 Mc 7,11: 14,46), directly ordained to eternal life (2 Mc 7,9.14.23.36). However, there is nothing to indicate that universal resurrection is intended. It is solely a question of the virtuous. God will not dispense the just from the common law of death, but they face death supported by the hope of immortality and the assurance of the resurrection (2 Mc 7,9.11.14,23.28.36). The problem of individual retribution is here again inseparable from the problem of the death of the just. But the author maintains strict reserve on the manner of the resurrection, and on when it will take place.

Clearly, the biblical revelation of the nature of paradise is incomplete. The beatitude of the just immediately after death is not clearly affirmed in the Book of Wisdom (3,2-3), while the Book of Daniel predicts the resurrection of the just, but only in general terms (12,2). However, the essential element of the promised happiness lies in a life-with-God forever. In the collective eschatology of the prophets, as in the individual eschatology of a later epoch, this life-with-God constitutes the core of the afterlife. At the two extremes of salvation history the image of an earthly paradise makes concrete the ideal of human happiness as life-with-God. Finally, the image of a "transference" of Enoch by God, exercising its influence on the Psalms (19(18),16; 49(48),16; 73(72),24) and on the Book of Wisdom (4,10-14), allows the representation of a mysterious super-terrestrial happiness with God reserved for the just. In the concept of an eschatological happiness in which the body of man will share; and especially in the hope of a life-with-God forever and the joy of living in his presence, the biblical revelation is entirely original.[43] It is to this central core of the Jewish expectation of eschatological happiness and life-with-God, as we shall see, that the Book of Enoch gives imaginative (or mythological) representation when it depicts the beatitude of the just in the eternal temple.

---

[42] See, P. BEAUCHAMP, op. cit. (n. 32) 510.

[43] For a survey of the other ancient beliefs in the afterlife, see P. GRELOT, op. cit. (n. 29) 102-107.

(c) GOAL OF THE TEMPLE.

(i) *Earthly Temple.* The temple was God's dwelling-place, the locus par excellence of his presence.[44] As such it was the source of divine blessings and life for Israel. These blessings which issued from God's presence in the temple were not simply "spiritual"; they were also closely linked with man's material welfare and prosperity. From the temple Yahweh decided the destiny of the nations (Am 1,2ff; Pss 47(46),8; 82(81); 96(95),10-13; 99(98),1f.). God's presence in the temple was also the assurance of the deliverance of his people (Pss 46(45); 48(47); 76(75)), and the possession of the land (Ex 34,23-24; Jer 7,1-15). But these blessings are not limited to victory over hostile armies; they extend to the bestowal of all blessings and fertility from the temple where Yahweh is to be found (Pss. 24(23),5; 65(64),5(4); 68(67),10-11(9-10); 128(127),5; 132(131),15; 133(132),3; 134 (133),3).

The image of a fertilising river which flows through Zion is vitally related to the temple as the source of blessings (Ps 46(45),4). The real significance of this river derives from Israel's belief in the river which fructifies the garden of paradise (Gn 2,10-14; comp. Ps 65(64),10(9); Is 33,21; Jl 4,18 (3,18); Ez 47; Ze 14,8; comp. also Ap 22,1f). The devout Israelite knew that in Yahweh's house there was a "fountain of life" and a "river of delights" (Ps 36(35),8-9). In a word, the temple was the source of salvation.

Understandably, then, the temple became the centre and goal of Israel's aspirations. The privilege of access to worship there was not lightly given (cf. Pss 15(14); 24(23),3-4; comp. Is 33,14-16; Jer 7,1ff).[45] To worship in the temple was to share in the outflow of divine blessings to Israel and to the land on which Israel was privileged to dwell as Yahweh's "sojourners" (*gērîm*). (comp. Lv 25,23; Ps 39(38),13(12)). Those who worship in Yahweh's house share in the blessings of Yahweh towards Israel, and dwell securely upon the land (Ex 34,24). Therefore, it was a particular privilege "to dwell" in the Lord's temple (Pss 23(22),6; 27(26),4; 61(60),4; 65(64),4; 84(83),4; 91(90),1.9; 134(133); 135(134),2; Is 38,20; comp. Is 5,4).[46] All, therefore, who worship in the temple enjoy the blessing of living as a member of Yahweh's people in his land. They can even be said to be "planted" in Yahweh's house (πεφυτευμένοι, Ps

---

[44] See, note, 29.

[45] There were conditions of entrance into Yahweh's temple. This is clear from the "entrance-tôrôt", which were part of a liturgical celebration for all who shared in the temple.

[46] The language of Ps 23(22),6 and 27(26),4 is not a sublime cult-mysticism, nor applicable only to Levitical temple personnel. It is relevant to every Israelite.

92(91),13(14); καταφύτευσον, Ex 15,17; 2 Mc 1,29; comp. also καταφυτεύσω, 2 Sm 7,10 = I Chr 17,9) just as Israel was "planted" in the land (καταφύτευσας, Ps 44(43),3(2); καταφύτευσας, Ps 80(79),8(9).10; comp. ἐφύτευσεν, v. 16).

Thus to attain to the goal of the temple is to be-with-God, and so to share in the blessings of salvation, as a member of the worshipping community.

(ii) *Eschatological Temple.*   In the OT a fertilising river issuing from the Jerusalem temple indicates it as the source of eschatological blessings. Ezekiel had seen a river flow from the rock underneath the temple (Ez 47,1-12). Zechariah announces that God will pour out on the house of David a spirit of compassion and supplication. He takes up the same idea again with the image of "a fountain" which "will be opened for the house of David and the citizens of Jerusalem" (13,1), only to tell us finally that "living water" (ὕδωρ ζῶν) shall flow out from Jerusalem at the end of time (13,8). So, too, Joel announces for the final age "that a fountain (πηγή) shall come forth from the house of the Lord" (4,18).

The blessings of salvation reserved for the eschatological age are also inseparably linked with the Jerusalem temple as the gathering-place of the nations. The parallel texts of Isaiah and Micah describe these benefits (Is 2,4; Mi 4,3). The exaltation of this eschatological temple inaugurates a new age of peace and happiness for all mankind.

However, it is only in the Book of Enoch[47] that the heavenly temple becomes designated explicitly as the goal of eschatological bliss. Here we have the fullest description of the heavenly temple in Jewish literature. It is a magnificent crystal building, and contains an inner house (i.e. holy of holies) in which God is enthroned in great majesty:

---

[47] The Books of Enoch include the Ethiopic and the Slavonic Enoch. I Enoch is preserved in an Ethiopic version of the lost Greek version of an Aramaic (or possibly Hebrew) original, also lost. The date of composition is by no means certain. For a full discussion, see D. S. Russell, *The Method and Message of Jewish Apocalyptic* (London, 1964). Russell himself dates it "from c. 164 onwards" (p. 51). P. Grelot maintains that the section entitled The Book of Parables, or The Similitudes of Enoch (I Enoch, ch.s 37-71), is certainly the most recent. He dates it between the first century, B.C. and the NT period. See, "Le messianisme dans les apocryphes de l'AT", in *La Venue du Messie* (RechBibl VII) Bruges-Paris, 1962) 48. J. T. Milik and M. Black date it as late as 250 A.D. See, *The Books of Enoch. Aramaic Fragments of Qumran Cave 4* (edited by J. T. Milik with the collaboration of M. Black) (Oxford, 1976) 6. See, also M. Black, "The 'Parables' of Enoch (I En 37-71) and the 'Son of Man'", *ExpT* 88 (1976-1977) 5-8. M. E. Stone, however, writes: "The Similitudes of Enoch (I Enoch chap.s 37-71) probably come from the last century B.C.". See "The Book of Enoch and Judaism in the Third Century B.C.", *CBQ* 40 (1978) 492. The evidence used in our study is confined to I Enoch, with references in the notes (where helpful) to some significant parallels in 2 Enoch (or Slavonic Enoch).

"In every respect it so excelled in splendour and magnificence and extent that I cannot describe to you its splendour and its extent. And its floor was of fire, and above it were lightings and the path of the stars, and its ceiling also was flaming fire. And I looked and saw therein a lofty throne: its appearance was a crystal ... And the Great Glory sat thereon, and His raiment shone more brightly than the sun and was whiter than any snow" (I En, 14,16-18.20).[48]

The cult in this heavenly temple is also described. The author tells how Levi travels through the heavens to the "highest of them all" where he sees the temple and its priesthood and cult:

"For in the Highest of all dwelleth the Great Glory, in the holy of holies, far above all holiness. And in (the heaven next to) it are the angels of the presence of the Lord, who minister (λειτουργοῦντες) and make propitiation (ἐξιλασκόμενοι) to the Lord for all the sins of ignorance of the righteous. And they offer to the Lord a sweet-smelling savour, a reasonable and bloodless offering (λογικὴν καὶ ἀναίμακτον προσφοράν)"(I En 3,4-6; comp. 5,1-2).

This "house" is the eschatological goal of the just. Israel is depicted as a flock of sheep, which in the time of Solomon is represented as grazing peacefully around the temple "a tower lofty and great ... (which) was built on the house for the Lord of the sheep" (89,50).[49] The old temple is torn down and in its place a magnificent new one is erected:

"And I stood up to see till they folded up that old house; and carried off all the pillars, and all the beams and ornaments of the house were at the same time folded up with it, and they carried it off and laid it in a place in the south of the land. And I saw till the Lord of the sheep brought a new house greater and loftier than that first, and set it up in the place of the first which had been folded up; all its pillars were new, and its ornaments were new and larger than those of the first, the old one which He had taken away, and all the sheep were within it" (90,28-9).

---

[48] For a translation of I Enoch, see, R. H. CHARLES, *The Book of Enoch (Oxford, 1912)*, also F. MARTIN, *Le Livre d'Hénoch (Paris, 1906)*. Our translation in this section may be found in R. J. McKELVEY, *The New Temple. The Church in the New Testament* (Oxford, 1969) 28-32.

[49] The "tower" represents the temple, and the "house" very likely stands for Jerusalem.

Besides, the peace and repose of the just in this heavenly temple is often evoked:

> "In those days a whirlwind carried me off from the face of the earth and placed me at the extremity of the heavens. And there I saw another vision: the dwellings of the saints and the places of repose of the just. There my eyes saw their dwelling-places with the saints ... The just and the elect will be innumerable before him for an eternity of eternities ... The just and the elect will shine before him as the lights of fire ..." (I En 39,3-8; cf. also 51; 58; 62,13-16).

So, too, a river flows from this heavenly temple as a source of blessings for the universe:

> "And I went from thence to the middle of the earth (i.e. to the temple), and I saw a blessed place in which there were trees with branches abiding and blooming (of a dismembered tree). And there I saw a holy mountain, and underneath the mountain to the east there was a stream and it flowed towards the south" (26,1-2).

Finally, the abode reserved for the just is none other than the place where the patriarch Enoch has been placed after his transference (I En 39,3-8ff). Enoch associates himself with the angelic liturgy in this heavenly temple of bliss. There the essence of his joy is a life-with-God beyond description, except in symbols.

This symbolism of Enoch can best be explained as a final culmination of the OT tradition. The author has taken the familiar OT world-picture of the Jerusalem temple as the goal and source of eschatological blessings, with the OT eschatological vision of the human condition radically transformed (Hos 2,14-23; Is 11,6-8; 51,3; 65,25; Ez 36.35; 47,7-12; Jl 4,18; Is 2,4; Mi 4,3-4) and the universe transfigured (Is 66,22; 65,22; comp. 43,19); and projected it into heaven. Ideas traditionally associated with the OT explanation of eschatological happiness and the eschatological temple are now predicted of the heavenly temple.

3. Application to Jn 14,2-3

(a) SIMILARITIES. It would be in line with Jewish tradition to interpret "the Father's house" of Jn 14,2-3 with reference to the heavenly temple. The disciples might easily have understood the image in line with the OT theme of the Jerusalem temple as the goal of salvation in general and of eschatological salvation in particular; and at the same time in line with all that the OT had foretold of the human condition radically transformed and the universe transfigured in the promised paradise of the eschatological age. All of this could now be understood as specified in a new way with reference to the heavenly temple in line with the culmination of a whole Jewish tradition represented by Enoch.[50] The Father's house would be a suitable image to designate this heavenly temple as the eschatological goal to which Jesus promises to take his disciples to share with him in the super-terrestrial happiness and intimacy of a life-with-God forever in the hereafter.

We may also detect the influence of the Nathan oracle on Jn 14,2-3. The motif of the son who will abide permanently in God's house forever in the Nathan oracle, as interpreted with reference to the temple in Targum I Chr 17,14, could be seen to correspond to the permanent condition of Jesus in "the house of my Father" in Jn 14,2-3. Jesus already dwells in the Father's house permanently (ὅπου εἰμὶ ἐγώ), or (in the language of Jn 14,2-3), has his μονή, by strict right as son, in the Father's house (ἐν τῇ οἰκία τοῦ πατρός μου).[51]

Thus the condition of Jesus in Jn 14,2-3 might be interpreted as the fulfilment of that line of Jewish tradition where the Davidic Messiah, who is to have a father/son relationship with Yahweh himself, is to abide permanently in the temple.

(b) DIFFERENCES. The term οἰκία is never found in the Jewish tradition to designate the temple, earthly or heavenly. It must be granted that the term οἶκος would appear at first sight to be the one best suited to Jn 14,2-3, if the evangelist wished to convey only the meaning "temple". It would conform to the OT use of the phrase οἶκος(τοῦ) Θεοῦ, which was the common term for the temple in the Jewish tradition.[52] It would also conform to John's own use of the phrase οἶκος τοῦ πατρός μου with reference to the Jerusalem temple in Jn 2,16 (comp. also 2,17).

To understand "my Father's house" as a designation either for the Jerusalem temple, or the heavenly temple, would undoubtedly be something quite new and original. There is no exact parallel in the Jewish tradition to the phrase in this sense. However, it could still be interpreted in line with the Jewish tradition of the Davidic Messiah, who is to address

---

[50] J.O. TUÑI-VANCELLS expresses this well: "Se trata de un versículo del cuarto evangelio que parece ser heredero de la concepción apocalíptica del libro de Enoch sobre la casa de Dios". See, *La verdad os hará libres: Jn 8,32. Liberación y libertad del creyente en el cuarto evangelio* (Barcelona, 1973) 181.

[51] The permanent character of the expected Messiah is stated explicitly in Jn 12,34. See, W.C. VAN UNNIK, "The Quotation from the Old Test. in John 12,34" *NovT* 3 (1959) 174-79.

[52] See, note, 8.

God as "my Father": "he will invoke me, 'my Father, my God'" (Πατήρ μου εἶ σύ, Θεός μου, Ps 89(88),27), and who is himself in turn addressed by God as Son: "you are my son, today I have begotten you" (Υἱός μου εἶ σύ, Ps 2,7). The phrase "the house of my Father", then, is a possible designation for the temple, if an original one, on the lips of the Son of David — Son of God (comp. 2 Sm 7,14; I Chr 17,13).

In fact, this mysterious father/son relationship between God and the Davidic Messiah is fulfilled in an entirely original way in Jn 14,2-3. Jesus is not only the expected Messiah who is the Son of Yahweh in some kind of metaphorical way (Ps 2,7; 89(88),27; 2 Sm 7,14; I Chr 17,13). The evidence of the fourth gospel in general points to Jesus as the Messiah, who is God in the strict sense, with a capital G (cf. Jn 5,18; 10,30.38).[53] Through his passion-resurrection the Son whom God has given to David will be manifested as the Son of God — equal to God (Jn 8,28). In this sense, Jesus makes an unheard of claim in Jn 14,2-3 equivalent to one of equality with God, implying a strictly divine Father/Son relationship between himself and God who is his Father.[54] It is as such also that Jesus dwells in his Father's temple as the exclusive property of Yahweh ("my house") with the strict right of a Son, who is one with God, his Father (cf. Jn 14,10-11.20; 17,21-23).

B. THE MANY ROOMS

1. Vocabulary: Rooms

(a) OLD TESTAMENT. The term μονή occurs only once in the OT (1 Mc 7,38). The structure of the verse is as follows:

a. ποίησον ἐκδίκησιν ἐν τῷ ἀνθρώπῳ τούτῳ καὶ ἐν τῇ παρεμβολῇ αὐτοῦ,

b. καὶ πεσέτωσαν ἐν ῥομφαίᾳ·

c. μνήσθητι τῶν δυσφημιῶν αὐτῶν

d. καὶ μὴ δῷς αὐτοῖς μονήν.

---

[53] It is only in the post-Paschal perspective that the profound implications of Jn 14,2-3, as underlined by J. H. BERNARD, are revealed: "The Temple is often described in the OT as 'the house of God', and Jesus so described it (Mk 2,26; Mt 12,4; Lk 6,4). It was to make an unmistakable claim for Himself to substitute for this familiar expression the words 'the house of my Father'". See, *op. cit.* 91.

[54] The remarkable phrase "my Father" occurs 26x in John (comp. Mt 16x; Lk 14x). Moreover, the title "Father" in John (absolute use, 90x) has almost become a synonym for God, and is the predominant title for God on the lips of Jesus.

The first two members (v. 38a; 38b) are clearly linked together by the conjunction καί (consecutive), and together they express one and the same wish: "take vengeance on this man and on his army, and (consequently) let them fall by the sword". The second two members (v. 38c; 38d) are also clearly linked together by the conjunction καί (consecutive), and continue the thought of v. 38a and v. 38b. They provide the reason for the invocation of death in vengeance, namely, for blasphemy: "remember their blasphemies, and (consequently) may you not give them μονή".[55] The parallelism in thought between v. 38a and v. 38c suggests a parallelism in thought also between v. 38b and v. 38d. Both v. 38b and v. 38d are linked to v. 38a and v. 38c by καί consecutive, respectively. These two members (v. 38b and v. 38d) would, then, both seem to express more or less the same idea in positive and negative form:

v. 38b may they perish by the sword   — positive.

v. 38d may you not give them μονή   — negative.

However, the meaning of v. 38b is clear: "may they perish" so that v. 38d should express more or less the same idea negatively. The phrase: "may they perish" now becomes, expressed negatively: "do not give them abiding", or equivalently: "may they not survive (live)," or: "may they not remain alive". In fact, the noun μονή should be rendered here primarily in a dynamic sense as a noun of action rather than as a static noun. The translations generally render the term μονή in I Mc 7,38 in this way. However, a connotation of "respite" or "repose" is also implied in view of the immediate context of the phrase as a prayer for victory against enemies.[56]

Thus both the context and the structure of this solitary use of the term μονή in the OT in the phrase μὴ δῷς αὐτοῖς μονήν of I Mc 7,38 seem to indicate primarily a meaning of "continued existence" or "permanent abiding", with the idea of "respite" or "repose" clearly implied.

---

[55] The term forms part of the prayer of the priests in the temple uttered against Nicanor, who threatens to destroy the temple with his army.

[56] Thus the *BJ* renders: "ne leur accorde pas de relâche" (ad loc.), and the TOB: "ne leur accorde pas de sursis" (ad loc.). These renderings capture the connotation of "respite" or "repose" implicit in the term. This idea of rest or peace after battle is clearly in context. See, note, 55.

(b) EXTRA-BIBLICAL. The term μονή occurs twice in Josephus. In one passage the term clearly signifies "an abode" or "dwelling-place":

"So Jonathan took up his residence in Jerusalem (τὴν μονὴν ἐποιεῖτο), making various repairs in the city and arranging everything according to his liking" (Antiq. xiii,2,1).[57]

Jerusalem became this "abode" or "abiding-place".

In the other passage the meaning of the term is less clear. The sentence is as follows:

"And he found in it a certain hollow cave, which he entered, and there made his abode for some time (καὶ διετέλει ποιούμενος ἐν αὐτῷ τὴν μονήν) (Antiq. viii,13,7).[58]

Here the term μονή appears at first sight to be used in the sense of a "resting-place", or a "station" for refreshment or repose on a journey; for it is applied to the stay of Elijah in the cave on Mount Horeb. But the context and construction alike show that here also the term signifies "an abode" or "abiding-place".

Thus the term μονή is also used in a static sense within the Jewish tradition to indicate an "abode" or "dwelling-place", with the stress on the idea of permanence or stability. However, the term is never used of room(s) in the Jerusalem temple, nor with reference to room(s) in the heavenly temple.

2. Themes

(a) ROOMS.

(i) *In General.*   The possession of a house in general is a sign in the OT of stability and success, just as to possess a royal house (or palace) designates the stable possession of power:

"I will build myself a great house with spacious upper rooms (οἶκον σύμμετρον, ὑπερῷα ῥιπιστά)" (Jer 22,14; comp. 2 Sm 7,1; 5,11)[59]

---

[57] Our translation is from the Loeb edition. See, *Jewish Antiquities* (London, 1926-65). W. WHISTON translates: "And thus did Jonathan make his abode". See, *Josephus. Complete Works* (Michigan, 1960).

[58] Our translation is from the Loeb edition. W. WHISTON renders: "he entered into it (cave), and continued to make his abode in it". See, *op. cit.* (n. 57).

[59] David says to Nathan: "see now, I dwell in a house of cedar" (2 Sm 7,1). In this way he expresses his attainment of victory and rest from his enemies, with peace and prosperity.

Little wonder, then, that we should find reference repeatedly in the OT to the rooms of an ordinary house, where one might flee for refuge and safety:

> "Ben-hadad also fled, and entered an inner chamber in the city (εἰς τὸν οἶκον... εἰς τὸ ταμίειον)" (I Kgs 20,30 = LXX 3 Kgs 21,30).[60]

Thus in Dt 32,25 terror inside the chamber is identified with the summit of affliction:

> "In the open the sword will bereave, and in the chambers shall be terror (καὶ ἐκ τῶν ταμιείων φόβος)" (Dt 32,25).

Moreover, the term "room" in the plural takes on an important eschatological significance in Isaiah's Song of victory:

> "Go into your rooms, my people (εἴσελθε εἰς τὰ ταμίειά σου), shut your doors behind you. Hide yourself a little while until the wrath has passed. For, see, Yahweh will soon come out of his dwelling, to punish the inhabitants of the earth for their crimes" (Is 26,20-21).

Here, we find the same term חדר (MT) that we find to describe the rooms of the Jewish temple in I Chr 28,11.[61]

(ii) *In the Temple.* The temple itself was constructed in three major parts: the Ulam or porch, the Hekal or main hall, the Debir or inner sanctuary.[62] Besides, the term αὐλή occurs frequently of the temple in the LXX (177x). It commonly designates the "open court or atrium" in front of the tabernacle, or temple (Ex 27,9; 2 Chr 6,14; Is 34,13; Jer 30,28; Ez, passim).[63] But the temple itself is often referred to in a transferred sense as the "courts" (αὐλαί: Pss 84(83),2-10; 135(134),2; 92(91),12; 100(99),3-4; 116(115),19; Neh 13,7).

However, there is ample evidence besides to show that the Jerusalem temple itself had several inner "rooms", or apartments:

> "David gave his son Solomon the plans for the temple (τὸ παράδειγμα τοῦ ναοῦ) and the building (καὶ τῶν οἴκων αὐτοῦ), the treasuries (τῶν ζακχω αὐτοῦ), the upper rooms (καὶ τῶν ὑπερῴων), the inner apartments (καὶ τῶν ἀποθηκῶν τῶν ἐσωτέρων)... He also gave him the plans (τὸ

---

[60] Comp. Dt 32,25; I Kgs 22,25; Jer 22,13-14; Is 26,20.

[61] The Hebrew term denotes a place of refuge, or escape, where one flies in terror for safety and concealment: "conclave pro conclavi (commutans), i.e. ab uno in aliud confugiens". See, F. ZORELL, *Lexicon Hebraicum et Aramaicum Veteris Testamenti* (Parisiis, 1955).

[62] On the divisions of the temple in general, see, R. DE VAUX, *op. cit.* (n. 17) 313-317.

[63] This is the more common use of the term, which occurs some 177x in the LXX.

παράδειγμα) which he had in mind for the courts of the temple of the Lord (τῶν αὐλῶν οἴκου κυρίου), all the surrounding apartments (καὶ πάντων τῶν παστοφορίων), the treasuries of the temple of God, and the treasuries of dedicated gifts (τῶν ἀποθηκῶν)" (I Chr 28,11-12).[64]

So, too, the eschatological temple of Ezekiel's vision has many compartments:

> "Then he brought me into the outer court (εἰς τὴν αὐλὴν τὴν ἐσωτέραν) and behold, there were chambers (παστοφόρια) and a pavement, round about the court; there were thirty rooms on the pavement (τριάκοντα παστοφόρια)" (Ez 40,17).[65]

The divisions of the temple are also clear from the Temple Scroll of Qumran.[66] The structure of the scroll begins with a description of the temple building.[67] The scroll affirms that a temple must exist in the land (Ex 25,8-9) and that its blueprint, which specifies its house installations, stairs, courts, and their chambers (I Chr 28,11-12), was known to David (I Chr 28,11f). The scroll distinguishes between this temple and the messianic temple which God himself will build on "the Day of Blessing" (cf. I En 90,29; Jub 1,15-17.26-29). Three square courts surround the sanctuary.[68] The plan of the courts is based on the wilderness camp (Nm 2-3). This is best illustrated by the chambers of the outer court assigned to the priests, the three Levitic families, and the twelve tribes which also were grouped around the wilderness sanctuary. Columns 40-46 describe this outer court. It is a square with twelve gates named for the tribes. Along the court's walls are three stories of stoae and chambers (cf. Neh 12,44; 13,7) for the tribes (cf. Neh 12,44; 13,7), the priests (Nm 3,38), and the Levitical families (cf. Nm 3,23.29.35.38). The chambers are to be cleansed when the course is changed at the end of the sabbath (cf. Neh 12,1f; 13,9). On the roof of the third storey are columns for the constructing of booths for the Festival of Booths to be occupied by the elders, tribal chieftains, and the commanders of thousands and hundreds (cf. Neh 8,16-17).

---

[64] Comp. I Kgs 6,5-6; 2 Chr 31,11; Ezr 8,29; Neh 12,44; 13,4-9; Jer 35,2.4; 36,10.

[65] Comp. Ez 41,6; also ch.s 40-42 (passim).

[66] See, J. MILGROM, "The Temple Scroll" *BA* 41 (n. 3) (1978) 105-120. We are dependent on this excellent article pending the publication of the Scroll.

[67] Cols 4-7: The Exterior Wings, Sanctuary, Porch, Adytum, Attic, Stoa (west of Temple); cols 30-31: The House of the Winding Staircase; cols 31-35: The House of the Laver; cols 33-34: The House of Vessels; cols 34-35: The House of Slaughter; col 35: The Stoa (parwar); cols 36-38: The Inner Court; cols 38-40: The Middle Court; cols 40-46: The Outer Court.

[68] The Inner Court (cols 36-38); The Middle Court (cols 38-40); The Outer Court (cols 40-46).

Thus there is ample evidence in the Jewish tradition for a division of the temple into "rooms".[69]

(iii) *In the Heaven(s)*. The commandment of Ex 20,4 divides the universe into three parts, heaven, earth, and the chaotic waters under the earth. These divisions are never referred to as "rooms". Moreover, the universe itself is never called οἶκος or οἰκία in the OT. We do find examples of free poetic imagery depicting the cosmos as a house with a balcony (עליה) as a cover (Ps 104(103),2-3; Am 9,6), or as an outstretched tent (Is 40,22; Ps 104(103),2). In heaven above are chambers for snow and hail (Jb 38,22), the winds (Jer 49,36; 37,9.12; Ps 135(134),7), and the water (Ps 33(32),7; Jb 38,37), which in a cycle, when it has fallen on the earth as rain, returns thither (Jb 36,27; Is 55,10).

The Greek OT term to designate heaven is οὐρανός. It is found 51 times in the plural. As such it serves to express the idea of a plurality of heavens. Understandably, a distinction was made in later Judaism between the heavens, varying from two, three, five, seven to ten.[70] These divisions of the heaven(s) are not referred to as "rooms".

(b) RESTING-PLACES.

(i) *In the Temple.* In the OT the temple is the place of the repose of God as the final resting-place of the ark:

> "Arise, O Lord, and go to thy resting-place (ἀνάπαυσις) thou and the ark of thy might" (Ps 132(131),8).[71]

The temple is designated repeatedly as the "resting-place of God" (cf. Is 66,1; I Chr 28,2; 2 Chr 6,14; Sir 36,12).

So, too, the temple also became in turn the place of rest for the people of God. Israel's final possession of the land was closely linked with the attainment of "rest", or "repose" (cf. Ex 33,14; Dt 3,20; 12,9-11; 25,19; Nm 10,33; Jos 1,13.15; 21,44; 22,4; 2 Kgs 8,56; 1 Chr 23,25; Ps 95(94),11; Jer 31(38),2). The loss of the land in turn was synonymous with the loss of a place of rest (cf. Dt 28,63-67). It is precisely this attainment of rest in the secure possession of the land which is repeatedly

---

[69] According to Y. YADIN, the Temple Scroll was composed probably during the reign of John Hyrcanus (134-104), or slightly earlier, i.e, during the second century, B.C.. See, *op. cit.* (n. 66) 119.

[70] See, H. Traub, *TDNT* V 511f.

[71] There is also extra-biblical evidence for this idea of the temple as the place of repose for a god. See, R. DE VAUX, "Le Lieu que Yahvé a choisi pour y établir son nom", in *Das Ferne und Nahe Wort* (Festschrift L. Rost: Beihefte zur *ZAW* 105) (Berlin, 1967) 224, also note, 22.

designated as the condition for building the temple (cf. 2 Sm 7,1.11; 1 Kgs 5,35 (LXX vv. 17-19); 8,56; I Chr 17,8-9). After the entrance in fact, this idea of rest in the secure possession of the land was transferred to the temple.

In this way the temple also becomes the place of rest for the people of God. It is the goal where the psalmist longs to rest permanently in close intimacy with God (cf. Pss 42(41)-43(42); 63(62); 84(83); 137(136); 143(142)). Every devout Israelite longs to dwell permanently as a member of the worshipping community in intimate communion with God ever present in the temple (cf. Pss 23(22),6; 27(26),4; 61(60),4; 84(83),4; 91(90),1.9; 134(133); 135(134),2; Is 38,20; comp. Ps 5,4). The eschatological temple is also the final place of rest to which God will gather his people at the end of time (cf. Ex 15,17; 2 Mc 1,29; 2 Sm 7,10/I Chr 17,4; 4QFlor).[72]

(ii) *In the Afterlife.* We have already considered the gradual evolution of belief in the afterlife within the Jewish tradition. In the OT sheol was the abode of all the dead, without distinction of dwelling-places. Later came the gradual emergence of belief in life after death and the resurrection, collective and individual, with a clear distinction between the destiny of the wicked and the just. However, the revelation of the OT on life after death is essentially incomplete. Entrance of the just into heaven immediately after death is not clearly affirmed. Hence, we find many descriptions of the habitation(s) or room(s) of the just in an intermediate state while expecting the final resurrection and the judgment.

Important evidence for this may be found in the later Jewish apocalyptic literature. IV Esdras gives perhaps the most significant description of the intermediate state of the just in expectation of the final resurrection. In chapter 7 Ezra speaks to God in these words:

> "If I have found favour in thy sight, O Lord, show this also to thy servant: whether after death, even now when every one of us must give back his soul, we shall be kept in rest until those times come in which thou shalt renew the creation, or shall we suffer torture forthwith?" (7,75).[73]

The answer given is that, when the soul departs from the body "that it may return to him who gave it", it adores the glory of the Most High first

---

[72] We will consider these texts more at length in our treatment of the term τόπος.

[73] For the text and translation we are following R. H. CHARLES, *The Apocrypha and Pseudepigrapha of the Old Testament*, (Oxford, 1913). W. O. E. OESTERLEY dates the Apocalypse of Ezra, or IV Esdras, "circa A.D. 100". See, *Esdras* (The Ezra Apocalypse) (London, 1933), Introduction, p. XXI. So, too, does D. S. RUSSELL "c.a.d. 90". See, *op. cit.* (n. 47) 38.

of all (7,78). Then at once the souls of the wicked and the souls of the just go their separate ways, the former to suffering and the latter to blessing. The condition of the souls of the wicked is first described:

> "Such souls shall not enter into habitations, but shall wander about henceforth in torture, ever grieving and sad in seven ways" (7,80).

A description is then given of the state of the souls of the righteous:

> "First of all they shall see with great joy the glory of him who receives them; and they shall rest in seven orders" (7,91).

Just as the souls of the wicked are tormented, so the souls of the righteous enter into bliss where they remain in resting-places (7,95), guarded by angels (7,95), until the time of the resurrection (7,32).[74] These abodes of the righteous departed are called "habitationes" (7,80), "habitacula" (7,85.101.121), and "promptuaria" (4,35; 7,32.95).[75] The meaning of these "abodes" is more fully explained in Rabbinical writings, echoing, doubtless, earlier ideas. The souls of the righteous, it is taught, go to the treasure-houses (אוצרות) under the throne of God; their chambers (מחיצות) are separated from the dwelling-place of the Almighty by a curtain (פרגוד); they may hear the voice of God, but they may not behold Him. These chambers of the just, at least as interpreted by the later Jewish tradition, would seem to be situated in some way within the heavenly temple under the throne of God.

A Nabataean inscription, dating from the beginning of the Christian era, also provides important evidence on the existence of a dwelling-place in the afterlife. The phrase כפרא ואונא (C.I.S. ii,202¹) is a very remarkable one to be found in an inscription from North Arabia.[76] In Syriac the word ﻝﺅﺝﻱ is sometimes employed of the abodes of the dead, and commonly does not suggest anything more than משכב את רפאם meaning "resting-places among the shades" (Phoen. Tabnith. 1.8; C.I.S. i 3⁸). Yet the term in the Nabataean inscription suggests something more than the mere resting-place of the dead. The use of two words is unique; the former denotes the sepulchre, the latter suggests something more: דנה כפרא ואונה, "this is the tomb and mansion", i.e. lodging, habitation. The

---

[74] In II Baruch, too, the souls of the righteous are preserved in "treasuries" (cf. 21,23; 23,4; 30,2), guarded by angels until the day of the final judgment. The Book of II Baruch, the Syrian Apocalypse of Baruch, is dated later than IV Esdras. D. S. Russell dates it "after A.D. 90". See, *op. cit.* (n. 47), Introd. xxxviii.

[75] See, W. O. E. Oesterley, *op. cit.* (n. 73) 37, note on IV Esdras 4,35.

[76] J. Courtenay James treats this inscription at length. See, "Mansiones Multae", *ExpT* 27 (1915-1916) 427-428.

idea is probably more elevated than בת עלמא, "house of eternity" (C.I.S. i,124; Eccl 12,5), which usually means "the grave". The central idea of אונא is rest with the suggestion of peace after conflict.[77] The term refers to a resting-abode, or state of rest, after the trials of life. It should be noted, however, that there is no question here of an abode, either in heaven itself or in the temple, earthly or heavenly.

The Book of Enoch also provides important evidence of dwelling-places in the afterlife. Before his journey to the Garden of the Just, Enoch visits the subterranean world where the souls of the dead await the final judgment (I En 22). Here we find a new kind of sheol, in striking contrast to the OT concept. The souls of the just await the final resurrection in a special part of sheol, where they are already separated from sinners (I En 22,5-9). At the final judgment this separation will be definitive.

However, in I En 70 we find a description of the "transportation" of Enoch to a paradise where he shares in the lot of the saints. There he awaits the final judgment when the whole earth will be transformed into paradise (I En 70). In this place, too, he is joined by Elijah after his "transportation" (I En 89,52).

Even in expectation of the final resurrection, then, the situation of the mass of the just in sheol differs from that of the Fathers, who by a special privilege of God are placed in a paradise of delights. But for all the final recompense is deferred until the final resurrection. Then sinners will see their condemnation to torture confirmed and all the just will eat of the Tree of Life in the Garden of delights, where they will occupy their eternal "dwelling-places" or "resting-places" and "the just and the elect will be innumerable before him for an eternity of eternities" in the heavenly temple (I En 39,3-8).

(c) INHABITANTS.

(i) *The Eschatological Temple.* Many of the OT expressions of universalism are linked with the eschatological temple. One of the central ideas of Jewish eschatology is the regathering, or reunion, of Israel at the divine dwelling-place (2 Mc 1,27-29; comp. 2,7-8.17-18). However, the extension of this concept to include the Gentiles marks an important new development (Is 2,2-4/Mi 4,1-4; Is 54,2; 56,6-7; 60,1-13; 66,18-21; Ze 8,20-23; 14,16-21; Tb 14,4-7; comp. 13,10-14).

Thus the Jerusalem temple becomes the goal of the final and universal salvation of the eschatological age, the centre of unity, not only for Israel, but also for all mankind.

---

[77] J. COURTENAY JAMES concludes: "It is to be presumed that the Aramaic word behind μοναί was אונא, and that Our Lord's vernacular ran: (or אבא) בית אבי אונא אנן סניאין. This is supported, if not confirmed, by the Peshitta". See, *op. cit.* (n. 76) 428.

(ii) *The Heavenly Temple.* In the OT the heavenly temple is inhabited by immortal beings. It is the dwelling-place of Yahweh's innumerable court (I Kgs 22,19f; Jb 1,6-12; 2,1-7; Is 6,1f; Ze 3,1-7; Dn 7,9f). There the just will abide with God (Wis 3,9). They will share the lot of the saints and be numbered among the angels (Wis 5,5).

So, too, Philo in his use of the Stoic conception of the cosmic temple says that the heavenly (or uppermost) part (the νεώς) of this temple is inhabited by immortal beings (Som 1,34), and has angels as priests (Spec 1,66) and the Logos for its high priest (Som 1,215).

The texts of Qumran also show the heavenly temple peopled by immortal beings:[78] "the servants of the presence of the Glory ... the godly ones ... the cherubim ... the holy angels (4QS1,40,2-18) ... saints (angels) ... sons of heaven (IQH 3,21f; cf. 4,24f) ... the angels of the Face (IQH 6,12f) ... the angels of the Presence (IQSb 4,25f)". The members of the community mingle with the angels even before death (IQH 3,19f; 7,22-25; 11,3f).[79]

There is also abundant evidence for heavenly inhabitants in the Book of Enoch (I En 20,40; 3,4-6: 39,3-8). Moreover, we also find the universalism which was linked with the eschatological temple in the OT again linked with the heavenly temple. The old temple is torn down and in its place a magnificent new one is erected (I En 90,28-29). The advent of the new temple will mark great happenings. The ancient hostility between the Jews and the Gentiles will come to an end, and the latter will worship in the temple (I En 90,33). As a token of their reconciliation the sword which had been given to the Jews to destroy their enemies is put away in the temple (I En 90,34f). The author concludes "And I saw that that house was large and broad and very full" (I En 90,36).

3. Application to Jn 14,2-3

(a) SIMILARITIES. To interpret the μοναί of Jn 14,2-3 as permanent dwelling-places would be in accord with the use of the term μονή in the Jewish tradition. Within a house, as in Jn 14,2-3, such a use of the term would clearly designate a "room".

However, the use of the term μονή in the Jewish tradition provides no basis for interpreting the μοναί of Jn 14,2-3 as "stations" on a road or "halting-places" (resting-places) on a journey. Thus there would be no support for interpreting these μοναί to designate the different stages

---

[78] See, A. Dupont-Sommer, *The Essene Writings from Qumran* (Oxford, 1961), 102. 109. 219.

[79] See, J. Strugnell, "The Angelic Liturgy at Qumran — 4Q serek sirot 'olat hassabat", *VetTSup* 7 (1960) 344.

through which Jesus would have to pass on his journey to the heavenly home, in line with the Jewish tradition of a division of the heavens.[80] Moreover, these divisions are never referred to as "rooms".

Neither can the μοναί refer to the divisions of the universe.[81] These μοναί of Jn 14,2-3 exist within the "house". But the universe is never described as a "house" in the Jewish tradition, and its divisions are never referred to as "rooms".

However, the μοναί of Jn 14,2-3 might easily be interpreted with reference ot the temple. There is ample evidence in the Jewish tradition for a division of the temple into "rooms". So, too, the μοναί might be interpreted with reference to the eschatological temple, which also has many "rooms" in the Jewish tradition. Such an understanding would be all the more easy, since the idea of a "room" itself takes on eschatological significance within this same tradition.

Moreover, the disciples might also have understood this OT image of the eschatological temple with many "rooms" as specified in a new way in line with the Jewish tradition represented by Enoch,[82] with reference to the heavenly temple with its many rooms, or dwelling-places, for the just in the hereafter. The "rooms" in the Father's house would be a suitable image to designate the possibilities for others to dwell there. To these same "rooms" Jesus would now promise immediate entrance to his disciples at some indefinite moment in the future, when he would return to take them into these eternal and heavenly dwelling-places reserved for the just in the eschatological temple.[83] There they would await in anticipation of the final judgment, the resurrection on the last day.

The connotation of "rest" or "repose" implicit in the use of the term μονή would also support an interpretation of "the house with many rooms" in line with the Jewish tradition of the temple as the "resting-place" of God and his people.[84] This, too, might be seen as specified in a new way in line with the Jewish expectation of

---

[80] Such a concept of ascent would be entirely foreign to John. In fact, John never once describes a journey of Jesus through the heavens, either by way of ascent or descent. D. MOLLAT makes this point well. See, "Remarques sur le vocabulaire spatial du quatrième évangile", *StudEv* I (TU 73) (1957) 328.

[81] O. SCHAEFER attempts to understand the Father's house in this way. See, "Der Sinn der Rede Jesu von den vielen Wohnungen in seines Vaters Hause und von dem Weg zu ihm (Jon. 14,1-2)", *ZNW* 32 (1933) 212-213. Again, such a concept would be quite un-Johannine.

[82] J. O. TUÑI-VANCELLS has already noted this background of Enoch to Jn 14,2-3. See, *op. cit.* (n. 50) 181, also note, 108.

[83] It is in this sense that P. GRELOT explains the paradise promised to the good thief in Lk 23,46. See, *op. cit.* (n. 29) 211.

[84] J. CORTENAY JAMES draws special attention to the connotation of "rest" in the term μονή. See, *op. cit.* (n. 76) 428.

"resting-places" for the just in the heavenly temple. Jesus would then first enter into his "resting-place" in this temple, and later return to take his disciples to their "resting-places" with him there. Such an interpretation of μοναί as "resting-places" would also be clearly in context. In Jn 14,1a Jesus encourages his disciples: "let not your hearts be troubled" (Μὴ ταρασσέσθω; comp. also 14,27), and then supports his words with the promise of 14,2-3 that he will return to take the disciples later to the μοναί in the Father's house. On the other hand, any hint even of future degrees of beatitude would be entirely out of place.

Finally, the numerical adjective "many" (πολλαί) which qualifies the "rooms" might be seen in line with the Jewish tradition where the temple is to become the centre of eschatological and universal salvation.[85] But here again this tradition could be seen as slanted by John in line with the extra-biblical tradition represented by Enoch to refer to the heavenly temple as the eschatological and universal goal of salvation. In line with this tradition the πολλαί would then be understood quantitatively, and not qualitatively. The "rooms" would be numerous, providing accommodation for many.

(b) DIFFERENCES. The term μονή is never used in the Jewish tradition to designate "rooms" in the temple, earthly or heavenly.

Finally, in the Jewish tradition the heavenly temple is peopled with immortal beings. However, Jn 14,2-3 must be seen to abstract entirely from this aspect of the tradition. We cannot determine from our text whether or not the μοναί in the Father's house are inhabited or not by celestial beings, or angels, prior to the preparation, or after it either. We only know that prior to the preparation, Jesus abides in the Father's house permanently, and after the preparation it will be peopled by the disciples. The text says no more. We must respect this economy of the text.

CONCLUSION

In Jn 14,2-3 we have the simple image of a spacious house, with many rooms. It is easily intelligible within the Jewish tradition with reference either to the Jerusalem temple, or the heavenly temple, as the eschatological goal of universal redemption; and even with reference to both the Jerusalem temple and the heavenly temple at the same time. Our study of the Jewish tradition has provided ample justification for the confusion in the minds of the disciples about the precise temple which is intended. In this house, whether it be the Jerusalem temple or the heavenly temple, there are rooms, or possibilities, enough for a great number to dwell there.

---

[85] A. SERRA has rightly underlined this aspect of the OT Jewish tradition by way of background to Jn 14,2-3. See, *Contributi dell'antica letteratura giudaica per l'esegesi di Giov. 2,1-12 e 19,27-29* (Roma, 1975), 380.

CHAPTER III

THE JOURNEY OF JESUS TO PREPARE A PLACE

A. THE JOURNEY OF JESUS

1. Vocabulary: Journey

The verb πορεύομαι [1] occurs repeatedly in the LXX in the literal sense of "to journey".[2] Although the technical term for going on pilgrimage to the temple is the verb ἀναβαίνω, still πορεύομαι is also frequently found of going to the temple (or to the tent of meeting):

> "I was glad when they said to me, 'Let us go to the house of the Lord' (εἰς οἶκον κυρίου πορευσόμεθα)" (Ps 122(121),1) (comp. ἀναβαίνω, v. 4).[3]

Besides, the verb forms part of the LXX exodus vocabulary in general,[4] but with special reference to God himself who walks before his people.[5]

> "For you shall not go out (ἐξελεύσεσθε) in haste, and you shall not go in flight (πορεύσεσθε); for the Lord will go before you (πορεύσεται γὰρ πρότερος ὑμῶν κύριος)" (Is 52,12).

So, too, the verb is used in the context of the entrance into Canaan,[6] and is also used to describe the entrance itself directly:

> "But Joshua the son of Nun and Caleb the son of Jephunneh remained alive, of those men who went to spy out the land (ἀπὸ τῶν ἀνθρώπων ἐκείνων τῶν πεπορευομένων κατασκέψασθαι τὴν γῆν)" (Nm 14,38; comp. Josh 2,1; 3,4).

---

[1] In the LXX πορεύομαι is used for several Hebrew verbs, but mainly for הלך, whose various senses it assimilates. See, F. Hauck/S. Schulz, *TDNT*, VI, 570.

[2] See, Gn 11,31; Ex 3,18; Dt 6,7; 2 Kgs 2,1.11(2x).16.18.

[3] See also Is 2,2; Mi 4,2; Ze 8,21(2x).23.

[4] See, Dt 1,7 εἰσπορεύομαι; 1,19 πορεύομαι; 1,30.33 προπορεύομαι; 1,31.33 πορεύομαι; Jgs 11,16 πορεύομαι; Ps 68(67), 8 ἐκπορεύομαι; Is 35,8 πορεύομαι.

[5] The theme of God walking before his people is expressed by πορεύομαι with several different prepositions, ἔμπροσθεν (Is 45,2), πρὸ προσώπου (Dt 1,30.33; 31,6), and πρότερος (Nm 14,14; Dt 1,33; Is 52,12). God walks before his people, not only at the first exodus (Dt 1,30.33; Nm 14,14), but also at the second one (Is 11,15-16; 43,16-21; 52,12).

[6] See, Dt 1,19.31.33.

We find the verb in a moral sense in general,[7] with ὀπίσω,[8] with ἐνώπιον,[9] with ἐναντίον.[10] But the verb is used especially in a moral sense, with reference to the observance of God's commandments,[11] and walking in the truth:

"Teach me thy way, O Lord, that I may walk in thy truth (ὁδήγησόν με, κύριε, τῇ ὁδῷ σου, καὶ πορεύσομαι ἐν τῇ ἀληθείᾳ σου)" (Ps 86(85),11).

It is important for an understanding of our text of Jn 14,2-3 to note the use of the verb, with a connotation of danger to be overcome,[12] even of battle.[13] The mission of Jacob, as heir to the promise of the possession of the land, is referred to as such a journey fraught with danger in fulfilment of God's design:

"Then Jacob made a vow, saying, 'if God will be with me, and will keep me in this way that I go (ἐν τῇ ὁδῷ ταύτῃ, ᾗ ἐγὼ πορεύομαι), and will give me bread to eat and clothing to wear, so that I may come again to my Father's house in peace (καὶ ἀποστρέψῃ με μετὰ σωτηρίας εἰς τὸν οἶκον τοῦ πατρός μου), then the Lord shall be my God'" (Gn 28,20-21).

So, too, the journey of Yahweh himself before his people into the land, with all the difficulties and dangers which it entails from enemies on the way, is also referred to with this same verb:

"The Lord your God who goes before you will himself fight for you (κύριος ὁ θεὸς ὑμῶν ὁ προπορευόμενος πρὸ προσώπου ὑμῶν αὐτὸς συνεκπολεμήσει αὐτοὺς μεθ' ὑμῶν κατὰ πάντα), just as he did for you in Egypt before your eyes in the wilderness" (Dt 1,30-31).

Closely akin to this use of πορεύομαι, with a connotation of danger and enemies to be overcome, is the use of the verb with reference to the journey of death:[14]

---

[7] See, I Kgs 8,36; Is 35,8-9; Mi 4,2-5(2x).
[8] See, Dt 6,14; 8,19; 28,14; Jgs 2,12; I Sm 12,14; Jer 2,5.8.
[9] See, I Kgs 2,4; 8,23; 9,4; I Chr 34,31; Tb 3,5; Is 38,3.
[10] See, 2 Chr 6,14.16.
[11] See, Dt 8,6(LXX); 10,12; 11,22; 19,9; 26,17; 28,19; 30,16.
[12] See, Pss 23(22),4; 138(137),7.
[13] See, Jgs 4,8(2x).9(2x); Dt 1,29-30; 2 Sm 17,11.
[14] Human life is conceived in the OT as a journey, which like everything earthly ends in death. When dying David says: πορεύομαι ἐν ὁδῷ πάσης τῆς γῆς (I Kgs 2,2; comp. Eccl 9,10; 12,5). Since death is the land of no return David complains that he can go to his dead child, but it cannot come to him (cf. 2 Sm 12,23; comp. Jb 10,21; 16,22).

"Are not the days of my life few?
Allow me to rest a little
before I depart whence I shall not return
(πρὸ τοῦ με πορευθῆναι ὅθεν οὐκ ἀναστρέψω)
to the land of darkness and gloom,
to the land of eternal darkness" (Jb 10,21).[15]

The compound form of the verb πορεύομαι with the preposition εἰς is found several times to designate the entrance of the high priest into the sanctuary on "Yôm hakkipurîm". Here the verb is closely linked in turn with the compound form of the verb ἔρχομαι:

"There shall be no man in the tent of meeting when he enters (εἰσπορευομένου αὐτοῦ) to make atonement in the holy place until he comes out (ἐξέλθῃ)" (Lv 16,17; comp. 16,2.23).

The journey of the nations to the eschatological temple is also described with this verb. So, too, is the life-style characteristic of the eschatological age:

"And many nations shall journey (πορεύσονται), and shall say: 'Come, let us go up (ἀναβῶμεν) to the mountain of the Lord, to the house of the God of Jacob, that he may teach us his way, and that we may walk in it (πορευσόμεθα)" (Is 2,3; comp. Mi 4,2; Ze 8,21).

We should also note the use of the verb πορεύομαι within the NT Jewish tradition prior to John. This would seem to clarify significantly John's use of the verb in our text. Here we find in general a repetition of the LXX use of the verb. It is used sometimes of a journey home (Lk 5,24) and of a journey to the temple (Lk 2,41). It is also used of a journey with a connotation of danger, even of death (Lk 22,33) and conflict with enemies (Lk 14,31). Besides, it describes moral conduct, both good (Lk 1,6; Acts 9,31; comp. 14,16) and bad (I Pt 4,3; 2 Pt 2,10; 3,3; Jude 11.16.18). It refers to the saving mission of the disciples of Jesus (Mt 10,6-7; 28,19; Mk 16,15) and that of Paul (Acts 18,6; 22,21; 28,26); and designates too the journey of Jesus to his death in Jerusalem, as part of God's saving design (Lk 9,51; 13,33; 22,22). But it is also used of a journey of Jesus himself to the next world (I Pt 3,19) and to heaven itself (Acts 1,10-11; I Pt 3,22).

Moreover, in the Synoptics the theme of "departure" is expressly linked with that of "return" in some of the Parousia-parables (e.g. Mt

---

[15] On the use of the verb πορεύομαι to designate the journey of death, see, I Kgs 2,2; Eccl 3,20; 5,14(2x); 6,4-6; 9,10; 12,5; Prv 2,10; Jb 16,22; Ps 55(54), 15 πορεύομαι = ἀναβαίνω; Is 8,10(l.v.); Wis 3,3 πορεία; comp. Ps 39(38),13 ἀπέρχομαι.

25,14-30; Lk 19,12-27; Mk 13,34-37). The terminology varies (πορεύομαι, Mt 25,16; Lk 19,12; comp. ἀποδημῶ, Mt 25,14.15). However, the verb πορεύομαι is expressly used with ἔρχομαι in the parable of the Talents (Mt 25,19.27; Lk 19,13.23). Here we have a Christological application. The "departure" refers to a period of absence by Jesus and the "coming" refers to his return as the Son of Man at the Second Coming.

The departure of Jesus is described expressly in Acts as a heavenly journey. It provides a significant parallel to our text. In Jn 14,2-3 and in Acts 1,10-11 the verb πορεύομαι is again closely linked with the verb ἔρχομαι:

> "And while they were gazing into heaven as he went (εἰς τὸν οὐρανὸν πορευομένου αὐτοῦ), two men stood by them in white robes, and said, "Men of Galilee, why do you stand looking into heaven (εἰς τὸν οὐρανόν)? This Jesus who was taken up (ἀναλημφθείς) from you into heaven (εἰς τὸν οὐρανόν) will come (ἐλεύσεται) in the same way as you saw him go into heaven (πορευόμενον εἰς τὸν οὐρανόν)" (Acts 1,10-11).

This description of the visible departure of the risen Jesus into heaven by way of conclusion to his earthly life is linked here with his return, as part of the early church's developing response to the problem of the Parousia (cf. Acts 1,6). The text has ἔρχομαι, which was earlier linked in the tradition with the Second Coming (Mk 13,26 par; 14,62). The explicit comparison made by the angel interpreters between the departure and return of Jesus points to an understanding of the Parousia as a visible intervention of Jesus at the end of time. The departure of Jesus and his return in Jn 14,2-3 could well be understood in line with this perspective of final eschatology. It is surely significant that the three main verbs of motion in our text have a parallel in this text of Acts (πορεύομαι, ἔρχομαι, ἀναλαμβάνω/παραλαμβάνω).

2. Themes

(a) ACCESS TO CANAAN.[16] Within the general biblical tradition of the exodus we find ample evidence for a tradition on the entrance into the land (Dt 1,19-45; Nm 13-14; comp. Ps 95(94); Dt 9,22-24). The Israelites poised on the threshhold of the promised land are invited to enter. It is a moment of decision. At this precise moment an expedition is sent before the people (Nm 13,1; Dt 1,22). They journey to explore the land (τῶν πεπορευομένων) (Nm 14,38). Joshua (Ἰησοῦς) was part of this preparatory expedition (Nm 13,8.16; 14,5). There is clearly a problem of difficulties and dangers, and enemies (Dt 1,28.30.41-44; Nm 13,18.28.33;

---

[16] For a stuty of this tradition in the OT, see A. VANHOYE, "Longue marche ou accès tout proche? Le contexte biblique de Hébreux 3,7-4,11", *Bib* 49 (1968) 9-26.

14,3.43-45). So the people have to be encouraged (Nm 14,9; Dt 1,21.29; comp. Jos 10,25).[17] On his return Joshua (Ἰησοῦς) announces the good news that the Lord will bring the people into the land (Nm 14,7-8; comp. the words of Moses, Dt 1,21-25). However, the exploration of the land proves to be inefficacious. The Israelites refuse to enter, and even speak of returning to Egypt (Nm 14,3-4). The biblical tradition interprets this refusal as unbelief or refusal to accept God's word (ἀπειθέω, Dt 1,26; Nm 14,43; Dt 9,23,24; οὐ πιστεύω, Dt 9,23; Ps 106(105),24; Dt 1,32 οὐκ ἐνπιστεύω, Nm 14,11).[18] However, it was not merely a question of refusal to enter, but also of an inability later to do so. The people did in fact decide afterwards to enter, and even attempted to do so (Nm 14,40-45; Dt 1,41-44). Moses tried to dissuade them (Dt 1,42; Nm 14,41), for God had sworn that they would not enter the land (Nm 14,21-23.28-30; Nm 32,10; Dt 1,34-35; Ps 95(94),11). So the enterprise was foredoomed (Nm 13,39-45; Dt 1,41-45). The Israelites not only refused to enter because of their unbelief, but as a consequence of this same unbelief they were unable to enter, when they did decide to do so.

However, in spite of everything there is the promise that Joshua (Ἰησοῦς) will enter (Dt 1,38; Nm 14,30-38). So, too, there is the same promise of an entrance also for a new generation. God condemns the fathers to a desert wandering in chastisement for their sins (Nm 14,32; Dt 1,40). But the promise to the "little children" is already expressed in Nm 14,21-24. It is taken up again in Nm 14,29-31 and Dt 1,35.39. So, too, Ps 95(94) evokes implicitly the same promise. The psalmist considers the faithful assembly he is addressing as the "little children" of the Israelites in the desert, for he warns them against the example of their fathers (v. 9). It is to these "little children" that God had in fact promised entry (πᾶν παιδίον νέον Dt 1,39; παιδία Nm 14,31).

(b) ACCESS TO THE TEMPLE.[19]   There is a marked tendency in the OT to transfer to the temple ideas linked earlier in the tradition with the exodus and the entrance into the land (e.g. Ex 15,1-18; comp. 2 Mc

---

[17] We find μὴ φοβεῖσθε twice as the words of Joshua in Nm 14,9. We may compare the words of Moses μὴ φοβεῖσθε μηδὲ δειλιάσητε in Dt 1,21, and his words again μὴ φοβοῦ μηδὲ δειλία in Dt 31,6.8; compare μὴ πτήξητε μηδὲ φοβηθῆτε in Dt 1,29. The words of Joshua counselling his warriors μὴ φοβηθῆτε αὐτοὺς μηδὲ δειλιάσητε in Jos 10,25 are to be noted, as they are the same words addressed by Yahweh to Joshua himself (Jos 1,9; 8,1; comp. 2 Mc 15,8; Is 13,7; Sir 22,6).

[18] Comp. ἠπειθήσατε, Dt. 1,26; ἀπειθοῦντες, Nm 14,43; καὶ ἠπειθήσατε τῷ ῥήματι κυρίου τοῦ Θεοῦ ὑμῶν καὶ οὐκ ἐπιστεύσατε αὐτῷ καὶ οὐκ εἰσηκούσατε τῆς φωνῆς αὐτοῦ, Dt 9,23; οὐκ ἐπίστευσεν τῷ λόγῳ αὐτοῦ, Ps 106(105),24; οὐκ ἐνεπιστεύσατε, Dt 1,32; οὐ πιστεύουσίν μοι, Nm 14,11.

[19] See, ch. 11, pp. 59-60.

1,27-29; Is 2,2-4; Mi 4,1-4). In this way the general theme of access to the temple takes on considerable importance (e.g. Pss 15(14); 24(23),3-6; 118(117),19-20.26-27). It had, however, a special importance on "Yôm hakkipurîm". This was the occasion for a solemn entrance by the high priest into the sanctuary (Lv 16,1ff; 23,26ff; Nm 29,7ff). The purpose of his entrance was to make atonement for himself, his family, and the whole congregation of the children of Israel (καὶ ἐξιλάσεται περὶ αὐτοῦ καὶ τοῦ οἴκου αὐτοῦ, Lv 16,6.11, with the addition of καὶ περὶ πάσης συναγωγῆς υἱῶν Ἰσραήλ, in v. 17).

However, the true significance of this ritual entrance cannot be understood apart from the divisions of the tabernacle. The tent, as we find it in exodus, like the temple in Jerusalem, was divided into two parts. One part served as sanctuary properly so called; the other part served as vestibule (Ex 26,31-33). The vestibule was generally accessible. But entrance into the other part was governed by strict laws. Only the high priest, once a year, could enter it by strict right when he carried in sacrificial blood in order to make expiation (Ex 30,10; Lv 16,2.14ff). After the solemn service the entrance to the sanctuary was closed. In this we see the restricted efficacy of the high priest's role. The purpose of his expiation was to establish communication between the people and God, by making atonement for sin. Still the people as such were excluded from access to the sanctuary. At the end of the liturgy the same restrictions were again imposed, and the same inability of access resulted. It is thus clear that neither had communication been established, nor had nearness to God been attained. This solemn rite of entrance into the sanctuary was no more than a kind of ineffectual mime. The high priest did not open up a path to God (comp. Heb 9,24; 9,7-8).[20]

(c) ACCESS TO HEAVEN.[21] The OT traditions of the transportation of Enoch[22] and Elijah[23] have a special importance for the understanding of our theme. These traditions represent in mythical[24]

---

[20] A. Vanhoye provides a good summary of this aspect of the Jewish tradition. See, "Par la tente plus parfaite ... (He 9,11)", *Bib* 46 (1965) 2-3.

[21] On this theme in general, see G. Lohfink, *Die Himmelfahrt Jesu. Untersuchungen zu den Himmelfahrts- und Erhöhungstexten bei Lukas* (München, 1971).

[22] See, Gn 5,24; Sir 44,16; 49,14.16 (Hebrew text). For a discussion of these texts, see P. Grelot, "La légende d'Hénoch dans les Apocryphes et dans la bible", *RecSR* 46 (1958), 5-26.181-210. The influence of Gn 5,24 on the subsequent development of the tradition has been well summed up by G. Lohfink. See, *op. cit.* (n. 21) 55.

[23] See, 2 Kgs 2,1-18; Sir 48,9.12; I Mc 2,58; comp. also Mal 3,22-23 (LXX) on the return of Elijah. The influence of 2 Kgs 2,1-18 on the later tradition has been well summed up again by G. Lohfink. See, *op. cit.* (n. 21) 58.

[24] We use the term "mythical" here in a technical sense to describe the symbolic representation of a reality otherwise inexpressible, except by means of symbols. This use has been well explained by P. Grelot. See, *De la mort à la vie éternelle* (Paris, 1971) 56.

language the OT theme of access to heaven for the just man.[25] The two stories are different representations, but the underlying idea is the same. Both men escape the common law of death,[26] by a bodily assumption into heaven.

This same idea of access to heaven also underlies the notion of "ascensio" which figures prominently in apocalyptic literature, where great men of early days and of biblical history are taken up to heaven.[27] Behind the description of all these journeys lies the current mythical cosmology of the times according to which God dwells in the heaven(s), inaccessible and remote from the world of men (Is 14,12), who are in turn separated by an abyss from the underworld (Is 14,15-19).

(d) VICTORY OVER SIN AND DEATH.

(i) IN GENERAL

In the OT death is the common lot of all men (Gn 3,19; Ps 90(89),3; Jb 23). However, this reality of death is presented in the OT by contrast with God's gift of life and communion (or life) with God on earth. Hence, it is conceived in terms of the absence of God, or separation from him.[28] Behind this understanding of death lies the OT mythical cosmology, with its three-tiered concept of the universe (heaven-earth-sheol). Sheol is the abode of the $r^e f\bar{a}'\hat{i}m$.[29] It is a mythical representation of the state of death as a nebulous mode of existence, more akin in fact to non-existence, in the afterlife. The place itself is an infernal abyss in a subterranean world separated from the world of men by waters. Biblical man is deeply conscious of an insurmountable barrier between heaven and earth (Is 14,12-14).[30] Sheol is the land of no return.[31]

---

[25] The OT phrase that "Enoch walked with God" (Gn 5,22.24) indicates that Enoch was a just man (comp. Gn 6,9; Mi 6,8; Mal 2,6).

[26] IV Esdras (Vg) expresses it as follows: "Et videbunt qui recepti sunt homines, qui mortem non gustaverunt a nativitate sua" (6,26).

[27] In later Judaism these journeys to the hereafter, or to heaven, are a favourite theme with reference to the great heroes of faith in the past, e.g. Enoch (17-19), with a doublet — first voyage (21-25) and second voyage (26-36), Abraham (Apc Abr 15ff), Ezra (IV Esd 14,9.49) and Baruch (2 Bar 48,20). See, G. LOHFINK, op. cit. (n. 21) 51-72.

[28] Death means severance from God, whether in punishment for the wicked or in peace for the just. This, however, is only one aspect of the OT idea of death, or sheol. See, R. MURPHY, " 'To Know Your Might is the Root of Immortality' (Wis 15,3)", CBQ 25 (1963) 90, note, 10.

[29] For a full description of the biblical idea of existence in sheol, see, P. GRELOT, op. cit. (n. 24) 57-59; also D. S. RUSSELL, The Method and Message of Jewish Apocalyptic (London, 1971) 355-356.

[30] Hence, the dramatic evocation of the descent into hell several times in the OT (Nm 16,33; Is 14,9-15; Ex 32,18-32; Ps 55(54)16; contrast I Sm 28,8-14).

[31] See, Wis 2,1.5; Prv 2,19; Jb 7,9; 10,18-22; 16,22; contrast I Sm 28,8-14.

Little wonder that such a concept of death became identified as a mysterious evil power hostile to man. Death is the powerful enemy. Jeremiah reflects the fear in a dirge that is reminiscent of the Canaanite divinity, Mot:[32] "Death has come up through our windows, has entered our palaces; it cuts down the children in the street, young people in the squares" (Jer 9,20). In Hosea Yahweh calls for the "plagues" and "sting" of death (nether world) in a passage which acknowledges the strong grip that death and sheol have upon man: "Shall I deliver them from the power (מיד) of the nether world?" (Hos 13,14). A similar idea is in the mind of the psalmist: "God will redeem me from the power (מיד) of the nether world" (Ps 49,16; cf. Ps 116,8; Dn 3,88). Thus death has its own realm, the nether world (which is used interchangeably for death), from which man has to be delivered (Ps 30,4; 86,13). Death reaches out its hand in the form of sickness: "any weakness in life is a form of death".[33] Hence the psalmist describes his sickness as a state of being in sheol (Ps 88,5-7), imprisonment in bonds (Ps 18,5f: 116,3) (חבלי-מות), behind bars (Jon 2,7).

However, death never formed part of God's plan for men. It was by the devil that death entered into the world (Gn 3,19; Wis 2,23-24). The common realities of sin and death are indissolubly linked with the evil power who induces to sin (Gn 3,1-6). Behind the figure of Satan lies the implacable Adversary of God's design (Is 27,1). In direct opposition to God's design we thus find the Power of the Abyss, the Infernal Power who is the originator of sin and death.

So, biblical man is faced with the evil of sin (Gn 3,1-8.10.23-24), and death (Jb 9,25-26; 14,1-12; 17,11-16), which lead to separation from God. However, God promises victory over Satan (Gn 3,15) and God possesses power over death (Ps 30(29),3-4; 68(67),20; Is 38,17-20; Jon 2,7; Hos 6,2). By faith in the might of Yahweh the spectre of death can be overcome.[34] Even if there is no cult — because no true life — in sheol,[35] the realm of death is not thereby outside Yahweh's dominion (Am 8,12; Ps 139,8; Prv 15,11). Yahweh is described as the author of both life and death (Dt 23,39; cf. I, Sm 2,6; Is 45,6f). Hence Yahweh alone has the strength to deliver from any power of death. In this way the power of sheol can be cancelled.

---

[32] Mot, the Canaanite God of death, is King of sheol. See, R. Murphy, *op. cit.* (n. 28) 90, note, 11.

[33] See, A. R. Johnson, *The Vitality of the Individual in the Thought of Ancient Israel* (Cardiff, 1949) 94; also K. Barth, *Die Errettung vom Tode* (Zollikon, 1957) 52f.

[34] It is in this sense that R. Murphy explains "to know your might is the root of immortality" in Wis 15,2. He says: "the experience of God's death-destroying power makes our immortality possible". See, *op. cit.* (n. 28) 93.

[35] This is the common motif in the Psalms of Lamentation, e.g. 6,6; 30,10; 88,11f.

This motif of the power of Yahweh over death pervades the whole book of Wisdom. In the monologue of the impious in Wis 2,1 the supreme power of the nether world is admitted; there is not one who has come back from Hades.[36] But for the author, who is proclaiming the message of a blessed immortality, Hades has lost its power. God has complete power (ἐξουσίαν) over it, leading people there and back (Wis 16,13). It has no "domain" (βασίλειον) on earth (Wis 1,14). Finally, it is called "powerless", as the night-darkness that covered the Egyptians is "powerless" (ἀδύνατον); and is described as coming "from the recesses of a powerless (ἀδύνατον) nether world" (Wis 17,14).

(ii) IN PARTICULAR

a. ESCHATOLOGICAL VICTORY. The final victory, however, over death belongs to Jewish eschatology (Ez 37,1-14; Is 65,17-25; 25,8; 27,1; 26,19; Hos 13,14). So, too, the final victory over sin is also eschatological. There is the promise of such a victory in the context of a new alliance which will establish a relationship between God and man which the alliance of Sinai was unable to do (Hos 2,16-22; Jer 31,31-34; Ez 36,25-28). An inner law will replace the external law, with a purification of the heart by a gift of the Spirit (Ez 36,25-27; Jer 31,31-34). All this implies a radical transformation of the human condition which only God can work as part of the eschatological gift of salvation.

b. SUFFERING SERVANT. One tradition on the manner of this eschatological victory of God over sin is particularly relevant to the theme of death. In the Servant Songs, the mysterious person who is presented as the artisan of eschatological salvation and the mediator of a New Alliance (Is 42,5-7) must innocently undergo the consequences of human sin (Is 53,5-8). But he will accomplish the expiation by a sacrifice which will purify men from their sins by sharing in the human condition of suffering and death (Is 53,10-12). Thus he becomes a means of redemption. This continues the OT tradition of personal sacrifice and its fecundity in the context of God's design.[37] The Suffering Servant offers his life (Is 53,10) and thus obtains together with the expiation of sin (Is 53,10) the justification of the multitudes (Is 53,11-12), and an outstanding glorification (Is 52,13).

---

[36] Possibly ἀναλύσας means "who has freed from" Hades.

[37] This OT idea has its foundation in the history of men like Isaac, Joseph, Moses, Job, the prophets, and the suffering just men of the psalms.

3. Application to Jn 14,2-3

(a) SIMILARITIES. The use of the verb πορεύομαι with reference to the Father's house and the many rooms in Jn 14,2-3 may rightly be understood in line with general LXX usage to evoke again the exodus.[38] John would, then, be presenting Jesus as a new leader who goes before his people to fight for them in a new exodus. The connotation of danger which this journey might involve for Jesus himself in fulfilment of his mission and for his disciples who wish to follow him (cf. Jn 13,37-38) would also accord with the LXX use of the term.

However, this new exodus of Jn 14,2-3 would seem to be conceived more precisely by John, not as a long journey of wandering in the desert, but at the exact moment of entrance into the land. It would seem to be a journey of access which Jesus makes as a mediator who first journeys before his disciples on their behalf. Jesus ('Ιησοῦς) would be a new Joshua ('Ιησοῦς), then, who enters before his disciples into the promised land.

The use of πορεύομαι itself may be interpreted in line with LXX usage to describe the preliminary journey of exploration by Joshua in preparation for the actual entrance of the people later into the land. In the person of Jesus, then, would be fulfilled the promise of entrance made to Joshua ('Ιησοῦς, Nm 14,30; Dt 1,30), and in the person of the disciples the promise of entrance made to the generation of "little ones" (cf. παιδίον, Dt 1,39; παιδία Nm 14,31; comp. τεκνία, Jn 13,33).[39]

Besides, the phrase μὴ ταρασσέσθω ὑμῶν ἡ καρδία (Jn 14,1a) with the additional μηδὲ δειλιάτω in the immediate context of Jn 14,2-3 (cf. also Jn 14,27) could also be seen to echo the counsel of Joshua to his warriors before entrance into the land.[40]

---

[38] Several exegetes have discerned a reference to the exodus behind John's use of πορεύομαι in 14,2-3. See, R. E. Brown, *op. cit.* 625; I. de la Potterie, "Je suis la voie, la vérité et la vie" (Jn 14,6)", *NRT* 88 (1966) 915, also notes, 21-22. On the general theme of the exodus in the fourth gospel, see J. Enz, "The Book of Exodus as a Literary Type for the Gospel of John", *JBL* 76 (1957) 208-215; T. F. Glasson, *Moses in the Fourth Gospel* (London, 1963); F. H. Smith, "Exodus Typology in the Fourth Gospel", *JBL* 81 (1962) 329-342.

[39] The τεκνία of Jn 13,33 is the diminutive form of the term τέκνον (cf. Jn 1,12; 8,39; 11,52). It would be well suited (in Johannine usage) to designate the new generation of believers in Christ prefigured by παιδία of Nm 14,31 (comp. also, πᾶν παιδίον Dt I,39).

[40] M.-E. Boismard has linked this phrase of Jn 14,1a with the tradition of entrance into the land. See, "L'évolution du thème eschatologique dans les traditions johanniques", *RB* 68 (1961) 520; also R. E. Brown, *op. cit.* 625. However, the addition of the verb δειλιάω in the parallel phrase of Jn 14,27 is also highly significant. It is the only use of this verb in the NT; and reinforces the link with the OT phrase (Dt 1,21.29; 31,8; Josh 10,25).

Furthermore, the incredulous Jews who refused to enter the land, and were unable to do so, because of their unbelief could easily be seen to prefigure the incredulous Jews of the fourth gospel referred to explicitly in the immediate context of Jn 14,2-3 (cf. 13,33). These are radically incapable of following Jesus on this journey because of their unbelief (cf. Jn 7,34-36; 8,21-24). The disciples by contrast are invited to believe in the immediate context of Jn 14,2-3 (cf. 14,1b; comp. 14,10-11.29), and promised access to the goal of Jesus' journey later (13,36) on the return of Jesus (14,3b).

All this would lend support to an interpretation of Jn 14,2-3 in line with the OT tradition of the entrance into the land.

However, the use of πορεύομαι could also be seen as a term well suited in line with the LXX terminology to indicate the journey of Jesus in Jn 14,2-3 as a journey on pilgrimage to the temple in general, and even more precisely to designate the great eschatological pilgrimage to the temple.

So, too, this journey may also be considered as a journey of Jesus by means of a bodily ascent into the heavenly temple after his death in line with NT usage of the term (cf. Acts 1,10-11). The departure of Jesus would then initiate a period of absence by Jesus prior to his Second Coming. But this same heavenly ascent could also be conceived as a journey of escape from the common law of death; and in this sense a journey of victory over death and its consequences, sin. Such a journey of Jesus would be in accord with the OT Jewish tradition of the transportation of Enoch and Elijah, and with the extra-biblical Jewish tradition of the "ascensio" represented especially in later Jewish apocalyptic literature.[41]

Moreover, the verb πορεύομαι may be interpreted with reference to a journey of Jesus to the heavenly temple through death. This would be also in accord with LXX usage of the term. Besides, the deeper possible meaning of the journey opened up by the Johannine phrase ψυχὴν τίθημι of Jn 13,37-38 (comp. 10,11.15.17.18)[42] would point to this journey of Jn 14,2-3 as an entrance of Jesus into communion with his Father in the temple by a sacrificial movement through his passion-death. In the broader perspective of the whole gospel the death of Jesus also involves the sacrificial shedding of his blood in atonement for sin (cf. 19,34; 1,29),[43]

---

[41] J. P. MIRANDA has shown, in considerable detail, that John's use of ἀναβαίνω comes from the Jewish traditions of the ascension of Moses, Elijah and others. See, *Der Vater der mich gasandt hat: Religionsgeschichtliche Untersuchungen zu Ekklesiologie* (European University Papers 23/7) (Bern, 1972) 66-82.

[42] See, ch. I, p. 37, also note, 30.

[43] See, *JB* ad loc., note, "r"; also S. LYONNET, *Sin, Redemption, and Sacrifice. A Biblical and Patristic Study* (Rome, 1970) 260.

and at the same time a victory over death (cf. 5,28-29) and Satan (cf. 12,31; 14,30; 16,33). The consequence of the journey of Jesus in Jn 14,2-3 is an at-one-ment of the disciples with God. This designates in equivalent Johannine terms the complementary positive effect of the removal of sin. As a consequence of his journey Jesus also becomes the perfect mediator between God and man, one-with-God (ὅπου εἰμι ἐγώ) and one-with-the-disciples (πρὸς ἐμαυτόν) in the temple of the Father's house (ὅπου εἰμι ἐγώ).

Our text, then, might be interpreted at this possible deeper level of meaning in line with the OT tradition of the entrance of the high-priest into the sanctuary to make atonement for sin. Such a journey of Jesus through his passion-death could also be seen as the fulfilment of the eschatological victory of God over evil in all its forms.

Finally, to interpret this journey of Jesus with additional moral implications would also be in line with LXX usage.[44] Jesus himself affirms that he undertakes this journey in submission to God's command (cf. Jn 14,31; comp. Jn 10,18). Besides, the immediate context of Jn 14,2-3 is full of the theme of submission to God's commandments (cf. 14,15.21; comp. 13,34-35). This journey of Jesus would thus provide an ideal pattern for the lifestyle of the new eschatological community. In the use of this term πορεύομαι, then, John might well be influenced especially by Is 2,2-3 (comp. Mi 4,1-4). Here we have a simple pericope with the verb πορεύομαι used both of the eschatological pilgrimage to the temple and of the lifestyle of the whole new eschatological age.

All these rich possibilities of the verb πορεύομαι in line with LXX and NT usage would help to explain the sudden (and unexpected) change from the use of ὑπάγω in Jn 13,33.36(2x) to πορεύομαι in Jn 14,2-3(2x) (comp. also ὑπάγω in Jn 14,4.5.28).[45]

(b) DIFFERENCES. However, the journey of Jesus in Jn 14,2-3 also breaks in some ways with these same Jewish traditions. It breaks with the tradition of the preparation of entrance by a preliminary exploration of the land. Like Joshua, Jesus also returns. But the exploration of the land by the new Joshua, unlike that of the first Joshua, is efficacious. The disciples will enter later into the Father's house. Moreover, this tradition

---

[44] It should be noted, however, that the term πορεύομαι is never used elsewhere in the fourth gospel in a direct and clear moral sense. It is the verb περιπατέω which takes on these moral connotations in the fourth gospel (cf. Jn 8,12; 12,35(x)). See, I. DE LA POTTERIE, "L'exaltation du Fils de l'homme (Jn 12,31-36)", Greg 49 (1968) 476.

[45] In general Johannine usage πορεύομαι and ὑπάγω are identical. Attempts to distinguish them are not convincing. See, D. E. HOLWERDA, The Holy Spirit and Eschatology in the Gospel of John. A Critique of Rudolf Bultmann's present Eschatology (Kampen, 1959) 17 Anm. 46.

of entrance into the land may now be seen as slanted by John in an original way to designate access to the heavenly temple.

So, too, John breaks with the Jewish tradition of access by the high-priest (or mediator) into the earthly sanctuary. Not only may John be seen again to nuance this theme in a new way to designate a journey of access by Jesus into the heavenly temple. But in contrast to the Jewish high-priest Jesus (who already dwells perpetually in the Father's house) enters the heavenly sanctuary by strict right as Son.[46] Besides, Jesus is not presented as entering the temple each year; he enters once only (ἐὰν πορευθῶ). In this way Jesus opens a permanent way of access to the heavenly temple, or communion with God there, for the disciples. His entrance, in contrast to that of the Jewish high-priest, is efficacious.

However, at a deeper possible Johannine level of understanding the new exodus of Jn 14,2-3 would be something entirely unique as a journey of Jesus into the heavenly temple through his passion-death. The journeys of Enoch and Elijah were by way of exception to the common law of death. Not so this journey of Jesus. Jesus actually died (cf. Jn 19,20.30.33-34). Thus death, synonymous in the OT with separation from God, becomes now itself the very means of victory over death by affording Jesus himself a way of access to God (and a way of access for his disciples after him). In his journey out of this world and access to the heavenly temple by his passion-death Jesus would overcome death and span the distance which separates men from God. Death would cease to be a sign of separation from God and a sign of the power of Satan to which it was linked from the beginning (Jn 8,44). The meaning of death would be radically changed by the death of Christ (comp. Hb 2,14-15).

B. THE PREPARATION

1. Vocabulary: Preparation

(a) OLD TESTAMENT. The verb ἑτοιμάζω[47] (and with it the adjective ἕτοιμος) is used of a house in general in the LXX, meaning "to prepare",[48] in the sense of to render accessible:

> "I have prepared the house and a place (ἐγὼ δὲ ἡτοίμακα τὴν οἰκίαν καὶ τόπον) for the camels" (Gn 24,31; comp. Tb 11,3; Ze 5,10-11).

---

[46] See, ch. I, note, 34.

[47] In the LXX ἑτοιμάζω is used for several Hebrew verbs, but mainly for כון, whose various senses it assimilates. See, W. GRUNDMANN, *TDNT*, II, 704-706.

[48] See, *L.S.* 903.

So, too, we find the use of the verb in general in the same sense with reference to a "room":

"Sister, prepare the other room (ἑτοίμασον τὸ ἕτερον ταμίειον) and take her into it" (Tb 7,15).[49]

However, the verb also takes on a profound religious significance in the LXX.[50] The term and its derivatives express God's whole creative and conserving action in nature and in history.[51] In this creative sense the verb has a special importance to designate the preparation of the land:

"On that day I took them by the hand to lead them out of the land of Egypt into the land which I have prepared for them (εἰς τὴν γῆν, ἣν ἡτοί-μασα αὐτοῖς)" (Ez. 20,6).[52]

The Hebrew verb תור, here rendered by ἑτοιμάζω in the LXX, means "to seek out, spy out, or explore";[53] and is the same verb which is used repeatedly meaning "to spy out" or "to explore" in the OT tradition of the exploration of the land (e.g. Nm 13,2.16.17.21.25.32(2x); 14,7,34.36.38; comp. Jgs 1,23).

Finally, the use of the verb with reference to the temple has a very special significance for our study. It is used:

(i) directly of the rooms in the temple:

"Then Hezekiah said to prepare rooms in the house of the Lord, and they prepared them (ἑτοιμάσαι παστοφόρια εἰς οἶκον κυρίου, καὶ ἡτοίμασαν)" (2 Chr 31,11; comp Neh 13,5.7).[54]

---

[49] Regretfully, this verse is not found either in the Aramaic or Hebrew fragments indicated by J. T. MILIK in "La Patrie de Tobie", *RB* 73 (1966) 522-530. The author gives the list of passages in Tobit which are present in 4QTob ar[A-D] and 4QTob hebr[a], but none of the texts. See, *op. cit.* 522, note, 3.

[50] In this religious sense the verb is found with reference to the prophetic task (Is 40,3; comp. Mt 3,3; Mk 1,3; Lk 3,4). There is a corresponding task for individuals and the people to prepare their hearts, or dispositions (Sir 2,7; Prv 23,12; Am 4,12; Mi 6,8; comp. Lk 1,17). This meaning is not directly relevant to our study.

[51] See, W. GRUNDMANN, *op. cit.* (n. 47) 706.

[52] See, also Ex 23,20 (LXX γῆ = מקום MT; comp. Ex 15,17).

[53] See, F. BROWN/S. R. DRIVER/G. A. BRIGGS, *A Hebrew and English Lexicon of the Old Testament* (Oxford, 1953).

[54] The verb is also used indirectly of the temple with reference to the sacrifices in general (Nm 13,1; 2 Chr 35,12), and to the passover lambs in particular (2 Chr 35,14.15.16); and also with reference to the furnishings of the temple and materials in general (I Kgs 5,18; I Chr 22,2.3.5(2x).14.28).

(ii) directly of the temple itself:

    a. "The place you have made your dwelling, Yahweh (ἕτοιμον κατοικητήριον) the sanctuary, Yahweh, prepared by your own hands (ὃ ἡτοίμασαν αἱ χεῖρες σου)" (Ex 15,17).[55]

    b. "Solomon reigned in the days of peace and God gave him rest on every side, that he might build a house for his name and prepare a sanctuary to stand forever (ἐτοιμάσῃ ἁγίασμα εἰς τὸν αἰῶνα)" (Sir 47,13).

    c. "Who in their days built the temple (ᾠκοδόμησαν οἶκον) and raised to the Lord a holy temple (l.v. people) (καὶ ἀνύψωσαν ναὸν ἅγιον κυρίῳ) ready for everlasting glory (ἡτοιμασμένον εἰς δόξαν αἰῶνος)" (Sir 49,12).[56]

    d. "Thou hast given command to build a temple (οἰκοδομῆσαι ναόν) on thy holy mountain and an altar in the city of thy habitation, a copy of the holy tent which thou didst prepare from the beginning (ἣν προητοίμασας)" (Wis 9,8).[57]

(iii) directly of a "place" for

a. a temple:

"And Solomon began to build the house of the Lord in Jerusalem (οἰκοδομεῖν τὸν οἶκον κυρίου) on Mount Moriah where the Lord had appeared to David, his father, at the place that David had appointed (τόπῳ, ᾧ ἡτοίμασεν Δαυιδ)" (2 Chr 3,1).

b. the ark:

"The inner sanctuary he prepared in the innermost part of the house (τοῦ δαβιρ ἐν μέσῳ τοῦ οἴκου ἔσωθεν ἡτοίμασεν – in A. B. omit) to set there the ark of the covenant" (I Kgs 6,19).[58]

"He prepared the place (καὶ ἡτοίμασεν τὸν τόπον) and pitched a tent for it, to bring up the ark of the Lord to its place, which he had prepared for it (εἰς τὸν τόπον, ὃν ἡτοίμασεν αὐτῇ) so that you may bring up the ark of the Lord, the God of Israel, to the place that I have prepared for it (οὗ ἡτοίμασα (ας) αὐτῇ (ην))" (I Chr 15,1.3.12).[59]

---

[55] F. M. CROSS, Jr. and D. N. FREEDMAN point to the antiquity of the phrases in Ex 15,17. See, "The Song of Miriam", *JNES* 14 (1955) 249-250. But whatever about the origin of the terminology, there is clear evidence in the Jewish traditions that Ex 15,17 was in fact interpreted with reference to the temple (cf. 2 Mc 1,29; 4QFlor).

[56] With reference to Zerubbabel and Joshua, building the second temple.

[57] Either the heavenly temple, or a heavenly prototype of the Jerusalem temple, or the tabernacle of Moses. See, *JB* ad loc., note "e".

[58] With reference to Solomon's construction of the temple.

[59] These examples are not to show that the term τόπος in I Chr 15,1.3.12 (comp.

By way of conclusion to this survey we note that the whole work of building, or constructing the temple from beginning to end is designated as a process of preparation:

> "Thus was prepared all the work of Solomon (καὶ ἡτοιμάσθη πᾶσα ἡ ἐργασία) from the day the foundation of the Lord's house (τὸν οἶκον κυρίου) was laid until it was finished" (2 Chr 8,16; comp. Ze 5,11).

So, too, we note the parallel texts of Mi 4,1 and Is 2,2, which are supremely important for our theme:

> "In the days to come the mountain (of the temple of the Lord = καὶ ὁ οἶκος τοῦ θεοῦ, an addition in Is 2,2) shall tower over the mountains and be lifted higher than the hills" (ἕτοιμον, Mi 4,1 = ὑψωθήσεται Is 2,2).[60]

Here, the eschatological temple as the goal of the pilgrimage of the nations is thus explicitly designated as a place "prepared".

(b) TARGUMS:[61] Dt 1,33. The Targum of Dt 1,33 provides further important evidence in support of our understanding of Jn 14,2-3 against the background of the Jewish tradition of the entrance into the land. There are clearly some literary links between Dt 1,33 (LXX) and the text and context of Jn 14,2-3:

ὃς προπορεύεται πρότερος ὑμῶν ἐν τῇ ὁδῷ ἐκλέγεσθαι ὑμῖν τόπον ὁδηγῶν ὑμᾶς ἐν πυρὶ νυκτὸς δεικνύων ὑμῖν τὴν ὁδόν, καθ' ἣν πορεύεσθε ἐπ' αὐτῆς, καὶ ἐν νεφέλῃ ἡμέρας.

προπορεύομαι	= πορεύομαι	(Jn 14,2-3 (2x)).
τόπος	= τόπος	(Jn 14,2-3(2x)).
ὁδός	= ὁδός	(Jn 14,4.5.6).
δείκνυμι	= δείκνυμι	(Jn 14,8.9).

---

also I Kgs 8,6 without ἑτοιμάζω) is necessarily the technical use of the term for the "sanctuary" or "temple"; but they do show that the temple or sanctuary itself was regarded in some sense as "a place prepared", and so may aptly be described in accordance with LXX usage as the object of a process of preparation. See, H. Köster, *TDNT*, VIII, 196, n. 64.

[60] See, H. Wildberger, "Die Völkerwallfahrt zum Zion. Jes. ii,1-5", *VetT* 7 (1957) 62-81.

[61] For a general introduction to the study of the Targums and proper methodology, see R. Bloch, "Note méthodologique pour l'étude de la littérature rabbinique", *RecSR* 43 (1955) 194-224; J. Bowker, *The Targums and Rabbinic Literature* (Cambridge, 1969); M. McNamara, *The New Testament and the Palestinian Targum to the Pentateuch,* (AnBib 27A) (Rome, 1966); G. Vermes, *Scripture and Tradition in Judaism* (Leiden, 1961). For more specific background on the Targum to the prophets, see P. Churgin, *Targum Jonathan to the Prophets* (New Haven, 1927); J.F. Stenning, *The Targum of Isaiah* (Oxford, 1949).

However, the possibility of dependence is further strengthened by the evidence of the Targum tradition:[62]

RSV	LXX	MT
to seek out	ἐκλέγεσθαι ὑμῖν	לתור לכם
a place	τόπον	מקום
to pitch your tents		לחנתכם

All the Targums (Pal. Tgs. and Onk.) and the Peshitta translate תור,[63] of Dt 1,33 as "prepare" from the root תקן, and חנה by the root שרי, meaning "to rest".[64] They render as follows:

Onk.   לאתקנאה לכון אתר בית מישרי לאשריותכון

Ps. Jon.   לאיתקנא לכון אתר בית משרוי לאשריותכון

= to prepare you a place, a place of encampment
(or: resting place)
for your encampment.

---

[62] The date to be assigned to the Targums of the Pentateuch is still a matter of debate. Some regard the Palestinian Targums of the Pentateuch, or at least Neofiti, as existing in the first century of our era, if not earlier; others maintain that the Aramaic in which they are written is from the second century A.D. at the earliest, although the traditions they contain may be earlier. see, M. McNamara, "Targum" in the *Interpreters Dictionary of the Bible*, Supp. Vol, 859-860. While this debate continues, it is preferable to establish the date for the passages used by such methods as the early versions of Scripture, and others noted by Bloch, *op. cit.* (n.61) and R. Le Déaut, *La Nuit Pascale* (Rome, 1963) 41-71, and M. McNamara, *Targum and Testament* (Shannon, 1972) 86-89. The Targum of the Former Prophets, and consequently Onkelos related to it in language, is believed by A. Tal (Rosenthal), to predate 135 at the earliest. See, *The Language of the Targum of the Former Prophets and its Position within the Aramaic Dialects* (Tel Aviv, 1975) in Hebrew, with an English summary, pp. vii-xii. A summary of Tal's book is now available in A. Diez Macho, *MS Neophyti, I., Vol. V, Deuteronomio* (Madrid, 1978).

[63] The Hebrew verb תור means "to seek out, spy out, explore". This same verb is used repeatedly in the OT tradition of the exploration of the land (e.g. Nm 13,2.10.17.21.23.32(2x); 14,7.34.36.38). In all occurrences of the Book of Numbers, apart from 10,33 and 15,19, the term means "to spy out the land". It is also translated by ἑτοιμάζω (LXX) with reference to the work of Yahweh for his people during the exodus, when he "prepared" the land for them in Ez 20.6.

[64] We have a similar uniformity in the rendering of all the Targums (Pa. Tgs. and Onk) and the Peshitta for the hebrew roots תור by תקן and חנה by שרי in Nm 10,33:

MT	מנוחה	להם	לתור
Onk	אתר בית מישרי	להון	לאתקנאה
TJI	אתר בית משרוי	להון	לאתקנא
Neof	אתר בית משרוי	להון	למתקנה
Pesh	בית משריא	להון	לתטיב

This uniformity of translation in all the Aramaic versions indicates that here we are in the presence of a well-established and ancient Palestinian exegetical tradition which leads to the conclusion that the rendering of Dt 1,33 and Nm 10,33 as "to prepare a place of encampment (or resting-place) for you" is very old and presumably pre-christian.

Neof.   למתקנה לכון אתר לשרוייכון
    = to prepare for you a place for your encampment
      (or: a resting place)

Peshitta   למתקנה לכון אתרא דתשרון בה
    = to prepare you a place in which you might encamp (or rest).[65]

In view of this uniform rendering there can hardly be any doubt that the tradition is ancient.

This Targum of the verb "to prepare" is surely significant, since, unlike the LXX ἐκλέγομαι, meaning "to choose", or the MT תור, meaning "to seek out" or "to spy out", it corresponds exactly to the verb "prepare" (ἑτοιμάζω) in Jn 14,2-3. However, "the place" here refers to the promised land as "the resting-place" (בית מישרי of the Targums) which God is to prepare, and not to the temple.

2. Themes[66]

(a) YAHWEH AS THE BUILDER OF THE ESCHATOLOGICAL TEMPLE. The provision of the eschatological temple is designated within the Jewish tradition in general as the work of Yahweh himself.[67] However, the text of 2 Sm 7,10-14 takes on a special importance within this tradition for an understanding of this theme. The midrash on this text from cave 4 (4QFlor) is one of the most intriguing as well as one of

---

[65] All forms of the Aramaic renderings come from the Aramaic verb שרי which has a wide range of meaning: (1) "to loose", "untie" (camels, etc.), "unharness"; "disengage"; "dismiss"; (2) "allow", "permit", "forgive (sin)", "absolve"; (3) "sit down for a meal" (unloose one's girdle; cf. Lk 17,8); (4) "begin", "start"; (5) "encamp (unloose camels, etc.)", "dwell", "rest". See, J. Levy, *Neuhebräisches und Chaldäisches Wörterbuch über die Talmud und Midraschim* (Vols. I-IV) (Leipzig, 1876) ad loc. The context must determine which term we are to choose to translate in any given occurrence, e.g. whether "camping-place" or "place of rest". As in 1,33 the Targums also speak elsewhere of the promised land as a "resting-place" which God is to prepare. The term מישרי is translated sometimes as "resting-place" and sometimes as "camping-place". Thus Dt 1,33 "para prepararlos un lugar de campamento" (Diez Macho) = "pour leur preparer un lieu de campement" (Le Déaut). So, also Ex 33,14 "y os preparare un lugar de repos" (Diez Macho) = "et vous préparerai un lieu de repos" (Le Déaut). Compare also, Nm 10.33. There seems to be little doubt that the targumist is thinking of the promised land uniformly in these several texts. For translations, see, A. Diez Macho, *op. cit.* (n. 62).

[66] The theme of the preparation, or exploration of the land is also relevant here. This has been adequately treated for our purpose in the previous section.

[67] See, Ez 37,26-28; Ze 3,14-17; Ze 2,14-15 (LXX). So, too, in extrabiblical eschatological expectation the temple is conceived as the work of Yahweh. See, *Jub* 1,18; *I En* 90,38-39; comp. *Exsec* 164-165.

the most elusive texts from Qumran.[68] There are several lacunae at crucial points in the midrash, which makes interpretation precarious. But about one fact there can be little doubt: the midrash regards Nathan's oracle as an eschatological prophecy.[69] The oracle, according to the interpreter, speaks about the "end of days" (באחרית הימים) (lines 2 and 12). Although the first lines of the midrash are missing, it seems likely that the interpretation begins with a comment on 2 Sm 7,10: "and I will appoint a place (מקום) for my people Israel". The text was presumably quoted through 2 Sm 7,11a, though this is by no means certain. The interpretation begins in line 2: This is the *house* ... (הואה הבית). The immediate question is where the "house" comes from. It has not been mentioned in the text from 2 Sm thus far, and in the text which is immediately quoted from Ex 15,17,[70] the term בית is not used. Further on in the midrash, however, there is reference to a "house" that God will build (line 10). And in the oracle from 2 Samuel there are two references to "houses", one in 7,11 (presumably referring to David's dynasty), and one in v. 13a (presumably referring to the temple David's seed is to build).[71] It appears, then, that the interpreter has related the "place" in 2 Sm 7,10 to one of the two "houses" mentioned in the oracle.

---

[68] For a complete study of this interpretation in Qumran, see, D. JUEL, *Messiah and Temple* (Missoula, 1977) 172-179; and for the text of 4QFlor. with English translation (ibid), p. 180. The text and translation for 4QFlor. are taken from the critical edition, DJDJ V 53-54. For alternative reconstructions of the text and different interpretations, see, J. STRUGNELL, "Notes en marge du volume V des Discoveries in the Judean Desert of Jordan", *RQ* 29 (1970) 220-222; and Y. YADIN, "A Midrash on 2 Sam vii and Ps. i-ii (4QFlorilegium)", *IEJ* 9 (1959) 95-98.

[69] The oracle is also viewed as a messianic prophecy: the "seed" promised David is identified in line 11 as the "Shoot of David" (צמח דוד), an expression used elsewhere in the scrolls as a designation for the Davidic Messiah (4QpIsa; 4QPB). B. GÄRTNER'S attempt to apply the title to the community is unconvincing. See, *The Temple and the Community in Qumran and the New Testament* (Cambridge, 1965), 35-39. There is widespread agreement that the comment beginning in line 10 interprets the oracle as a promise of the Davidic Messiah. See, L. SILBERMAN, "A Note on 4QFlorilegium" *JBL* 78 (1959) 158-159; D. FLUSSER, "Two Notes on the Midrash on 2 Sam vii", *IEJ* 9 (1959) 104; A. DUPONT-SOMMER, *The Essene Writings from Qumran* (New York, 1967) 313. 315; N. A. DAHLS, "Eschatology and History in the light of the Qumran Scrolls", *The Future of our Religious Past* (New York, 1971), 16.

[70] On Ex 15,17, see, note, 55.

[71] D. JUEL argues very cogently that the omission from the midrash of the phrase in 2 Sm 7,13a ("He shall build a house for my name"), the text according to which the Messiah will build the eschatological temple, is not accidental, but intentional. The midrash perhaps even reflects a conscious correction of a traditional view according to which the Messiah was expected to build the temple. In the light of the sect's eschatological beliefs, it is not surprising that no attempt is made to increase substantially the stature of the royal Messiah by acknowledging his role as builder of the eschatological "house". See, *op. cit.* (n. 68) 178-179.

This house is then identified with the מקרש which, according to Ex 15,17, God is to build. This verse is used elsewhere to describe the eschatological temple that God is to erect, and that seems to be the most likely meaning here. By appealing to Ex 15,17, therefore, the interpreter identifies the "place" in 2 Sm 7,10 with the "house" in line 2 meaning the eschatological sanctuary.

But the text of the midrash also seems to assume the meaning "temple" in line 10. The text from 2 Sm 7,11 reads כי בית יעשה לך יהוה. Instead of the more neutral עשה, however, the midrash reads בנה. The "house" to be "built" is clearly the temple, the sanctuary to be built by God's hands. The interpreter seems to have read the term בית in 2 Sm 7,11 as "temple".

Thus the Nathan oracle is viewed by the interpreter as an eschatological text, promising both the "Shoot of David" (lines 10-11) as well as a "house" to be built by Yahweh at the end of time as his sanctuary. The midrash is the only unambiguous piece of evidence that this text has been so interpreted.

(b) THE MESSIAH AS THE BUILDER OF THE ESCHATOLOGICAL TEMPLE.[72]

The link between the Messiah and the building of the eschatological temple is also deeply embedded in the Jewish tradition in general.[73] But perhaps the most important evidence of all derives within this tradition from the Targums. The Targum Zechariah 6,12 is the most straightforward.[74] The Hebrew text says that the man whose name is the Branch (or Shoot = צמח) will build the temple of God.[75] The targumist simply interprets for his readers the term צמח: he translates it משיחא. The same translation occurs in 3,8, where the expression עבדי צמח (my servant

---

[72] BEN F. MEYER observes in general that "In the light of substantially attested biblical and post-biblical traditions deriving from the oracle of Nathan it is clear that 'the building of the temple' could easily be made to carry messianic connotations". See, *The Aims of Jesus*, (London, 1979) 180.

[73] In the Psalms of Solomon (c. 70-40, B.C.) the restoration of the temple is made one of the chief offices of the Messiah (cf. 17,32f). Moreover, there are also significant allusions to 2 Sm 7 (cf. 17,5.23). Apparently, the Messiah's work in respect to the eschatological temple is thought of as in some sense fulfilling the prediction of Nathan's prophecy concerning the son of David and the temple. The evidence from the Sibylline Oracles is no less explicit (c. 140, B.C.-70, A.D.). The fifth Oracle states that the new temple will be erected by the Messiah (cf. v. 424f).

[74] For the full text of Ze 6,12, see, D. JUEL, *op. cit.* (n. 68) 181.

[75] For examples of the use of צמח as a designation for the Messiah, see, D. JUEL, *op. cit.* (n. 68) 189. Here this same author writes: "We can learn from other sources a) how widely צמח was regarded as a designation for the Messiah and b) what evidence there is that this particular passage from Zech. was recognized as messianic. Such information can help locate the particular targumic tradition in time".

the branch) is rendered עבדי משיחא (my servant, the Messiah).[76] In the next line the targumist adds עתיד ד־, making certain that the events to be described are understood as future. He translates the strange expression מתחתיו יצמח = "shall grow up from his place",[77] with two verbs, the first (יתגלי, be revealed)[78] being considerably more than a mere translation. The passage is clearly messianic. It describes events which are to take place in the future, the most important of which will be the revealing of the Messiah and his building the temple of the Lord (היכלא דייי).[79]

However, the text of the Nathan oracle again takes on a special importance within this Targum tradition for an understanding of our theme. In the Targum 2 Sm 7,13-14 it is highly probable that the targumist interprets the one who "shall build a house for my name" (הוא יבנה בית לשמי) with reference to the future Son of David, the Messiah.[80] We know from Qumran (4QFlor) that the oracle of Nathan has been interpreted to refer to the Messiah. There is no clear evidence in the Targum that the targumist agrees with such a reading of the text, but more importantly, there is no suggestion that he does not accept its messianic significance and is attempting to historicise the text. He simply renders the text in Aramaic, following the Hebrew quite literally. In v. 14, however, there are indications that the targumist is more concerned about careful translation. His translation makes quite clear that the father/son language is purely symbolic, that the Son of David is not literally God's son. It seems reasonable to infer from the obvious sensitivity reflected in the translation that the passage has traditionally been taken to refer to someone other than Solomon. This is a strong indication that the passage has been important in messianic discussions.

The Targum to the parallel text of I Chr 17,12-13 also seems to view the text as messianic. The modifications in the translations are slight. The targumist uses the more common בית מקדש for בית, and he has attempted

---

[76] This text has probably been the source of the "servant tradition", in which passages speaking about "my servant" (עבדי) are interpreted to refer to the Messiah. See, P. SEIDELIN, "Der 'Ebed Jahwe' und die Messiagestalt in Jesaiatargum", *ZNW* 35 (1936) 194-231, esp. 226-228.

[77] "from his place", see, BROWN, DRIVER, BRIGGS, *op. cit.* (n. 53), re תחת, II,2a.

[78] The word seems to be a technical term for the appearance of the Messiah. For a discussion, see, M. MCNAMARA, *op. cit.* (n. 61) 249, and the literature there cited. The same expression is used of the appearing of the Messiah in: TJI Gn 35,21; PT Ex 12,42; Tg Jer 30,21; Tg Zech 3,8. The verb רבה (in Ze 6,12) is used of the Messiah also in Tg Is 11,1.

[79] D. JUEL provides ample indirect evidence for an early dating of this Targum in the first century. See, *op. cit.* (n. 68) 191.

[80] See, note 68. We also know from the NT that the Nathan Oracle has been interpreted to refer to the Messiah (cf. Lk 1,32-33; Jn 7,42; Acts 2,30; Heb 1,5).

to include both the reading from 2 Sm and the reading from I Chr (both לי and לשמי). Verse 13 is evidence that the version of Nathan's oracle in Chronicles has not escaped the attention of the careful translator. Here he is even more careful to demonstrate the purely figurative character of the father/son imagery. As in the case of Targum 2 Sm 7,14 the sensitivities suggest that the text is messianic in the mind of the targumist.

The evidence of Targum Is 53,5 is much more striking still, because the phrase about building the eschatological temple is so clearly an insertion of an entirely new idea into the text and not simply a translation. We can easily observe the mechanics of the insertion. What makes it possible is the reading of the participle מחלל to mean "profaned" instead of "pierced" or "wounded".[81] The rest of the verse is appropriately referred to the destruction of the temple, not the mishandling of the servant. The rebuilding of the temple by the Messiah ("my servant the Messiah" in 52,13) is not derived from the text but is inserted into the verse as something entirely new.[82] Thus the theme of the Messiah as the builder of the eschatological temple rejoins the prophecy of the Suffering Servant.[83]

The sum of this evidence from the Targums suggests that the building of the eschatological temple was a fixed part of the constellation of messianic traditions.

3. Application to Jn 14,2-3

(a) SIMILARITIES. The use of the verb ἑτοιμάζω with reference to the Father's house with the many rooms as its (indirect) object might well be interpreted in harmony with LXX usage, as meaning to render the house with the rooms accessible, or to open it up for the coming of the disciples. So, too, it might be interpreted with reference to a "place", meaning "a temple" as (direct) object, in the creative sense of providing a temple. Moreover, the verb would be appropriate to designate the preparation of the eschatological temple, which is explicitly designated in LXX usage as a place "prepared" (ἕτοιμον, Mi 4,1); and may thus aptly be described as the object of a process of preparation (cf. I Chr 15,1.3.12).

---

[81] It is probably not even necessary to repoint this participle, as suggested by BROWN, DRIVER, BRIGGS, op. cit. (n. 53). For a discussion of the problem, see, H. HEGERMANN, Jesaia 53 in Hexapla, Targum und Peschitta, (Gütersloh, 1954), 79, n. 3.

[82] It is already taken for granted that the reader will not be taken totally by surprise, but is already familiar with the idea. See, D. JUEL, op. cit. (n. 68) 189.

[83] A. VANHOYE has already noted the importance of the Targum Isaiah, 53,3 for an interpretation of the NT. See, Structure and Theology of the Accounts of the Passion in the Synoptic Gospels (Minnesota, 1967) 30, n. 1. D. JUEL considers this Targum more completely in the interpretation of Mark. See, op. cit. (n. 68) 182-187.

However, the verb might be interpreted in accordance with LXX exodus vocabulary as evoking the tradition of the preparation of the land, and especially in harmony with the terminology of the Targum tradition of the preparation of the land as evidenced particularly by Targum to Dt, 1,33: there is an exact correspondence between the verb "to prepare" in Jn 14,2-3 and Targum to Dt 1,33.

The claim of Jesus to provide a "temple" or "sanctuary" in Jn 14,2-3 (if τόπος be so interpreted) may be seen as an implicit (or veiled) claim to be the Messiah to whom the building of the eschatological temple is ascribed in the Jewish tradition. It could hardly be interpreted as a claim of Jesus to be God Himself, since John is careful to distinguish clearly between Jesus and the Father in our text.

Finally, the journey of preparation is also open to interpretation at a deeper possible level of meaning with reference to the passion-death of Jesus as the means of providing a "sanctuary" or "temple" (if τόπος be so interpreted). Jn 14,2-3 could then be seen in line with that Jewish tradition where the Messiah as the Suffering Servant is designated as the builder of the future eschatological temple. The theme of the temple in Jn 14,2-3 could be seen to rejoin the prophecy of the Suffering Servant.

(b) DIFFERENCES. John's specific choice of ἑτοιμάζω seems to have been influenced in a special way by the use of the term in the Targum tradition of the preparation of the entrance into Canaan. But this tradition is nuanced in an original way by John in our understanding of Jn 14,2-3 with reference to the preparation of entrance into the eschatological temple, whether it be the earthly temple or the heavenly one.

C. THE PLACE

1. Vocabulary: Place

(a) OLD TESTAMENT.

(i) *In General.* In the LXX τόπος indicates for the most part a "place" in the spatial sense of some kind of physical "space".[84] It is a simple topographical designation. In this spatial sense there is a curious use of the term to describe the place where the priest Eli sleeps in the sanctuary at Shiloh:

---

[84] See, Gn 24,25.31; 28,10(3x); Nm 32,1; Dt 23,12.16.

"At that time Eli, whose eyesight had begun to grow dim, so that he could not see, was lying down in his own place (ἐν τῷ τόπῳ αὐτοῦ = (MT) במקומו...) and Samuel was lying down within the temple of the Lord (ἐν τῷ ναῷ = (MT),בהיכל) where the ark of God was" (I Sm 3,2-3; comp. I Sm 3,9).

In this general spatial sense the term may also refer to heaven, even the heavenly temple:[85]

"And let the Lord God be a witness against you, the Lord from his holy temple (Κύριος ἐξ οἴκου ἁγίου αὐτοῦ). For behold, the Lord is coming forth out of his place (Κύριος ἐκπορεύεται ἐκ τοῦ τόπου αὐτοῦ), and will come down and tread upon the high places of the earth" (Mi 1,2-3).[86]

However, the term has a technical sense in the LXX when it refers to the land:

"You have seen how the Lord your God bore you, as a man bears his son, in all the way that you went until you came to this place (εἰς τὸν τόπον τοῦτον)" (Dt 1,31).[87]

The term also has a technical sense when it refers to the sanctuary or temple. It designates the sanctuaries prior to the conquest of the land, and also the Jerusalem temple itself.[88] The prayers which are made on earth in this sanctuary Yahweh will hear in the place of his dwelling in heaven:

"yet have regard to the prayer of thy servant ... that thy eyes may be open night and day toward this house, the place (εἰς τὸν οἶκον ... εἰς τὸν τόπον) of which thou hast said, 'My name shall be there', that thou mayest hearken to the prayer which thy servant offers towards this place (εἰς τὸν τόπον τοῦτον). And hearken thou to the supplication ... when they pray towards this place (εἰς τὸν τόπον τοῦτον); yea, hear thou in heaven thy dwelling-place ... (ἐν τῷ τόπῳ τῆς κατοικήσεώς σου ἐν οὐρανῷ)" (I Kgs 8,28-30).[89]

---

[85] Comp. Hos 5,15. This text is also significant for its use of πορεύομαι to designate a journey of Yahweh to his heavenly dwelling-place: "I will go and I will return to my place".

[86] "Honour and majesty are before him; strength and joy are in his place (ἐν τόπῳ αὐτοῦ)" (I Chr 16,27) becomes in the parallel text "in his sanctuary" (Ps 96(95),6).

[87] See, Dt I,31.33; 9,7; I Chr 17,19; 2 Kgs 18,25; Jer 7,20; 7,3-7.

[88] See, Gn 28,16.17.19; Dt 12,2.3.13. On this theme, see, P. R. ACKROYD, Exile and Restoration (London, 1976) 156, also note, 11.

[89] See, I Kgs 8,33-34; 2 Chr 6,40; 7,12; 2 Mc 1,29; 2,18. It is still a matter of conjecture whether Jerusalem was already a τόπος in the technical sense of "sanctuary' or "holy place" before the arrival of the ark. For a discussion of this problem, see, R. DE VAUX, Ancient Israel. Its Life and Institutions (London, 1973) 310-311.

In this technical sense of the temple[90] the term is found repeatedly in the Deuteronomical formula: "the place (τόπος) where Yahweh has chosen to establish/place his name" (Dt 12,5; comp. Dt. 12,11).[91]

(ii) *In Particular*. There is one LXX use of the term which requires special attention. It seems to have a special importance within the Jewish tradition as part of the Nathan oracle.[92]

2 Sam 7,10. | I Chron 17,9

"And I will appoint *a place*	καὶ θήσομαι τόπον
for my people Israel	τῷ λαῷ μου(τῷ) Ἰσραήλ
and will plant them,	καὶ καταφυτεύσω αὐτόν,
that they may dwell in their own place	καὶ κατασκηνώσει καθ' ἑαυτὸν
and never be disturbed again;	καὶ οὐ μεριμνήσει οὐκέτι,
and violent men shall afflict them no more.	καὶ οὐ προσθήσει υἱὸς ἀδικίας τοῦ ταπεινῶσαι αὐτόν.

Here the verbs are in the future.[93] David has just conquered Jerusalem and brought the ark there (cf. 2 Sm 6,17; 1 Chr 15,3.12.28-29; 16,1). Accordingly, the Nathan oracle, with its vision of the future, can scarcely refer to the conquest. What seems to be in question here is the future building of the temple. Such an interpretation of τόπος is much more in harmony with the general perspective of the Nathan oracle, which may be regarded almost as a *locus classicus* for the Jewish temple tradition. Such an interpretation would also be in line with the general LXX technical use of the term τόπος to designate the sanctuary.[94] A reference to the temple, then, seems to fit better into the concrete historical circumstances of the Nathan oracle, and the general LXX technical usage of the term τόπος, meaning temple.

---

[90] On this technical sense of the term, see, H. Köster, *TDNT, VIII, 196.*

[91] We have two slight variations of this formula:

(i) "to establish his name there" (לשכן) (Dt 12,11; 14,23; 16,2.6.11; 26,2, (cf. also Neh 1,9).

(ii) "to place his name there" (לשום) (Dt 12,5.21; 14,24).

Both variations of the formula are equivalent to one another and both have the same meaning. The "place" (τόπος) is never identified by name, but later ages recognise it as Jerusalem and the temple where Josias would centralise the nation's worship. For a full discussion of the formula, see, R. DE VAUX, "Le Lieu que Yahvé a choisi pour y établir son nom", in *Das Ferne und Nahe Wort — Festschrift L. Rost* (Beihefte zur *ZAW* 105) (Berlin, 1967), 219-228.

[92] On the Nathan oracle in general, see, ch. 11, note, 18.

[93] For a full discussion of the tenses of the verbs in the MT and in the ancient versions, see, A. GELSTON, "A Note on II Samuel, 7,10", *ZAW 84 (1972) 92-94.*

[94] See, ns. 87. 88.

(b) EXTRA-BIBLICAL LITERATURE.

(i) *Qumran.* The evidence of 4QFlor from Qumran[95] is highly significant for the interpretation of 2 Sm 7,10 within the Jewish tradition. We have already observed that this midrash regards Nathan's oracle from 2 Sm 7 as an eschatological prophecy.[96] However, the midrash is fragmentary.[97] But it seems to begin with a quotation from 2 Sm 7,10ff, ending at עַל עַמִּי יִשְׂרָאֵל in v. 11, and followed immediately by a comment, "This is the house that ...", with a quotation from Ex 15,17. It appears, then, that the interpreter has related the "place" in 2 Sm 7,10 to one of the two houses mentioned in the oracle. This house is then identified with the מקדש which, according to Ex 15,17, God is to build. By appeal to Ex 15,17, therefore, the interpreter identifies the "place" in 2 Sm 7,10 and one of the two "houses" with the eschatological sanctuary.

(ii) *Targums.*

a. *In General.* There are signs of a significant evolution, or development in general within the Targum tradition itself. We have already considered the text of Dt 1,33,[98] and seen that the hebrew verb תור is rendered uniformly by the Aramaic versions as "to prepare".[99] So, too, the Hebrew term meaning "a place of encampment" (from the root חנה) is rendered in these same Aramaic versions by words which can be translated either as "place of encampment" or "resting-place".

However, this phrase "to prepare a place of encampment or a resting-place" is also common elsewhere in the Targums.[100] In the context of the desert wanderings, Nm 10,33 speaks precisely of the journey from the mount of the Lord "to seek a resting-place for them". The various translations of the Targums are again uniform, rendering the hebrew תור by תקן (meaning "to prepare") and חנה by שרי (meaning "to rest").

Besides, in Ex 33,14 Yahweh tells Moses: "My presence (lit.: my face) will go with thee and give thee rest" (והנחתי). This is rendered in a rather literal fashion in most of the Targums, except that Onkelos avoids the anthropomorphism by paraphrasing "my face" as "my Shekinah" (i.e. presence). Neofiti, however, paraphrases as follows: "The glory of my Shekinah will go (lit.: lead, accompany) among you, and I shall prepare a resting-place for you" ("you", plural in both instances) ואתק(י)ן לכון בית משרוי.

---

95 See, n. 68.

96 See, pp. 93-95; also n. 69.

97 See, pp. 93-95; also n. 69.

98 See, pp. 91-93.

99 See, n. 64.

100 For these arguments we are indebted to the study of M. McNamara. See, "'To prepare a resting place for you'. A Targumic expression and John, 14,2f', *MillSt* 3 (1979) 100-107.

Occasionally, however, one or other of the targumic texts paraphrases rather literally the Hebrew term for "rest". Thus Dt 12,9 where the Hebrew reads: "You have not yet come to rest (המנוחה) and to the inheritance", Onkelos and Neofiti render literally, except that the latter renders "rest" as "place of rest" (בית ניחא). For Pseudo-Jonathan the "rest" is the sanctuary or temple: "For you have not yet come to the sanctuary (lit. בית מקדש = house of holiness) which is the house (or: place) or rest (בית נייחא) and the land of Israel which is called inheritance".

We have a similar occurrence in the translations of Gn 49,15, which in the Hebrew text reads: "He (i.e. Issachar) saw a resting-place (מנחה) that it was good". The Fragment Targum renders as: "And he saw the sanctuary (lit: house of holiness), which is called rest (מנוחה), that it was good". This text is also found in the margin of Neofiti.

From the manner in which the Aramaic translations (the Peshitta included) render the terms תור, מנוחה and related words, we can conclude that the expression "to prepare a resting-place for you" was an established interpretation in the NT period. In the Pentateuch, the resting place, or place of encampment, would refer to the stations of the desert wanderings. But in latter times it would have meant the land itself and the sanctuary.

b. *In Particular.* The Nathan oracle again takes on special importance within the Jewish tradition of the Targums. The Targum I Chr 17,9[101] has some important modifications of the LXX text:

"And I will make (or appoint) for my people a prepared place (אתר מתקן לעמי), and they shall dwell in their place (וישרון באתרהון), and they shall not tremble more".[102]

---

[101] For the text, see, R. Le Déaut/R. J. Robert, *Targum des Chroniques (Cod. Vat. Urb. Ebr. I), I, (introduction et traduction); II, (texte et glossaire), (Rome, 1971).*

[102] Much has been made of the plural form "places" which S. Aalen reads in this Targum text of 1 Chr 17,9: "The Targum inserts the important word "prepared" and speaks of "places" instead of the singular used in the Hebrew original". See, " 'Reign' and 'House' in the Kingdom of God", *NTS* 8 (1962) 238. So, too, G. Fischer also insists on the importance of the plural form "places". See, *Die himmlischen Wohnungen. Untersuchungen zu Joh 14,2f,* (Frankfurt/M, 1975), 118, n. 8. However, R. Le Déaut/J. Robert rightly render in the singular as "ils demeureront a leur place". See, *op. cit.* (n. 101), Vol. I, 80. The vocalisation of the manuscript must be presumed faulty; the plural would require a consonantal ן באתריהו. In the vocalisation of the manuscript edited by R. Le Déaut/J. Robert (*op. cit.* (n. 101) 19-21), Tg. I Chr 17,9 is identical (with a few exceptions of different synonyms in adverbs) with Tg 2 Sm, 7,10 (which also reads באתרהון, and which it probably follows). See, R. Le Déaut/J. Robert, *op. cit.* (n. 101) 23. Thus Tg. Chron. adds nothing in this respect, it would seem, to Tg. 2 Sm 7.10, since Tg 2 Sm 7,10 also has "a place" (אתר מתקן). Abraham Tal (Rosenthal) has argued that this Targum antedates the year 125, A.D. See, *op. cit.* (n. 62).

Here we note that the Targum inserts the important word "prepared". There seems to be little doubt that the targumist is thinking here of the promised land as "a prepared place".[103] However, in view of the links between Ex 15,17 and 2 Sm 7,10 within the temple tradition as evidenced by Qumran, and in view of the general evolution or development of the phrase "to prepare a place" within the Targum tradition the text of I Chr 17,9 (parallel to 2 Sm 7,10) would leave itself open for application in the general development of the Jewish tradition to the temple as the goal of later Jewish eschatological expectations.

2. Themes: The temple as the goal of unity

(a) A DEUTERONOMICAL FORMULA.[104] The theme of the temple as the goal of unity can be clearly seen behind the gradual evolution of the term τόπος.[105] It occurs some 34 times in Deuteronomy, of simple geographical location twice (23,12.16), of the promised land 7 times (1,31.32; 9,7; 11,5.24; 26,9; 29,7), of the "holy places" or "sanctuaries" prior to the temple 3 times (12,2.3.13); and on every other occasion, that is 21 times, in a distinctly Deuteronomical formula. The "place" itself is never identified by name, but later ages recognise it as Jerusalem and the temple where Josias would centralise the nation's worship. In this rich Deuteronomical formula "the place where Yahweh has chosen to establish/place his name", which is constantly repeated, in all 21 times, either in complete or incomplete form, the Jerusalem temple is called the "place" = τόπος = מקום.[106]

The reasons that motivated the demand for centralisation are not wholly agreed upon by scholars, and various suggestions have been offered.[107] Suffice it here to note that the unification of Israel's worship by the concentration of it on a single centre in Jerusalem at the temple

---

[103] It is probably better not to seek a fully worked out reinterpretation of biblical exegesis in the text of the Targums. We have seen that the Targums speak continually of the promised land as a "resting-place" which God is to prepare. See, n. 65. In the light of the whole general Targum Tradition this would also seem to be the most obvious sense for the term "place" (אתר) in I Chr 17,9.

[104] See, n. 91.

[105] See, R. E. CLEMENTS, God and Temple. The Idea of the Divine Presence in Ancient Israel (Oxford, 1965). Note especially, Ch. 6: "The Prophetic Reaction and the Deuteronomic Reform".

[106] The Deuteronomistic historians explicitly identified Yahweh's chosen sanctuary as the Jerusalem temple. (I Kgs 8,15ff,29; 11,36; 14,21; 2 Kgs 21,4.7). See, R. E. CLEMENTS, op. cit. (n. 105) 92, n. 6.

[107] For a brief outline of these suggestions, see, R. E. CLEMENTS, op. cit. (n. 105) 92, n. 5.

finds expression in this Deuteronomical formula, and is all part of a long process by which the Jerusalem temple gradually replaces the various other shrines and cultic centres which Israel found in the land, and are also referred to in the OT as מקום (Dt 12,2.3.13).

The influence of this Deuteronomical formula is extensive. Already in the Deuteronomistic I Kgs 8,29 we find: εἰς τὸν οἶκον τοῦτον..εἰς τὸν τόπον..εἰς τὸν τόπον τοῦτον. The same term τόπος is commonly used in prophetic passages from Deuteronomy onwards, especially in prophecies of disaster in Jerusalem.[108] But here the phrase seems to have combined a double sense. At first Jerusalem mostly, its habitants (2 Kgs 22,16-20), and the whole land of Judah (2 Kgs 18,25; Zeph 1,4; Jer 7,20), seems to dominate. However, the meaning of "temple" also seems to infiltrate (Jer 14,13; comp. 14,15; also 28(35),3f).

The same problem of a double meaning occurs in passages more strongly influenced by Deuteronomy, especially the temple address in Jer 7. The meaning of "land" seems to be present at first:

> "I will cause you to dwell in this place (ἐν τῷ τόπῳ τούτῳ) (Jer 7,3), that is, I will cause you to dwell in this place, in the land (ἐν τῷ τόπῳ τούτῳ ἐν γῇ)" (Jer 7,7).

Then in the continuation of the passage we read:

> "But go you now to my (holy) place (εἰς τὸν τόπον μου) which was in Shiloh (comp. εἰς οἶκον κυρίου ἐν Σηλωμ, 1 Sm. 1,24; Ps 78(77),60), where I caused my name to tabernacle at first" (Jer 7,12).

and then finally:

> "Therefore will I do to this house (τῷ οἴκῳ τούτῳ) over which my name is named and in which you trust, and the place (τῷ τόπῳ) which I gave to you and to your fathers, as I have done to Shiloh" (Jer 7,14).

The term τόπος seems to have a double sense here. So, too, in other passages in Jeremiah. This intentional multiplicity of meaning is to be explained by the artificial Deuteronomical linking of τόπος as shrine with the idea of τόπος as the land, or the place where Yahweh causes his people to dwell.

---

[108] Again in parts influenced by Deuteronomy. See, Jer. 16,2-9; 19,3-6.12; 32,37; 33,10.12, and the Deuteronomic saying: "Innocent blood does not flow in this place", Jer 22,3. See, P. R. ACKROYD, op. cit. (n. 88) 156; also, H. KÖSTER, TDNT, VIII, 198.

(b) NEHEMIAH, 1,9. We seem to have a similar fusion of meaning in Neh 1,9 (LXX II Esdras 11,8-9):

"If you are unfaithful, I will scatter you among the peoples; but if you return to me and keep my commandments and do them, though your dispersed be under the farthest skies, I will gather them thence and bring them to the place which I have chosen, to make my name dwell there (εἰς τὸν τόπον, ὅν ἐξελεξάμην κατασκηνῶσαι τὸ ὄνομά μου ἐκεῖ)."

Here the reunion of the people around the sanctuary seems to be inextricably bound up with their possession of the land, and the term τόπος seems to designate at one and the same time both the "land" and "sanctuary".

(c) MACCABEES.

(i) *2 Mc 1,27-29.* The Book of Maccabees has an importance all its own for our theme. Already by the time of Maccabees the theological understanding of τόπος is fully orientated to the temple as the holy place.[109] In 2 Mc the temple emerges decisively as "the place" where the scattered exiles shall be reunited. The prayer of Nehemiah in 2 Mc 1,27-29 clearly reflects this Jewish expectation:

v. 27. "Gather together (ἐπισυνάγαγε) our scattered people (τὴν διασπορὰν ἡμῶν), set free those who are slaves among the Gentiles, look upon those who are rejected and despised, and let the Gentiles know that you are God."

v. 28. "Afflict those who oppress us and affront us by their insolence."

v. 29. "Plant your people in your Holy Place, as Moses said (καταφύτευσον τὸν λαόν σου εἰς τὸν τόπον τὸν ἅγιόν σου)"

This passage which is a significant interpretation of Ex 15,17 with reference to the temple, serves to evoke again the Babylonian exile and the subsequent restoration of the scattered people of God, which it centres on the temple.[110] As such it reflects contemporary expectations. By a kind of literary fiction the aspirations of an earlier generation become those of a later one (comp. Is 43,16-20).

(ii) *2 Mc 2,17-18.* We have further evidence of this same contemporary Jewish expectation of the gathering of the people of God to the temple in

---

[109] "In 1,2.3. and 4 Macc. the land is never called τόπος. 'The holy place where God has planted his people' in 2 Macc. 1,29 is not the land but the temple. Cf. 2 Macc. 5,19f". See, H. KÖSTER, *TDNT*, VIII, 198.

[110] Compare, 4QFlor where the text of Ex 15,17 is also appealed to as a description of the eschatological temple. See, pp. 93-95.

yet another technical use of the term τόπος = "temple" in the letter(s) sent by the Jews of Jerusalem to their compatriots in Egypt. By way of conclusion to this document we read:

> v. 17. "to conclude ... God who has saved his whole people, conferring on all the heritage, kingdom, priesthood and sanctification",
>
> v. 18. "as he promised through the Law, will surely, as our hope is in him, be swift to show mercy and gather us together (ἐπισυνάξει) from everywhere under heaven to the Holy Place (εἰς τὸν ἅγιον τόπον) since he has rescued us from great evils and has purified the temple (τὸν τόπον)" (2 Mc 2,17-18).

Again, the unity of the people is inseparably linked with the temple: "however, the Lord has not chosen the people for the sake of the place, but the place for the sake of the people (ἀλλ' οὐ διὰ τὸν τόπον τὸ ἔθνος, ἀλλὰ διὰ τὸ ἔθνος τὸν τόπον ὁ κύριος ἐξελέξατο)" (2 Mc 5,19).[111] But this same theme of an indissoluble link between the unity of the people and the temple may also be found elsewhere in Maccabees (cf. I Mc 3,43. 58-59; comp. Jn 11,48).

Thus the final unity of the people cannot be separated from the temple in the Jewish expectations of a later epoch represented by the Book of Maccabees, and the theme of the temple as the expected gathering-place of the scattered people of God would be easily evoked by the use of the term τόπος, meaning "sanctuary" or "temple".

(d) EXODUS, 15,17.[112] Finally, the original source of the Jewish temple tradition which culminates in 2 Mc 1,29 is explicitly designated in this text as Ex 15,17. This text of Exodus forms part of "The Song of Miriam". It has its own "Heilsgeschichte" conceived as a divinely guided pilgrimage of the people of God to the goal of the sanctuary.[113] The text is as follows:

"lead them in and plant them on the mountain of your inheritance,[114]	εἰσαγαγὼν καταφύτευσον αὐτοὺς εἰς ὄρος κληρονομίας σου,
your prepared abode	εἰς ἕτοιμον κατοικητήριόν σου,
which you have made,	ὃ κατειργάσω, κύριε,
the sanctuary, O Lord,	ἁγίασμα, κύριε,
which your hands have prepared."	ὃ ἡτοίμασαν αἱ χεῖρές σου.

---

[111] This priority of people over religious institutions is a remarkable anticipation of the Gospels. See, *JB* ad loc. note, "d".

[112] On Ex 15,17, see, M. Cross, Jr. and D. N. Freedman, *op. cit.* (n. 55); also, R. E. Clements, *op. cit.* (n. 105) 52-53; D. N. Freedman, "A Letter to the Readers". *BA* 40 (n. 2) (1977) 46-48.

[113] To appreciate the point of this hymn, we must recall that in the common Israelite view history was "Heilsgeschichte", that is, history formed and guided by God and, in particular, by the word of God, not simply a juxtaposition and sequence of events. It is history with a divine plan or purpose.

[114] D. N. Freedman locates the mountain of Ex 15,17, not on Mt. Zion, but on Mt.

There is no doubt that Ex 15,17 is linked in the Jewish tradition with the eschatological temple. It is this later interpretation such as we find it in the Qumran text of 4QFlor., (comp. 2 Mc 1,27-29), read back again into the ancient ode, which gives special weight to Ex 15,17, within the context of the whole unified composition of the Song of Miriam, for an understanding of the Jewish temple tradition. Here we have a presentation of Israel's origins as a divinely guided pilgrimage which reaches its climax in the establishment of the people on the holy mountain as the site of Yahweh's temple.[115]

Thus the history of the Exodus is retold in intimate association with the sanctuary which becomes the goal of this divinely guided pilgrimage through the desert. It is hardly surprising that such a song of victory should become the source of inspiration for later Jewish eschatological expectations of a final reunion of the congregation of the poor in the Qumran text of 4QFlor.

By way of conclusion, we note that an interpretation of τόπος in 2 Sm 7,10//I Chr 17,9 and Dt 1,33 with reference to the eschatological temple would be in harmony with the Jewish tradition represented by 4QFlor., where this same text of Ex 15,17 is again explicitly evoked.[116]

3. Application to Jn 14,2-3

(a) SIMILARITIES. The use of the term τόπος as the direct object of the preparation in Jn 14,2-3 might easily be interpreted in line with LXX usage as a simple topographical designation, meaning "place" in the physical (spatial) sense of "space".[117] However, the term τόπος is also open to interpretation in line with that same LXX usage in a highly technical sense, meaning "land" or "sanctuary" and "temple". To interpret τόπος in any of these ways would be in accord with LXX usage of the term.

Sinai/Horeb; and distinguishes the temple, not as the Jerusalem temple, but as the eternal temple on which the "tent of meeting" or "tabernacle" was modelled (Ex 25,8.40). See, *op. cit.* (n. 112) 46-48. It should be noted, however, that such an interpretation is not that of 2 Mc 1,27-29. Besides, if the poem envisages only the installation of the people on Mt. Sinai then one cannot help wondering why the inhabitants of Philistia, Edom, and Canaan are terrified (Ex 15,14-16).

[115] J. SCHREINER points out that Ps 78(77) also expresses the belief that the conquest of Canaan finds its proper goal in the building of the temple. See, *Sion-Jerusalem, Jahwes Königssitz*, (München, 1963) 210. On the phrase "And he built his Sanctuary" in v. 69, see, N. D. FREEDMAN, *op. cit.* (n. 112) 48.

[116] There is a further important literary link established between Ex 15,17, 2 Sm 7,10 = I Chr 17,9, and 2 Mc 1,29 by the common use of the verb καταφυτεύω. See, Ch. II, p. 60.

[117] The object of the process of preparations is directly τόπος and indirectly the Father's house with the many rooms. See, Ch. I, n. 35.

Moreover, the τόπος could also be seen as particularly apt to designate at one and the same time both the land itself and the temple, as the eschatological gathering-place of the people of God. Interpreted in this sense, the use of the term τόπος in 2 Sm 7,10 might be seen to have exercised a special influence on the choice of the term τόπος in Jn 14,2-3 in view of the interpretation of that text within the Jewish tradition inspired by Ex 15,17 and evidenced by the Qumran text of 4QFlor. Moreover, the text of I Chr 17,9 which is parallel to 2 Sm 7,10, with its explicit reference to "a place prepared" in the Targum tradition would add further support to this line of interpretation.

Interpreting the τόπος of Jn 14,2-3 in this way, then, the phrase θήσομαι τόπον τῷ λαῷ μου (2 Sm 7,10/I Chr 17,9) would provide an intelligible interpretation of the phrase ἑτοιμάσω τόπον ὑμῖν as follows:

τίθημι = ἑτοιμάζω in the sense of to give, or place, or provide.

τόπος = τόπος in the sense of eschatological "sanctuary", as interpreted in the Jewish tradition evidenced by 4QFlor.

λαός = ὑμῖν in the sense that the group of the disciples might be seen to represent a new people of God as the nucleus of the eschatological community.

This phrase of Jn 14,2-3 is at least open to interpretation with reference to the eschatological temple in line with the general Jewish temple tradition. Such an interpretation is all the more likely as I Chr 17,9 and the parallel text of 2 Sm 7,10 form an integral part of the Nathan oracle, the *locus classicus* of the Jewish temple tradition.

Finally, the Targum rendering of Dt 1,33 as "to prepare a place of encampment/resting-place" might be seen to have also exercised a special influence on the formation of Jn 14,2-3. Again, this would not be so directly, but in line with the gradual evolution of the phrase within the general Targum tradition to designate the preparation of the land/sanctuary, and also in line with the general Jewish tradition inspired by Ex 15,17 and evidenced by the Qumran text of 4QFlor and 2 Mc 1,29.

(b) DIFFERENCES. The disciples of Jn 14,2-3 may be invested at a possible deeper level of understanding with a wider significance as representatives of all future believers. If we interpret in this way, then the τόπος would be prepared for the disciples as a type of the new people of God. To interpret in this way, however, would be to break with strict LXX usage, where the term τόπος designates the temple as the gathering-place of the scattered people of God, by extending the significance of the term τόπος to designate the temple as the gathering-place of all believers. Such an interpretation would be in line rather with the more universal perspective of the OT tradition of the

Jerusalem temple as the gathering-place, not just of the people of God (cf. 2 Mc 1,27-29; 2,18), but of all the nations (cf. Is 2,2-4; Mi 4,1-4; Ze 14,16-21).[118]

Moreover, any suggestion that the τόπος of Jn 14,2-3 might be interpreted at this same possible deeper level of meaning in line with Jn 2,21, with reference to the temple, or sanctuary of the body of Jesus, would be a radical and complete break with the whole Jewish temple tradition. The New Temple of the body of the risen Jesus which is prepared by the passion-resurrection is something unique — a new creation.

CONCLUSION

In Jn 14,2-3 we have a simple statement that Jesus is about to journey to the Father's house to prepare a place there for the disciples. This is intelligible within the Jewish tradition with reference to a journey of Jesus to the Jerusalem temple. So, too, it is intelligible within this same tradition with reference to a journey of Jesus to the heavenly temple either through death, or after his death, or by way of exception to the common law of death, in order to render the Father's house accessible to the disciples. At a deeper possible level of meaning it is also understandable in line with the same Jewish tradition to designate a journey of Jesus in order to provide a "sanctuary" or "temple" as the eschatological gathering-place of the disciples. The originality of John's style is to choose language which is open to these two possible levels of meaning in line with LXX usage. By one and the same journey Jesus would thus render the Father's house accessible to the disciples and provide the eschatological temple, or sanctuary, as their gathering-place.

---

[118] See also, Is 56,6-7; 60,1-13; 66,18-21; Jer 3,17; Tb 13,10-14; 14,4-7; Ze 8,20-23.

CHAPTER IV

THE RETURN OF JESUS TO TAKE THE DISCIPLES

A. RETURN OF JESUS

1. Vocabulary: Return

The phrase πάλιν ἔρχομαι of Jn 14,2-3 indicates the return of Jesus after his departure (ἐὰν πορευθῶ). It is implicit in the text that Jesus will return from the Father's house, his temple, which is the goal of his journey; and that he will return to his disciples (comp. πρὸς ὑμᾶς, 14,18.28). The purpose of this intervention is expressly stated to be in favour of his disciples. It is further implicit in the text that Jesus will intervene in order to take the disciples with him to the Father's house. Hence, the perspective of our text is that of a salvific intervention of Jesus on his return from the temple in order to take the disciples with him there.

The verb ἔρχομαι is extremely common in the LXX.[1] It is frequently used in a physical sense to designate movement in space. But it also takes on at times a religious import. It is used to designate salvific intervention in general. It usually indicates that something is happening in history which affects the destiny of men's lives.[2] It may be a question of daily incidents, or events of radical significance (I Sm 10,7; Jb 6,8; Prv 11,2; Is 5,19; 44,7). This use of the term generally implies that God is leading history, or man's destiny, and causes these things to happen.

The verb is also used of persons, as in our text. When it is used in this sense, it means to intervene in history (cf. Gn 49,10; Ez 21,32). It may refer to the coming of God himself (Ps 80(79), 2(3)).[3] Sometimes, God is

---

[1] It occurs some 1,200 times and some 300 times in a religious sense. There it renders some 35 Hebrew terms, mostly the verb בוא. See, E. HATCH-M. A. REDPATH, *A Concordance to the Septuagint and Other Greek Versions of the Old Testament* (Including the Apocryphal Books) (Oxford, 1897) 548-53; also J. SCHNEIDER, *TDNT*, II, 666-76.

[2] S. AALEN expresses this general use of the verb well. See, "'Reign' and 'House' in the Kingdom of God in the Gospels", *NTS* 8 (1962) 224.

[3] Comp. Hos 10,12; 11,9; Is 66,18; Ze 2,14 (LXX); 9,9 (LXX); Is 40,9-10; Mal 3,1; 3,22-24 (LXX); Ps 96(95),13; comp. I Chr 16,33.

said to "come", when he intervenes in order to save in distress, or to punish (Hos 6,3; 10,10.12; 11,9). He also intervenes to save at the end of time (Is 66,18).[4] But God may intervene in salvation history, not directly, but through others. The verb ἔρχομαι is used to describe the coming of the Son of Man (Dn 7,13)[5] and the coming of the Messiah (Ps 118(117),26).[6]

There is also clear evidence for a frequent and varied use of ἔρχομαι in the other NT writings, apart from the fourth gospel.[7] Again, the material or physical sense prevails.[8] But the verb is frequently found, too, with a religious import in the context of salvation (Mk 10,14; Mt 19,14; Lk 18,16; I Tm 1,15; Gal 4,4-5), revelation (Mk 1,14; 2,13; I Tm 2,4), Elijah (Mt 11,14; 17,10), the Messiah (Mt 3,11; 11,3; Mk 11,9; Lk 7,19.20; 19,38),[9] the Son of Man (Mt 24,30; Mk 14,62), and eschatology (Mt 16,28; Mk 10,30; Lk 11,30; I Thes 5,2). Besides, the use of the verbal tenses is noteworthy. The present indicative of ἔρχομαι is used mainly to express the eschatological-messianic import and the aspect of judgment (Mt 17,11; Mk 13,35; Lk 11,40; I Cor 15,35), the present participle mainly to express the Coming of the Messiah (Mt 3,11; Mk 11,9.10; Lk 7,19.20), and the future mainly to express the Parousia (Mt 9,15; Mk 2,20; Lk 17,22; Acts 1,11; 2 Pt 3,3). In our text of Jn 14,2-3, we find the present indicative of the verb. This is used in general by John to stress the eschatological-messianic Coming of Jesus (Jn 4,21.23; 5,25.28; 12,15; 16,25.32).

The adverb πάλιν is found several times in the LXX (89x).[10] It is used mostly of place to designate back or backwards (cf. Gn 42,24; 43,2; 44,25; Jos 6,13; 2 Mc 12,17); and of time to designate once more or again

---

[4] The verb is also used to designate the eschatological intervention by which God dwells among his people as in a temple: "Behold, I come and I will dwell in your midst" (cf. Ze 2,14 (LXX); comp. Ez 37,21.26.28; Ze 3,14.15.17). On this aspect of OT thought, see, A. SERRA, *Contributi dell'antica letteratura giudaica per l'esegesi di Giovanni 2,1-12 e 19,25-27* (Roma, 1977) 312-313. However, this perspective does not correspond to that of Jn 14,2-3, but rather to that of Jn 14,23.

[5] Again, the perspective of Dn 7,13 does not correspond to that of Jn 14,2-3, for the Son of Man does not "come" to men, but to God.

[6] On this theme of the coming of the Messiah, see, S. MOWINCKEL, *He That Cometh* (Oxford, 1956).

[7] For a more extensive treatment of the verb in the OT and NT, see, V. PASQUETTO, *Incarnazione e Comunione con Dio. La venuta di Gesù nel mondo e il suo ritorno al luogo d'origine secondo il IV vangelo* (Roma, 1982) 98-101.

[8] This sense is found especially with the formulae ἔρχεσθαι εἰς and ἔρχεσθαι πρός. See, W. J. MOULTON-A. S. GEDEN-H. K. MOULTON, *A Concordance to the Greek Testament* (Edinburgh, 1978⁵), ad loc.

[9] Here we mostly find the formula ὁ ἐρχόμενος.

[10] On the general use of πάλιν, see, ch. I, p. 41, n. 47.

(cf. Gn 8,10.12; 24,20; Jgs 19,7; Is 25,8; Jer 18,4). It is found several times with the verb ἔρχομαι in its compound forms (cf. Gn 42,24; Lv 14,43; Jos 6,13(14); 2 Chr 19,4; Jb 6,29; 2 Mc 5,7).[11] It is used with these compound forms of the verb to designate the physical movement of return (Gn 42,24; Jos 6,13(14)). However, the simple form of the verb ἔρχομαι is never found with πάλιν in the LXX.

Hence, there is no LXX text which may be cited by way of parallel to the use of the phrase πάλιν ἔρχομαι in Jn 14,2-3. However, we can see from our brief survey of LXX usage that the phrase is indeed suited in line with LXX usage of the verb ἔρχομαι to designate some kind of salvific intervention by Jesus, with the additional connotation of return supplied by the adverb. Finally, it should be further noted that the phrase πάλιν ἔρχομαι is never found either in any eschatological-messianic texts of the NT, apart from Jn 14,2-3.

2. Themes

(a) RETURN OF MOSES. We find a parallel to the perspective of Jn 14,2-3 in the figure of Moses. The salvific intervention of God through him in favour of his people is significantly set within the framework of a departure and return (Ex 19,2-25; comp. 34,2-29). The exodus account of the theophany on Sinai begins with the departure of Moses (Ex 19,3), and it concludes with his return to the people (Ex 19,25).

Moreover, this departure and return of Moses is carefully linked with the theme of revelation, which dominates the whole narrative (cf. Ex 19,9). Moses departs from his people and receives the revelation of God (Ex 19,3.20.24). He returns afterwards as God's agent to communicate it to the people of God (Ex 19,10.14.21). This revelation is the law of God (cf. Ex 20). It is designated explicitly as a revelation "from heaven" (Ex 20,22). A later tradition was to identify this law with wisdom (cf. Sir 24,9-27).

However, Moses alone could ascend the mountain, and with him Aaron later (Ex 19,24). The mountain remained totally inaccessible to the general mass of the people (Ex 19,12). They could approach the mountain of God (Ex. 19, 13-17.22), but in no way could they ascend the mountain with Moses (or with Aaron) (Ex 19,12.23-24), or even touch it at the peril of death (Ex 19,12).

The same pattern of departure and return occurs again at the renewal of the covenant (Ex 34). Moses departs to ascend Mt. Sinai and there he receives the law (Ex 34,1; comp. also Ex 34,2.4). He returns afterwards with it to the people (Ex 34,29). So, too, the mountain of revelation itself remains totally inaccessible to the mass of the people (Ex 34,3).

---

[11] Always as a translation of the Hebrew term שוב.

However, later Jewish tradition also tended to invest Moses as the mediator of the Torah with an eschatological role. Hence, we find the expectation of an eschatological prophet-like-Moses (Dt 18,15-18).[12] There is evidence for the expectation of the coming of a prophet who could solve legal problems on the pattern of Moses (I Mc 4,46). At Qumran the Essenes are told to cling to the Torah and the ancient laws of the community until a prophet comes — presumably the prophet-like-Moses.[13] The biblical reference to this prophet is given a prominent place in a Qumran collection of passages dealing with the eschatological triumph over enemies (4Q Testimonia).[14] There is also clear evidence of this same expectation at the time of Jesus (cf. Acts 3,22).[15]

(b) RETURN OF ELIJAH. We have seen that the OT tradition of the transportation of Elijah would seem to have a special importance for an understanding of the πορεύομαι of Jn 14,2-3 (cf. 2 Kgs 2,1-18; Sir 48,9-10; I Mc 2,58).[16] A tradition linked with Elijah might well provide us also with the background for an understanding of the phrase πάλιν ἔρχομαι.

In post-exilic expectations Elijah was to return before the day of the Lord. In Malachi 3,1 [17] there is a reference to the angel who would prepare the way of the Lord and the prophet later identifies this messenger as Elijah (Mal 3,23).[18] The idea that Elijah was still alive and active, after he had been taken up to heaven in a chariot, was fostered by the strange appearance of a letter from him some time later (2 Chr 21,12). The tradition of the departure of Elijah, then, has a complementary aspect in the Jewish expectation of his return (Mal 3,23-24).

This salvific return of Elijah was to remain an important feature of Jewish eschatology: "you who are ready at the appointed time, it is written, to calm the wrath of God before it breaks out in fury, to turn the heart of the father to the son, and to restore the tribes of Jacob" (Sir

---

[12] On this theme, see, H. M. Teeple, *The Mosaic Eschatological Prophet* (JBL Monograph) (1957).

[13] See, L. H. Silberman, "The Two 'Messiahs' of the Manuel of Discipline", *VetT* 5 (1955) 79-81; also R. E. Brown, "The Messianism of Qumran", *CBQ* 19 (1957) 59-61.

[14] This collection is wrongly called a messianic anthology. See, P. Skehan, "Miscellanea Biblica. A New Translation of Biblical Texts", *CBQ* 25 (1963) 121-122.

[15] Acts 3,22 identifies Jesus as the prophet-like-Moses. (cf. Jn 6,14; 7,40; comp. 7,52). R. Schnackenburg provides more details. See, "Die Erwartung des Prophetens nach dem Neuen Testament und den Qumran-Texten", *StudEvang* I (Tu 73), 622-39.

[16] See, ch. III, pp. 81-82.

[17] Around 450 B.C.

[18] Possibly a slightly later addition to the book (3,23 (MT) = 4,5 (LXX)).

48,10).[19] Again, Enoch pictures Elijah's return before the judgment and before the appearance of the great apocalyptic lamb in its elaborate animal allegory of history (En 90,31; 89,52).[20]

This expectation of the return of Elijah was also evidently widespread in Palestine at the time of Jesus (Mk 8,28; 9,11). In popular belief it was expected that Elijah would come to the rescue of the godly in time of need (comp. Mt 17,11; 27,47.49). This expectation of a return of Elijah even continued into the Judaism of the post-Christian age.[21] Hence, the tendency in later Jewish tradition to assimilate the eschatological role of Elijah with that of Moses is perfectly intelligible.[22]

(c) RETURN OF THE HIGH PRIEST. We have already referred to the importance of the entrance of the high priest into the sanctuary on the feast of Atonement (Lv 16,1ff.; 23,26ff.; Nm 29,4ff.) by way of background to our understanding of πορεύομαι in Jn 14,2-3.[23] This rite of atonement might also shed some light on our understanding of the phrase πάλιν ἔρχομαι. It might be understood in relation to the return of the high priest to the people, after his entrance into the holy of holies (cf. εἰσπορευομένου αὐτοῦ ἐξιλάσασθαι ἐν τῷ ἁγίῳ, ἕως ἄν ἐξέλθῃ ... ἐξελεύσεται, Lv 16,17-18; εἰσελεύσεται Ααρων εἰς τὴν σκηνὴν τοῦ μαρτυρίου..εἰσπορευομένου αὐτοῦ εἰς τὸ ἅγιον ... ἐξελθών, Lv 16,23-24). However, the purpose of the rite was to establish communication between the people and God. In fact, the sanctuary was closed after the solemn entrance of the high priest. Hence, the restricted efficacy of the high priest's entry: the people did not have access to the sanctuary.

3. Application to Jn 14,2-3

(a) SIMILARITIES. The return of Jesus described in Jn 14,2-3 with the verb ἔρχομαι might be seen in line with the NT usage of the verb, and interpreted with reference to the final Coming of Jesus as the Son of Man at the Parousia (comp. Jn 13,31-32). As such the verb would complement John's use of the verb πορεύομαι in our text, if we interpret it of the departure of Jesus prior to his return at the Second Coming. So, too, the return of Jesus could be understood in line with the OT expectation of

[19] Around 200 B.C.
[20] On the dating of Enoch, se, ch. II, n. 47.
[21] See, StB I, 1042; also A. EDERSHEIM, The Life and Times of Jesus the Messiah, vol. 11, (London, 1901) 706-9.
[22] See, W.A. MEEKS, The Prophet-King. Moses Traditions and the Johannine Christology (SNT 14) (Leiden, 1967).
[23] See, ch. 111, pp. 80-81.

the return of either of the two great OT figures of Moses and Elijah. Such interpretations would find support in the eschatological overtones of the text and immediate context of Jn 14,2-3 (cf. ἔρχομαι, 14,2.18; ἔτι μικρόν, 14,19; ἐν ἐκείνῃ τῇ ἡμέρᾳ, 14,20).[24]

We have suggested that the entrance of Jesus into the temple of the Father's house may be interpreted in line with the OT tradition of the entrance of the high priest into the sanctuary to make atonement for sin.[25] So, too, the return of Jesus may likewise be interpreted in relation to the return to the people of this same high priest, after his entrance into the holy of holies. Against this background, the "departure" of Jesus and his "return" may be seen as complementary aspects of one sacrificial movement. Such an interpretation would also harmonise perfectly with the sacrificial connotation of the immediate context of Jn 14,2-3 (cf. 13,37-38).[26]

Finally, the return of Jesus to his disciples in Jn 14,2-3 might also be understood in line with the return of Moses to the people with the revelation of the law after his ascent of Mt. Sinai. Clearly, there is nothing in the text of Jn 14,2-3 to evoke directly the scene on Mt. Sinai. However, it would seem that this scene was not far from John's mind in the immediate context of Jn 14,2-3 (comp. ἐμφανίζω, Jn 14,21-22(2x); Ex 33,13).[27] Moreover, all of this would harmonise well with the theme of revelation (cf. ἀλήθεια, Jn 14,6; λόγος, Jn 14,23-24) and the response to it by faith (πιστεύω, Jn 14,1(2x).10-12(4x).29), which dominate the immediate context of Jn 14,2-3.

(b) DIFFERENCES. The use of πάλιν with ἔρχομαι is without parallel in the Jewish tradition to designate any kind of salvific intervention. The phrase is an original creation of John.

Moreover, the return of Jesus reveals a striking difference to the return of Moses to the people after his ascent of Sinai. The mountain of the OT remains totally inaccessible to the people of God. However, Jesus returns precisely in order to give the disciples access to the Father's house (παραλήμψομαι ὑμᾶς πρὸς ἐμαυτόν).

Finally, the return of the high priest to the people, after his entrance into the sanctuary on the Day of Atonement, is also notably different

---

[24] See, ch. 1, p. 40; also ns 44. 45.

[25] See, ch. 111, pp. 86-87.

[26] See, ch. 1, n. 30.

[27] A double use of the verb ἐμφανίζω in Jn 14,21-22 is surely significant. The verb is used only in the NT (Mt 27,53; Acts 23,15.22; 24,1; 25,2.15; Heb 9,24; 11,24). However, it is an appropriate term to evoke the theophany of Sinai. Moreover, the phrase ἐμφάνισόν μοι σεαυτόν in Ex 33,13 is parallel to the phrase δεῖξόν μοι τὴν σεαυτοῦ δόξαν in Ex 33,18 (comp. δείκνυμι in Jn 14,8-9). Hence, some such glorious manifestation analogous to that of Sinai would seem to be expected by the disciples.

from our understanding of Jn 14,2-3, where Jesus promises to return precisely in order to give the disciples access to the sanctuary of the Father's house. The efficacy of the high priest's entry is no longer restricted in the case of Jesus. Besides, the return of Jesus may be seen no longer just as a return after the entrance of the high priest into the holy of holies in the Jerusalem temple. It may also be seen to be slanted in a new way by John to designate the return of the high priest after his entrance into the heavenly sanctuary.

B. THE TAKING OF THE DISCIPLES

1. Vocabulary: Taking

(a) OLD TESTAMENT. We find the verb παραλαμβάνω repeatedly in the LXX in the literal sense of "to take along with oneself".[28] We even have a striking linguistic parallel to the use of the verb in Jn 14,2-3:

> "And Uzziah took him from the assembly to his own house (καὶ παρέλαβεν αὐτόν Οζιας ἐκ τῆς ἐκκλησίας εἰς οἶκον αὐτοῦ)" (Jdt 6,21).[29]

However, the simple form of the verb λαμβάνω in the LXX provides several interesting parallels to the use of παραλαμβάνω in Jn 14,2-3. We find the simple form of the verb three times to designate the eschatological intervention of Yahweh to gather[30] the scattered[31] children of God:

> "Behold, I take (λαμβάνω) the whole house of Israel from the nations where they have gone; and I will gather them (συνάξω) from all sides, and bring them (εἰσάξω) to the land of Israel" (Ez 37,21; cf. Dt 30,4-5; Ez 36,24).[32]

---

[28] See, Gn 22,3; 31,23; 45,18; 47,2; Nm 22,4; 23,27; Jgs 9,43; 11,5; 1 Sm 17,57; Ct 8,2; Jer 39,7; Dn 5,13. G. DELLING sums up the LXX use of the verb παραλαμβάνω: "In the LXX παραλαμβάνω means 'to take to (and with) oneself', mostly". See, *TDNT*, IV, 13.

[29] It is to be noted, however, that the link here is purely linguistic, not thematic.

[30] The verb παραλαμβάνω is not one of the common LXX verbs to describe the gathering-together of the scattered people of God. The action of gathering itself is generally described by such verbs as συνάγω, ἄγω, εἰσάγω, ἀνάγω, ἐπισυνάγω, εἰσδέχομαι, ἀποστρέφω, ἐνδέχομαι, ἐπιστρέφω, λαμβάνω. For a complete list of the uses of these verbs in the LXX in this sense, see, A. SERRA, *op. cit.* (n. 4) 306, ns. 7-16. To this list we may add the use of προσάγω, in Ex 19,4.

[31] The condition of being "scattered" in the LXX is generally designated with such verbs as διασκορπίζω, σκορπίζω, διασπείρω, λικμάω. For a complete list of the uses of these verbs in the LXX in this sense, see, A. SERRA, *op. cit.* (n. 4), 306, ns. 17-20.

[32] In view of the phrase πρὸς ἐμαυτόν in Jn 14,2-3, the text of Ex 19,4 has a significant variation for "the land" as the goal of the gathering activity of Yahweh:

The use of the verb λαμβάνω is parallel to συνάγω in Dt 30,4 and Ez 37,21, and to εἰσάγω in Ez 36,24 and Dt 30,5. This use of the simple form of the verb marks significantly that the authors do not wish to indicate the land of Israel as the habitation of God.[33] God speaks of taking them "into your land" (εἰς τὴν γῆν ὑμῶν, Ez 36,24 = εἰς τὴν γῆν τοῦ Ἰσραήλ, Ez 37,21). This makes the use of the simple form rather than the composite necessary in these texts.

Besides, there is one highly significant use of the simple verb λαμβάνω (Ps 49(48),16) and two uses of the composite form προσλαμβάνω (Pss 18(17),17; 73(72),24) to designate victory over death, or deliverance from the powers of sheol:

"Lead me into your council (MT. תנחני = LXX ὡδήγησάς) and with glory take me to yourself (MT תקחני = προσελάβου με)" (Ps 73(72),24).[34]

It is this same verb both in its simple (2 Kgs 2,3.5)[35] and in its composite form of ἀναλαμβάνω (2 Kgs 2,9.10.11; I Mc 2,58; Sir 48,9; 49,14) which we find in the LXX to describe the transportation of Elijah from earth to heaven. The event is summed up briefly:

"And Elijah was taken up (ἀνελήμφθη) in a whirlwind to heaven (εἰς τὸν οὐρανόν)" (2 Kgs 2,11).[36]

Significantly, it is the same Hebrew verb לקח which we find repeatedly in this description of the transportation of Elijah (2 Kgs 2,3.5.9.10).[37] So,

---

"you have seen what I did to the Egyptians, and how I bore you (ἀνέλαβον) on eagles' wings and brought you to myself (προσηγαγόμην ὑμᾶς πρὸς ἐμαυτόν)".
We might also note the use of the compound form of λαμβάνω in Jer 31,32: "I took them by the hand to bring them out of the land of Egypt" (ἐπιλαβομένου μου).
[33] The land of Israel is sometimes designated as Yahweh's dwelling-place, "my house", which is thus considered as a sanctuary of God, a kind of extension of the temple (cf. Ex 15,17; Jer 12,7; Hos 9,15; Ze 9,8). See, ch. 11, n. 10.
[34] For this translation, see, M. DAHOOD, Psalms II (New York, 1973) 187. The author interprets the Hebrew לקח as a technical word to signify "to take to oneself, to assume". He notes that this is the verb used by biblical writers to signify "assumption". What the psalmist is asking is that God will take him to himself, just as he took Enoch and Elijah. In other words he is asking for an "assumption". The verb לקח is precisely that used in Gn 5,24; 2 Kgs 2,3.5.9; Sir 42,15; 48,9, as well as in Ps 49 (48),16; Ps 18(17),1.7. See, op. cit. 301.
[35] Comp. ἀνάγω in 2 Kgs 2,1.
[36] Comp. ἀναλαμβάνω, Mk 16,19; Acts 1,2.11.22; I Tm 3,16; also ὑπολαμβάνω, Acts 1,9. On these NT uses of ἀναλαμβάνω, see, G. LOHFINK, Die Himmelfahrt Jesu. Untersuchungen zu den Himmelfahrts- und Erhöhungstexten bei Lukas (SANT, 26) (München, 1971) 57-59.
[37] The sole exception is in 2 Kgs 2,11, where עלה (MT) = ἀναλαμβάνω (LXX).

too, it is לקח in the MT of all three above-mentioned psalms (Pss 18(17),17; 49(48),16; 73(72),24).[38] The link between these psalms and the Elijah narrative with the Enoch narrative of Gn 5,24 has long since been recognised.[39]

It is easy to see how the verb לקח used to describe the transportation of Enoch and Elijah should acquire a special religious resonance, a technical sense, with reference to victory over death (negative aspect) and access to heaven (positive aspect).[40] Both the tradition of Enoch and that of Elijah express in mythical language, each in its own way, the same theme of escape from the common lot of death, and access of the just man to heavenly beatitude.[41] Thus behind the Hebrew verb לקח in the description of the deportation of Enoch and Elijah (Gn 5,24; 2 Kgs 2,3.5.9.10) and the victory of the just man over death (Pss 18(17),17; 49(48),16; 73(72),24), and the corresponding use of the verb λαμβάνω in its simple and composite forms (Pss 18(17),17; 49(48),16; 73(72),24; 2 Kgs 2,3.5.9.10.11; Sir 48,9), we find evidence for an important OT belief in victory over death and access to heavenly beatitude.[42]

(b) EXTRA-BIBLICAL LITERATURE. In the extra-biblical Jewish tradition a special interest also attached to men who had, according to the scriptures, been transported so as never to die. Such were Enoch and Elijah: "and they shall see the men that have been taken up (qui recepti sunt homines), who have not tasted death from their birth" (IV Esdras 6,26). The influence of this OT tradition[43] of Enoch[44] and Elijah[45] is considerable. However, the Enoch tradition takes on a special

---

[38] In Ps 18(17), it is more a question of the psalmist being rescued from "the waters deep", or equivalently death. The phrase "my powerful foe" in v. 18 refers to death. So, too, it is liberation from sheol or death which is directly intended in Ps 49(48),16. In Ps 73(72), 24, however, the positive aspect of "assumption" or transportation of God is emphasised. Here the לקחני is parallel to תנחני where נחה is the terminus technicus "to lead into paradise". See, M. DAHOOD, op. cit. (n. 34) 195.

[39] See M. DAHOOD, op. cit. (n. 34) 195; G. LOHFINK, op. cit. (n. 36) 55, n. 16; P. GRELOT, "La légende d'Hénoch dans les apocryphes et dans la bible. Origine et signification", RecSR 46 (1958) 209.

[40] We find the same Hebrew verb, לקח again in the MT of Gn 5,24, but with the verb μετατίθημι in the LXX rendering: "Enoch walked with God. Then he vanished because God took him (ὅτι μετέθηκεν αὐτὸν ὁ Θεός) (comp. μετατίθημι (2x).. μετάθεσις, Heb 11,5). This same verb is also found to describe the same event in Sir 44,16 (μετετέθη) as compared with ἀναλαμβάνω in Sir 29,14, ἀνελήμφθη.

[41] See, ch. 111, pp. 81-82.

[42] For a brief summary of the evidence, see, G. LOHFINK, op. cit. (n. 36) 73.

[43] On the influence of the OT tradition in general, see P. GRELOT, op. cit. (n. 39) 210.

[44] See, G. LOHFINK, op, cit. (n. 36) 55.

[45] See, G. LOHFINK, op. cit. (n. 36) 58.

importance. I Enoch provides several accounts of the transportation of Enoch himself: "and it came to pass after this that his name during his lifetime was raised aloft to that Son of Man and to the Lord of Spirits from amongst those who dwell on the earth. And he was raised aloft on the chariots of the spirit and his name vanished among them" (I En 70,1-2). It is a question of a true transportation of Enoch ("from amongst those who dwell on the earth").[46] Also interesting is the description of I Enoch 12,1: "Before these things Enoch was hidden, and no one of the children of man knew where he was hidden, and where he abode, and what had become of him (ἐλήμφθη Ἐνώχ, καὶ οὐδεὶς τῶν ἀνθρώπων ἔγνω, ποῦ ἐλήμφθη καὶ ποῦ ἔστιν καὶ τί ἐγένετο αὐτῷ)".[47] The double use of the verb λαμβάνω is striking. However, it should be noted that it is by no means certain that here we have a description exclusively of the heavenly transportation of Enoch.[48]

In the Psalms of Solomon, 4,20[49] we find death expressed by the strange word ἀνάλημψις[50] = "assumption". These Psalms of Solomon are translated from a semitic original, with a number of translations in Greek substantives that are proof of this. It would be quite natural to assume that ἀνάλημψις is another of these, derived from the Hebrew of the Aramaic root הסתלק, meaning, "to be taken up", "to die". The "receptio" of the Assumption of Moses, 10,12,[51] in apposition to

---

[46] The phrase corresponds to the Greek phrase ἐξ ἀνθρώπων, as G. LOHFINK aptly observes. See, op. cit. (n. 36) 56, n. 163.

[47] For the text of Enoch, 12,1, cf. J. FLEMMING-L. RADERMACHER, Die Griechischen Christlichen Schriftsteller der ersten drei Jahrhunderte. Das Buch Henoch (Leipzig, 1901). R. H. CHARLES comments on the text: "ἐλήμφθη Eth. "was hidden". This — the usual Eth. rendering of נקל, μετέθηκεν, and ἐλήμφθη, in connexion with Enoch — is due to the influence of the Enoch myth". See, The Book of Enoch (Oxford, 1893).

[48] "Hier könnte auch das Wandeln Henochs mit Gott von Gn 5,22.24 M im Hintergrund stehen". See, G. LOHFINK, op. cit. (n. 36) 56.

[49] The original of the Psalms of Solomon is probably in Hebrew. They are extant in Syriac and Greek. For the Greek text with French rendering, see, J. VITEAU, Les Psaumes de Salomon. Introduction, texte grec et traduction (Documents pour l'étude de la bible) (Paris, 1911) 266f. There is an English translation by Gray in R.H. CHARLES, The Apocrypha and Pseudepigrapha of the Old Testament, vol. 11 (Oxford, 1913) (reprint 1963) 637f.

[50] Outside the Psalms of Solomon, 4,20 and Lk 9,51 the word does not occur in this same sense in Greek.

[51] For an English translation, see, R.H. CHARLES, The Assumption of Moses (London, 1897). CHARLES, however, takes "receptio" to refer to Moses' "assumption into heaven" rather than to "death". In this he is followed by E. KAUTZSCH. See, Die Apokryphen und Pseudepigraphen des Alten Testaments, vol. II (Tübingen, 1900) 312.328. SCHMIDT and MERX (referred to in Kautzsch, p. 329, n. "e"), however, took "mors"and "receptio" as a double rendering of the same phrase, and probably rightly so. It is possible that we have another instance of "to be taken up" = "to die" in the apocryphal Gospel of Peter, Fragment I, I,19: "And the Lord cried out aloud saying: My power, my power (= Heli, Heli of Mt 27,46?), thou hast forsaken me. And when he has so said, he was taken up". See, M.R. JAMES, The Apocryphal New Testament (Oxford, 1955) 91.

"mors", may also be none other than a synonym for "death". This extra-biblical tradition is in line with the biblical tradition, where the premature death of the just man is likened to a similar assumption (cf. Wis 4,10-14).[52]

(c) NEW TESTAMENT LITERATURE. There is also clear evidence for a frequent and varied use of the simple, and compound use of the verb λαμβάνω with παρά in the other NT writings,[53] apart from the fourth gospel.[54] The passive use of this compound form occurs in a highly technical sense to designate "receiving" the tradition (I Cor 11, 23; 15,1.3). But we find it most frequently used actively in a material or physical sense (Mt 4,5.8; 27,27; Mk 10,32; Lk 9,10; Acts 15,39). Again, it means "to take along with oneself". It is sometimes followed by the preposition μετά with the reflexive pronoun (Mt 12,45; 18,16; Mk 4,36; 14,33). But the idea of accompaniment is already contained in the compound verb itself, even without the additional preposition, as in Jn 14,2-3 (Mt 17,1; 20,17; Mk 4,36; 9,2; Lk 9,28; Acts 15,39). The compound form of the verb also has an eschatological import in a Parousia-parable about the Last Judgment and the Coming of the Son of Man (Mt 24,40-41; Lk 17,34-35). Moreover, the idea conveyed by this eschatological use of the compound verb is not without parallel elsewhere in the NT (Mt 13,27; I Thes 4,17).

2. Themes

Several strands of Jewish tradition might be seen by way of background to our understanding of the παραλήμψομαι of Jn 14,2-3.

(a) MOSES. The OT records a special intervention of God to save his people through Moses.[55] We have several accounts of this salvific intervention (Ex 3,1-12; comp. 6,2-18; 6,28-7,7). The narrative of Ex

---

[52] In Wis 4,10 we find the same Greek verb μετατίθημι which we find in Gn 5,24 (cf. also Sir 49,16), and it describes the transportation of the just man to God through death: "There was one who pleased God and was loved by him, and while living among sinners he was taken up (μετετέθη, comp. ἡρπάγη, v. 11; ἔσπευσεν, v. 14). The dependence of this text on Gn 5,24 has also been recognised. The text of Wis 4,7-14 has been described as a midrash on Gn 5,23-24. See, P. GRELOT, op. cit. (n. 39) 219.

[53] The compound form of the verb occurs 49 times in the NT; but 3 times only in John (Jn 1,11; 14,3; 19,16). G. FISCHER studies the NT use of the term at length. See, Die himmlischen Wohnungen, Untersuchungen zu Joh 14,2f (Frankfurt/M, 1975) 98-102.

[54] See, ch. I, note, 55.

[55] On this aspect of the Jewish tradition, see, R. DE VAUX, "God's Presence and Absence in History: The Old Test. View", Conc 10 (n. 5) (1969) 5-11.

3,1-12 begins and ends on Sinai. Moses reaches Horeb "the mountain of God (εἰς τὸ ὄρος Χωρηβ)" (Ex 3,1). There he receives his "mission" (ἀποστέλλω) (Ex 3,10-13(2x)). He is to take the people of God with himself out of the land of Egypt (ἐξάγω (3x)) (Ex 3,10-13) in order that they may serve God on Sinai "upon this mountain (ἐν τῷ ὄρει τούτῳ)" (Ex 3,12).

At Sinai, then, Moses receives his mission from God to deliver his people from Egypt and lead them out with himself in order to serve God on this same mountain. The movement of the narrative of the mission of Moses thus comes full circle, beginning at Mt. Sinai and returning to it as to its goal.

(b) JOSHUA. By his saving intervention in the OT God was able to lead the people out of Egypt into the land (cf. Ex 3,8). Moses was one of his instruments. However, Moses could lead God's people out of Egypt only to Mt. Sinai, and within sight of their goal (Dt 34,4). It was the role of yet another great leader, Joshua, to lead God's people on the final stage of their journey into the promised land (Jos 1,6).

We have already treated of this tradition of the entrance to Canaan at some length (Dt 1,19-45; Nm 13-14; comp. Ps 95(94); Dt 9,22-24).[56] Here we merely recall briefly some relevant details. Joshua ('Ιησοῦς) forms part of an exploratory expedition sent to prepare the entrance of the people into the land (Nm 13,8.16; 14,5). On his return Joshua announces the entrance of the people (Nm 14,7-8). However, the Israelites not only refused to enter because of their unbelief (Nm 14,3-4), but as a consequence of this unbelief they were unable to enter, when they did decide later to do so (Nm 14,40-45). As a result, the exploration of the land was inefficacious.

But in spite of everything there remained the promise: Joshua would enter later (Dt 1,38; Nm 14,30-38), and with him a new generation of Israelites (Nm 14,21-24; 14,29-31; Dt 1,35-39; comp. Ps 95(94)). It was the mission of Joshua to lead the people of God into the promised land (cf. Jos 1,6). The narrative of this entrance is recorded in the Book of Joshua.

(c) THE WISE MAN. The saving intervention of God may also be seen under a different aspect in the OT wisdom tradition. There we find a general invitation to enter the school of wisdom (cf. Wis 6,11). But wisdom itself is eternal and exists with God (Wis 7,25-26; 8,3-4; 9,4-9), who is the source of wisdom for men (Wis 7,15; 8,21; 9,6.10.17). Hence, we find a movement of ascent to heaven which is directed towards the attainment of this wisdom and a complementary movement of descent

---

[56] See, ch. III, pp. 79-80.

which is directed in turn towards the communication of this same heavenly wisdom to men (Wis 9,16-18; Dt 30,12; Prv 30,4; Bar 3,29; cf. also IV Esd 4,8).

The fruits of this wisdom are described as a kind of heavenly beatitude. They are friendship with God (Wis 7,14.27), intimacy with God (Wis 6,19), immortality (Wis 6,18; 8,13.17), repose, gladness and joy, without bitterness and pain (Wis 8,16-18). In this way, men are saved by wisdom (Wis 9,18).

Understandably, then, we find that the wise man who has discovered wisdom for himself returns to men to guide them towards it. His mission might be summed up as follows:

"What I learned without self-interest, I pass on without reserve;
I do not intend to hide her riches.
For she is an inexhaustible treasure to men,
and those who acquire it win God's friendship,
commended as they are to him by the benefits of her teaching" (Wis 7,13-14).

(d) THE MESSIAH. The revelation of God is said to direct men to the goal of the temple. In Ps 43(42), 3-4 the psalmist envisages a pilgrimage and prays:

"Send forth your light and your truth (τὸ φῶς σου καὶ τὴν ἀλήθειάν σου); let them lead me and bring me to thy holy hill, and to thy dwelling-place".

Here, the psalmist personifies God's salvific intervention emanating as "light" and "truth", and prays that they may lead him home from exile into the temple.[57]

Besides, the prophet Isaiah envisages the eschatological temple as a school of instruction:

"Come, let us go up to the mountain of the Lord, and to the house of the God of Jacob; that he may teach us his way and that we may walk in it (καὶ πορευσόμεθα ἐν αὐτῇ). For out of Sion shall go forth the law (ἐξελεύσεται νόμος) and the word of the Lord from Jerusalem (λόγος)" (Is 2,3 = Mi 4,2).

The "law" and the "word" of God will emanate from the eschatological temple so that men may walk according to God's will. In this vision of the prophet the new life style of the eschatological age is here described as a pilgrimage of the nations ascending to the temple[58] to which there is a complementary salvific intervention of God emanating from the temple.

---

[57] See, E. VOGT, "The Place of Life of Ps. 23", Bib 34 (1954) 195-211, especially, 209.
[58] See, ch. II, p. 72.

Thus we have a reciprocal movement of truth, law and light emanating from the eschatological temple and the nations at the end of time on pilgrimage to the temple guided by that same light.

In the Targums, however, this tradition would seem to be slanted in a new way. The LXX has only one solitary example of the precise form παραλήμψομαι. On this basis alone several commentators[59] have pointed to a link between the παραλήμψομαι of Canticles 8,2 and Jn 14,2-3. However, it should be noted that the perspective of Canticles and that of our text are quite different. In Canticles 8,2 we read:

"I will take you and lead you into the house of my mother (παραλήμψομαί σε, εἰσάξω σε εἰς οἶκον μητρός μου) and into the chamber of her that conceived me".

Here it is Israel that leads the Messiah to the Jerusalem temple.[60] The imagery evoked seems to be that of a solemn procession[61] to mark some great feast such as we find evidence for elsewhere in the OT (Pss 24(23),7-10; 68(67),25-28; 118(117); Neh 12,31-41).

The whole problem of the interpretation of the Canticle is still an open question.[62] However, in the Targum and midrash to Canticles this poem is reread in an allegorical sense from beginning to end.[63] In the Targum to Canticles there is evidence of a Jewish tradition and our text of Jn 14,2-3 is open to interpretation in line with it.[64] However, there is

---

[59] See, W. BAUER, op. cit. 178; J. H. BERNARD, op. cit. 535; R. BULTMANN, op. cit. 600, n. 3; also, O. SCHAEFER, "Sinn der Rede Jesu von den vielen Wohnungen in seines Vaters Hause und von dem Weg zu ihm (Joh. 14,1-7)", ZNW 32 (1933) 214.

[60] This is at least one possible interpretation followed by the JB. ad loc., n. "c": "To the Temple, 3:4, where the messianic King, descended from David, will have his throne, Is 11:10; Mi 4;8; Ze 6,9-15; 9:9-10; Ps 2:6; 110:2". For a similar interpretation with reference to the temple in Cant. 8,2, see, A. ROBERT-R. TOURNAY, Le Cantique des cantiques (Paris, 1963) 288. The same authors provide the alternative interpretations (op. cit. 135-36).

[61] ROBERT-TOURNAY note that the two Hebrew verbs of the MT are not synonymous: "נהג designe le déroulement de la procession et הביא, l'entrée au Temple. Ils sont joints symétriquement de sorte qu'on pourrait presque traduire: 'Dans une marche solennelle, je t'introduirais'". See, op. cit. (n. 60) 288.

[62] On this whole problem of whether the Canticle is to be interpreted in a naturalistic or in an allegorical sense, see, A. FEUILLET, Le cantique des cantiques — étude de théologie biblique et réflexions sur une méthode d'exégèse (Paris, 1953); A. ROBERT-R. TOURNAY, op. cit. (n.60) 41-55. G. NOLLI, Cantico dei cantici-antica interpretazione ebraica (Roma, 1976), 31-45.

[63] See, R. LOEWE, "Apologetic Motifs in the Targum to the Song of Songs", in Studies and Texts, vol. III, Biblical Motifs — Origins and Transformations (Cambridge, Massachusetts, 1966), 160.

[64] Again, the dating of the traditions represented in this Targum creates a problem. R. LOEWE dates the Targum to Canticles in the seventh century, A.D.; but he adds that "it contains exegesis for which midrashic parallels are extant, some of them in Tannaitic sources". See, op. cit. (n. 63) 167-168.

no direct link between the text of Canticles 8,2 and Jn 14,2-3. There is only a very indirect one, and in this link the verb παραλήμψομαι itself has not got a role of any great importance.

In the Targum to Canticles 8,2 the perspective is again, like that of the MT and LXX, that of Israel leading its Messiah to the Jerusalem temple:

"I will lead you, O King Messiah, and I will bring you up to my temple." [65]

This perspective clearly does not correspond to that of Jn 14,2-3. However, in the Targum this perspective of Israel leading its Messiah to the Jerusalem temple is closely linked in the preceding verse of Canticles 8,1 with another tradition where the Messiah accompanies, or in turn leads, the assembly of Israel to the temple as to a place of instruction in the law. In the Targum to Canticles 8,1 we read:

"When King Messiah appears to the Congregation of Israel, they will say to Him: Come, be to us a brother and let us go up to Jerusalem, and we will suck with you the judgments of the Law, as a suckling sucks his mother's breast".

The tradition opened up in this perspective indicates a possible understanding of Jn 14,2-3. The evidence for this tradition in the Targums to Canticles also emerges in the Targum to Canticles, 1,8 which records that day when God will send the exiles their Messiah to lead his brethren to the security of the tabernacle which is the house, the sanctuary or temple:

"Let her (i.e. Israel) teach (or lead) her children, compared to the kids of goats, to go to the Assembly House and to the House of Learning; then by that merit, they will be sustained in the Exile until the time when I send the King, the Messiah, who will lead them to rest in their Dwelling, the Sanctuary which David and Solomon, the shepherds of Israel, will build for them."

Moreover, the final vision of the Targum to Canticles 8,14 is once again that of a solemn procession of the exiles to the temple:

"So look on us and regard our pains and afflictions from the high heavens, until the time when you will be pleased with us and redeem us and bring us up to the mountain of Jerusalem and there the priests will offer up before you incense of spices".

---

[65] Our translation of the Targum to Canticles is taken from M. H. POPE. He provides the Targum to each text as he comments on each successive verse. See, M. H. POPE, *Song of Songs* (The Anchor Bible) (New York, 1977).

Finally, it is significant that the phrase "mother's house" of Canticles 8,2 also occurs in Canticles 3,4:

> "Till I brought him to my mother's house (εἰς οἶκον μητρός μου), to the chamber (εἰς ταμίειον) of her who conceived me".

The Targum made the mother's house the Tent of Meeting and turned the chamber to classrooms for instruction in the law, with Moses and Joshua as the teacher:

> "Then after a little time, YHWH turned from His fierce anger and He commanded Moses, the prophet, to make the Appointment-Tent and the Ark and He caused His Presence to dwell in the midst of it. And the people of the House of Israel offered their sacrifices and were occupied with the words of the Law in the chamber of the House of Study of Moses, their Master, and in the classroom of Joshua, son of Nun, his assistant".

3. Application to Jn 14,2-3

(a) SIMILARITIES. The use of the compound form of the verb λαμβάνω with παρά in Jn 14,2-3 indicates a journey of Jesus-with-the disciples. Such a journey as a result of the salvific intervention of Jesus (after the preparation of a place) may well be seen against the background of the role of Moses at the exodus, who receives his mission from God to go and lead his people out of Egypt and then return with them to the same goal of Mt. Sinai from whence he departed on his mission. Jesus would, then, fulfil his role, like a new Moses, by taking the disciples back with him to the source and goal of his mission.

However, this journey of Jesus with the disciples might also be interpreted, even more appropriately, in line with the promise of entrance into the land. Jesus would, then, fulfil his role in taking the disciples with him, like a new Joshua, leading a new generation of Israelites with him into the promised land. But we have already referred to this tradition of entrance by way of background to the understanding of our text, and also stressed its relevance within the immediate context of Jn 14,2-3.[66] This use of παραλήμψομαι merely lends additional support.

So, too, the verb παραλήμψομαι may be interpreted alternatively in line with the OT wisdom tradition. The role of Jesus, then, might be seen like that of the wise man who has discovered heavenly wisdom for himself and so returns to guide disciples towards it. The entrance of the disciples into the Father's house with Jesus might be interpreted as an entrance by them with Jesus into that heavenly beatitude, which we have seen is the fruit of wisdom.

---

[66] See, ch. III, pp. 79-80.

The return of Jesus to take the disciples to the temple of his Father's house could also be interpreted against the general OT background of God's revelation emanating from the goal of the Jerusalem temple to guide the pilgrim home from exile; and even more precisely with reference to a pilgrimage of all the nations at the end of time in the light of this same revelation of God, which emanates from the goal of the eschatological temple. But this return of Jesus to take his disciples may be interpreted against this same Jewish background as it is slanted in a new way in the Targums. The use of the precise form παραλήμψομαι might be taken to evoke (at least indirectly) through the Targum to Canticles the Jewish tradition of the Messiah leading the children of Israel to the eschatological temple as the place of instruction in the law. Against this background "the house of my Father" with "the many rooms" in Jn 14,2-3 would correspond to "the house of my mother" in Canticles 8,2 understood in line with the Targum tradition as a reference to the temple, with its classrooms for instruction in the law.

Such an interpretation would be clearly in place in the immediate context of Jn 14,2-3. There Jesus who will take the disciples to himself presents himself in Jn 14,6 as "the truth", which is the replacement of the law (comp. Jn 1,17).[67] Jesus also presents himself in Jn 14,7-9 as the revelation of God/Father in person, and designates himself as the means of attaining to the knowledge of God/Father. This would in turn help to explain the change from "the house of my mother" in Canticles 8,2 to "the house of my Father" in Jn 14,2-3. In Jn 14,7-9, too, we have a highly significant use of the verb "to see" (comp. Jn 14,19) to describe the revelation of the Father such as it will be "seen" by the disciples. In this pilgrimage of the disciples to the Father's house in Jn 14,2-3, set as it is in this immediate context, we may see the fulfilment of the eschatological pilgrimage of the sons of Israel led by their Messiah going up to the temple as the place of instruction in the law, and in this sense also going up "to see the face of God" or "to seek the face of God", that is, to discover God's design of salvation.

But the παραλήμψομαι of Jn 14,2-3 might be interpreted in line with LXX use of the verb λαμβάνω in its simple and compound form to designate the journey of the disciples by means of a bodily ascent into the heavenly temple, with consequent escape from the common law of death, and in this sense a journey of victory over death and its consequences, sin. Such a journey of the disciples (after the preparation) could be seen

---

[67] This is one of the central ideas of the work of S. A. PANIMOLLE *Il dono della legge e la grazia della verità* (Roma, 1973). See, also W. MICHAELIS, *TDNT*. V, 82; S. PANCARO, *The Law in the Fourth Gospel. The Torah. Moses and Jesus, Judaism and Christianity according to John* (SNT 42) (Leiden, 1975).

as parallel to the journey of Jesus (before the preparation) and would be in accord with the Jewish tradition of the transportation of Elijah and Enoch.

So, too, the παραλήμψομαι could be interpreted eschatologically in line with NT usage to designate a transportation of the disciples as a result of the final intervention of the Son of Man (comp. Jn 13,31-32). But this in turn may be understood at a deeper level of a journey by the disciples with Jesus through death (after the preparation of a place) parallel to the journey of Jesus through death (before the preparation). Such an interpretation would be intelligible in line with OT Jewish tradition of the transportation of the just man to God through death (cf. Wis 4,10-14), and the extra-biblical Jewish tradition of the "assumptio" or "receptio".[68]

Finally, the use of παραλήμψομαι in Jn 14,2-3 might be interpreted in line with LXX exodus vocabulary. The specific use of the verb could be seen as parallel to LXX use of the simple form, which evokes the eschatological intervention of Yahweh to save his people by gathering them to the land. The effect of the future salvific intervention of Jesus indicated by παραλήμψομαι could, then, be seen as the fulfilment of the eschatological intervention of Yahweh to save his people through Jesus, who will journey with his people in a new exodus. Such a use of παραλήμψομαι would also be in harmony with the exodus theme evoked by the double use of πορεύομαι in Jn 14,2-3.[69]

(b) DIFFERENCES. The choice of παραλήμψομαι in Jn 14,2-3 reveals the originality of John. The use of the composite form with its additional connotation of "along with" or "in the company of" (παρά) underlines (such as the simple form could never do) the identity between the journey of Jesus alone (before the preparation is complete) and the journey of the disciples with Jesus (after the preparation is complete). By the same path first traced out by himself Jesus takes the disciples along with himself later. The παραλήμψομαι also indicates that the distance traversed by Jesus first alone (before the preparation) is now traversed by the disciples later (after the preparation) through the intervention of Jesus, and in his company.

However, if the παραλήμψομαι is interpreted in line with the LXX use of the simple form λαμβάνω to evoke the eschatological intervention

---

[68] Lk 9,51 would provide us with a parallel to an interpretation of παραλήμψομαι in Jn 14,2-3 with reference to death. The ἀνάλημψις of Luke refers to Christ's death in Jerusalem, but also embraces the entire process of Christ's "exaltation", i.e. his resurrection.

[69] See, ch. III, p. 76.

of Yahweh to gather the scattered children of God in a new exodus, then
we would have in Jn 14,2-3 an unheard of promise by Jesus to fulfil in
person the great final intervention of Yahweh. But this new exodus of the
disciples with Jesus may be seen to be slanted in a new way in our
understanding of Jn 14,2-3 to indicate a journey through death, or one by
way of exception to the common law of death. If in turn the tradition
evoked is that of the Messiah leading the children of Israel to the
eschatological temple as the place of instruction in the law, this too could
be seen as slanted in a new way to indicate Jesus as the future promised
Messiah who accompanies the children of Israel on their eschatological
journey to the goal of the heavenly temple.

Moreover, interpreted at a deeper possible level of meaning as a
journey of access by the disciples with Jesus along the same path
already traced out by Jesus previously through his death, the use of
παραλήμψομαι (like that of πορεύομαι) would in a sense also indicate
a complete break with the Jewish tradition, where death was a sign of
separation from God and the power of Satan. According to Jn 14,2-3
the journey of the disciples with Jesus (παραλήμψομαι), like the
journey of Jesus himself before the preparation is complete, would
become a way of access to the heavenly temple through death, and at
the same time a victory of the disciples with Jesus over death, and its
consequences, sin.

CONCLUSION

In Jn 14,2-3 we have a simple statement that Jesus will return
(from the Father's house) in order to take the disciples to be reunited
with him (in the Father's house). This return of Jesus is clearly
intelligible within the Jewish tradition with reference to an
eschatological intervention of Jesus from the Jerusalem temple to take
the disciples to be reunited with him there. So, too, it is quite
intelligible within this same tradition with reference to an
eschatological intervention of Jesus from the heavenly temple to take
the disciples either through death, or by way of exception to the
common law of death, in order to be reunited with him there.

Moreover, the salvific intervention of Jesus in Jn 14,2-3 may be
interpreted more precisely with reference to the eschatological temple as
the goal and source of revelation and the person of Jesus identified with
the Messiah who is to lead the people of God in pilgrimage to this
eschatological temple as to the place of instruction in the law. The theme
of revelation in the immediate context of Jn 14,2-3 would lend support to
this line of interpretation.

RECAPITULATION

By way of conclusion to Part I of our thesis we recapitulate briefly. Our interpretation of Jn 14,2-3, with its possibilities of a deeper level of understanding, is clearly intelligible in line with the Jewish tradition. However, it is also greatly enriched by a comparison with it. Moreover, it bears the stamp of Johannine originality.

A. *Continuity of the Jewish tradition*

(i) IN GENERAL. Our approach to the Jewish tradition through the vocabulary of our text is amply justified. The terminology used to designate the Father's house with the many rooms may rightly be interpreted with reference to the Jerusalem temple, or the heavenly temple, as the goal of eschatological salvation; or with reference to both at the same time in a confused manner such as the misunderstanding of Jn 14,5 would seem to suggest. The image aptly describes the possibility for the disciples of a life-with-God in the promised temple of the eschatological age. Ideas traditionally associated with OT explanations of eschatological happiness and the eschatological temple might be seen to be predicated in Jn 14,2-3 of the heavenly temple in line with the Jewish apocalyptic tradition.

In Jn 14,2-3 we also have echoes of the OT exodus vocabulary. This vocabulary would seem to be deliberately chosen to describe this journey as a new exodus. However, it is an exodus which must be conceived not after the manner of the endless wandering of the Israelites in the desert, but precisely at the moment of entrance into the promised land. The journey of Jn 14,2-3, both for Jesus and the disciples, is a journey of entrance or access.

Moreover, the vocabulary used to describe the journey of preparation and return in Jn 14,2-3 may also be understood within the Jewish tradition with reference to a journey to the temple in general, and with reference to the great eschatological journey to the temple in particular. The journey of Jesus in our text may be properly understood of a journey to the eschatological temple in order to render it accessible to the disciples, and the journey of the disciples with Jesus later as a journey of access into this same temple, once it has been opened for the disciples by Jesus.

The journey of Jn 14,2-3 may be interpreted at a possible deeper level of meaning as an entrance into the temple of the Father's house by a sacrificial movement through his passion-death in line with the OT tradition of the entrance of the high-priest into the sanctuary to make atonement for sin. Such an interpretation would provide our text with a cultic *Sitz im Leben*.

(ii) IN PARTICULAR. Some specific biblical texts seem to have influenced the formulation of Jn 14,2-3 in a particular way, if not directly at least indirectly.

a. *Is 2,2-3/Mi 4,1-4*

Is 2,2-3	Mi 4,1-4	Jn 14,2-3
ὁ οἶκος τοῦ Θεοῦ	*ἐμφανὲς τὸ ὄρος*	*οἰκίᾳ τοῦ πατρός*
ἐπ' ἄκρων τῶν ὀρέων...	*τοῦ κυρίου, ἔτοιμον*	*ἑτοιμάσαι/ὦ*
	ἐπὶ τὰς κορυφὰς	
	τῶν ὀρέων, ...	
πορεύσονται ἔθνη	*πορεύσονται ἔθνη*	*πορεύομαι/θῶ*
πολλά...ἀναβῶμεν...εἰς	*πολλά..ἀναβῶμεν...εἰς*	
τὸν οἶκον τοῦ Θεοῦ...	*τὸν οἶκον τοῦ Θεοῦ .....*	*οἰκία τοῦ πατρός*
..τὴν ὁδὸν αὐτοῦ,	*τὴν ὁδὸν αὐτοῦ,*	
καὶ πορευσόμεθα	*καὶ πορευσόμεθα*	*πορεύομαι/θῶ*
ἐν αὐτῇ ·	*ἐν ταῖς τρίβοις αὐτοῦ ·*	
ἐκ γὰρ Σιων	*ὅτι ἐκ Σιων*	
ἐξελεύσεται νόμος	*ἐξελεύσεται νόμος*	*ἔρχομαι*
καὶ λόγος κυρίου	*καὶ λόγος κυρίου*	
ἐξ Ἰερουσαλημ.	*ἐξ Ἰερουσαλημ.*	

These direct contacts with our text itself are strengthened by the additional direct verbal contacts with the context also (comp ὁδός, Is 2,3; Mi 4,2; Jn 14,6). Moreover, the phrase νόμος καὶ λόγος of Is 2,3 and Mi 4,2 may be expressed in equivalent Johannine terms with the ἀλήθεια of Jn 14,6. Here we find ample support for an interpretation of Jn 14,2-3 in line with the Jewish OT tradition as the fulfilment of the promised eschatological pilgrimage of the nations to the Jerusalem temple as to a place of revelation.

b. *2 Sm 7,4-17/1 Chr 17,3-15*

We may detect the special influence of the oracle of Nathan on our text. This is not so directly, but rather indirectly as this oracle was interpreted in Jewish tradition with reference to the Davidic Messiah, and the temple. There would appear to be several points of contact.

The motif of the son who is to abide permanently in God's house forever καὶ πιστώσω αὐτὸν ἐν οἴκῳ μου is interpreted with reference to the temple in Targum I Chr 17,14. This line of tradition may be seen to be fulfilled in our understanding of Jn 14,2-3, where Jesus dwells permanently in the temple of the Father's house. Moreover, the father/son relationship implicit in the phrase "my Father (πατρός μου)" of Jn 14,2-3 may be seen as the fulfilment of the father/son relationship of the Nathan oracle: ἐγὼ ἔσομαι αὐτῷ εἰς πατέρα, καὶ αὐτὸς ἔσται μοι εἰς υἱόν (2 Sm 7,14/1 Chr 17,3).

Likewise, the promise of a secure place for the people of Israel καὶ θήσομαι τόπον is interpreted with reference to the temple within the Jewish tradition. A reference to the temple here as the τόπος would seem to accord best with the future perspective of the LXX tradition of the oracle. Such an interpretation would derive support from the Jewish tradition represented by 4QFlor. of Qumran. This text, by appeal to Ex 15,17, seems to identify this τόπος with the eschatological sanctuary. The more precise designation of this τόπος as "a prepared place" in the Targum I Chr 17,9 (which is parallel to 2 Sm 7,10) lends additional support to the influence of the Nathan oracle on Jn 14,2-3, with its explicit reference to the preparation of a place (ἑτοιμάσαι/άσω τόπον). To interpret the phrase "to prepare a place" in Jn 14,2-3 as a promise to provide the eschatological sanctuary could be seen to fulfil this line of Jewish tradition.

Moreover, the interpretation of 4QFlor. also seems to have read the term "house" = בית (MT) = οἶκος (LXX) in 2 Sm 7,11 as the eschatological "temple". It refers to the promise of Yahweh "to build a house". So, too, it is highly probable that Targum 2 Sm 7,13-14 interprets the one who shall build "a house" = בית (MT) = οἶκος (LXX) with reference to the future son of David, the Messiah. The Targum of the parallel text of I Chr 17,12-13 uses the more common בית מקדש, which is an unequivocal reference to the temple or sanctuary. Our understanding of Jn 14,2-3, then, may be rightly traced back to its source in one of the traditional interpretations of the Nathan oracle, which assign the building of the eschatological temple to the Messiah.

c. *Dt 1,33*

This text would also seem to have influenced the formulation of Jn 14,2-3. Again this is not so directly, but indirectly by means of the Targum tradition. All the Targums (Pal. Targums and Onk.) and Peshitta translate the LXX phrase ἐκλέγεσθαι ὑμῖν τόπον of Dt 1,33 as "to prepare a resting-place". Here we have an explicit reference to the preparation of the land. This is significant since it provides an exact verbal link with our text of Jn 14,2-3 (ἑτοιμάζω). Thus it would seem that John deliberately evokes this whole tradition of the preparation of the land when he uses the phrase "to prepare a place" in Jn 14,2-3. Jesus would, then, go before his people in Jn 14,2-3 as a new Joshua (Ἰησοῦς) to prepare their entrance into the promised land.

Moreover, an interpretation of this phrase "to prepare a resting-place" with reference to the sanctuary or the place where God had chosen to make his name to dwell (and not merely with reference to the promised land) would be in harmony with the final evolution of the phrase within the Targum tradition itself by the NT period, and also in harmony with the general evolution of the meaning of the term τόπος within the OT tradition to designate the sanctuary, or temple, of the eschatological age.

d. *Ct 8,2*

Ct 8,2	Jn 14,2-3
παραλήμψομαί σε, εἰσάξω σε εἰς οἶκον μητρός μου καὶ εἰς ταμίειον τῆς συλλαβούσης με.	παραλήμψομαι ὑμᾶς πρὸς ἐμαυτόν ἐν τῇ οἰκίᾳ τοῦ πατρός μου μοναὶ πολλαί εἰσιν.

There are two direct verbal links between Ct 8,2 and Jn 14,2-3. It may be argued that the παραλήμψομαι of Ct 8,2, which is the only use of this precise form of the verb παραλαμβάνω in the LXX, has exercised some influence on the formulation of Jn 14,2-3. If this is so, then it can be said to do this very indirectly, and even then the verb παραλήμψομαι itself apparently has no direct influence as such. It may be said in favour of a link, however, that the text of Ct 8,2 is closely linked through the Targum to Ct 8,1 with the tradition of the Messiah who leads his people to the eschatological temple as to the place of instruction in the law. It may also be argued that the phrase οἶκον μητρός μου of Ct 8,2 has exercised some influence also on the formulation of Jn 14,2-3. Again, this would seem to be only very indirectly in line with the Targum to Ct 3,4, where the "mother's house" becomes the "tent of meeting" and the "room", the "classrooms" for instruction in the law. Our understanding of Jn 14,2-3 may rightly be seen as the fulfilment of this Jewish tradition of the Messiah leading his people to the eschatological temple as to the place of instruction in the law.

B. *Break with the Jewish tradition*

The terms οἰκία and μονή are never found in the Jewish tradition with reference to the temple, earthly or heavenly. However, to interpret the phrase "my Father's house" as designating either the Jerusalem temple or the heavenly one would not represent a radical break with Jewish tradition. It could be interpreted in line with Jewish tradition of the Davidic Messiah, who is to address God as "my Father" (Ps 89(88),27) and who is himself in turn addressed by God as "Son" (Ps 2,7). The phrase "my Father's house", then, is a possible designation for the temple, if an original one, on the lips of the Son of David — Son of God (comp. 2 Sm 7,14; I Chr 17,13).

The choice of the familiar OT exodus theme to designate an eschatological journey of entrance, not into the Jerusalem temple, but into the heavenly temple would also represent an original fusion of ideas. Moreover, this journey of preparation which is effective for the disciples in Jn 14,2-3 would break with the exodus tradition which it evokes, where the preparation of the land is ineffective.

So, too, John would break with the Jewish tradition if we interpret the term τόπος at a possible deeper level of meaning to designate the "temple" of the body of Jesus and the process of preparation as the passion-death of Jesus which provide the τόπος prepared, or the New Temple of the risen Jesus. An understanding of the term τόπος at this same possible deeper level of meaning to designate the gathering-place of all believers would also extend the more restricted meaning of the OT term as the gathering-place of the people of God.

The choice of παραλήμψομαι in Jn 14,2-3 reveals the originality of John. The use of the composite form is admirably suited to indicate the identity between the journey of Jesus (alone before the preparation is complete) and the journey of the disciples (with Jesus after the preparation is complete) to the temple in this new exodus of the new people of God.

Finally, the use of πάλιν with ἔρχομαι is without parallel in the Jewish tradition to designate any kind of salvific intervention. The phrase is an original creation of John.

PART II: TEXT AND CONTEXT

CHAPTER V

LITERARY QUESTIONS

A. TEXTUAL PROBLEMS

The manuscript evidence in favour of our text is strong.[1] However, there are two alternative readings which merit consideration.

1. First Variant Reading: πολλαὶ μοναὶ παρὰ τῷ πατρί [2]

We note that there is considerable patristic evidence for this reading.[3] M.-E. Boismard argues that it is the original one.[4] However, such a conclusion would seem to be unwarranted. It is entirely without manuscript support.[5]

Besides, the short reading can be adequately explained. The shorter reading πολλαὶ μοναὶ παρὰ τῷ πατρί corresponds to the μονὴν παρ'αὐτῷ ποιησόμεθα of Jn 14,23. It may well be an attempt to harmonise. The temptation to do this would be rendered even greater by the use of μονή in both texts. These are the only two uses of the term in the NT. Thus the longer reading of our text is clearly the lectio difficilior.

Some commentators[6] also underline a similarity between our text and Luke 2,49 ἐν τοῖς τοῦ πατρός μου, with its variant "in domo Patris mei".[7] Both texts, they maintain, refer to the temple. Here again we may detect an attempt to harmonise.

---

[1] For the complete text, see, ch. I, p. 29.

[2] This shorter form of the text was already noted by F. BLASS, *Evangelium sec. Johannem cum variae lectionis delectu* (Leipzig, 1902).

[3] M.-E. BOISMARD provides us with the patristic evidence. See, "Critique textuelle et citations patristiques", *RB* 57 (1950), 389-390, with notes.

[4] See, *op. cit.* (n. 3), 390-391.

[5] Hence, it is rightly omitted from the critical editions. See, ch. I, n. 1. So, too, it is rightly omitted from B. M. METZGER, *A Textual Commentary on the Greek New Testament* (Stuttgart, 1971).

[6] See, C. K. BARRETT, *op. cit.* 381; J. H. BERNARD, *op. cit.* 91; R. BULTMANN, *op. cit.* 124, n. 1; and several others.

[7] Ta+ svyp ar ggⁱ Did Thdt. See, A. MERK ad Lc 2,49.

We find no compelling evidence, then, in favour of the shorter reading. However, it is not entirely without significance for the understanding of our text. It highlights an important literary link between Jn 14,2-3 and Jn 14,23, and may well represent a theological interpretation of the phrase ἐν τῇ οἰκίᾳ τοῦ πατρός μου, which provides us with an important clue to its meaning.[8]

Finally, we accept the possibility of a link with Luke 2,49. This parallel text may also provide us with a clue to the meaning of Jn 14,2-3; and support an interpretation of our text with reference to the temple in line with Augustine: "Quippe cum dixerit, in domo Patris mei mansiones multae sunt: quid putamus esse domum Dei, nisi templum Dei".[9]

2. Second Variant Reading: omission of ὅτι [10]

The conjunction ὅτι is omitted from several witnesses. However, there is excellent, if not absolutely conclusive manuscript evidence for retaining it. This we do with the best textual editions[11] and most commentators.[12]

Besides, the reading with ὅτι is clearly the lectio difficilior. An omission of ὅτι would apparently make better sense. But such an omission could easily be explained as a simplification introduced by copyists who took it as ὅτι recitativum, which is often omitted as superfluous.[13]

There is also the problem of how to render ὅτι. It may be rendered "that" (recitativum) or "because" (causal). Moreover, the whole phrase "εἰ δὲ μή, εἶπον ἂν ὑμῖν ὅτι" may be a question.[14] This makes possible four different readings of the text:

---

[8] R. E. BROWN suggests this. See, *op. cit.* 627. The same point is also well made by I. DE LA POTTERIE. See, *La vérité dans saint Jean, II. Le croyant et la vérité* (Rome, 1977), 861.

[9] See, Augustine, *In Jo.* LXVIII, 2; PL 35, 1814.

[10] R. SCHNACKENBURG makes the rather bizarre suggestion that the text originally contained a ὑπάγω before the πορεύομαι. See, "Das Anliegen der Abschiedsrede in Joh. 14", in *Wort Gottes in der Zeit* (Festschrift für K. H. Schelkle) (Düsseldorf, 1973), 97. However, such a conjecture is without manuscript support. G. FISCHER provides a satisfactory treatment of this second variant reading. See, *Die himmlischen Wohnungen. Untersuchungen zu Joh 14,2f,* (Frankfurt/M, 1975), 35-56.

[11] The ὅτι is retained by Nestle, Merk, *GNT* in their critical editions. B. M. METZGER assesses the value of the manuscript evidence. See, *op. cit.* (n. 5), ad loc.

[12] R. E. BROWN is a notable exception. See, *op. cit.* 620.

[13] B. M. METZGER explains the omission in this way. See, *op. cit.* (n. 5) ad loc.

[14] It is a question in the *GNT*.

(i)   If it were not so I would have told you, because I am going to prepare ...

(ii) If it were not so would I have told you so, because I am going to prepare ...?

(iii) If it were not so I would have told you that I am going to prepare ...

(iv) If it were not so would I have told you that I am going to prepare ...?

To take ὅτι causally results inevitably in a triviality. So it might seem better to take ὅτι as explicative, introducing either direct or indirect speech. In either case this is improbable, since the disciples are at once told that Jesus is going to prepare a place for them. Neither does it solve the problem to take the phrase εἰ δὲ μή εἶπον ἄν ὑμῖν as a parenthesis.[15] This would in turn lead again inevitably to a causal sense, for ὅτι would no longer depend on εἶπον.

It would seem best, then, to render the phrase as a question,[16] although this in turn also raises some difficulties. There is apparently no evidence that Jesus previously told his disciples that he goes to prepare a place for them. Some commentators would appeal to the ἵνα clause of Jn 14,3c which recalls the wording of Jn 12,26 (comp. Jn 17,24).[17] But this is hardly sufficient to justify Jn 14,2b as a self-quotation.

We note in reply to this difficulty that the fourth gospel is full of Jesus' self-quotations (Jn 1,50; 3,7; 4,10; (5,28); 6,65; 8,24; 13,33; 14,28; 15,20; 16,15; 16,19; 18,8). They are an integral part of Johannine dialogue and serve to advance the development of thought. We find in their backward movement of repetition and their forward movement of development evidence of the spiral movement typical of John. However, the self-quotation in John does not always refer to a definite word of Jesus (cf. Jn 10,25; 11,40; 6,36; 10,36). It is used at times by John to evoke what is at least implicit in a whole line of thought. This vague and indefinite aspect of the self-quotation contributes to the typical Johannine technique of misunderstanding. It also leaves the text itself open to interpretation at a second deeper level of understanding. Several examples of such self-quotations of Jesus may be found in the immediate context of Jn 14,2-3 (cf. 13,33; 14,28; 15,20; 16,15; 16,19). It would hardly be out of place, then, in the text of Jn 14,2-3 itself.

---

[15] C. K. BARRETT explains it is this way: "There will be many abiding-places (and if it had not been so I would have told you)". See, op. cit. 381.

[16] Thus several translations, e.g. KNOX, R.S.V.; and PHILLIPS, The Gospels in Modern English. It is also taken as a question by J. MARSH, op cit. 502; R. BULTMANN, op. cit. 601, n. 4.

[17] See, J. MARSH, op. cit. 502-503; R. BULTMANN, op. cit. 601, n. 4; B. F. WESTCOTT, op. cit. 201; also, B. NOACK, Zur johanneischen Tradition (Kopenhagen, 1954) 148.

The phrase εἰ δὲ μή of itself looks to what precedes. There the departure of Jesus and the inability of the disciples to follow him is announced (Jn 13,33). This inability is later qualified as temporary (Jn 13,36). After the journey of Jesus, however, the inability disappears (Jn 14,3a). Then the Father's house becomes accessible to the disciples and Jesus returns to take them to it. So it is implicit at least in what precedes that Jesus must first go to prepare a place, if his disciples are to follow him later. Thus the εἰ δὲ μή as a question is in line with the whole tenor of what precedes. It also keeps open as a question the possibility of interpretation at a deeper level of understanding with reference to the passion-resurrection of Jesus.

We conclude that the self-quotation of Jn 14,2b is a Johannine literary technique. It is true that Jesus has not said before directly (or explicitly) what he now says in Jn 14,2b. But he has said so indirectly (or implicitly). This is typical of John's style.[18]

B. FAREWELL DISCOURSE(S) (Jn 13,1-17,26)[19]

1. In General

The context of Jn 14,2-3 provides important indications to direct our interpretation. Our text forms part of the so-called farewell discourses (Jn 13,1-17,26). After a brief introduction (Jn 13,1-3),[20] we have a solemn prologue which records the footwashing of the disciples (Jn 13,4-30). Two discourses proper run parallel to each other (Jn 13,31-14,31; 15,1-16,33). The section ends with a prayer of Jesus (Jn 17,1-26). Such discourses were a very definite literary form of the day, and a concluding prayer such as we find in John formed a significant part of this literary form.[21]

---

[18] We can accept with B. F. Westcott that there is an abruptness in our text, if Jn 14,2b is to be taken as a question. See, op. cit. 201. We have already drawn attention to further evidence of unevenness in our text. See, Introduction (pp. 23-24). But a question here, however abrupt or unexpected, may well be designed by John to open up for us a possible deeper level of meaning in our text. We will treat more at length later in this chapter of John's use of the question.

[19] On the general structure of the discourse, see, C. Charlier, "La présence dans l'absence (Jean 13,31-14,31)", BVC 2 (1953) 61-75; A. Niccacci, "L'unità letteraria di Gv. 18,1-38", in Euntes Docete XXIX, Fasc. II. Aug. (1976) 291-323; J. M. Reese, "Literary Structure of Jn 13:31-14,31; 16:5-6.16-33", CBQ 32 (1970) 341-366, especially pp. 358-59; C. H. Dodd, Interpretation of the Fourth Gospel (Cambridge, 1960) 403-409; Y. Simoens, La gloire d'aimer. Structures stylistiques et interprétatives dans le discours de la cène (Jn 13-17) (Analecta Biblica, 90) (Rome, 1981).

[20] W. K. Grossouw rightly calls these three verses "a kind of minor prologue". See, "A Note on John XIII, 1-3", NovT 8 (1966) 129; also, A. Niccacci, op. cit. (n. 19) 298.

[21] This literary genre has been carefully studied by J. Munck. See, "Discours d'adieu dans le Nouveau Testament et dans la littérature biblique", in Aux sources de la tradition chrétienne (Mélanges M. Goguel) (Neuchâtel, 1950), 155-170.

This whole section is clamped together into a close literary unit by a large semitic inclusion, ἀγαπάω [22] beginning and ending the section (Jn 13,1(2x); 17,26; also ἀγάπη, Jn 17,26). The theme of love is a leading one in the whole section. It occurs again and again.

Besides, there is a highly significant link between these farewell discourses and the immediately succeeding narrative of the passion (Jn 18,1-19,42). The typical Johannine link formula ταῦτα εἰπών which introduces the passion narrative points to what follows as an illustration closely linked to what precedes. [23] Before the actual events, then, are described a long farewell message of Jesus explains their meaning. Our text forms part of this explanation.

A closer examination of the discourses will help us to isolate the more immediate context of Jn 14,2-3 and direct our interpretation more securely. The introductory verses of Jn 13,1-3 are composed of two phrases in strict parallelism. An inclusion brackets them as a unit. The same phrase formulation in practically the same terms opens and closes the passage and condenses the meaning: εἰδώς (v. 1) .... εἰδώς (v. 3) μεταβῇ ..... πρὸς τὸν πατέρα (v. 1) ... πρὸς τὸν Θεὸν ὑπάγει (v. 3). This return from the end of the pericope to the beginning indicates a cyclic movement of thought. However, this cyclic movement once complete also advances. The episode of the footwashing which follows immediately is in turn parallel to the supreme love of Jesus mentioned in the introduction. We might indicate this as follows:

before the passover ...   knowing (εἰδώς) he loved them ....

during the meal ... to betray him, knowing (εἰδώς) ..... he began to wash the feet.

There is then a reverse movement and an advance movement. And this provides us with a valuable clue to the spiral movement of John's thought as the discourse unfolds.

The circumstances described in these introductory verses are also important for our interpretation. They open perspectives which govern what follows. Everything unfolds in the light of a passover which is imminent. The phrase is designedly vague and indefinite πρὸ δὲ τῆς ἑορτῆς τοῦ πάσχα. This temporal indication is a final link in a chain of previous references to an imminent passover (comp. πρό, Jn 12,1; ἐγγύς,

---

[22] The verb ἀγαπάω occurs 25x in the farewell discourse including the final prayer, and the noun ἀγάπη 6x. C. H. DODD would regard the theme of love as the fundamental theme of chapters, 13-17. See, *op. cit.* (n. 19) 398-399.

[23] A. NICCACCI comments aptly on this Johannine link-formula: "suggerisce una connessione immediata (cf. 7,10)". See, op. cit. (n. 19) 307.

Jn 2,13; 6,4; 11,55). These all form part of the Johannine theme of the replacement of the Jewish feasts.[24] This final reference to the passover is explicitly linked with the passage of Jesus out of this world to his Father (μεταβαίνω, v. 1. ὑπάγω, v. 3), which is accomplished through his passion-resurrection.

Moreover, the "hour" has arrived. It is a long-awaited "hour" (cf. Jn 7,30; 2,4; 8,20; 12,23.27(2x)).[25] It refers to the "hour" of the passion-resurrection of Jesus. It is inseparable in John from the glorification of Jesus (comp. Jn 12,23; 17,1). It is the glorification of this "hour" which dominates our text within its more immediate context (Jn 13,31-32). This "hour" is already effective here and now as the discourse unfolds.[26]

These opening verses also introduce the theme of the return of Jesus to his Father. Its importance is emphasised by repetition (Jn 13,1.3). It is intimately linked in turn with the heavenly origin (ἀπὸ Θεοῦ ἐξῆλθεν) and destiny of Jesus (ἐκ τοῦ κόσμου τούτου πρὸς τὸν πατέρα/Θεόν). This same theme pervades the whole discourse (Jn 13,33.36(2x); 14,4.5; 14,28; 15,26; 16,7.28). It is explicit in our text (Jn 14,2b.3a). This is the journey of the "hour" of Jesus through his passion-resurrection.

Moreover, at the centre of these introductory verses we also find a striking clash between the love of Jesus (ἀγαπήσας..ἠγάπησεν) and the betrayal of Judas, instigated by the devil (παραδοῖ). Satan and the betrayer are placed in strict relationship with this journey of Jesus to the Father. John's mind is clearly echoing to contrasts. It will continue to do so throughout the discourse.[27] This will help to explain some apparent breaks in the sequence of thought as the discourse unfolds.

Everything in these discourses, then, should be interpreted with reference in some way to these introductory verses. So, too, our text within its more immediate context. The future passover of the passion-resurrection of Jesus is imminent. It is the "hour" of the return of Jesus to his Father through his glorifying passion-resurrection. This is the perspective which will govern our interpretation of Jn 14,2-3. Besides, we have a clue in these introductory verses to the working of John's mind. He winds his way in a spiral movement into the discourse, with his mind ever open to the clash of opposites.

---

[24] D. MOLLAT accepts these Jewish feasts in John as the basis for his structure of the Gospel. See, *JB,* Introduction to St. John, p. 141. R. E. BROWN also stresses this theme of replacement in John. See, *op. cit.* 411.

[25] J. FERRARO studies the significance of the "hour" in John at length. See, *L'ora di Cristo nel quarto vangelo* (Analisi di strutture letterarie) (Roma, 1970).

[26] In a real sense, it is the risen and glorified Christ who speaks throughout the farewell discourses. See, C. H. DODD, *op. cit.* (n. 19) 397; also, R. E. BROWN, *op. cit.* 581.

[27] Judas is contrasted with the disciples (13,10), Jesus with Satan (14,30), the world with Jesus (14,27) and the disciples (14,17.19.22); love (15,1-17) with hatred (15,18-25), darkness with glory (13,30-32), betrayal (13,38) with belief (14,1), Judas with the Beloved Disciple (13,21-23).

2. In Particular

In our view the discourse which follows the footwashing is not just a single discourse. It is composed of two parallel discourses.[28] The final prayer of Jesus apart (Jn 17,1-26), we accept a division of the farewell discourses (Jn 13,31-16,33) into a first discourse (Jn 13,31-14,31) and a second discourse (Jn 15,1-16,33). The first discourse concludes with the enigmatic words of Jesus "come, let us go hence" (Jn 14,31). We agree that this concluding verse would naturally introduce chapter 18. But we cannot accept any rearrangement theory to explain this kind of incongruity in the fourth gospel.[29] In our view the gospel has an overall unity as it stands. In its final form it is a one man composition. Jn 14,31 is perfectly intelligible in our two-discourse theory.[30] The second discourse ends with the triumphant cry of Jesus: "have confidence; I have overcome the world" (Jn 16,33).[31]

The more immediate context of Jn 14,2-3, then, is the first farewell discourse (Jn 13,31-14,31). This is clearly separate from the second discourse which follows it (Jn 15,1-16,33). However, we cannot at the same time overlook the link between both of these discourses within the whole unified section of Jn 13,1-17,26.[32] Nearly all the dominant ideas of the first discourse reappear in the second, nuanced and deepened as if by prolonged and prayerful meditation. This provides further evidence for the spiral movement of John's thought. The two discourses are clearly parallel. In order to give the first discourse (Jn 13,31-14,31) its full resonance the corresponding and complementary developments of the second discourse (Jn 15,1-16,33) should be constantly kept in mind. The same is true of our text. The corresponding developments of the second discourse clarify its meaning.

---

[28] C. Charlier is a fine exponent of this theory. See, *op. cit.* (n. 19). Besides, Y. Simoens treats of several alternative structures proposed for the discourses. See, *op. cit.* (n. 19), I-51. However, J. M. Reese challenges this theory of duplicate discourses. See, *op. cit.* (n. 19) 330.

[29] A. Feuillet provides us with a general review of these rearrangement theories. See, *Johannine Studies* (New York, 1964) 129-136.

[30] For an alternative solution to the problem of Jn 14,31, see, C. H. Dodd, *op. cit.* (n. 19), 406-409.

[31] C. H. Dodd stresses the parallel between Jn 16,33 and Jn 14,31, which he describes as a "stirring battle-cry". See, *op. cit.* (n. 19), 408, note, I.

[32] We have already referred to the large semitic inclusion between Jn 13,1 and Jn 17,26. See, p. 141.

C. LITERARY TECHNIQUES[33]

1. Division of the Discourse (Jn 13,31-14,31) [34]

There are several literary devices used by John in the first farewell discourse (Jn 13,31-14,31) which help us to locate our text more exactly within its immediate context and throw considerable light on its meaning. Perhaps the most important of these devices is that of dialogue. It is a typical Johannine technique.[35] In relation to John's use of dialogue, the first farewell discourse (Jn 13,31-14,31) may be divided into three large sections (Jn 13,31-35; 13,36-14,24; 14,25-31). The first section (Jn 13,31-35) precedes the dialogue proper, which begins with the question of Peter (Jn 13,36). It is a monologue of Jesus. These few verses form an introduction, or prologue. They are an epitome of subsequent developments, and contain the whole discourse in miniature, or in embryo. The second section is the body of the discourse (Jn 13,36-14,24). This central section unfolds entirely by means of the dialogue, questions and answers. It is an expansion of John's thought already expressed succinctly in the introductory verses of the first section (Jn 13,31-35); and is the longest section of the discourse. The third section, like the first section, is also a monologue of Jesus (Jn 14,25-31). It forms a conclusion or epilogue, which draws together all the strands of the discourse right from the outset. At this point the dialogue has ceased.

We may thus divide the first farewell discourse conveniently as follows:

Section I: Introduction, or Prologue   (Jn 13,31-35)

Section II: Dialogue, or Development   (Jn 13,36-14,24)

Section III: Epilogue, or Conclusion   (Jn 14,25-31)

All of these three sections will contribute, each in its own way, to a better understanding of our text.

---

[33] We must agree fully with D. DEEKS when he writes: "The fourth evangelist was not only a brilliant theologian; he was also a master of a very specialised literary technique". See, "The Structure of the Fourth Gospel", *NTS* 15 (1968) 126.

[34] C. CHARLIER divides the discourse (13,31-14,31) into a progressive series of five cycles. See, *op. cit.* (n. 19), 66-67. This structure, however ingenious, appears to us unduly contrived.

[35] For a fine example of the Johannine structure and mode of composition based on the technique of dialogue, see, I. DE LA POTTERIE, "Naître de l'eau et naître de l'Esprit — Le texte baptismal de Jean 3,5", in *La Vie selon l'Esprit. Condition du Chrétien* (Unam Sanctam, 55), 41-53.

(a) *Introduction (Jn 13,31-35)*

It has been claimed that these verses which form the introduction, or prologue to the discourse are thrown together in a haphazard way, without any inner coherence or unity.[36] Nothing could be farther from the truth. All of these verses link back to the general introduction of Jn 13,1-3. The glorification of Jesus announced in Jn 13,31-32 is inseparable in the fourth gospel from the "hour" of Jn 13,1 (comp. Jn 12,23.27-28). The departure of Jesus in Jn 13,33 (ὑπάγω) takes up again the first mention of departure in Jn 13,3 (ὑπάγω). It is the same journey of Jesus to the Father through his passion-resurrection. The theme of love announced in Jn 13,34-35 which rounds off our first section (ἀγαπάω (3x); ἀγάπη) also takes up again the first reference to love in Jn 13,1 (ἀγαπάω, (2x)). Far from being thrown together in a haphazard way, these introductory verses to the first farewell discourse (Jn 13,31-35) are composed of three phrases, which all evoke again the general introduction to the larger unified section of Jn 13,1-17,26. Moreover, they also contain the whole subsequent development of the first discourse in embryo.

(i) Glorification (Jn 13,31-32)

All three phrases which make up the introduction to the discourse proper are clearly distinct. The first phrase merits a special word of attention (Jn 13,31-32). It stands apart, even within this introduction. Moreover, it is important for an understanding of the discourse as a whole and our text in particular. We find it before Jesus addresses his disciples formally as "little children" (τεκνία, Jn 13,33).[37] Besides, it is the only part of the discourse where Jesus is referred to in the third person, and as the Son of Man. It is also clamped together in itself as a minor unit by means of the link-term δοξάζω (5x). John effectively structures Jn 13,31-32 to act as a prism. The light of glory is refracted through these verses on every part of the discourse, and the figure of the Son of Man dominates the whole subsequent discourse.

---

[36] L. CERFAUX sums up the opinions well. See, "La charité fraternelle et le retour du Christ (Jo. XIII, 33-38)", *ETL* 24 (1948), 321. Indeed, some commentators would even regard Jn 13,34-35 as an interpolation. See, F. BECKER, "Die Abschiedsreden Jesu im Johannesevangelium",*ZNW 61 (1970) 220.

[37] We may compare Jn 12,23 within the structure of Jn 12,23-36. See, I. DE LA POTTERIE, "L'exaltation du Fils de l'homme (Jn 12,31-36)", *Greg* 49 (1968) 463.

The concentric structure of the phrase is also important:

a Νῦν ἐδοξάσθη ὁ υἱὸς τοῦ   b′ καὶ ὁ Θεὸς ἐδοξάσθη ἐν αὐτῷ.
ἀνθρώπου,
b εἰ ὁ Θεὸς ἐδοξάσθη ἐν αὐτῷ,   a′ καὶ ὁ Θεὸς δοξάσει αὐτὸν ἐν
ἑαυτῷ,
καὶ εὐθὺς δοξάσει αὐτόν.

We understand the ἐδοξάσθη as an ingressive aorist.[38] The manifestation of the salvific intervention of God has already begun in the glorification of Jesus through his passion-resurrection. This is in harmony with the perspective of the "hour" in the general introduction of Jn 13,1-3, which has already come (Jn 13,1). A future process of glorification (δοξάσει) is distinguished from an immediate future glorification (εὐθὺς δοξάσει) which in the logical sequence of events will set it in motion.[39] This immediate future glorification is left suspended in Jn 13,32. The εὐθύς is taken up again in the ἔτι μικρόν which announces the immediate future departure of Jesus to his passion-resurrection. It is this same journey of Jesus to his Father which is explicitly referred to in our text of Jn 14,2-3 (πορεύομαι, (2x)). This is the glorifying journey of the Son of Man in the immediate future, which will in turn set in motion a continual future process of glorification (comp. Jn 14,13; 16,14).

(ii) The Journey of Jesus (Jn 13,33)

Jesus introduces the theme of departure in Jn 13,33 by addressing his disciples formally as "little children" (τεκνία). It is a diminutive form of τέκνον (comp. Jn 1,12; 8,39; 11,52). As such it is charged with affection and tenderness. The term is found nowhere else in the fourth gospel. It softens the harsh announcement of departure in the same verse. This will be an immediate future departure (ἔτι μικρόν), followed by a period of absence (ζητήσετε). The evangelist announces with this departure a parallel situation of the Jews and the disciples: an inability to follow Jesus. The cyclic structure of this second clause stresses this inability:

---

[38] Others would explain this aorist as "complexive", with reference to the whole passion, death, resurrection, and ascension which take place in the "hour" of Jesus. See, R. E. BROWN, op. cit. 610. Here, however, a "complexive" would appear somewhat out of place. It would indicate that everything had been already accomplished. This could hardly be reconciled with the future tenses of Jn 13,32.

[39] The glory of Jesus was already visible throughout his ministry (cf. 2,11; 11,4; comp. 17,4) in anticipation of the supreme manifestation of his glory in the "hour" of his passion-resurrection (cf. 7,39; 12,23.27-28). But the glory of Jesus will continue to be revealed after the passion-resurrection, and because of it (cf. 14,13; 15,8; 16,14; 17,10).

a καὶ καθὼς εἶπον τοῖς Ἰουδαίοις

                                 b ὅτι ὅπου ἐγὼ ὑπάγω ὑμεῖς οὐ

a′ καὶ ὑμῖν λέγω ἄρτι.   δύνασθε ἐλθεῖν,

The emphatic position of ἄρτι seems to invest this term with a special importance. The disciples are not able to follow Jesus, but only for "now" (ἄρτι). This prepares us in turn for the subsequent development of the discourse (comp. Jn 13,36c). In its emphatic position the "now" (ἄρτι)[40] also links back with the "now" (νῦν) of Jn 13,31b, and anticipates the νῦν of Jn 13,36, and the ἄρτι of Jn 13,37. The disciples cannot follow Jesus "now" (νῦν/ἄρτι) in his passion-resurrection. In the repetition of temporal adverbs an immediate future perspective of the passion-resurrection (εὐθύς, Jn 13,32... ἔτι μικρόν, Jn 13,33) and a present perspective (νῦν, Jn 13,31 ... ἄρτι, Jn 13,33) seem to fuse.

Jn 13,33 contains an explicit self-quotation. It evokes directly Jn 7,33-34 and Jn 8,21-22. A comparison of these texts will help to explain the deeper spiritual import of the journey of Jesus referred to in Jn 13,33 and Jn 14,2-3; and reveal the subtlety and delicacy with which the evangelist constructs Jn 13,33. There are clear verbal links between all three texts (Jn 13,33; 7,33-34; 8,21-22), as we shall see. Besides, the phrase ὅπου ἐγὼ ὑπάγω ὑμεῖς οὐ δύνασθε ἐλθεῖν of Jn 8,21-22(2x) is repeated verbatim in Jn 13,33, and initiates the development of the dialogue leading up to Jn 14,2-3. There the dialogue is a direct variation of the same theme. So, too, the variation of the phrase ὅπου ἐγὼ ὑπάγω of Jn 8,21-22(2x) which we find in the ὅπου εἰμὶ ἐγώ of Jn 7,34 (also in Jn 7,36) is again repeated verbatim in Jn 14,2-3.

Both of the texts evoked by Jn 13,33 (Jn 7,33-34; 8,21-22) contain a typical Johannine use of the question. In Jn 7,33 an enigmatic statement of Jesus about his future departure (ὑπάγω) elicits a question from the Jews: "does he intend to go (πορεύομαι, Jn 7,35(2x)) among the Greeks and to teach the Greeks?". The question is artfully left in suspense. It is open to both a negative and positive reply. Negative, because the departure (ὑπάγω/πορεύομαι) is not a journey in a physical or material sense to the land of the Greeks. In some such manner Peter understands the journey of Jesus in Jn 13,33. But the answer is also positive. Jesus will depart by passing from this world to the Father through death (Jn 13,1; 16,28). It is only in this way that Jesus will be able to teach the pagan world (comp. Jn 12,20-24).

---

[40] R. BULTMANN notes this emphatic position, but construes it with reference to the following verse. See, *op. cit.* 525, note, 2.

Again it is a question of the departure of Jesus in Jn 8,21-22 (ὑπάγω) (3x). This time the Jews have an intimation of a journey to a heavenly home. It was again perhaps some such intimation that prompted Peter in Jn 13,37. So the Jews now ask the question: "does he intend to kill himself?" (ἀποκτενεῖ, Jn 8,22). Again the question is left suspended. Paradoxically, the reply is both yes and no. In the physical sense the answer is negative. Jesus does not intend to commit suicide. His enemies cause his death (cf. Jn 5,18; 7,1.19.20.25; 8,37.40; 11,53). But the answer is also positive at a deeper spiritual level. Jesus goes to his death, but he is entirely free (Jn 10,17-18). This is the meaning of the journey of Jesus in our text of Jn 14,2-3 — a journey through death to the Father.

Both of these texts evoked by Jn 13,33 also help to clarify the meaning of the goal to which Jesus will take his disciples in Jn 14,2-3 (ὅπου εἰμὶ ἐγώ). We first compare Jn 7,33-34 and Jn 13,33:

Jn 7,33-34	Jn 13,33
ἔτι χρόνον	ἔτι ( )
μικρὸν	μικρὸν
μεθ' ὑμῶν εἰμι	μεθ' ὑμῶν εἰμι·
καὶ ὑπάγω	( )
πρὸς τὸν πέμψαντά με.	( )
ζητήσετέ με	ζητήσετέ με,
καὶ οὐχ εὑρήσετε,	( )

LINK
καὶ καθὼς εἶπον τοῖς Ἰουδαίοις ὅτι

καὶ ὅπου εἰμὶ ἐγὼ	( ) ὅπου ἐγὼ ὑπάγω
ὑμεῖς οὐ δύνασθε ἐλθεῖν.	ὑμεῖς οὐ δύνασθε ἐλθεῖν.

The subtle difference in the parallel texts "where I am" (ὅπου εἰμὶ ἐγώ, Jn 7,34) and "where I am going" (ὅπου ἐγὼ ὑπάγω, Jn 13,33) is significant. Jesus does not say to his disciples in Jn 13,33 "where I am you cannot come" (ὅπου εἰμὶ ἐγώ), as he does to the incredulous Jews in Jn 7,34. It is a radical inability for the Jews. Hence Jesus says to them explicitly in Jn 7,34 "you will not find me". This phrase is significantly omitted from Jn 13,33. The possibility of coming to Jesus remains ever open to the disciples. In fact, Jesus promises in our text of Jn 14,2-3 that he will return after his departure precisely to take the disciples to "where I am" (ὅπου εἰμὶ ἐγώ, Jn 14,3). Jesus merely says to the disciples that they cannot come "where I am going" (Jn 13,33), because it is only for the present that the way is not open to them. This explains the emphatic position of ἄρτι (Jn 13,33), left in suspense awaiting future development (cf. Jn 13,36-37).

A comparison with the parallel text of Jn 8,21-22 also reveals an omission which is no less significant:

Jn 8,21-22   Jn 13,33

                                  τεκνία, ἔτι μικρὸν μεθ' ὑμῶν εἰμι·
ἐγὼ ὑπάγω καὶ   (   )
ζητήσετέ με,   ζητήσετέ με,

LINK

καὶ καθὼς εἶπον τοῖς Ἰουδαίοις ὅτι

καὶ ἐν τῇ ἁμαρτίᾳ ὑμῶν ἀποθανεῖσθε·   (   )
ὅπου ἐγὼ ὑπάγω   ὅπου ἐγὼ ὑπάγω
ὑμεῖς οὐ δύνασθε ἐλθεῖν.   ὑμεῖς οὐ δύνασθε ἐλθεῖν.

The Jews "will die in their sin". This is explained in turn as the sin of unbelief in the parallel text of Jn 8,24. The circular movement of the phrase helps to emphasise this:

a ἀποθανεῖσθε ἐν ταῖς ἁμαρτίαις ὑμῶν·
b ἐαν γὰρ μὴ πιστεύσητε ὅτι ἐγώ εἰμι,
a′ ἀποθανεῖσθε ἐν ταῖς ἁμαρτίαις ὑμῶν.

The multiplicity of "sins" may be reduced to a single "sin".[41] This is "the" sin of deliberate unbelief (Jn 9,41; 15,22(2x).24; 16,8.9; 19,11). The Jews will reject Christ definitively, die in their unbelief. For this reason they are radically incapable of following Jesus. Not so the disciples. Their situation is parallel to that of the Jews, but also quite distinct. Hence, the omission of the phrase from Jn 8,21 in Jn 13,33. However, the deliberate parallel with Jn 8,21-22 which John explicitly evokes does indicate that at the back of the evangelist's mind in Jn 13,33 there lies the general understanding of faith as a means of "coming" to Jesus (comp. Jn 3,18.21; 6,35; cf. Jn 7,37-38),[42] — the Johannine theme of following Jesus by faith as his disciples.

(iii) Love (Jn 13,34-35)

The formal address τεκνία of Jn 13,33 already prepares us for the introduction of the theme of "love" in Jn 13,34-35 (ἀγαπάω (3x), ἀγάπη).

---

[41] There is a general tendency in John to reduce multiplicity to unity (14,23; comp. 14,24; 13,34; comp. 14,15.21; 17,4; comp. 5,36).

[42] In these texts we find the phrase ἔρχομαι πρὸς parallel to πιστεύω εἰς.

This theme easily links back with the term τεκνία of Jn 13,33, and helps to make more precise the inner nature of the filial relationship between Jesus and his disciples. A circular movement in Jn 13,34 again indicates the central phrase which bears the stress:

ἵνα   ἀγαπᾶτε ἀλλήλους,

                                καθὼς ἠγάπησα ὑμᾶς,

ἵνα καὶ ὑμεῖς   ἀγαπᾶτε ἀλλήλους.

The double ἵνα is explanatory. It defines the new commandment as love for one another (ἀλλήλους). Moreover, the central phrase καθὼς ἠγάπησα ὑμᾶς again links back with the ἀγαπάω in the solemn introduction (Jn 13,1(2x)).

These final introductory verses of Jn 13,34-35 also evoke the theme of discipleship (μαθητής, Jn 13,35) [43] and explain it in terms of love. But the theme of love itself is left in suspense here for the moment. It will be taken up again later in the central section of the discourse (Jn 14,15.21.23.24.28) and in the conclusion (Jn 14,28). However, it is one of the curious features of Jn 14,2-3 that it refers only to the activity of Jesus himself. This is due, of course, to the limitations imposed by our choice of this text. But the activity of Jesus there who "will take the disciples to himself" (παραλήμψομαι) may be fittingly complemented in Johannine terms by the activity of the disciples described in these introductory verses and elsewhere in the discourse as an activity of love. These introductory verses already seem to point in that direction.

(b) *Dialogue (Jn 13,36-14,24)*

     (i) Questions [44]

In the discourse we find a subtle Johannine use of the question. It is left in suspense, as it were, on the lips of Jesus, without an answer (Jn 13,38; 14,9.10). Such a use of the question forms part of the general enigmatic quality of the fourth gospel (cf. Jn 10,6; 16,25). But this openness of the Johannine question must be respected. It is the "double-think" in a subtle form (comp. Jn 7,35; 8,22). [45]

One such question on the lips of Jesus is: "will you lay down your life for me?" (Jn 13,38). The answer may be negative or positive. A negative

---

[43] On the Johannine theme of discipleship, See, I. DE LA POTTERIE, *La vérité dans saint Jean* (Rome, 1977) 562-65.

[44] A. VANHOYE explains the subtlety of the Johannine use of the question in his exegesis of Jn 2,4. See, "Interrogation johannique et exégèse de Cana (Jn 2,4)", *Bib* 55 (1974) 157-167.

[45] See, A. VANHOYE, *op. cit.* (n. 44), 157, note, 1.

answer is suggested by the text itself. Far from laying down his life, Peter will deny Jesus three times (Jn 13,38b; comp. 18,27). But the question remains a question. As such it is also open to a positive reply. There is a real sense in which Peter will lay down his life for Jesus by following him in his martyrdom (cf. Jn 21,18-19). This is a very subtle use of Johannine "irony".[46] It leaves the question open to a second deeper level of meaning, which can only be understood in the light of the passion-resurrection (comp. Jn 10,17-18). It stamps the departure of Jesus referred to in our text of Jn 14,2-3 with a sacrificial import.[47]

The Johannine question also has a similar role on the lips of the disciples in the discourse. It plays an essential part in the development of the dialogue. It opens a second deeper level of meaning in quite a different way. But this use of the question is also conscious literary art. One aspect of "irony" in the fourth gospel is precisely to have questions voiced which do not receive the expected answer (comp. Jn 4,12; 8,53.57). It is a curious feature of our discourse that the questions on the lips of the disciples never receive a direct reply. The question always receives an unexpected answer, which in turn directs attention to the person of Jesus. We may illustrate this as follows:

Jn 13,36:	Question:	where are *you going*?
	Reply:	where I am going you *cannot follow* me now ... only later.
Jn 13,37:	Question:	why can I not follow you now ...?
Jn 13,38:	Reply:	you will *deny me* three times.
Jn 14,5:	Question:	we do not know *where you are going* ...?
	Reply:	I am the way ...
Jn 14,8:	Question:	show us the Father ...?
Jn 14,9:	Reply:	so long a time ... and you do not *know me*.
Jn 14,21:	Question:	why will you *reveal yourself* to us ...?
Jn 14,23:	Reply:	we (Jesus and the Father) will come and make our abode with him.

These replies of Jesus are unintelligible at the moment to the disciples. But by means of this technique of indirect reply John succeeds in keeping open the possibility of a deeper understanding of the mystery of the person of Jesus. It allows for a deeper insight into this mystery in the light of the passion-resurrection. The answer to the question is a true answer, even if indirect, but only at this deeper level of meaning.

---

[46] D. W. WEAD provides an extensive study of Johannine irony. See, *The Literary Devices in John's Gospel* (Basel, 1970) 47-66. See, also H. CLAVIER, "L'ironie dans le quatrième évangile", *StudEvang* I (TU 73) (1959) 261-276.

[47] See, ch. I, note, 30.

(ii) Misunderstanding[48]

The theme of misunderstanding (or partial understanding) is inseparable in the discourse from the Johannine use of the question. It provides a valuable indication of the whole purpose of the discourse, which is designed precisely to correct this misunderstanding. It points to the meaning of our text at the first level of understanding. But it also indicates by contrast with this misunderstanding how our text is to be reinterpreted in its immediate context at a second deeper spiritual level of understanding.

It is the interplay of dialogue, question and answer, which brings out precisely this lack of understanding. Something which Jesus says is taken up in a material (or physical) sense by one of his disciples. A question on one of the disciples' lips then gives expression to some misunderstanding. As yet the disciples cannot grasp the deeper spiritual[49] sense of Jesus' words without the Spirit. The disciples and Jesus are on two entirely different planes of thought.

Peter asks: "where are you going?" (Jn 13,36). But he imagines the journey in a material sense as a movement in space (comp. Jn 7,35). He asks further: "why can I not follow you now? I will lay down my life for you" (Jn 13,37). Peter here imagines a journey that may involve the danger of death (comp. Jn 8,22) and so a journey possibly in this sense to his heavenly home. Then Thomas reveals his lack of understanding when he says: "we do not know where you are going" (Jn 14,5). It seems that he is anxious to know where the Father's house is located in space.[50] Philip says: "show us the Father" (Jn 14,8). Jesus has just spoken of his "coming" (Jn 14,3). But his words of reproach to Philip show that the disciple was expecting some kind of external theophany visible to the bodily eye, a marvellous external intervention. The final question is that of Judas: "why will you show yourself to us and not to the world?" (Jn 14,22). It also reveals the same kind of tragic misunderstanding as that of Philip in a material and physical sense. Jesus has again just spoken of his "coming" (Jn 14,18). The error of Judas springs from a typical Jewish

---

[48] On the theme of Johannine misunderstanding, see, H. LEROY, *Rätsel und Missverständnis. Ein Beitrag zur Formgeschichte des Johannesevangeliums* (Bonn, 1968).

[49] We use the term "spiritual" here in connection with the Spirit (comp. I Cor 2,14-16). The "spiritual" meaning is opened up to perfect faith by the risen Jesus through the gift of the Spirit. Y. CONGAR explains the term well in this sense. See, *The Mystery of the Temple* (London, 1962) 148-149.

[50] O. SCHAEFER explains the spatial implications of Peter's question. See, "Der Sinn der Rede Jesu von den vielen Wohnungen in seines Vaters Hause und von dem Weg zu ihm (Joh. 14,1-7)", *ZNW* 32 (1933), 211.

understanding that the final "coming" must be a glorious external manifestation (cf. Jn 13,31-32), a definitive triumph over the enemies of God visible to all men. He asks, then, why the promised experience is reserved only for the privileged few (comp. Acts 10,40-41: "not for all the people").[51] This latter part of the discourse would seem to be designed to reinterpret traditional Jewish eschatological expectations.

In line with this kind of misunderstanding, or partial understanding, our text of Jn 14,2-3 would be taken by the disciples to designate in a spatial sense a physical journey of Jesus (πορεύομαι) to a material dwelling-place of his Father (οἰκία τοῦ πατρός μου) located somewhere indefinite in space; and his later "coming" (ἔρχομαι) would be understood by them as a final glorious intervention of Jesus to visibly save his people (παραλήμψομαι) by reuniting them with himself in the Father's dwelling-place (πρὸς ἐμαυτόν) at the end of time. All this, however, will take on a deeper spiritual sense at a second deeper level of understanding in the light of the passion-resurrection. This is exactly what we find in the immediate context of Jn 14,2-3.

a. *Departure*. — A glance at the following diagram will show how the themes of "going" and "coming" seem to dominate the discourse:

Introduction (Jn 13,31-35)	Jn 13,33: Going (ὑπάγω) (comp. Jn 13,36(2x); 14,4.5.28)
Dialogue (Jn 13,36-14,24)	Jn 13,36: Going (ὑπάγω) (2x) (comp. Jn 14,28; 13,33)
	Jn 14,2 : Going (πορεύομαι) (comp. Jn 14,3.12.28)
	Jn 14,3 : Going (πορεύομαι) (comp. Jn 14,2.12.28)
	Jn 14,3 : Coming (ἔρχομαι) (comp. Jn 14,18.23.28.30)
	Jn 14,4 : Going (ὑπάγω) (comp. Jn 13,33.36(2x); 14,5.28)
	Jn 14,5 : Going (ὑπάγω) (comp. Jn 13,33.36(2x); 14,4.28)
	Jn 14,12: Going (πορεύομαι) (comp. Jn 14,2.3.28)
	Jn 14,18: Coming (ἔρχομαι) (comp. Jn 14,3.23.28.30)
	Jn 14,23: Coming (ἔρχομαι) (comp. Jn 14,3.12.28.30)
Epilogue (Jn 14,25-31)	Jn 14,28: Going (ὑπάγω) (comp. Jn 13,33.36(2x). 14,4.5.28)
	Jn 14,28: Going (πορεύομαι) (comp. Jn 14,2.3.12)
	Jn 14,28: Coming (ἔρχομαι) (comp. Jn 14,3.18.23.30)
	Jn 14,30: Coming (ἔρχομαι) (14,3.18.23).

---

[51] See, ch. I, pp. 39-40.

It is the same journey of Jesus which is described in the discourse alternatively by πορεύομαι (Jn 14,2.3.12.28) and ὑπάγω (Jn 13,33.36(2x); 14,4.5.28). The meaning of both verbs is identical in John.[52] This journey of Jesus is first mentioned in Jn 13,33 (ὑπάγω). It is an immediate future departure (ἔτι μικρόν). At the first level of meaning it is understood by the disciples in the immediate context as a physical movement in space. But this ὑπάγω of Jn 13,33 takes up again the last use of the verb in Jn 13,3, where it designates the journey of the "hour" of Jesus through his passion-resurrection. At this deeper level of understanding the journey is neither a physical movement in space, such as a bodily ascension into heaven, nor is it the physical act of dying. It is a spiritual ascent to God. Although this journey is still in the future, it is also in some mysterious way already in the process of being realised. The ὑπάγω is a futuristic present in Jn 13,33.[53]

So, too, the vocabulary is carefully calculated to relate this journey of Jesus to his passion-resurrection as an eschatological event.[54] The ἔτι μικρόν of Jn 13,33 had already announced the impending death of Jesus (comp. Jn 8,35). Jesus affirms that Peter cannot follow him "now" (νῦν). This term echoes the νῦν of Jn 13,31, which signals the start of the passion of Jesus (comp. νῦν, Jn 12,27.31(2x)).[55] The alternation of νῦν (Jn 13,36) with ἄρτι (Jn 13,37) supports this. The Johannine phrase ἀπ' ἄρτι (Jn 14,7b) designates the eschatological period initiated by the passion-resurrection of Jesus.[56] No less decisively does the phrase ψυχὴν τίθημι evoke in Johannine terms the passion-death of Jesus (comp. Jn 10,11.15.17).[57]

The πορεύομαι of Jn 14,2-3 is thus to be understood in its immediate context with reference to the passion-resurrection of Jesus as an eschatological event. This is the deep spiritual meaning of the term which emerges by contrast with the disciples' material understanding (or misunderstanding) of it as an outward, external, physical movement in space.

b. *Return.* — It is the verb ἔρχομαι which is used exclusively in the discourse to describe the return of Jesus (Jn 14,3.18.23.28). This return is

---

[52] See, ch. III, note, 45.

[53] See, *BDF*, 323.

[54] C. H. Dodd is right when he designates the intention of the evangelist as "to interpret the death and resurrection of Jesus as the eschatological event in the fullest sense". See, *op. cit.* (n. 19) 399.

[55] I. de la Potterie explains at length how this temporal adverb "now" in John points to the centre of salvation history. See, *op. cit.* (n. 37), 465-467.

[56] Again, I. de la Potterie explains the import of the phrase. See, *op. cit.* (n. 37), 465.

[57] See, ch. I, note, 30.

first mentioned in Jn 14,3. There it is left in suspense, totally undetermined with reference to any particular "coming". It is understood (or misunderstood) in the immediate context as a glorious and visible eschatological intervention of Jesus (Jn 14,8). The ἔρχομαι of Jn 14,3 is taken up again with the ἔρχομαι of Jn 14,18. Here it is again understood (or misunderstood) by the disciples in the immediate context as a glorious and visible intervention of Jesus (Jn 14,22). However, the "coming" is explicitly designated here as an immediate future coming (ἔτι μικρόν, Jn 14,19). This immediate future "coming" refers to the appearances of the risen Jesus (comp. ἔρχομαι of Jn 20,19.24.26; also 21,13).[58] There is no other immediate future coming of the risen Jesus in the fourth gospel.

This "coming" is described in a context of vision. The disciples will see Jesus alive (Jn 14,19).[59] The vision is described by the verb θεωρέω.[60] In Johannine usage it designates a vision of faith.[61] This vision is further specified in terms of a knowledge of the inner mystery of Jesus: his union with the Father and the disciples (γινώσκω, Jn 14,20).[62] That it is a vision of faith is further confirmed by the contrast (δέ, adversative) with the "world" (κόσμος), which will not "see" Jesus (θεωρέω, Jn 14,19). This contrast is clearly related to the previous contrast between the disciples and the "world" (κόσμος), which cannot open by faith to receive the Spirit because it neither "sees" him (θεωρέω) nor knows him (γινώσκω) (Jn 14,17). In this theophany the risen Jesus becomes the object of an inner vision by faith under the action of the Spirit.

To this inner vision of faith under the revealing action of the Spirit there is a corresponding epiphany of Jesus (ἐμφανίσω αὐτῷ ἐμαυτόν, Jn 14,21).[63] The recipient of this manifestation is specified in the immediate

---

[58] John is the only evangelist who uses ἔρχομαι in his account of the resurrection apparitions, with Jesus as the subject (20, 19.24.26; 21,13). In this regard a comparison between Lk 24,36 (without ἔρχομαι) and Jn 20,19 (with ἔρχομαι) is particularly significant. Although Jesus is already present in Jn 21,13, the evangelist still uses the rather strange expression: "Jesus comes" (ἔρχεται).

[59] We accept the reading of J. DUPONT, who maintains that the ὅτι introduces a complement which together with με forms the double object of θεωρεῖτε. See, *Essais sur la christologie de saint Jean* (Bruges, 1951) 208-209. C. TRAETS provides a complete list of alternatives for the interpretation of ὅτι. See, *Voir Jésus et le Père en lui selon l'évangile de saint Jean* (Rome, 1967), 173-174, note, 23.

[60] We read the θεωρεῖτε of Jn 14,19 as a futuristic present. See, *BDF*, 323. It refers here to a "seeing" in the immediate future, which initiates a continual process of "seeing" throughout a prolonged future period.

[61] However, the verb θεωρέω by no means excludes physical vision (cf. Jn 2,23; 6,2.19; 7,3; 10,12). See, E. A. Abbott *Johannine Vocabulary* (London, 1905), n. 1598.

[62] For a study of the relationship between faith and knowledge in John, see, I DE LA POTTERIE, Ὄιδα et γινώσκω. Les deux modes de la connaissance dans le quatrième évangile", *Bib* 40 (1959) 709-725, especially, 720, note, 1.

[63] B. F. WESTCOTT rightly explained this phrase with reference to the action of the Spirit, who manifests Christ. See, *op. cit.* 207.

context as the one who loves Jesus (ὁ (δὲ) ἀγαπῶν με(2x), Jn 14,21). Even the disciples themselves understood that this theophany was promised to them as believers in contrast to the "world" (κόσμος, emphatic, Jn 14,22). It is an epiphany of the Father's love in Jesus.[64] This is skilfully indicated by the variation in form from the passive to the active (ἀγαπηθήσεται/ἀγαπήσω, Jn 14,21). Moreover, the vocabulary designates this theophany as the eschatological intervention of Jesus (ἔτι μικρόν, Jn 14,19; comp. Jn 13,33 ... ἐν ἐκείνῃ τῇ ἡμέρᾳ, Jn 14,20).[65] The ἔρχομαι of Jn 14,18 understood by the disciples in line with the Jewish eschatological expectations of a glorious intervention of Jesus at the end of time (as the ἔρχομαι of Jn 14,3 was also understood in Jn 14,8) is to be understood in a deeper spiritual sense with reference to the "coming" of the risen Jesus working through the inner revealing action of the Spirit of truth engendering faith in the believer.

However, the "coming" cannot be confined to the visible "coming" of the risen Jesus with the gift of the Spirit in the immediate future at the resurrection (cf. Jn 20,22). The ἔρχομαι of Jn 14,18 is a futuristic present.[66] It refers to a future "coming", specified as immediate in Jn 14,19.[67] But it also refers to a whole process of "coming", which this immediate future "coming" will initiate. Jesus promises by his "coming" not to leave his disciples orphans. His "coming", then, can hardly be confined to transient interventions of the risen Jesus. So, too, there is no reason to confine the verb ἐμφανίσω to the resurrection appearances (Jn 14,21).[68] As a simple future it also fits an event which repeats itself. A continual process of "coming" is thus intended, ushered in by an immediate future "coming" of the risen Jesus, with the inner enlightening action of the Spirit.

But this "coming" of Jn 14,18 also implies something more. Jesus does not reply directly to the question of Judas in Jn 14,22 which voices

---

[64] C. H. Dodd is thus quite correct when he explains that this epiphany is essentially an epiphany of love, and not an outward manifestation, after the manner of popular eschatological expectations. See, op. cit. (n. 19), 405-406.

[65] See, ch. I, ns. 44. 45.

[66] See, BDF, 323.

[67] C. Traets provides extensive arguments in favour of interpreting the ἔρχομαι of Jn 14,18 with reference to the resurrection appearances. See, op. cit. (n. 59) 173-176.

[68] The manner of the manifestation is not made clear in this verse. The verb as such may refer either to the resurrection appearances, or a spiritual revelation of Jesus, or the final appearance of Jesus in glory; or even to all three at the same time. See, C. K. Barrett, op. cit 388. The verb is well suited, then, to designate the immediate future intervention of the risen Jesus at the resurrection appearances (Jn 14,18), with the gift of the Spirit (Jn 14,16-17), which inaugurates a continual process of intervention by the risen Jesus with the gift of the Spirit in anticipation of the final manifestation of the risen Jesus at the Parousia.

his misunderstanding. We have seen that this is conscious literary technique. The answer of Jesus seems to ignore the question. But in fact Jesus does reply at a deeper spiritual level of meaning. The ἐλευσόμεθα of Jn 14,23 takes up again the ἔρχομαι of Jn 14,18. Jesus explains further the implications of this ἔρχομαι: he will come with the Father to dwell permanently in the believer (ἐλευσόμεθα καὶ μονὴν παρ' αὐτῷ ποιησόμεθα, Jn 14,23). The "coming" of the risen Jesus with the enlightening action of the Spirit within the hearts of believers will also be accompanied by the inner abiding of Jesus with his Father in the believer.[69] This "coming" of the risen Jesus is not only self-revealing through the working of the Spirit (ἐμφανίσω αὐτῷ ἐμαυτόν, Jn 14,21), but also self-communicating (comp. Jn 17,26). It establishes a permanent link or union between Jesus (with the Father) and the believer.

The material (or physical) understanding (or misunderstanding) of the "coming" by Judas (Jn 14,22) in traditional Jewish eschatological terms is thus to be interpreted further in a deep spiritual sense with reference to a whole process of the "coming" of the risen Jesus inseparably linked with the inner revealing activity of the Spirit and an indwelling of Jesus with the Father in the believer, which is all initiated by the immediate future intervention of the risen Jesus at the resurrection. This is the meaning which the ἔρχομαι of Jn 14,2-3 takes on when it is taken up again in its immediate context in Jn 14,18 and interpreted in a deep spiritual sense as the eschatological event by contrast with the material understanding (or misunderstanding) of the disciples.

(c) Epilogue (Jn 14,25-31)

This monologue of Jesus fittingly concludes the discourse. It forms a unity in itself. This is achieved by an adroit use of link-terms. The phrase ταῦτα λελάληκα (Jn 14,25) aptly introduces a conclusion to the discourse (comp. Jn 15,11; 16,1.4.6.25.33). The ταῦτα sums up everything that Jesus has spoken to them.[70] By contrast (δέ, adversative, Jn 14,26), the role of the Paraclete is described (παράκλητος). His task is revelatory (διδάσκω/ὑπομιμνήσκω) like that of Jesus (λαλέω); and is also centered entirely on the words of Jesus (πάντα ἃ εἶπον ὑμῖν ἐγώ).[71]

---

[69] X. LÉON-DUFOUR comments perceptively on Jn 14,23: "The pattern of an outward process, assumed by seeing and even by hearing, is replaced by that of 'making our home'", see, *Resurrection and the Message of Easter* (London, 1974), 234.

[70] The parallel with the same phrase in Jn 16,33, which concludes the second farewell discourse, is most striking. See, R. E. BROWN, *op. cit.* 650.

[71] The role of the Paraclete in relation to Jesus is well treated by I. DE LA POTTERIE. See, *op. cit.* (n. 35), 85-105.

No new theme is introduced in this conclusion. The dialogue is finally ended. The repetition of one important phrase and several terms link the conclusion back to the discourse proper. There is an unmistakable parallel in the phrase:

Jn 14,1a: μὴ ταρασσέσθω ὑμῶν ἡ καρδία.

Jn 14,27: μὴ ταρασσέσθω ὑμῶν ἡ καρδία μηδὲ δειλιάτω.

So, too, several link-terms take up again and fuse together various strands of the discourse:

λαλέω	: Jn 14,25.30; comp. 14,10
παράκλητος	: Jn 14,26; comp. 14,16
ἐν τῷ ὀνόματί μου	: Jn 14,26; comp. 14,13.14
κόσμος	: Jn 14,27.31; comp. 14,17.19
ἀκούω	: Jn 14,28; comp. 14,24.
ὑπάγω	: Jn 14,28; comp. 13,33.36(2x); 14,4.5
ἔρχομαι	: Jn 14,28.30; comp. 14,3.18
ἀγαπάω	: Jn 14,28.31; comp. 13,34(3x).35; 14,15.21(4x).23.24
πορεύομαι	: Jn 14,28; comp. 14,3.12
πατήρ	: Jn 14,26.28(2x).31(2x); comp. 14,2.6.7.8.9(2x).10(3x).11(2x).12.13.16.20.21.23.24.
πιστεύω	: Jn 14,29; comp. 14,1b(2x).10.11(2x).12

Thus the conclusion (Jn 14,25-31) draws together by way of synthesis the various strands of the discourse, and provides it with an epilogue. By a natural Johannine complement the conclusion to the epilogue is parallel to the beginning (ποιέω Jn 14,31; λαλέω, Jn 14,25; comp. ποιέω/λαλέω, Jn 14,10), and links back with it. The epilogue in itself, then, forms a neatly unified section (Jn 14,25-31).

2. Dramatic Movement

(a) *Advance Movement* [72]

The discourse has a complex movement. This is the result of an adroit use of link-terms. It ensures a progressive linking up of the discourse by a smooth advance movement from the introduction to the end of the dialogue. We may illustrate this as follows:

---

[72] Here we are largely indebted to the structure proposed by C. CHARLIER. See, *op. cit.* (n. 19).

Introduction	where I am going *(ὅπου ἐγὼ ὑπάγω)* you cannot come (ἐλθεῖν).

Dialogue	where are you going? *(ποῦ ὑπάγεις;)*
	 where I am going *(ὅπου ὑπάγω)*
	 you cannot follow me now (οὐ..... νῦν ἀκολουθῆσαι)
	 but you will follow me later (ἀκολουθήσεις δὲ ὕστερον).
	 why can I not follow you now? *(ἀκολουθῆσαι ἄρτι;)* I will
	     lay down my life for you *(τὴν ψυχήν μου ὑπὲρ σοῦ θήσω);*
	 will you lay down your life for me? *(τὴν ψυχήν σου ὑπὲρ*
	     ἐμοῦ θήσεις;)
	 you know the way *(τὴν ὁδόν)*
	 where I am going *(ὅπου ἐγὼ ὑπάγω);*
	 we do not know where you are going *(ποῦ ὑπάγεις);*
	     how can we know the way? *(τὴν ὁδόν)*
	 I am the way *(ὁδός)* ... no one comes to the Father (πρὸς
	     τὸν πατέρα) except by me;
	 if you know me (εἰ ἐγνώκατέ με), you will know my Father
	     also *(τὸν πατέρα μου γνώσεσθε);*
	 from now on you know (the Father) *(γινώσκετε αὐτόν)* and
	     have seen him *(ἑωράκατε);*
	 show us the Father *(δεῖξον ἡμῖν τὸν πατέρα);*
	 so long a time ... and do you not know me? *(οὐκ ἔγνωκάς*
	     με;)
	 he who has seen me has seen the Father also *(ὁ ἑωρακὼς*
	     ἐμὲ ἑώρακεν τὸν πατέρα);
	 I will manifest myself to him *(ἐμφανίσω αὐτῷ ἐμαυτόν);*
	 why will you manifest yourself to us? (ἡμῖν μέλλεις
	     ἐμφανίζειν σεαυτόν;)

This advance movement of the discourse points to our text as a climax. It is achieved by the art of suspense. Two questions are asked:

(i) where are you going? (ὑπάγεις;) (13,36a)

(ii) why can I not follow you now? (οὐ ..ἀκολουθῆσαι ἄρτι;) (13,37a)

To neither of these questions does Jesus reply directly.

He answers as follows:

(i) you cannot follow me now (οὐ... νῦν ἀκολουθῆσαι)
     only later (ὕστερον) (13,36bc).

(ii) you will deny me three times (ἀρνήσῃ με τρίς) (13,38b).

The questions themselves are artfully left in suspense. However, we do find an answer to them, not directly, but at least indirectly in Jn 14,2-3. There the goal of Jesus' journey is indicated implicitly as the Father's house with the many rooms. It is also indicated there implicitly that Jesus will later take his disciples to this same goal, after the preparation.

Even the style itself indicates this advance movement of the discourse as a kind of ascent by a staircase movement to the goal of the Father's house:

a where are you going? (ποῦ ὑπάγεις;)
a′ where I am going (ὅπου ὑπάγω).

b you cannot follow me now (οὐ δύνασαί μοι νῦν ἀκολουθῆσαι).
b′ why can I not follow you now? (οὐ δύναμαί σοι ἀκολουθῆσαι ἄρτι;)

c I will lay down my life for you (τὴν ψυχήν μου ὑπὲρ σοῦ θήσω).
c′ will you lay down your life for me? (τὴν ψυχήν σου ὑπὲρ ἐμου θήσεις;)

This gradual ascending movement is a literary device called "anadiplosis". It is a stylistic quality common in the so-called "Songs of Ascent" (cf. Ps 122 (121)).[73] These "Pilgrim Songs" were in fact meant to provide devotional inspiration to those on pilgrimage to the temple. The use of "anadiplosis", then, would be admirably suited to evoke the theme of the temple, and with it the people of God on pilgrimage to it.

(b) *Reverse Movement*

The discourse also reveals a reverse movement. This, too, is the result of an adroit use of link-terms. It explains the sudden emergence in the discourse of themes already introduced, either explicitly like the themes of "glory" (Jn 13,31-32) and "love" (Jn 13,34-35), or implicitly like the theme of unity in the ὅπου εἰμὶ ἐγώ of Jn 14,2-3. These themes are left suspended, as it were, awaiting development. This reverse movement also highlights in yet another way the significant place of our text within the whole discourse. The following diagram will help to illustrate this:

---

[73] L. SABOURIN explains the device more at length. See, *The Psalms — their Origin and Meaning* (New York, 1974), 10.

The πορεύομαι of Jn 14,12 directs our thoughts back to the last use of πορεύομαι in Jn 14,2-3, where the term is introduced for the first time and repeated twice. There, too, we have a rather unexpected change from ὑπάγω (Jn 13,33.36(2x)) to πορεύομαι (Jn 14,2-3(2x)), with a sudden abrupt return to ὑπάγω in Jn 14,4.5. The Johannine use of both verbs is identical.[74] Hence, the unexpected use of πορεύομαι in Jn 14,2-3(2x) takes on a special significance in the structure of the discourse. The change forms part of the literary technique. The repetition of πορεύομαι in Jn 14,12, then, directs the mind back directly to Jn 14,2-3, which is the only previous use of the verb.

The mind is then directed further back with the introduction of δοξάζω in Jn 14.13 to the same term δοξάζω in Jn 13,31-32. There the term is introduced for the first time and repeated five times. This term has been left suspended, as it were, in the introduction to the discourse awaiting further development.

Later in the discourse a similar reverse movement repeats itself. The ἀγαπάω of Jn 14,15 (comp. also Jn 14,21(4x).23.24) directs our thoughts back to the last previous use of the verb in Jn 13,34-35. There the term is introduced for the first time in the discourse (ἀγαπάω(3x); ἀγάπη) and left suspended awaiting further development. At the same time the ἔρχομαι of Jn 14,18 also directs our thoughts back to the last use of the verb in Jn 14,2-3, where this term is introduced for the first time in the discourse and there left suspended also awaiting further development. It should be noted that this ἔρχομαι introduced for the first time in the discourse at Jn 14,2-3 highlights a complementary aspect of the verb πορεύομαι which is in turn introduced into the discourse for the first time in this same text.

---

[74] See, ch. III, note, 45.

Thus there is a significant reverse movement in the discourse back to Jn 14,2-3 and even further back to Jn 13,31-35. It points to our text as the great turning-point on which the whole discourse pivots. This significant place of Jn 14,2-3 within the movement of the discourse helps us to draw out some of the further implications of our text.

(i) Discipleship [75]

The question "where are you going?" (ποῦ ὑπάγεις) of Jn 13,36a, which introduces the development of the discourse proper (Jn 13,36-14,24), clearly links back with the "where I am going" (ὅπου ἐγὼ ὑπάγω) of Jn 13,33. Peter here wishes to know the goal of Jesus' journey. But Jesus does not reply directly to the question. In typical Johannine fashion he opens up with an indirect reply the deeper spiritual import of his journey for the disciples in the light of his passion-death.

The reply of Jesus is a subtle variation of the phrase which it takes up again from Jn 13,33:

13,33   ὅπου ἐγω ὑπάγω ὑμεῖς οὐ δύνασθε   ἐλθεῖν.

13,36b   ὅπου   ὑπάγω   οὐ δύνασθε μοι νῦν ἀκολουθῆσαι.

A typical verb of discipleship ἀκολουθέω replaces the more neutral ἔρχομαι.[76] It continues the theme of discipleship explicitly evoked previously by the μαθηταί of Jn 13,35. But Jesus also adds the all-important qualification "now" (νῦν). The inability of the disciples is only temporary (νῦν). This is at least implicit in the "now" (νῦν) of Jn 13,36b. It will become explicit in the ὕστερον of Jn 13,36c.

Peter questions further about why he cannot follow Jesus "now" (ἄρτι, Jn 13,37). The emphatic position of this "now" (ἄρτι) indicates that it bears the stress (comp. ἄρτι, Jn 13,33). However, no answer is yet given for this temporary inability of the disciples to "follow" Jesus as his disciples, nor is there any explanation of why they will only follow him later. Moreover, the question about the goal of Jesus' journey which sets the dialogue in motion still remains unanswered.

The verb ἀκολουθέω is taken up from Jn 13,36, where it was twice repeated. We find it again in the second question of Peter (Jn 13,37). Here John clearly wishes to develop the theme of discipleship. But again Jesus does not reply directly to the question. He takes up the phrase ψυχὴν

---

[75] See, note, 43.

[76] The importance of this change from one verb to the other has not passed unnoticed by the commentators. See, I. DE LA POTTERIE, "Je suis la voie, la vérité et la vie (Jn 14,6)", *NRT* 88 (1966) 914.

τίθημι from that question of Peter (Jn 13,37)[77] and opens up with an indirect reply in the form of a further question the deeper spiritual import of "following" Jesus on his journey. This question on the lips of Jesus "will you lay down your life for me?" (Jn 13,38) is an example of Johannine "irony".[78] The question surely suggests a negative answer. Peter will deny Jesus three times (ἀρνήσῃ με τρίς, Jn 13,38; comp. Jn 18,17.25.27). But the answer to the question of Jesus "will you lay down your life for me?" (Jn 13,38) is also positive. The phrase ψυχὴν τίθημι evokes the sacrificial death of Jesus (cf. Jn 10,11.15.17.18; 15,13; comp. I Jn 3,16). In a real profound sense, then, Peter will "lay down his life" for Jesus in death (comp. Jn 21,19).

The unanswered questions of Peter (Jn 13,36.37) now receive a reply, not directly, but indirectly in our text of Jn 14,2-3, which provides a climax to the advance movement of the discourse. The Father's house is where Jesus is going (οἰκία τοῦ πατρός μου). It is the goal of Jesus' journey and the place where Jesus himself also abides permanently (ὅπου εἰμὶ ἐγώ). As such this is also the goal of discipleship. We find confirmation of this in two parallel texts, where the goal of discipleship is described in almost identical terms:

Jn 14,3 :	ὅπου εἰμι ἐγὼ	καὶ ὑμεῖς	ἦτε.
Jn 17,24:	ὅπου εἰμι ἐγὼ	καὶ ἐκεῖνοι	ὦσιν.
Jn 12,26:	ὅπου εἰμι ἐγὼ ἐκεῖ καὶ ὁ διάκονος ὁ ἐμὸς		ἔσται.

So, too, the reason for the temporary inability of the disciples to follow Jesus as his disciples to this same goal now receives an explanation. Jesus must first go by means of his passion-death to prepare a place. Then Jesus will return to take the disciples to the goal of the Father's house and this temporary inability will disappear. The promise of Jesus that his disciples will be able to follow him "later" (ὕστερον) will then be fulfilled, after his passion-death.

(ii) Unity

The text of Jn 14,23 has a special importance for an understanding of our text. There are significant links from that text back to our text of Jn 14,2-3 (μονή/ἔρχομαι).[79] In Jn 14,2-3 the goal promised to the

---

[77] See, ch. I, note, 30.

[78] See, note, 46.

[79] Several commentators have underlined this important link. See, M.-E. BOISMARD, op. cit. (n. 3), 391; R. H. GUNDRY, "'In my Father's house there are many Μοναί' (John, 14,2-3)", ZNW 58 (1967) 69-70; J. M. REESE, op. cit. (n. 19), 324.

disciples is the Father's house with many dwelling-places there to which Jesus will take his disciples on his return, and where Jesus himself also dwells permanently with the Father (ὅπου εἰμὶ ἐγώ). Now in Jn 14,23 Jesus promises to come with the Father to make their dwelling-place in the disciples. In both texts it is the same deep spiritual union which is described. But it is expressed in complementary Johannine terms.

This becomes clear as the theme of unity gradually unfolds in the discourse.[80] We may express this development schematically as follows:

v. 10   ἐγὼ ἐν τῷ πατρὶ
                    καὶ
                    ὁ πατὴρ ἐν ἐμοί
                    ὁ δὲ πατὴρ ὁ ἐν ἐμοὶ μένων.

v. 11   ἐγὼ ἐν τῷ πατρὶ
                    καὶ
                    ὁ πατὴρ ἐν ἐμοί.

v. 20   ἐγὼ ἐν τῷ πατρί μου
                    καὶ ὑμεῖς ἐν ἐμοὶ
                    κἀγὼ ἐν ὑμῖν.

v. 23   μονὴν παρ' αὐτῷ ποιησόμεθα.

The theme of unity is explicitly introduced in Jn 14,10-11. Here it explains the deeper meaning of the "where I am" (ὅπου εἰμὶ ἐγώ) of Jn 14,3 in terms of the spiritual union between Jesus and the Father: "I am in the Father" (ἐγὼ ἐν τῷ πατρί, Jn 14,10.11). But there is a further development of the theme: the Father is also in Jesus (ὁ πατὴρ ἐν ἐμοί, Jn 14,10,11). This complementary aspect of the union receives emphatic expression in the phrase "the Father who abides in me" (ὁ δὲ πατὴρ ὁ ἐν ἐμοὶ μένων). There is nothing in the ὅπου εἰμὶ ἐγώ of Jn 14,3 to even suggest such a development. However, it is the same union between Jesus and the Father indicated by the phrase ὅπου εἰμὶ ἐγώ which is described equivalently in typical Johannine complementary terms in the phrase ἐγὼ ἐν τῷ πατρὶ καὶ ὁ πατὴρ ἐν ἐμοί of Jn 14,10-11 (comp. Jn 10,38; 17,21).

The phrase "I am in the Father" (ἐγὼ ἐν τῷ πατρί) which introduces the theme of unity again in Jn 14,20 links back with Jn 14,10-11. The theme is now developed still further. The disciples are in Jesus "you in me" (ὑμεῖς ἐν ἐμοί). Since it is expressly stated here that the disciples are in Jesus (ὑμεῖς ἐν ἐμοί) and has been already expressly stated that Jesus is in the Father (ἐγὼ ἐν τῷ πατρί, Jn 14,10.11), it can be inferred that the

---

[80] On this theme of unity in the fourth gospel in general, see, J. F. RANDALL, "The Theme of Unity in John: 17,21-23", *ETL* 41 (1965) 373-94; J. L. D'ARAGON, "La notion johannique de l'unité", *ScEcc* 11 (1959) 111-119; C. H. DODD, *op. cit.* (n. 19) 187-200.

disciples are in the Father by being in Jesus. This is the unity which is promised in Jn 14,2-3, when Jesus returns to take the disciples to himself in the Father's house: a unity of the disciples with Jesus in the Father (comp. αὐτοὶ ἐν ἡμῖν ἓν ὦσιν, Jn 17,21).

However, there is still further development of this theme of unity in Jn 14,20: Jesus is also in the disciples (κἀγὼ ἐν ὑμῖν). There is nothing in Jn 14,2-3, nor in Jn 14,10-11, to suggest any such development. But since it has been already expressly stated that the Father is in Jesus (ὁ πατὴρ ἐν ἐμοί, Jn 14,10.11) and now that Jesus is in the disciples (κἀγὼ ἐν ὑμῖν), it can be further inferred that the Father is also in the disciples by being in Jesus (comp. ἐγὼ ἐν αὐτοῖς καὶ σὺ ἐν ἐμοί, Jn 17,23).

Thus the union of the disciples with Jesus (ὑμεῖς ἐν ἐμοί) in union with his Father (ἐγὼ ἐν τῷ πατρί) which is the deep spiritual significance of what is promised in Jn 14,2-3 (as explained in the discourse) may be expressed equivalently in complementary Johannine terms as a union of the Father with Jesus (ὁ πατὴρ ἐν ἐμοί) in the disciples (κἀγὼ ἐν ὑμῖν). These are two correlative and inseparable aspects of the same deep spiritual union. It is precisely the establishment of this union of Jesus with the Father in the disciples which is described as the effect of the "coming" of Jesus (with the Father) in Jn 14,23: "we will come to him and make our dwelling with him". As a result of the taking in Jn 14,2-3 we have an "in-being" of the disciples in Jesus (in union with his Father) and as a result of the "coming" of Jn 14,23 we have an "in-being" of Jesus (with the Father) in the disciples. Hence a mutual or reciprocal μένειν ἐν.

But Jn 14,2-3 and Jn 14,23 also complement each other in yet another way. The activity of Jesus in Jn 14,2-3 is directed solely to the disciples as a group, or to the community which they represent.[81] Jesus will take them to the dwelling-places (μοναί) in the Father's house. In Jn 14,23, however, Jesus will come with the Father to make his dwelling-place (μονή) in every believer. As believers have dwelling-places (μοναί) with the Father in union with Jesus in Jn 14,2-3, so Jesus and the Father have an abiding-place (μονή) in every believer in Jn 14,23. The plural form μοναί of Jn 14,2-3 emphasises the individuality of the places which all believers have with Jesus in the Father. Inversely, the singular of Jn 14,23 emphasises the dwelling-place of the Father with Jesus in each disciple individually.[82] In Jn 14,2-3 the Father becomes the spiritual area where the whole community of believers dwells individually in union with Jesus; in Jn 14,23 each individual believer becomes the spiritual area where the Father dwells in union with Jesus.

---

[81] The representative role of the disciples will be discussed in detail by way of conclusion to this chapter.

[82] This point is well made by R. H. GUNDRY. See, op. cit. (n. 79), 70.

Once this union of Jn 14,23 is established, then the temporary inability of the disciples to follow (ἀκολουθέω) (Jn 13,36bc) Jesus "where I am going" through his passion-death disappears, and the goal of discipleship "where I am" (Jn 14,3) is attained at least initially, although the whole unifying process described in Jn 14,2-3 will only be fully realised in heaven at the end of time. This initial union of Jn 14,23 becomes possible with the immediate future "coming" of the risen Jesus (ἔρχομαι, Jn 14,18) to enlighten the believer by faith which issues in love through the inner working of the Spirit (ἐμφανίσω αὐτῷ ἐμαυτόν, Jn 14,21). It is this enlightening or revealing action of the risen Jesus through the Spirit issuing in love which creates the spiritual area for the indwelling of the Father with Jesus (μονή) in the believer-lover, and sets in motion the whole unifying process of Jn 14,2-3.

3. Structure (Jn 14,1-4) [83]

Here we consider in detail our text of Jn 14,2-3 itself only and the two verses which provide the immediate framework for it. The structure of this section of the discourse is important for an understanding of our text. We find two transitional verses, one preceding our text by way of introduction (Jn 14,1) and the other following it by way of introduction to what follows (Jn 14,4). We will first consider each of these transitional verses in turn, and then the text of Jn 14,2-3 itself.

(a) *Transitional Verses (Jn 14,1.4)*

(i) Jn 14,1a: Encouragement

The first phrase of Jn 14,1 links back with the immediately preceding verse of Jn 13,38. An exhortation not to be troubled is appropriate after the prediction of Peter's betrayal (Jn 13,38b). It is also appropriate at the thought of Jesus' separation from his disciples. This theme dominates the whole preceding section of the discourse (Jn 13,31-38, comp. Jn 16,6). Moreover, the disciples are still uncertain about the goal of Jesus' journey (Jn 13,36) and the reason for their temporary inability to follow him (Jn 13,37).[84] Both of these unanswered questions leave them perplexed. Besides, these words of encouragement serve to anchor the discourse in its concrete historical circumstances.[85]

---

[83] See, note, 19.

[84] This point is well made by O. SCHAEFER, see, *op. cit.* (n. 50), 211.

[85] The first farewell discourse (13,31-14,31) is much more firmly embedded in the context of Jesus' departure than the second one (15,1-16,33), or even the concluding prayer (17,1-26).

But the Johannine use of the verb ταράσσω opens up the possibility of an even deeper meaning. The disciples themselves had seen Jesus "troubled" (ἐταράχθη, Jn 13,21)[86] at the prospect of his own betrayal by Judas who is clearly the tool of Satan (Jn 13,26; comp. 6,70-71). Jesus was also "troubled" at the immediate prospect of his passion-death from which he prays to be saved (τετάρακται, Jn 12,27). So, too, Jesus was "troubled" before the power at work in the death of Lazarus (ἐτάραξεν, Jn 11,33). This is the power of the devil who was a "murderer from the beginning" (Jn 8,44). This "troubling", then, indicates the reaction of Jesus to the hostile power of Satan and death at work in his passion-death. Jesus links the disciples with himself in the last words of the discourse when he goes to meet the Prince of this world in his passion-death (ἐγείρεσθε, ἄγωμεν ἐντεῦθεν, Jn 14,31).[87] So these words of encouragement are also singularly appropriate for the disciples united with Jesus in their conflict with evil (comp. Jn 16,33).

These words of encouragement have a clear parallel in the epilogue of the discourse:[88]

Jn 14,1a: μὴ ταρασσέσθω ὑμῶν ἡ καρδία.

Jn 14,27: μὴ ταρασσέσθω ὑμῶν ἡ καρδία μηδὲ δειλιάτω.

This repetition, with its addition,[89] in the concluding summary of the discourse ties together a whole skein of motives to allay the sorrow of the disciples at their impending separation from Jesus. But it is the verses which follow immediately on our text of Jn 14,2-3 which provide them with their first direct motive for consolation.

(ii) Jn 14,1b: Faith[90]

An exhortation of Jesus to faith in Jn 14,1b follows immediately on Jn 14,1a. It makes explicit the theme of faith already implicit in Jn 13,33.

---

[86] R. SCHNACKENBURG explains the precise meaning of the verb in John. See, "Das Anliegen der Abschiedsrede in Joh. 14", in *Wort Gottes in der Zeit*, (Düsseldorf, 1973), 100, note, 11.

[87] C. H. DODD explains the deep spiritual import of these words. See, *op. cit.* (n. 19) 409.

[88] Some commentators would regard these parallels as an inclusion. See, C. CHARLIER, *op. cit.* (n. 19), 65. In our interpretation of the discourse, however, they do not form an inclusion strictly so called, as they do not begin and end a literary unit.

[89] On the significance of the additional verb, see, ch. III, note, 40.

[90] On the Johannine theme of faith, see, A. VANHOYE, "Notre foi, oeuvre divine d'après le quatrième évangile", *NRT* 86 (1964) 337-354. S. A. PANIMOLLE provides a list of all the Johannine uses of the verb πιστεύω. See, *Il dono della legge e la grazia della verità* (Rome, 1973), 50, note, 101. For an extensive bibliography on the theme of faith in John, see, J. McPOLIN, *The "Name" of the Father and of the Son in the Johannine Writings. An*

Again this phrase also links back with Jn 13,38 which immediately precedes it. Such an additional exhortation to faith is appropriate after the prediction of Peter's failure in a crisis of faith (comp. Jn 16,32; 18,17.25.27). Both phrases in Jn 14,1 run parallel to each other.[91] The latter (positive) one complements the former (negative) one: faith is to replace sorrow at the prospect of separation from Jesus.

The chiastic formation of the phrase is striking.

a πιστεύετε   b εἰς τὸν Θεόν,
                 καὶ
b′ εἰς ἐμὲ   a′ πιστεύετε.

A corresponding relationship between the phrase "believe in God" (πιστεύετε εἰς τὸν Θεόν) and the phrase "believe in me" (εἰς ἐμὲ πιστεύετε) is suggested by the parallelism of the phrases. This parallelism also suggests further a close relationship between the objects of faith, belief in God and belief in Jesus. Elsewhere in the fourth gospel these two objects are identified: believing in God is believing in Jesus (cf. Jn 12,44; comp. Jn 10,30; 14,10-11). The chiastic structure is well adapted to suggest that the Father is the goal of faith through the mediation of Jesus. We interpret the καί of the phrase as ascensive.[92] It marks the gradual ascending movement of the text. It also emphasises the christocentric nature of the phrase: the phrase is directed towards ἐμέ (Jesus) and through the ἐμέ (Jesus) to God. The Johannine use of the proposition εἰς stresses the dynamic movement of the phrase; access to God by faith is a dynamic movement through Jesus as Mediator.[93]

We read πιστεύετε as imperative.[94] A double imperative suits the context best. It seems most natural to take πιστεύετε in this way. The preceding imperative (ταρασσέσθω) suggests that these following verbs should be taken as imperatives also. A sudden change to the indicative would be singularly abrupt. However, we suggest that the evangelist also meant these verbs (πιστεύετε) of Jn 14,1b to be taken as a statement of fact: "you believe in God and you believe also in me". Here and now the disciples believe in God and in Jesus with imperfect faith. However, there

---

Exegetical Study of the Johannine Texts on Onoma with Reference to the Father and the Son (Rome, 1972) 46, note, 36.

[91] M.-J. LAGRANGE is right when he observes: "Le premier verset doit donc être un peu détaché de ce qui suit immédiatement; c'est presque un titre". See, *op. cit.* 392.

[92] On καί ascensive, see, *BDF*, 442,2.

[93] See, I. DE LA POTTERIE, "L'emploi dynamique de 'εἰς' dans saint Jean et ses incidences théologiques", *Bib* 43 (1962) 376.

[94] R. BULTMANN reads the first phrase as a question and the second as a statement: Do you believe in God? Then believe also in me; for you have only to believe in God through me!". See, *op. cit.* 600.

is also a real sense in which the disciples do not yet believe with perfect faith.[95] Hence the imperative is also in place.

This verb πιστεύετε of Jn 14,1b should be further interpreted in the light of its repetition in Jn 14,10-11, with which it forms an inclusion. There the object of faith is clearly indicated as both Jesus and the Father in their intimate unity. Besides, a typical Johannine use of the question also indicates there that the disciples are believers with imperfect faith, but not yet believers with perfect faith. Hence, the need for encouragement with the final imperative πιστεύετε of Jn 14,11. The double repetition of πιστεύετε in Jn 14,11 and its emphatic position at the end reinforces the link back with the πιστεύετε of Jn 14,1. We understand Jn 14,1, then, in the light of Jn 14,10-11 as a statement of the present imperfect faith of the disciples and as an imperative exhorting them to the perfect faith which is foreseen in Jn 14,29 of the epilogue.

This verse of Jn 14,1 is neatly detached from what follows.[96] However, it does suggest a possible interpretation of our text of Jn 14,2-3. The two distinct, but closely related members of this chiasm of Jn 14,1b treat of God and of Jesus respectively. They thus correspond in general to two members of our text of Jn 14,2-3, which treat respectively of what pertains to the Father — his house with many rooms — and what pertains to Jesus — his departure to prepare a place and his return to take the disciples with him. Both of these members of our text, like the members of the chiasm, are also clearly distinct from one another. The correspondence of the two members of the chiasm in Jn 14,1b suggests, then, that a similar link may also exist between the two distinct members of our text, namely, that the way of access to the Father's house with the many rooms is through Jesus. It further suggests that such a journey to the Father's house through Jesus should be interpreted with reference to faith. However, this would have to be interpreted with reference to perfect faith; for the movement of the disciples to the Father's house is only possible after the passion-death of Jesus (ἐὰν πορευθῶ).

One further important link between the chiasm of Jn 14,1b and our text should also be noted. The preposition εἰς in the chiastic verse corresponds to the preposition πρός in our text. In John both prepositions always have a dynamic import.[97] With the movement of the chiastic phrase centered on the person of Jesus and through him on God the gradual and progressive penetration into the mystery of the person of

---

[95] C. K. BARRETT lists three possible combinations: indicative-indicative, imperative-imperative, and indicative-imperative, all of which he considers possible from the context. See, op. cit. 380.

[96] See, note, 91.

[97] See, note, 93.

Jesus by faith is a gradual and progressive penetration into the mystery of God/Father. The clear emphasis on this dynamic aspect in the two parallel members of the chiasm of Jn 14,1b suggests a direct link primarily with the dynamic element of our text. The movement into Jesus and the Father in the chiasm is parallel to the dynamic movement "into Jesus" (πρὸς ἐμαυτόν) where he is in union with his Father (ὅπου εἰμὶ ἐγώ) in Jn 14,3; and the dynamic movement of faith (πιστεύετε) of Jn 14,1b would correspond to the dynamic movement of Jesus taking the disciples in Jn 14,3 (παραλήμψομαι). Both the πιστεύετε and the παραλήψομαι would thus emphasise two complementary and essential aspects of one and the same movement of faith into the mystery of Jesus and through Jesus into God, namely, the movement of the disciples actively penetrating into the mystery of Jesus by faith and their passivity being actually taken by Jesus.

(iii) Jn 14,4: The Way and the Goal

A study of this other transitional verse of Jn 14,4 which immediately succeeds our text is no less revealing. The l.v. has καί.....καί instead of the simple καί.[98] The omission of this second καί, together with the emphatic position of the τὴν ὁδόν, stresses the new idea of "the way", which is now introduced for the first time in the discourse. This prepares us for the shift in emphasis from the goal to "the way" in the subsequent development of the discourse (ὁδός, Jn 14,5.6).

However, the l.v. does clarify the meaning of our text. Jesus assures his disciples that what he has just said in our text indicates to his disciples both (καί) "where he is going" (the goal of his journey or his destiny) and (καί) "the way" to it. This clearly suggests that we interpret where Jesus is going (his goal or destiny) with reference to the Father's house with the many rooms and the way of access to it with reference to the departure of Jesus to prepare a place, his return, and his taking of the disciples to himself.

This evidence of the second transitional verse confirms the evidence of the first that the way of access to the Father's house with the many rooms is through Jesus as Mediator.

(b) Text *(Jn 14,2-3): A Journey to the Father's House*

(i) Division

The way is now prepared for us to consider the structure of our text itself. We distinguish two members, Jn 14,2a and Jn 14,2b-3, as suggested

---

[98] There is considerable evidence for this l.v., so much so that even *GNT* shows hesitancy.

by the transitional verses. The first describes the goal (Jn 14,2a) and the second describes the way (Jn 14,2b-3). The subtleties of Johannine style also provide us with a solid basis in the text itself for this division into two distinct members.

A present perspective dominates the first member. There are existing here and now many rooms in the Father's house (εἰσιν). By contrast a future perspective dominates the second: Jesus will go (πορεύομαι), will return (πάλιν ἔρχομαι)[99], and will take the disciples to himself (παραλήμψομαι ὑμᾶς πρὸς ἐμαυτόν).

Moreover, the first member is static. A static verb "there are" (εἰσιν) describes a house with rooms — something permanent and stable and static. By contrast the second member is dynamic — going (πορεύομαι), returning (πάλιν ἔρχομαι), preparing (ἑτοιμάσαι/ω), and taking the disciples to himself (παραλήμψομαι ὑμᾶς πρὸς ἐμαυτόν).

Finally, there is clearly a definite and well defined aspect to the first member. The house is defined and specific. It is a definite place clearly defined as a certain specific house by the immediate determinations of the definite article (τῇ), the possessive genetive (τοῦ πατρός), and the personal pronoun (μου). This specific house which is referred to in Jn 14,2a is unmistakably the one which belongs to Jesus' Father. By contrast the second member is indefinite and undefined. There is no indication of the manner, the "how" of Jesus' going, preparing, returning, and taking of the disciples to himself. Besides, the τόπος is indefinite, without the article and in the singular. As such it cannot be referred directly either to "the house" in the singular (οἰκία) with the definite article (ἡ), or to the "rooms" in the plural (μοναί).

Thus in the structure of the text the first member must be kept quite distinct from the second member. Only in this way can we avoid the confusion of some exegetes who identify the Father's house with the person of Jesus, without further qualification or clarification.[100] The Father's house exists permanently prior to any mention of the journey of Jesus or of his disciples after the preparation. This goal of Jesus' journey is clearly distinct (and must be distinguished) in some way at least from Jesus himself who is about to make a journey there and also from his disciples whom he will take there with him later.[101]

---

[99] Both of these verbs are futuristic presents.

[100] This confusion we find in R. H. GUNDRY: "Could it be clearer from the context that the first thing we are to think of when reading, 'In my Father's house are many μοναί', is not mansions in the sky, but spiritual positions in Christ". See, *op. cit.* (n. 79), 70. However, this is by no means so. The first and obvious meaning of Jn 14,2-3 is that the Father's house (goal) and Jesus (who journeys to it) are in some way quite distinct.

[101] Again, R. H. GUNDRY fails to make this prior distinction between the Father's house and the disciples when he writes: "the Father's house is no longer heaven, but God's household or family". See, *op. cit.* (note, 79) 70.

(ii) Unity

In our structure of the text, then, its two members are clearly distinct. However, the inner movement of the text also indicates a close unity between them. This was already suggested by the chiastic form of Jn 14,1b. We may illustrate this movement of Jn 14,2-3 schematically as follows:[102]

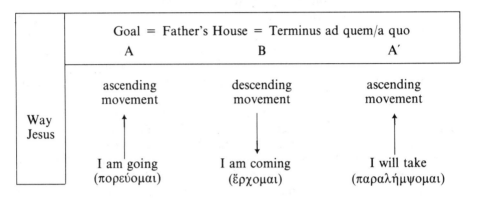

	Goal = Father's House = Terminus ad quem/a quo		
	A	B	A′
Way Jesus	ascending movement ↑ I am going (πορεύομαι)	descending movement ↓ I am coming (ἔρχομαι)	ascending movement ↑ I will take (παραλήμψομαι)

In Jn 14,2-3 we find a great movement of ascent directed entirely towards the goal of the Father's house (A/A′). There is an ascending movement of Jesus alone first through his passion-death (πορεύομαι) (A). This in turn is parallel to the ascending movement of the disciples later with Jesus (παραλήμψομαι) (A′). Both journeys are distinct, the one before (A) and the other after (A′) the passion-death of Jesus is complete. But they are both directed to the same goal of the Father's house. Moreover, the use of concatination (πορεύομαι ἑτοιμάσαι τόπον ὑμῖν......... ἐὰν πορευθῶ καὶ ἑτοιμάσω τόπον ὑμῖν) strongly underlines the absolute necessity of the journey of preparation by Jesus himself alone through his passion-death before his return to take the disciples with him is possible.

However, this ascending movement to the Father's house has a complementary descending movement from the Father's house (ἔρχομαι) (B). This ἔρχομαι is a futuristic present. It indicates a continual process of "coming", in anticipation of an ever future event. The πορεύομαι in turn indicates an action of some duration. Thus we find in Jn 14,2-3 a movement of ascent (A) to the Father's house by Jesus alone through his

---

[102] The ascending/descending movement is implicit in our understanding of the Father's house in Jn 14,2-3 at a second level of meaning as a reference to the heavenly temple. We shall return to this point more in detail in the following chapter, and develop its implications for an understanding of our text and its immediate context.

passion-death, and a perpetual descending (B) and ascending (A´) movement between the Father's house and the disciples after the passion-death is complete. The Jesus of Jn 14,2-3 may be described as on the way by an ascending movement to the Father's house through his passion-death, and after his passion-death as perpetually on his way by a descending movement from the Father's house to the disciples and with them perpetually on his way to the Father's house by an ascending movement after his passion-death. It follows that the risen Jesus, after his passion-death, becomes the mediator of an unbroken exchange between the Father's house and the disciples.

This movement of Jn 14,2-3 is important in order to help us to distinguish what is explicit and what is implicit in our text. Jesus does not say explicitly that he is going to the Father's house, but only that he is going to prepare a place (πορεύομαι, ἑτοιμάσω τόπον ὑμῖν). However, he does say so implicitly: he goes to prepare a place for the disciples (explicit) in the Father's house (implicit). This is indicated by the inner movement of the text. So, too, Jesus does not say explicitly that he will take the disciples with him to the Father's house.[103] Only a reunion of the disciples with Jesus himself personally after the preparation is promised (παραλήμψομαι ὑμᾶς πρὸς ἐμαυτόν). However, the promise of an entrance of the disciples with Jesus into the Father's house is implicit in the text. This, too, is indicated by the inner movement of Jn 14,2-3. Thus the whole inner movement of the text suggests implicitly an important relationship between the Father's house, the preparation of a place for the disciples there, and Jesus himself after the preparation is complete. We will be able to specify this relationship more exactly in our analysis of the text itself.

4. Universal Perspective

There is also one more important aspect of our text which emerges ever more clearly as the discourse unfolds. The activity of Jesus in Jn 14,2-3 is directed solely to the disciples as a group (ὑμῖν (2x) ..... ὑμᾶς ... ὑμεῖς). By a subtle literary technique, however, these same disciples are made to take on a wider and more universal role elsewhere in the discourse. This is achieved in several ways.

---

[103] R. H. GUNDRY regards this peculiar feature of our text as the clue to its deeper meaning: "The most striking feature of the passage — one that holds the clue to a deeper and truer understanding of it — is that Jesus does not promise that upon his return he will take his disciples to the "rooms" or "mansions" (AV, ASV) in the "Father's house". See, op. cit. (note, 79) 69.

It is a curious feature of the farewell discourses (Jn 13,1-17,26) that the role of the individual disciple disappears entirely in the second parallel discourse (Jn 15,1-16,33).[104] So, too, there is a significant transition from the singular to the plural in our discourse (ἀρνήσῃ, Jn 13,38.. μὴ ταρασσέσθω ὑμῶν ἡ καρδία..πιστεύετε..ὑμῖν, Jn 14,1), and from the plural to the singular and back again to the plural (δεῖξον ἡμῖν.... Jn 14,8..οὐ πιστεύεις, Jn 14,10 ..πιστεύετε, Jn 14,11). The individual disciple is clearly meant to represent the group.[105]

More significant still is the feature of the discourse whereby Jesus gradually and almost imperceptibly moves from addressing all the disciples, either as a group or through an individual, to a more general, indefinite and universal mode of address. We find striking examples of this in John's repeated use of the so-called definition-sentence and the indefinite clause.

These definition-sentences punctuate the discourse (ὁ ἑωρακώς, Jn 14,9; ... ὁ πιστεύων, Jn 14,12 ... ὁ ἔχων...καὶ τηρῶν....ὁ ἀγαπῶν......ὁ ἀγαπῶν, Jn 14,21.. ὁ μὴ ἀγαπῶν.......... Jn 14,24). Here we have a statement, such as a definition, which applies to all cases in a particular category which it defines, without reservation. Hence, the universal, general and all-embracing nature of the phrase.

The indefinite clause is less common. However, there is one example in the discourse of the use of the indefinite τις. It is found in the direct answer of Jesus to Judas. This disciple is addressed by Jesus in the singular (εἶπεν αὐτῷ, Jn 14,22), and still the statement of Jesus is a general (universal) condition in the (atemporal) present referring to anyone whatsoever who loves Jesus: "if anyone loves me (ἐὰν τις ἀγαπᾷ με)" (Jn 14,23).[106]

The alternative use of the two expressions in the two parallel clauses, positive in Jn 14,23 and negative in Jn 14,24, show how closely, if not entirely identical, the indefinite clause (Jn 14,23) and the so-called definition-clause (Jn 14,24) are as indefinite, general and all embracing statements of the truth.

The use of the indefinite οὐδείς in Jn 14,6b is no less significant. The validity of the οὐδείς is not restricted to the circle of the disciples who are addressed. We do not find οὐδεὶς ἐξ ὑμῶν, as we might expect. We find οὐδείς simply. It has a general and universal application.[107]

---

[104] C. H. Dodd thus attempts to fit chapters 14-16 under the general pattern of "dialogue giving place to monologue". See, op. cit. (n. 19), 400.

[105] It is by no means foreign to Jewish thought that a group should be represented by an individual in this way. See, H. Robinson, "The Hebrew Conception of Corporate Personality", in Werden und Wesen des A.Ts (Berlin, 1936) 49-62.

[106] M. Zerwick explains Jn 14,23 in this way. See, Biblical Greek (Rome, 1963), note, 325.

[107] W. B. Michaelis makes precisely the same point. See, TDNT, V, 80.

The representative role of the disciples is also underlined by the repeated contrast between them and the world (κόσμος) in the discourse (Jn 14,17.19.22). The term κόσμος has different meanings in the discourse. It is used of mankind in general in need of God's saving love (Jn 14,31; comp. πάντες, Jn 13,35). But it is used here in opposition to the disciples in its fully negative sense of that "world" which is represented by all those who deliberately refuse to believe (comp. Jn 15,22-24). The disciples by contrast would represent all believers.

We find that the activity of the disciples in the discourse is defined dominantly in terms of believing (Jn 14,1.10.12.29) and of loving (Jn 13,34-35; 14,15.21.23.24.28). As a group, then, they are meant to represent all those who believe in Jesus and love him — a universal community of faith and love.

CONCLUSION

We have provided arguments to support the longer reading ἐν τῇ οἰκίᾳ τοῦ πατρός μου μοναὶ πολλαί εἰσιν for our text, and with it the inclusion of ὅτι. Moreover, it would seem best to take the phrase εἰ δὲ μή, εἶπον ἄν ὑμῖν ὅτι as a question. A self-quotation of this kind is in the manner of John's style.

Our text of Jn 14,2-3 is firmly embedded in the general context of the so-called farewell discourses (Jn 13,1-17,26). These explain in anticipation the meaning of Christ's passion-resurrection. However, the more immediate context of our text is the first farewell discourse (Jn 13,31-14,31); and this in turn is clearly distinct from the second farewell discourse (Jn 15,1-16,33).

John's use of dialogue helps us to isolate further three large sections within the first discourse (Jn 13,31-35; 13,36-14,24; 14,25-31). The question is an integral part of this dialogue. John uses it to keep open throughout the discourse a second deeper level of understanding. Intimately linked in turn with the question is the Johannine theme of misunderstanding. This helps to confirm our interpretation of the text at a first level of meaning, as the disciples understood it in a literal sense. But it also helps us to determine, by John's correction of this same misunderstanding, the deeper spiritual import of our text.

At this deeper level of meaning the "journey" of Jn 14,2-3 refers to the passion-resurrection of Jesus as an eschatological event, and the "coming" of Jesus there is open to interpretation with reference to every possible intervention of the risen Jesus to take believers to himself, as part of that same eschatological event. This "coming" of Jn 14,2-3, however, is taken up again in the development of the discourse (Jn 14,18) and reinterpreted with reference to an immediate intervention of the risen Jesus at the resurrection (Jn 14,18). This in turn sets in motion a whole process of his "coming", with the gift of the revealing Spirit and an indwelling of Jesus (with the Father) in the believer (Jn 14,23).

A complex movement in the discourse highlights the significance of our text. The advance movement points to our text as a climax, where the first two unanswered questions of Peter (Jn 13,36.37) are finally resolved, not directly, but indirectly: the goal of Jesus' journey is the Father's house with the many rooms, which is also the goal of discipleship; and the disciples will be able to follow Jesus there later, when Jesus first prepares a place for them and then returns to take them to it.

The reverse movement explains the emergence in the discourse of themes already introduced, but left suspended, as it were, awaiting development. The union of the disciples with Jesus in the Father "where I am" described in Jn 14,2-3 is complemented perfectly in reciprocal Johannine terms by the union described in Jn 14,23. It is this union of Jn 14,23 in the believer which initiates in time the whole unifying process of Jn 14,2-3 in anticipation of the final union in the heavenly temple of the Father's house at the end of time. Once this union of Jn 14,23 has been established the temporary inability of the disciples to follow Jesus "where I am going" through his passion-death in Jn 13,36 disappears; and the goal of discipleship "where I am" in Jn 14,2-3 is initially, if not yet fully, attained.

The structure of Jn 14,1-4 also helps us to a better understanding of our text. The chiasm of Jn 14,1b suggests that the dynamic activity of Jesus, who will take the disciples to himself in Jn 14,2-3, should be interpreted with reference to the dynamic movement of faith which this first transitional verse describes, the one movement complementing the other. Moreover, the first transitional verse (Jn 14,1b) and the second (Jn 14,4) both seem to suggest that the way of access to the goal of the Father's house with the many rooms in Jn 14,2-3 is through Jesus as Mediator.

Finally, the structure of our text itself (Jn 14,2-3) reveals two distinct members (Jn 14,2a; 14,2b-3), the first describes the goal (Jn 14,2a) and the second the way (Jn 14,2b-3). But the inner movement of the text indicates a close unity between them. This in turn enables us to distinguish clearly what is implicit and what is explicit in the text: Jesus goes to prepare a place for the disciples (explicit) in the Father's house (implicit) and will return to take the disciples to himself (explicit) in the Father's house (implicit). Moreover, the disciples themselves in our text and in the discourse as a whole take on a universal role as representatives of the Christian community. All of this is important for our interpretation of Jn 14,2-3 at a second deeper level of meaning. To this we now turn our attention in greater detail.

CHAPTER VI

A SECOND LEVEL OF MEANING

We have seen the limitations of our initial interpretation of the text of Jn 14,2-3.[1] However, we distinguish two levels of meaning in our text.[2] So we must now see if its anomalies can be satisfactorily resolved at a second deeper level of understanding. This deeper level of meaning only emerges in the light of the glorifying passion of Jesus. In a literary sense, it becomes clear when the account of the passion-resurrection of Jesus has been read; and the gospel is then reread in the light of this conclusion.

A. THE FATHER'S HOUSE WITH THE MANY ROOMS

1. Double Meaning of οἰκία

(a) οἶκος. At this second level of meaning there is no doubt that the Father's house refers to the heavenly temple, not the Jerusalem temple; for Jesus travels there through his passion-death (πορεύομαι). If this is so, then it is hardly surprising that the term οἰκία is used instead of the more common LXX term for the Jerusalem temple οἶκος. Neither is there anything in the Johannine use of the term οἶκος which renders it more apt than οἰκία to designate a heavenly temple, or dwelling-place.

Both terms οἶκος (Jn 2,16(2x).17; 7,53 (l.v.); 11,20) and οἰκία (Jn 4,53; 8,35; 11,31; 12,3; 14,2) occur in the fourth gospel. The term οἶκος is used with explicit reference to the Jerusalem temple (Jn 2,16(2x).17). However, it must be remembered that Jn 2,16 is an implicit reference to Zechariah, 14,21: καὶ οὐκ ἔσται Χαναναῖος οὐκέτι ἐν τῷ οἴκῳ κυρίου παντοκράτορος ἐν τῇ ἡμέρᾳ ἐκείνῃ, and the evangelist himself refers explicitly in Jn 2,17 to Ps 69(68), 9(10): ὁ ζῆλος τοῦ οἴκου σου κατέφαγέν (καταφάγεταί, in John) με.[3] To some extent, then, John was confined in

---

[1] See, ch. I, pp. 43-45.

[2] We have explained this distinction of levels of meaning at length in the outline of our method. See, Introduction, pp. 24-26.

[3] Scholars in general admit this implicit reference to Ze 14,21. R. BULTMANN is a notable exception. See, op. cit. 124, n. 1.

his choice of the term οἶκος to designate the Jerusalem temple. That leaves only one further clear use of the term οἶκος in Jn 11,20.[4] There it refers to an earthly "house" in its primary sense of a material building or dwelling-place, where Mary stays while Martha in contrast goes to meet Jesus.[5]

Accordingly, in Johannine usage the term οἶκος is always used of an earthly house, once in the literal sense of a building or dwelling-place (Jn 11,20) and three times in a metaphorical sense with reference to the Jerusalem temple, twice to designate it as "a house of God" (Jn 2,16.17) and once as "a house of market" (Jn 2,16). There is no compelling reason why John should use the term οἶκος again to designate a heavenly temple in Jn 14,2-3.

(b) οἰκία. However, there is little obvious difference (in our view) between the use of οἶκος in Jn 11,20 and the use of οἰκία in Jn 11,31:

Jn 11,20: Μαριὰμ δὲ ἐν τῷ οἴκῳ ἐκαθέζετο.

Jn 11,31: οἱ οὖν Ἰουδαῖοι οἱ ὄντες μετ' αὐτῆς ἐν τῇ οἰκίᾳ.

These texts seem to point to an alternative use of the terms οἶκος and οἰκία in the literal (material) sense of a building, or dwelling-place. Certainly, the use of the term οἰκία in John does seem to have predominantly the meaning "family". This is clearly the case in Jn 4,53 and Jn 8,35. But the use of οἰκία in Jn 11,31 and Jn 12,3 does not seem to convey necessarily the meaning "family", and by no means necessarily excludes the primary meaning of a building as a dwelling-place. The fragrance of the ointment which filled the "house" (οἰκία) in Jn 12,3 does not seem to signify, even primarily, the "family" or "household", but rather the "house" itself, or the whole material building. So, too, the text of Jn 11,31, especially if compared with Jn 11,20, argues rather to the meaning of the house (οἰκία) as a material building, not as a family. The carefully nuanced statement of J. O. Tuñi-Vancells seems to correspond exactly to the Johannine usage: "Juan emplea en otra occasión la palabra οἰκία en el sentido de familia, *más que* en sentido de edificio".[6]

Thus there is no reason to definitely exclude the meaning of a building, whether it be understood literally of a material house (where people dwell) or metaphorically of a house (where God dwells), from the οἰκία of Jn 14,2-3, and to conclude that it must necessarily (and solely)

---

[4] The use of the term in Jn 7,53 is a l.v., without any considerable manuscript evidence.

[5] I. DE LA POTTERIE rightly observes that the infrequent use of the term οἶκος in John always has a material sense. See, *La vérité dans saint Jean* (Rome, 1977) 860, also, n. 249.

[6] See, *La verdad os hará libres, Jn. 8,32. Liberación y libertad del creyente en el cuarto evangelio* (Barcelona, 1973) 182, also n. 113.

designate a "family" or "household".[7] Moreover, the Johannine usage of οἰκία seems to be better adapted to take on a double meaning of "house" understood as a building or dwelling-place (Jn 11,31; 12,3), whether it be in the transferred sense of a "temple" (where God dwells) or of a "family" and "household" (Jn 4,53; 8,35) (where God may also be said to dwell).

Finally, it should be noted also that had John used the term οἶκος in Jn 14,2a the reference to the Father's house would much more readily have been understood of the Jerusalem temple only. All the more so with the definite article. The only other use of the phrase "the house of my Father" with the term οἶκος (and the definite article) in the fourth gospel to designate a specific place is with reference to the Jerusalem temple (Jn 2,16-17). The use of οἶκος in Jn 14,2a would have this one immediate and direct meaning. There would, then, be less justification for the confusion of Jn 14,5.

2. The Family of God: Jn 8,35

(a) LINKS WITH JN 14,2-3. This text of Jn 8,35 would seem to have a special importance for an understanding of Jn 14,2-3. There are significant links between both of these texts.[8] The phrase ἐν τῇ οἰκίᾳ is identical in both texts. The verb μένω in Jn 8,35(2x) corresponds to the term μονή (which derives from the verb μένω) in Jn 14,2-3. Moreover, there is the same inner relationship in both texts between the verb μένω (Jn 8,35)(2x)) and the noun μονή (Jn 14,2a) with the phrase ἐν τῇ οἰκίᾳ.[9] In both cases the preposition indicates a relationship of abiding "in" the house. Finally, we have a filial relationship expressed in both texts. It is explicit in Jn 8,35 (ὁ υἱός) and implicit in Jn 14,2a (τοῦ πατρός μου).

No less significant are the links between both contexts. Jn 13,33 evokes directly Jn 7,33-34 and Jn 8,21-22 in the immediate context of Jn 8,35.[10] Moreover, both contexts are dominated by the theme of discipleship, explicit in the term μαθητής (Jn 8,31; 13,35), and developed in terms of following Jesus by faith (πιστεύω, Jn 8,30.31; comp. 8,24.45.46; 14,1(2x).10-11(3x).12.29). All these striking verbal and thematic links seem to indicate that the evangelist designedly frames the text of Jn 14,2-3 in order to recall Jn 8,35, and with it the whole immediate context.

---

[7] We regard such an exclusion by R. H. GUNDRY of any reference to a building in the οἰκία of Jn 14,2-3 as a limitation in his exegesis. See, " 'In my Father's house there are many Μοναί' (John, 14,2-3)", *ZNW* 58 (1967) 68-72.

[8] The link between Jn 14,2-3 and Jn 8,35 has been underlined to great effect by several commentators. R. BULTMANN, however, rejects any such link. See, *op. cit.* 440, n. 2.

[9] O. SCHAEFER expresses this relationship well. See, "Der Sinn der Rede Jesu von den vielen Wohnungen in seines Vaters Hause und von dem Weg zu ihm (Joh. 14,2-3)", *ZNW 32 (1933) 213.*

[10] See, ch. V, pp. 146-149.

(b) STRUCTURE OF JN 8,31-36. There appears to be a rather abrupt transition in the immediate context of Jn 8,35 from the theme of liberty (Jn 8,32.33.36) to that of permanence in the household (Jn 8,35).[11] A glance at the general structure of Jn 8,31-36 will help to clarify.[12]

8,31	a	..ἀληθῶς μαθηταί μού ἐστε..
8,32	b	καὶ ἡ ἀλήθεια ἐλευθερώσει ὑμᾶς..
8,33b	c	..οὐδενὶ δεδουλεύκαμεν πώποτε·
8,33c	d	πῶς σὺ λέγεις ὅτι ἐλεύθεροι γενήσεσθε;
8,34	c′	..πᾶς ὁ ποιῶν τὴν ἁμαρτίαν δοῦλός ἐστιν.......
8,35b		..ὁ υἱὸς μένει εἰς τὸν αἰῶνα.
8,36a	b′	ἐαν οὖν ὁ υἱὸς ὑμᾶς ἐλευθερώσῃ,
8,36b	a′	ὄντως ἐλεύθεροι ἔσεσθε.

Here we have a concentric structure. At the centre (d) lies an open question: "how" to become free? The whole pericope pivots around this question and provides an answer to it in a movement forward (Jn 8,31-33b), and backward (Jn 8,34-36). There is a striking opposition between "slavery" (cc′) and "freedom" (bb′). It is a question, then, of liberation from slavery. But here we are dealing with the spiritual sense of slavery. It is freedom from the slavery of "sin", or "unbelief".[13] Such a liberation from "sin" is the negative aspect of "freedom". The parallel between Jn 8,31 (a) and Jn 8,36b (a′) indicates the true disciple of Jesus as the one who is truly free. The other parallel between Jn 8,32 (b) and Jn 8,36a (b′) designates the means by which this freedom is rendered possible. It is the work of "the Son" (b′), and of "the truth" (b). In contrast to the slave of sin, then, the disciple of Jesus is the one who is truly set free from the sin of unbelief by the intervention of Jesus. In a word, the believer (in contrast to the slave) is the disciple of Jesus, who is truly free.

(c) TEXT OF JN 8,35. The text of Jn 8,35 has only a secondary role within this structure. It is not related directly to the central question on "freedom" (d), except indirectly through the condition of "the slave", which is opposed to "freedom" (Jn 8,32-33b.34-36a) and to the condition of the son (Jn 8,35b). The text itself is built on a contrast in antithetical parallelism. Only the first member contains the words ἐν τῇ οἰκίᾳ (Jn 8,35a), but it is implicit in the second member also (Jn 8,35b):

---

[11] I. DE LA POTTERIE draws attention to this awkward twist in the pericope. See, op. cit. (n. 5) 859. 826.

[12] We are indebted to I. DE LA POTTERIE for this basic structure. See, op. cit. (n. 5) 827.

[13] It is clear from the immediate context that we are dealing with the sin of unbelief (cf. 8,24.37.47; comp. 9,41).

8,35a ὁ δὲ δοῦλος οὐ μένει ἐν τῇ οἰκίᾳ εἰς τὸν αἰῶνα.

8,35b ὁ υἱὸς   μένει (   ) εἰς τὸν αἰῶνα.

The imagery of Jn 8,35 seems to be drawn from the social scene:[14] a slave is not a permanent member of the household; a son is a permanent member. The two figures are contrasted in respect of a single characteristic: permanence as a member of the household. Behind the metaphor, however, lies a deeper spiritual sense. This is already suggested by the contrast between the slave (Jn 8,34c; 8,35a) and the son (Jn 8,35b). So, too, the additional words: εἰς τὸν αἰῶνα indicate a deeper spiritual meaning.[15] They are not on the level of imagery and metaphor. It is no longer a question merely of a son who abides momentarily in a temporal household or family. The phrase "the Son abides forever" affirmed of Jesus would indicate his profound personal union with the Father as God's Son (cf. Jn 10,30.38). The metaphor indicates directly this deeper spiritual reality of a filial relationship with God, expressed in terms of indwelling.[16]

The text of Jn 8,35 itself expresses a general truth. However, it is no simple comparison. It is an allegory.[17] In the second member of the text "the Son" (ὁ υἱός) applies directly to Jesus (Jn 8,35b).[18] It is closely linked by οὖν with the following verse (Jn 8,36):[19] the Son who abides permanently in the household (Jn 8,35b) is the Son who sets free. It is from his permanent union with the Father as the Son that the capacity of Jesus to free others derives.[20]

---

[14] C. H. Dodd writes: "we have a true parable, drawing attention to a familiar feature of the social scene". See, *Historical Tradition in the Fourth Gospel* (Cambridge, 1963) 381.

[15] This has been well expressed by C. H. Dodd who says that the phrase "lends itself to the theological (allegorical) interpretation of the parable, but in itself it need not mean more than 'perpetually', 'permanently'". See, *op. cit.* (n. 14) 381. I. de la Potterie writes in a similar vein. See, *op. cit.* (n. 5) 859.

[16] R. Laurentin makes precisely this point. See, *Jésus au temple. Mystère de Pâques et foi de Marie en Luc 2,48-50* (Paris, 1966) 130.

[17] A point well made by A. Loisy. See, *op. cit.* 569-570.

[18] The Christological interpretation is generally accepted by the commentators. See, C. H. Dodd, *op. cit.* (n. 14) 380; O. Schaefer, *op. cit.* (n. 9) 210; R. Bultmann, *op. cit.* 440.

[19] John uses this favourite link-word to indicate that what follows is closely connected with what has immediately preceded. The conjunction οὖν occurs 194x in the fourth gospel. See, *BDF* 451,1, and especially E. A. Abbott, *Johannine Grammar* (London, 1906), 2191-2200; F. Zorell *Lexicon Graecum Novi Testamenti* (Parisiis, 1961) Co. 957, n. 2a.

[20] W. Grundmann expresses our conclusion for us well: "Die Freiheit aber ist ..... die Öffnung des Vaterhauses zum Bleiben in him durch den Sohn (8,30-36)". See, *Zeugnis und Gestalt des Johannesevangeliums* (Stuttgart, 1960) 48.

(d) CONTEXT OF JN 8,35. The verb μένω occurs twice in Jn 8,35. This repetition in itself stresses its importance (comp. Jn 1,38.39(2x)).[21] Moreover, this verb also occurs in the immediate context in a similar turn of phrase (Jn 8,31):

Jn 8,31   ἐὰν ὑμεῖς   μείνητε ἐν τῷ λόγῳ τῷ ἐμῷ.

Jn 8,35   .... οὐ μένει   ἐν τῇ οἰκίᾳ.[22]

Only in a spiritual sense is it possible "to abide in the word" of Jesus (Jn 8,31; comp. 5,38). The verb μένω in Jn 8,35 takes on this same deep spiritual import. It is used in this deep spiritual sense elsewhere in John to describe the permanence of a deep spiritual relationship of communion between Jesus and the Father (Jn 14,10), and the disciple and Jesus (Jn 15,4(2x).5.6.7.9.10(2x); comp. 6,56; I Jn 2,24).[23]

So, too, the preposition ἐν used repeatedly in John to designate this relationship of in-dwelling describes alternatively both the Father and the Son as the "milieu" in which the other person dwells permanently (Jn 10,38; 14,10-11.20). It also designates the "milieu" in which the Christian moves: the believer "walks" in the truth (2 Jn 4; 3 Jn 3), in the commandments of Jesus (1 Jn 4,6); as the fruit-bearing branch dwells "in" (ἐν) the vine (closely united to it) so the believer dwells in Christ, in his love (Jn 15,9.10; cf. 1 Jn 4,16), in the word (Jn 8,31), in his teaching (2 Jn 9). These are just so many ways of expressing the deep spiritual reality of "Johannine space". It is in this deeper spiritual sense that we understand the οἰκία of Jn 8,35 — the inner spiritual "space" where the believer as a son abides in union with Jesus in his intimate personal union with the Father.

Finally, in the immediate context of Jn 8,35 we also find the phrase παρὰ τῷ πατρί to describe what Jesus has seen "in the company of the Father" (Jn 8,38; comp. Jn 17,5(2x)). The phrase underlines the intimacy of the personal relationship.[24] The proximity of the phrase to Jn 8,35 is hardly accidental.[25] It would seem to suggest that the phrase ἐν τῇ οἰκίᾳ

---

[21] A similar repetition of the same verb in Jn 1,38-39 also has a deep import. See, R. BOHEN, "The Fourth Gospel as Dramatic Material", *JBL* 49 (1930) 300.

[22] For a more detailed consideration of these two texts, see I. DE LA POTTERIE, *op. cit.* (n. 5) 863.

[23] See, ch. I, ns. 15. 16.

[24] On παρά with the dative meaning "nigh, near, beside... And not just immediate proximity (Lk. 9,47....). On the other hand, "in someone's home" (Lk 19,7; Jn 1,40; A. 10,6) or with a group of people (Rev. 2,13)". See, *BDF, n. 238.*

[25] I. DE LA POTTERIE expresses it thus: "Le rapprochement entre le v. 35 et le v. 38 s'impose: ἐν τῇ οἰκίᾳ τοῦ πατρός, dans le contexte, peut et doit se comprendre au sens de παρὰ τῷ πατρί". See, *op. cit.* (n. 5) 861.

of Jn 8,35 should be interpreted in this same sense of παρὰ τῷ πατρί.[26] This in turn would support our understanding of Jn 8,35 in a spiritual sense of personal intimacy with the Father.

(e) APPLICATION TO JN 14,2-3.

(i) *Similarities.* In our interpretation of Jn 8,35 within its immediate context the phrase ὁ υἱὸς μένει (ἐν τῇ οἰκίᾳ) ἐις τὸν αἰῶνα would correspond to the phrase ὅπου εἰμὶ ἐγώ with reference to Jesus in Jn 14,2-3. This latter phrase refers at least implicitly (or indirectly) to the οἰκία of Jn 14,2-3 as the place "where I am", that is, the house where Jesus (the Son) is or dwells forever permanently in union with his Father. In the immediate context of Jn 14,2-3 this is expressed in the equivalent Johannine terms of ἐγω ἐν τῷ πατρί (μου) (Jn 14,10.11.20).[27] This striking parallel supports an interpretation of the οἰκία of Jn 14,2-3 in line with Jn 8,35 at a deeper level of meaning. Indeed, the several additional links between both texts and contexts seem to suggest further that the evangelist intended such an interpretation. To interpret the οἰκία of Jn 14,2-3 as the inner spiritual "space" where Jesus abides as Son in close personal union with his Father, then, would be at least in line with the deeper spiritual meaning of οἰκία in Jn 8,35, and supported also by the evidence of the immediate context of Jn 14,2-3.

(ii) *Differences.*   Such an application of the spiritual meaning of the οἰκία of Jn 8,35 fits perfectly the present condition of Jesus in Jn 14,2-3. Not so the present condition of the disciples. They are still at a distance from the οἰκία of Jn 14,2-3. However, the οἰκία of Jn 8,35 is for them also as believers the inner spiritual "space", where they too are to dwell as sons united with Jesus in his intimate personal union with the Father. But this is only possible for the disciples of Jn 14,2-3 after the journey of Jesus to prepare a place, and his return to take the disciples to be with him in the οἰκία. Hence, only after the passion-resurrection of Jesus. The full spiritual import of the οἰκία of Jn 8,35 only applies in Jn 14,2-3, when the disciples are reunited with Jesus after the passion-resurrection in his intimate union with the Father.[28] Only then does the οἰκία of Jn 14,2-3 become the inner spiritual "space" where the believers as sons

---

[26] This suggestion is also made by R. LAURENTIN. See, *op. cit.* (n. 16), 130-131.

[27] See, ch. V, pp. 163-166.

[28] The statement of O. SCHAEFER, then, needs to be qualified: "Die allgemeine Wahrheit von 8,35 findet in 14,2a eine spezielle Anwendung". See, *op. cit.* (n. 9) 213. This author fails to take into account the necessity of preparation in Jn 14,2-3. The full spiritual import of οἰκία in Jn 8,35 applies to the οἰκία of Jn 14,2-3 only after the passion-resurrection of Jesus.

actually abide in union with Jesus in his intimate personal union with the Father. In a word, the οἰκία of Jn 14,2-3 can be identified as the community, or the family, or the household of the sons of God united with Jesus in the Father only after the passion-resurrection of Jesus. Prior to the departure and preparation of a place there are possibilities (enough and more than enough) for the disciples to abide spiritually in Jesus. But they have not yet their "spiritual positions" in union with Jesus.[29]

We have already seen that there is considerable patristic evidence for reading παρὰ τῷ πατρί instead of ἐν τῇ οἰκίᾳ τοῦ πατρός.[30] This we may accept as evidence of a theological interpretation of the phrase ἐν τῇ οἰκίᾳ by the Fathers. Well did they understand that to dwell "in the house of the Father" in Jn 14,2-3 (comp. Jn 8,35) means in equivalent Johannine language to dwell "with the Father" (comp. Jn 8,38). Such is precisely the meaning which the phrase ἐν τῇ οἰκίᾳ takes on as it is integrated into the over-all Johannine theology, especially that of the farewell discourses (Jn 13,1-17,26). Besides, when the reciprocal aspect of the union of Jn 14,2-3 is described in Jn 14,23 we find significantly the phrase παρ᾽ αὐτῷ, which corresponds exactly to the phrase ἐν τῇ οἰκίᾳ[31] understood in the spiritual sense of an intimate personal relationship.

Finally, for the οἰκία of Jn 14,2-3 to take on its full spiritual import, the disciples must already occupy the "rooms" (μοναί) rendered accessible to them in the Father's house by the preparation of a place However, these possibilities of dwelling in the Father's house are "many" (πολλαί) — enough and more than enough for everyone.[32] Every believer (not just the disciples of Jesus in Jn 14,2-3) can have a "spiritual position" (μονή) in union with Jesus in the Father. At this level of understanding the representative role of the disciples takes on its full significance.[33] As a group they represent all those who believe in Jesus and love him — a universal family of faith and love. The πολλαί of Jn 14,2-3 is perfectly intelligible in line with the Johannine perspective of universal redemption for all who believe in Christ (cf. Jn 4,42; 8,12; 9,5; 12,32). The whole universal family of believers can have their μοναί in the Father's house.

---

[29] The phrase "spiritual positions" is borrowed from R. H. GUNDRY, op. cit. (n. 7) 70. Several commentators accept this explanation, without reservation or qualification. D. W. WEAD is the only exegete (to our knowledge) who notes a double meaning for the term τόπος. See, c. I, n. 21.

[30] See, ch. V, pp. 137-138.

[31] See, n. 24.

[32] On the meaning of πολλαί, see, ch. I, pp. 33-34.

[33] On the representative role of the disciples in the discourse, see, ch. V, pp. 173-175.

B. THE PREPARATION OF A PLACE

1. Double Meaning of τόπος

The term τόπος is common in the fourth gospel, seventeen times in all. It is used mostly in its primary literal sense, meaning "place", some kind of physical space, or spatial area (Jn 5,13; 6,10.23; 10,40; 11,30; 18,2; 19,13.17.20.41; 20,7.25). But there is also a highly technical use of the term twice to designate in a transferred sense "a temple" (Jn 4,20; 11,48). In both texts the term bears the definite article. Hence, it designates a definite, specific "temple". It is interpreted in both Jn 4,20 and in Jn 11,48 almost unanimously in line with LXX usage as a reference to the Jerusalem temple (comp. Mt 24,15; Acts 6,13; 21,28).[34] Clearly, the Johannine usage of τόπος is well suited to take on a double meaning of "place", with reference to some kind of physical space and with reference to "a temple".

Besides, we have already seen that the τόπος of Jn 14,2-3 is indefinite, without the article and in the singular.[35] As such it cannot be referred directly either to "the house" in the singular (οἰκία) with the definite article (τῇ), or the "rooms" in the plural (μοναί). Hence, it is not stated directly (nor explicitly) that Jesus goes to the Father's house to prepare a place for the disciples there. The text says so only indirectly (or implicitly). This we conclude from the whole movement of the text. It is stated directly (and explicitly) only that Jesus goes to prepare "a place". Clearly, then, there is nothing in the text to exclude the interpretation of τόπος as "sanctuary" or "temple". In itself the text is entirely open to it.

2. The New Temple of the risen Jesus: Jn 2,13-22

The question still remains to be answered in what sense can this journey of Jesus in Jn 14,2-3 be said to prepare "a place", meaning "a temple" or "a sanctuary". To resolve this problem we turn to the redactional comment of Jn 2,21. This text states explicitly that the body of Jesus is "a temple": ἐκεῖνος δὲ ἔλεγεν περὶ τοῦ ναοῦ τοῦ σώματος αὐτοῦ. The σῶμα clearly refers to the physical body of Jesus (comp. Jn 19,31.38(2x).40). This text is significantly located near the text of Jn 2,16-17. We will now consider this important text again and with it that of Jn 2,21, together with the scene of the Cleansing of the Temple as a whole (Jn 2,13-22).

---

[34] See, *BJ* ad loc., n. "a".
[35] On this aspect of our text, see, ch. V, pp. 170-171.

(a) LINKS WITH JN 14,2-3. This scene would also seem to have a special importance for an understanding of our text. We have already stressed the significant verbal link between τὸν οἶκον τοῦ πατρός μου of Jn 2,16 (comp. also Jn 2,17) and the ἐν τῇ οἰκίᾳ τοῦ πατρός μου of Jn 14,2-3.[36] There is a clear reference to the temple in Jn 2,16. But this scene of Jn 2,13-22 is also unique in the fourth gospel for the frequency and variety of its temple vocabulary.[37] Moreover, it is centered entirely on the temple itself as the Jewish place of worship, and unfolds within its precincts (cf Jn 2,14; comp. Jn 7,10-8,59). The redactional comment of Jn 2,21 explicitly refers the words of Jn 2,19 about the Jerusalem temple to the body of Jesus. So, too, the theme of the temple is evoked with the implicit reference in Jn 2,16 to Zechariah, 14,21. The whole scene is clearly dominated by the temple theme.

So, too, the general chronological setting of an immediate future passover is identical for both Jn 2,13-22 and Jn 14,2-3 (cf. ἐγγὺς ἦν τὸ πάσχα, Jn 2,13; πρὸ.....τοῦ πάσχα, Jn 13,1; cf. also, Jn 11,55; 12,1; comp. Jn 6,4). Also, the general topographical framework of a pilgrimage to the Jerusalem temple is common to both (ἀνέβη εἰς Ἰεροσόλυμα, Jn 2,13; ἀνέβησαν πολλοὶ εἰς Ἰεροσόλυμα, Jn 11,55-56; 12,20). The scene of the Cleansing of the Temple (Jn 2,13-22) and that of the Last Supper (Jn 13,1-17,26) both unfold after Jesus has gone up on pilgrimage to the Jerusalem temple and in the perspective of an immediate future passover. Thus John designedly places both Jn 2,13-22 and Jn 14,2-3 within a similar topographical and chronological setting, and provides an obviously important verbal link between them.[38] It would seem that John has deliberately done this in order to underline a theological similarity of meaning at a deeper level of understanding.

(b) STRUCTURE OF JN 2,13-22. The section of Jn 2,13-22 forms a compact unit in itself. It is preceded and followed by typical Johannine transitional verses (Jn 2,12; 2,23-25; comp. Jn 3,22-23; 4,43-45). The topographical and chronological details of Jn 2,13 provide the setting. The dramatic action in the temple proper then develops in a double

---

[36] See, ch. I, p. 30.

[37] All the Johannine equivalents for the temple occur here more than once, except the term τόπος (cf. Jn 4,20; 11,48); and two of them οἶκος and ναός occur nowhere else with reference to the temple:
(i) ἱερόν   (Jn 2,14.15).
(ii) οἶκος   (Jn 2,16.17).
(iii) ναός   (Jn 2,19.21).

[38] On the theological significance of chronological and topographical details in the fourth gospel, see, D. MOLLAT, "Remarques sur le vocabulaire spatial du quatrième évangile", StudEvang I (TU 73) (1959) 322-28.

movement. We have a symbolic action of cleansing the temple (Jn 2,14-17) followed by the promise of a future "sign" (Jn 2,18-22).[39]

However, the link between both sections is also clear. It is the words and actions of Jesus in the first movement which triggers off the dialogue in the second (ἀπεκρίθησαν οὖν, Jn 2,18). So, too, the phrase ἐμνήσθησαν οἱ μαθηταὶ αὐτοῦ (Jn 2,17.22) by way of conclusion to both sections underlines that both sections are carefully structured to emphasise their related significance by means of the parallelism (comp. Jn 10,30.38).

Thus in spite of the break between Jn 2,14-17 and Jn 2,18-22 there is a continued and gradual progressive development of thought from one section to the next. The two sections should be kept clearly apart, and yet closely linked in any interpretation of the scene.

(c) TEXT OF JN 2,13-22. In Jn 2,19 Jesus accedes to the request of the Jews for a "sign" (cf. Jn 2,18). This required "sign" is to authenticate the action of Jesus in Jn 2,14-17 (comp. Jn 6,30). The reply of Jesus must be interpreted in the immediate context with reference to the Jerusalem temple. But the response of the Jews in Jn 2,20 shows that it is quite unintelligible to them at this level of meaning. The λύσατε of Jn 2,19 is a typical semitic use of the imperative as a condition, meaning, "if you destroy".[40] It is clear from Jn 2,20 in fact that the Jews will certainly not comply with this condition and destroy their cherished temple. Hence, the exercise by Jesus of this power which he claims to rebuild the temple is purely hypothetical. The promised future "sign" of Jn 2,19 does no more than affirm a claim of Jesus to have the power to rebuild the temple. In no way should we look for another material temple to appear. In a sense, then, the reply of Jesus in Jn 2,19 to the request for a "sign" in Jn 2,18 is equivalently a refusal: no "sign" (in the sense understood by the Jews) will be given (comp. Mt 12,38-39; Mk 8,11-12; Lk 11,16).[41]

In one sense, then, the reply of Jn 2,19 is a refusal. But in another deeper sense it is not so. This whole scene must be interpreted at a second deeper level of meaning in the light of the passion-resurrection of Jesus. This perspective already opens up in the setting to the scene (cf. Jn 2,13). The verb ἀναβαίνω has a double meaning (comp. Jn 20,17(2x)). It is a technical term for a pilgrimage to the temple (comp. Jn 5,1;

---

[39] It is rightly understood by the disciples as a symbolic action since they interpret it as the fulfilment of Ps 69(68), 9(10). The "recalling" of Jn 2,17 refers both to a pre-Paschal and post-Paschal understanding.

[40] C. H. Dodd explains this use of the imperative well. See, *The Interpretation of the Fourth Gospel* (Cambridge, 1960), 302, n. 1.

[41] X. Léon-Dufour wrongly (in our view) disowns this comparison with the "sign" of Jonas. See, "Le signe du temple selon saint Jean", *RecSR* 39 (1951), 158.

7,8(2x).10(2x).14; 11,55; 12,20). But it is also used in a deeper sense to designate the spiritual ascent of Jesus to his Father through his passion-resurrection (cf. Jn 20,17(2x); comp. Jn 3,13; 6,62). So, too, the phrase καὶ ἐγγὺς ἦν τὸ πάσχα is a stereotype formula which punctuates the gospel (cf. Jn 6,4; 11,55; comp. Jn 12,1). It opens a perspective on an immediate future passover. In Jn 13,1 this same perspective refers to the passion-resurrection. Finally, the phrase ἐμνήσθησαν οἱ μαθηταὶ αὐτοῦ of Jn 2,22 explicitly indicates a deeper post-Paschal understanding of the scene (comp. Jn 2,17).[42]

This perspective of the passion-resurrection of Jesus also seems to have coloured even the choice of vocabulary in Jn 2,19. When we compare the Johannine expressions with their Synoptic parallels we find a striking change in the key-terms. The verb καταλύω (Mt 26,61; Mk 14,58) becomes λύω (Jn 2,19) and the οἰκοδομέω (Mt 26,6; 27,40; Mk 14,58; 15,20; comp. Jn 2,20) becomes ἐγείρω (Jn 2,19; comp. Jn 2,20.22). In each case the Synoptic terms are applicable to the destruction and reconstruction of a building. But they are not applicable to the destruction and reconstruction of a human body. The Johannine terms are seemingly specifically chosen because they are so applicable.[43] So, too, the phrase "in three days" (ἐν τρισὶν ἡμέραις) of itself may be taken to mean no more than "a brief space of time". But by comparison with the Synoptic parallels it cannot fail to take on a deeper significance also with reference to the passion-resurrection of Jesus (comp. ἐν τρισὶν ἡμέραις, Mt 27,40; Mk 15,29).

Even the OT allusion to Ps 69(68), 9(10) in Jn 2,17 takes on a deeper meaning in the light of the passion-resurrection of Jesus.[44] The future καταφάγεται of John (in contrast to the aorist κατέφαγεν of the LXX) stamps the quotation as a true prophecy about the death of Jesus. This future is characteristic of the understanding of the psalms as prophecy.[45] It predicts (in a negative sense) that zeal for the temple will consume Jesus even to the extent of bringing him to his death.[46] But it also predicts (in a positive sense) that Jesus will be consumed in his death with

---

[42] On the Johannine use of the verb "recall", see, I. DE LA POTTERIE, *The Christian Lives by the Spirit* (New York, 1970) 64.

[43] This is a point well made by E. C. HOSKYNS, *op. cit.* 194-195; also, D. W. WEAD, *The Literary Devices in John's Gospel* (Basel, 1970) 65.

[44] The "recalling" of Jn 2,22 explicitly designates a deeper post-resurrectional understanding (comp. Jn 2,17). The "scripture" of the same verse refers directly to Ps 69(68), 9(10) in Jn 2,17 (comp. Jn 10,35; 20,9; also Jn 19,24.28.36.37), but also indirectly to the other implicit OT allusions of the scene (e.g. Ze 14,21 in Jn 2,16). All these OT allusions (explicit and implicit) take on a deeper significance in the light of the passion-resurrection.

[45] R. BULTMANN rightly explains the future in this way. See, *op. cit.* 124, n. 3.

[46] C. H. DODD explains this implication of the text: "Just as the Righteous Sufferer of the Psalms paid the price of his loyalty to the temple, so the action of Jesus in cleansing the temple will bring him to grief". See, *op. cit.* (n. 40), 301, also n. 3.

zeal for the temple. In thus accepting his death Jesus will in some way build up the temple.

At this deeper level of understanding the λύσατε of Jn 2,19 becomes more than a mere condition. It is an ironical imperative such as we find in the OT prophets (comp. Am 4,4; Is 8,9).[47] The meaning, then, is: if you destroy this temple (as you most certainly will). Jesus thus designates the Jews as the agents of the destruction of the Jerusalem temple. Moreover, by the redactional comment of Jn 2,21 the author does not try to turn us away from this reference to the Jerusalem temple. Rather, he directs our attention to a double meaning which he intends. In Jn 2,19, then, we have an example of irony and of double meaning.

The irony of the text is couched in the first phrase. Jesus is telling the Jews that they will certainly destroy the Jerusalem temple. But by his remark in Jn 2,21 the evangelist invests the term "temple" with a double meaning. It is applicable, however, to both parts of Jn 2,19, which thus combines a statement about the temple of his own body and the Jerusalem temple.[48] We have already seen that it is impossible in one sense to apply the meaning of the Jerusalem temple to the second part of the text. However, in saying this we do not wish to exclude all reference there to the Jerusalem temple. Jesus speaks simultaneously of the Jerusalem temple and the temple of his body in both parts of Jn 2,19.[49] But the reference to the reconstruction of the temple cannot be understood with reference to a material building as the Jews understood it (Jn 2,20). It designates something entirely new: the New Temple of the glorified body of Jesus, which replaces the Jerusalem temple. At this deeper level of meaning we pass to a higher spiritual plane.[50] God abolishes only to fulfil.

The meaning of Jn 2,19 in the light of the passion-resurrection of Jesus, then, is: if you destroy the temple of my body (and you most certainly will) you will also destroy this Jerusalem temple, and I will raise up the New Temple of my glorified body to replace it. In this interpretation an inseparable solidarity is established between the Jerusalem temple and the temple of the body of Jesus. Moreover, the

---

[47] "impératif prophétique". See, X. Léon-Dufour, *op. cit.* (n. 41) 166, n. 29.

[48] A failure to recognise this seems to be at the root of much of the misinterpretation of this scene. For an outline of these false interpretations, see, X. Léon-Dufour, *op. cit.* (n. 41) 157-59.

[49] We agree entirely with the observation of X. Léon-Dufour: "Jésus parlait non pas uniquement du temple de pierre ou de son corps, mais simultanément de l'un et de l'autre". See, *op. cit.* (n. 41) 158.

[50] This has been well expressed by F. Godet: "Le Messie périt: c'est le Temple qui se relève; sous une forme nouvelle sans doute, car, dans le règne de Dieu, il n'y a jamais simple restauration du passé". See, *op. cit.* 217.

negative action of the destruction of both temples is assigned to the Jews (λύσατε), who are responsible for the death of Jesus (cf. Jn 19,11; comp. Jn 9,41). This is not to say that Jesus is entirely passive. It is he who gives the command: "destroy" (λύσατε). In a real sense, then, everything also depends in some way on his will (comp. Jn 13,27). The evidence of the whole gospel indicates that the rejection of Jesus by the Jews leads to his death (cf. Jn 7,30.44; 11,53; 15,22). However, the positive action of rebuilding the New Temple through his resurrection is attributed solely to Jesus himself (ἐγερῶ).[51] Besides, we have a question on the lips of the Jews in Jn 2,20, which leaves itself open to a double response in typical Johannine style.[52] It shows that the Jews are closed to any possible deeper meaning. But at the same time it remains open to such a possibility in the light of the passion-resurrection: Jesus will raise up the New Temple of his glorified body (note the emphatic σύ).

Thus in a sense the promised future "sign" will not be given as the Jews understood the words of Jesus, for we must not expect another material temple. Yet in another far deeper spiritual sense as the disciples understood the words of Jesus after his death-resurrection this future "sign" will be given — the "sign" of the New Temple of the risen Jesus.[53] In a sense far beyond the understanding of the Jews the words of Jesus are profoundly prophetic (Jn 2,19). So, too, is the question on the lips of the Jews themselves (Jn 2,20).

(d) APPLICATION TO JN 14,2-3.

(i) *Similarities.* At first sight there is apparently a considerable difference between the texts of Jn 2,13-22 and Jn 14,2-3, and their contexts. However, at a deeper level of meaning our text may be explained in line with the Johannine perspective of the former one. Jn 2,13-22 points to the "sign" of the New Temple as the effect of the passion-resurrection of Jesus. But the τόπος of Jn 14,2-3(2x) may be interpreted with reference to "the temple of his body" as in Jn 2,21, that is, τόπος (Jn 14,2-3(2x)) = ὁ ναός τοῦ σώματος αὐτοῦ (Jn 2,21). The journey of Jesus to his Father through his passion-resurrection (πορεύομαι) (2x), then, would be the process which prepares this temple of the body of Jesus. Thus our text of Jn 14,2-3 would describe in the process of preparation what is described in Jn 2,13-22 as the effect of the passion-resurrection of Jesus: the New

---

[51] This distinction between the negative and positive aspect is equivalently made by F. GODET. See, *op. cit.* 217.

[52] On the Johannine use of the question, see, ch. V, pp. 150-151.

[53] We are dealing here with the common NT theme of the spiritualisation of the temple. I. DE LA POTTERIE sums up this important theme for us at length. See, *op. cit.* (n. 5) 699.

Temple of the glorified body of Jesus. Once the journey is complete (ἐὰν πορευθῶ), we would then have the same effect in Jn 14,2-3 as in Jn 2,13-22. The τόπος prepared would become the New Temple. By one and the same process of preparation Jesus would render the Father's house (with the many rooms) accessible to the disciples, and provide the New Temple of his glorified body. This may be expressed schematically as follows:

CAUSE	EFFECT
2,13-22: Passion-Resurrection.	2,13-22: New Temple of risen Jesus
14,2-3 : Departure thro' passion-resurrection.	14,2-3 : Place prepared = New Temple = Father's house (with the many rooms) accessible.

(ii) *Differences*. The spiritual reality of the New Temple of the risen Jesus which emerges from the passion-resurrection is the same in both texts. However, the vocabulary used by John to designate it differs (ναός, Jn 2,20.21; τόπος, Jn 14,2-3(2x)). Besides, Jn 2,13-22 also clarifies what is implicit in the process of preparation in Jn 14,2-3. We distinguished a negative and a positive effect of the passion-resurrection of Jesus in Jn 2,13-22, ascribed respectively to the agency of the Jews (negative) and to the agency of Jesus (positive). We may express it as follows:

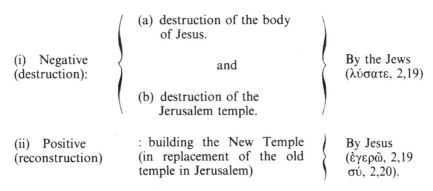

(i) Negative (destruction):	(a) destruction of the body of Jesus. and (b) destruction of the Jerusalem temple.	By the Jews (λύσατε, 2,19)
(ii) Positive (reconstruction)	: building the New Temple (in replacement of the old temple in Jerusalem)	By Jesus (ἐγερῶ, 2,19 σύ, 2,20).

Jn 14,2-3 designates only the positive action of Jesus (πορεύομαι..ἐὰν πορευθῶ καὶ ἑτοιμάσω) in providing the New Temple of his glorified body, but this positive action has a complementary aspect in the negative action of the destruction of the body of Jesus and the Jerusalem temple by the Jews. There is a total transformation of the material body of Jesus through the passion-resurrection of Jesus into the spiritual reality of the New Temple of his glorified body, which replaces the Jerusalem temple. The destruction is the effect of the passion-death of

Jesus of which the Jews are the cause, even if not exclusively so; the reconstruction is the effect of the resurrection of Jesus. Thus in a sense Jn 2,13-22 complements (as well as supports) our understanding of Jn 14,2-3.

C. RETURN OF JESUS

1. Coming (ἔρχομαι)

This return of Jesus is conditional on the departure of Jesus through his passion-resurrection (ἐὰν πορευθῶ). Hence, this return must designate the intervention of the risen Jesus. Besides, it is a heavenly intervention from the Father's house (implicit in the text). The questions of the disciples show that they interpret this ἔρχομαι of Jn 14,2-3 in the crude material sense of an eschatological intervention by Jesus (Jn 14,8; 14,22). But the whole thrust of the dialogue is to direct the minds of the disciples to a deeper spiritual understanding of this same eschatological intervention. Moreover, the ἔρχομαι is a futuristic-present. It describes a present continual process of "coming" [54] in anticipation of an ever future "coming". As a description of the eschatological intervention of God, then, a double perspective of realised and future eschatology fuse in the ἔρχομαι of Jn 14,2-3. [55]

Besides, the undetermined and indefinite nature of the text must be respected. [56] It is open to interpretation with reference to every possible intervention of the risen Jesus in anticipation of an ever future one. [57] Hence, in itself the ἔρχομαι may be interpreted of the intervention of the risen Jesus at death (Jn 11,25b), [58] at martyrdom (Jn 13,38; comp.

---

[54] In the words of M. J. LAGRANGE: "perpétuelle venue, toujours renouvelée". See *op. cit.* 387.

[55] On this double perspective of the fourth gospel, see, M.-E. BOISMARD, "L'évolution du thème eschatologique dans les traditions johanniques", *RB* 68 (1961) 507-524.

[56] This point is well made by R. BRÊCHET: "Le présent de venir laisse une certaine indétermination, le Christ vient plusieurs fois et un jour". See, "Du Christ à l'Église. Le dynamisme de l'incarnation dans l'évangile selon saint Jean", *DivThom* 56 (1953) 89.

[57] L. CERFAUX expresses the general idea: "En réalité, toutes ces perspectives, résurrection, Pentecôte, expérience de la présence actuelle du Christ dans la communauté, parousie se mêlent dans notre évangile". See, "La charité fraternelle et le retour du Christ (Jo., XIII, 33-38)", *ETL* 24 (1948) 324. See, also, B. F. WESTCOTT on Jn 21,22f, *op. cit.* 201.

[58] Some commentators would exclude any reference to the intervention of the risen Jesus at death from the "coming" of Jn 14,2-3. Thus R. H. GUNDRY, *op. cit.* (n. 7) 69. We agree with those commentators who refuse to exclude such a reference to death. See, R. BRÊCHET, *op. cit.* (n. 56) 89. We base our interpretation on Jn 11,25b, which promises eternal life after physical death.

21,19),[59] at the Eucharist celebration (Jn 21,13),[60] through the gift of the Spirit (Jn 16,8), at the indwelling (Jn 14,23), at the resurrection appearances (Jn 20,19.24.26), at the Second Coming (Jn 21,22.23). No particular application exhausts the possibilities of the text. Thus the ἔρχομαι of Jn 14,2-3 designates the whole eschatological period after the passion-resurrection of Jesus as a period of continual intervention by the risen Jesus in anticipation of the Second Coming — a whole indivisible process of intervention. Jesus is the one who is continually "coming" — on the way. This is the deep spiritual reality designated by the ἔρχομαι of Jn 14,2-3.

2. Again (πάλιν)

So, too, the use of the indefinite adverb πάλιν leaves the text still vague and undetermined. In no way does it specify the "coming" of Jn 14,2-3 with reference to any particular "coming" of the risen Jesus. However, this adverb πάλιν is clearly a preferred Johannine term (42x).[61] The evangelist seems to use it at times for a deep theological purpose. It often highlights links with the past in the development and structure of his narrative (e.g. Jn 4,54; comp. 2,11; 6,15; comp. 6,3; 10,31; comp. 8,59; 11,38; cf. 11,33; 12,28).[62]

Literally, πάλιν means "in the opposite direction". When it is applied to place, or movement in space, it means "back" or "backwards", a movement in reverse; and when it is applied to time it means "again" or "once more". We have seen that its use in Jn 14,2-3 may be understood in a temporal and spatial sense at a first level of understanding.[63] The promise of Jesus may thus be taken to mean that Jesus will "return", a movement which is the reverse of his "departure"; and it may also indicate that he will come "once more", or a second time. In both cases it refers to the Parousia.

---

[59] We find a reference to the martyrdom of Peter in the subtle irony of the question of Jesus in Jn 13,38: "will you lay down your life for me?".

[60] D. MOLLAT remarks: "En présentant l'apparition de Jésus ressuscité comme une "venue" (20,19.24.26; 21,13), les récits johanniques pourraient refléter cette conception liturgique". See, "L'apparition du Ressuscité et le don de l'Esprit: Jn 20,19-21", in Fête de la Pentecôte (AssSeign 30) 55.

[61] Comp. Mt (16x); Mk (28x); Lk (3x); Jn (42x); Acts (5x); Paul (38x); also, Jas 5,18; 2 Pt 2,30; I Jn 2,3; Ap 10,8-11.

[62] John uses this adverb very effectively in his narrative of the passion to link closely the exit and entrance of Pilate (Jn 18,33.38; 19,4.9). It helps to heighten the dramatic tension of the scene, and provides an external reflection of the inner wavering in the mind of Pilate.

[63] See, ch. I, p. 41.

But πάλιν does not have a merely temporal and spatial application. It also expresses contrast in logical sequence. For example, Jesus lays down his life "in order that (ἵνα) he may take it up again (πάλιν)" (Jn 10,17). This use of πάλιν serves to link two complementary aspects of the mission of Jesus (comp. Jn 16,27-28), his passion-death (laying down) and his resurrection (taking up). Moreover, the passion-death (laying down) is necessarily linked (ἵνα) in God's design (ἐντολή) to the resurrection (taking up). This ἵνα is significantly replaced by καί in the following parallel verse: Jesus has the power to lay it down and (καί) to take it up again (πάλιν) (Jn 10,18). It is in some such way that the πάλιν ἔρχομαι of Jn 14,2-3 should be linked to πορεύομαι (2x) in the same text.

The πάλιν emphasises a close and indissoluble link between the "return" and the "departure" of Jesus. The one is ordained directly to the other. It would seem, then, that we should read the first καί of Jn 14,3a as almost the equivalent of ἵνα, by analogy with the Johannine change from ἵνα to καί in Jn 10,17-18. This is all the more convincing, since this καί and the πάλιν ἔρχομαι are separated from each other only by subordinate clauses:

πορεύομαι ἑτοιμάσαι τόπον ὑμῖν; καὶ (ἐὰν πορευθῶ

καὶ ἑτοιμάσω τόπον ὑμῖν), πάλιν ἔρχομαι.

The πάλιν links inseparably the ascending/descending movement of the text, the journey of Jesus "going" to the Father through his passion-resurrection and the continual "coming" of the risen Jesus in anticipation of his intervention at the Parousia. They are both complementary aspects of one spiritual reality.

D. THE JOURNEY IN UNION WITH JESUS

Apart from Jn 14,2-3, the verb παραλαμβάνω is found only twice in John's Gospel (1,11; 19,16). In both cases it is used in a passive sense of "receiving" what is offered. In Jn 1,11 it is used negatively (οὐ παρέλαβον) of refusal by the Jews to "accept" or "receive" the Word by faith. Later, in Jn 19,16 it describes the Jews who "receive" Jesus, after he has been proclaimed by Pilate — ironically! — as their King, and handed over to them by him. Neither of these uses provide us with a parallel to John's use of the same verb actively, with Jesus as the subject in Jn 14,2-3.

The use of the verb παραλαμβάνω in Jn 14,2-3 indicates the effect of the continual intervention of the risen Jesus in anticipation of the Second Coming. Again the indefinite and undefined nature of the text must be respected. It is open to interpretation with reference to the effect of every possible intervention of the risen Jesus. It gives no indication whatever of the manner of this journey of the disciples with Jesus.

However, the use of the verb with the preposition παρά must be given its full force.[64] At this deeper level of meaning the intimacy with Jesus which the compound form of the verb indicates becomes a deep spiritual union between the believers and Jesus. The reciprocal aspect of this same union is described precisely with this preposition in the παρ' αὐτῷ of Jn 14,23. Hence, this journey of the disciples "with Jesus" (παρά) after the passion-resurrection indicates strictly a journey in intimate union with the risen Jesus. It is absolutely dependent on the permanent union of Jn 14,23 already established between the risen Jesus and the believer. Only when this union of Jn 14,23 is realised can the full implications of the παραλήμψομαι be adequately and fully explained. It designates a journey of the disciples already intimately united with the risen Jesus.

But the use of the preposition παρά also indicates something more. This journey of the disciples in union with the risen Jesus (after the preparation) is parallel to the journey of Jesus alone (prior to the preparation). Besides, the use of the παρά with λαμβάνω also indicates an important identity between this ascending movement of Jesus alone through his passion-resurrection (πορεύομαι) and that of the disciples in union with him after the passion-resurrection (παραλήμψομαι). The disciples in union with Jesus (after the preparation) travel along the same way previously traversed by Jesus in his passion-resurrection. What Jesus accomplishes alone through his passion-resurrection is accomplished by the disciples in union with the risen Jesus. The disciples in union with Jesus are caught up into the same movement of access into the heavenly temple of the Father's house through the passion-resurrection of Jesus. Thus the παραλήμψομαι of Jn 14,2-3 indicates this entrance of the disciples in union with the risen Jesus by the way of his passion-resurrection. This is the deeper spiritual reality indicated by the παραλήμψομαι of Jn 14,2-3.

The phrase πρὸς ἐμαυτόν also takes on a deeper significance at this level of understanding. It indicates union with the risen Jesus himself as the goal of this journey of the disciples in union with the risen Jesus. Thus the way and the goal are one: union with the risen Jesus. However, the Johannine use of the preposition πρός stresses the dynamic aspect of the ascending movement of the disciples into union with the risen Jesus.[65] Hence, the disciples in union with the risen Jesus (παραλήμψομαι) enter

---

[64] On this verb meaning "to take along with", see, ch. I, p. 41.

[65] See, ch. I, n. 54.

ever more deeply into union with him (πρὸς ἐμαυτόν). The complete phrase παραλήμψομαι ὑμᾶς πρὸς ἐμαυτόν indicates, then, a continual unifying action of the risen Jesus — an ever deepening movement of the disciples already in union with the risen Jesus into an ever deeper union with him. The goal (ἐμαυτόν) is already attained on the way (παραλήμψομαι) in the risen Jesus; but not yet fully attained.

At this point we can also see the profound implications of the relationship between the Father's house with the many rooms (οἰκία... μοναὶ πολλαί), the preparation of a place for the disciples there (τόπος), and Jesus himself after the preparation is complete (πρὸς ἐμαυτόν) which is suggested (at least implicitly) by the whole movement of the text.[66] After the preparation of a "place" Jesus himself becomes the τόπος prepared, a spiritual "space", or the New Temple in his risen body. But by the same process of preparation Jesus renders the Father's house with the many μοναί, where he himself dwells perpetually, accessible to the disciples. Afterwards, Jesus who is now the New Temple in his glorified body, or the τόπος prepared, takes the disciples in union with himself into union with himself, where he is perpetually, in the Father's house now rendered accessible to the disciples in the New Temple of the risen Jesus, or the τόπος prepared.

Thus at this deeper level of understanding the relationship suggested by the whole movement of the text becomes one of synonymous parallelism: the Father's house with the many rooms in it accessible to the disciples = the τόπος prepared = the risen Jesus (ἐμαυτόν). The disciples have access to the heavenly temple in the New Temple of the risen Jesus. In this New Temple, too, the goal of the heavenly temple and the way to it are one.

E. THE GOAL OF DISCIPLESHIP

1. Identification with Jesus: Jn 12,26b

(a) LINKS WITH JN 14,2-3. The goal of discipleship is described in almost identical terms in Jn 14,2-3 and Jn 12,26b:[67]

14,3c ἵνα ὅπου εἰμὶ ἐγὼ   καὶ ὑμεῖς   ἦτε.

12,26b καὶ ὅπου εἰμὶ ἐγώ, ἐκεῖ καὶ ὁ διάκονος ὁ ἐμὸς ἔσται.

---

[66] See, ch. V, pp. 172-173.

[67] This fact has not passed unnoticed by the critics. See, R. BULTMANN, *op. cit.* 426.432-3.

Besides, there is a further significant link between our text and the immediate context of Jn 12,26b:

14,3 ἐὰν πορευθῶ   παραλήμψομαι ὑμᾶς πρὸς ἐμαυτόν.

12,32 ἐὰν ὑψωθῶ ἐκ τῆς γῆς, πάντας ἑλκύσω   πρὸς ἐμαυτόν.

Here we find some who are the passive recipients of the future activity of Jesus himself. Besides, Jesus is presented as the goal of his own future activity "drawing" to himself in Jn 12,32 and "taking" to himself in Jn 14,3. So, too, the vocabulary of Jn 12,32 has an important literary link with the OT description of the eschatological pilgrimage of the nations to the temple through the ὑψόω of Is 2,2. This verbal link between Jn 12,32 and Is 2,2 is all the more significant in the general topographical framework of a pilgrimage to the Jerusalem temple, which Jn 12,32 shares with Jn 14,2-3 (ἀνέβησαν πολλοὶ εἰς Ἰεροσόλυμα, Jn 11,55; Ἕλληνές τινες ἐκ τῶν ἀναβαινόντων, Jn 12,20).[68]

Also, the general chronological setting of an immediate passover is identical for Jn 12,26b and Jn 14,2-3 (ἐγγὺς τὸ πάσχα, Jn 11,55.... πρὸ ἓξ ἡμερῶν τοῦ πάσχα, Jn 12,1; comp. also Jn 2,13; 6,4..πρὸ δὲ τῆς ἑορτῆς τοῦ πάσχα, Jn 13,1). It would seem that John again has deliberately placed the two texts of Jn 12,26b (also Jn 12,32) and Jn 14,2-3 within a similar topographical and chronological setting, with a significant verbal link between them, to underline a similarity between them at a deeper level of understanding.[69]

Finally, we have the theme of the glorification of the Son of Man opened up in the immediate context of both texts in identical terms:

13,31   ἐδοξάσθη ὁ υἱὸς τοῦ ἀνθρώπου.

12,23   δοξασθῇ ὁ υἱὸς τοῦ ἀνθρώπου.

(b) STRUCTURE OF JN 12,20-33. This section of Jn 12,20-33 falls easily into two distinct parts:

Jn 12,20-22:   Episode of the Greeks.

Jn 12,23-33:   Discourse.[70]

---

[68] Jesus himself also went up on pilgrimage (cf. Jn 11,56; 12,13).

[69] Compare the general topographical and chronological setting for the scene of the Cleansing of the Temple (Jn 2,13-22). See, p. 186.

[70] The structure of this discourse has been treated extensively by I. DE LA POTTERIE, "L'exaltation du Fils de l'homme (Jn 12,31-36)", Greg 49 (1968) 461-63. The author borrows the essentials of his analysis from X. LÉON-DUFOUR, "Trois chiasmes johanniques", NTS 7 (1961) 249-255. J. FERRARO provides a constructive criticism of this structure. See, L'ora di Cristo nel quarto vangelo (Roma, 1970) 45, n. 44.

Jn 12,26b forms part of the discourse of Jn 12,23-33. This discourse in turn is triggered off by the episode of the Greeks in Jn 12,20-22.

The discourse itself is clamped together as a unit by an inclusion (εἰς τὴν γῆν, Jn 12,24.... ἐκ τῆς γῆς, Jn 12,32 ... ἀποθνήσκω, Jn 12,24(2x); Jn 12,33, also θάνατος). Within this unified framework, the general statement of Jn 12,23 stands somewhat apart in isolation, as it were, and dominates the subsequent development of the discourse (comp. Jn 13,31-32). However, it is also closely linked with what follows by the solemn Johannine revelatory formula: ἀμὴν ἀμήν. The structure of Jn 12,24-25 is built on antithesis. The first verse contains a type of miniature parable or comparison, without the tertium comparationis (ἐὰν μὴ..ἀποθάνῃ..ἐὰν δὲ ἀποθάνῃ, Jn 12,24).[71] In the next verse this parable is applied in general antithetical terms (ὁ φιλῶν τὴν ψυχὴν..ἀπολλύει..ὁ μισῶν τὴν ψυχὴν..ζωὴν..φυλάξει, Jn 12,25). But the antithesis is curiously omitted from the text of Jn 12,26, where one might reasonably expect it again. However, it is the theme of discipleship which is introduced explicitly for the first time (ἀκολουθέω). But the image of the "seed" in Jn 12,24, and its general application in Jn 12,25, has no direct application in Jn 12,26. It is first applied directly only in Jn 12,32. This is underlined by the verbal links (εἰς τὴν γῆν, Jn 12,24... ἐκ τῆς γῆς, Jn 12,32). Jesus is the tertium comparationis[72]: just as the seed, if it dies, bears much fruit so too Jesus, if he dies, will bear much fruit. This fruit-bearing is illustrated by Jesus drawing all men to himself.

(c) TEXT OF JN 12,26b.[73] The text of Jn 12,26 is built on parallelism and contains a chiasm:

$$
\begin{array}{ll}
& \text{εἰμὶ} \quad \text{ἐγώ,} \\
\text{ἐὰν ἐμοί τις διακονῇ, ἐμοὶ ἀκολουθείτω, καὶ ὅπου} & \text{ἐκεῖ καὶ} \\
& \text{ὁ διάκονος..ἔσται·} \\
\text{ἐὰν τις ἐμοὶ διακονῇ (} \qquad \text{) τιμήσει αὐτὸν ὁ πατήρ.}
\end{array}
$$

Both conditional statements (ἐάν) have a universal application. In the first member there is a command to follow Jesus addressed to everyone who would serve him[74], and in addition a future goal is assured to the

---

[71] E. Rasco expresses this point well. See, "Christus, granum frumenti (Jo 12,24)", *VD* 37 (1959) 5.

[72] The Christological interpretation is generally accepted by the commentators. E. Rasco sums up the position well. See, *op. cit.* (n. 71) 5.

[73] The Johannine paternity of the text has been well established by E. Rasco. See, *op. cit.* (n. 71) 13-14. J. Ferraro also defends the present order of the discourse. See, *op. cit.* (n. 70) 30.

[74] It is by no means clear that the imperative ἀκολουθείτω of Jn 12,26 should be interpreted, with R. Bultmann, as "an imperative of promise". See, *op. cit.* 425-426. In the NT the imperative of ἀκολουθέω is a commandment, and not a promise (comp. Mt 8,22; 9,9; 16,24; 19,21; Mk 2,14; 8,34; Lk 5,27; 9,23; Jn 1,43).

follower of Jesus: the servant of Jesus must follow him and he will attain in the future to the goal where Jesus is at present. There will be some kind of identification between the disciple and Jesus in the future. The present εἰμί is not the equivalent of a future "shall be".[75] The full force of the present εἰμί is to be retained in contrast to the future ἔσται. The goal is already in some way attained by Jesus, even at present (εἰμί), but access to Jesus there, or identification with him, is only possible for his follower in the future (ἔσται). No reason is given for this.

(d) CONTEXT OF JN 12,26b.

(i) *Jn 12,32.* However, the text of Jn 12,32 explains the condition of this future access to Jesus: κἀγὼ ἐὰν ὑψωθῶ ἐκ τῆς γῆς, πάντας ἑλκύσω πρὸς ἐμαυτόν. The πάντας is to be retained.[76] It refers to all men, without exception.[77] The nature of the "drawing" is not specified, but it is clearly designated to give access to Jesus (πρὸς ἐμαυτόν), exactly what is promised to the follower of Jesus in Jn 12,26b. It is the same goal of access to Jesus, or identification with him, which is promised in Jn 12,26b and Jn 12,32. In Jn 12,32, however, this access is absolutely conditional on the "exaltation" of Jesus (ἐὰν ὑψωθῶ) through his passion-resurrection.[78] The miniature parable of the "seed" (Jn 12,24) applies to Jesus in his passion-death: if Jesus dies he bears much fruit, or draws all men to himself. Thus access to Jesus where he is becomes possible to all men, but only on the condition of his passion-death, his "exaltation".

The access to Jesus which is promised in Jn 12,26b, but with no explanation of how this is possible, is now clarified. All men (πάντας) can have access to Jesus (πρὸς ἐμαυτόν) where he is (ὅπου εἰμὶ ἐγώ) on the condition of his "exaltation". However, Jn 12.,32 is explicitly universal. Not so Jn 12,26b. The possibility of access to Jesus is opened up to all men by the "exaltation" of Jesus in Jn 12,32. But the promise of actual access to Jesus is given only to the follower of Jesus in Jn 12,26b.[79] The

---

[75] R. BULTMANN gives the present of the verb "to be" a future meaning in Jn 12,26; 14,3; 17,24; *op. cit.* 307, n. 6.

[76] As in A. MERK, E. NESTLE, and *GNT*. The Vulgate has "omnia".

[77] There is interesting attestation, including P⁶⁶, for a neuter plural reading which would make the lifting up of Jesus effective on all things. However, *BDF*, 138 suggests that it is simply a neuter used here for a general masculine reference. A neuter may also be adequately explained in accordance with Johannine style.

[78] The perspective of the "hour" of the passion-resurrection opens up in Jn 12,23 (comp. 12,27). In this perspective ὑψόω (Jn 12,32) and δοξάζω (Jn 12,23) are identical in meaning. See, ch. I, n. 29. On the double meaning of ὑψόω, see, D. W. WEAD, *op. cit.* (n. 43), 34-36; also, I. DE LA POTTERIE, *op. cit.* (n. 70).

[79] R. BULTMANN comments perceptively in this manner on Jn 12,32: "it is self-evident that he certainly offers this possibility to all men, but that this is realised only in those who belong to him, who as his servants will be with him (v. 26; 14,3; 17,24)". See, *op. cit.* 432.

fruits of the passion-resurrection of Jesus are offered to all men (comp. Jn 3,16: 8,12), but not all men accept these benefits by faith (comp. Jn 8,45; 12,37-39). All men do not necessarily become the disciples of Jesus (Jn 3,11; 3,32; 5,38.43; 6,36; 7,5; 8,19.43.46).

Thus the two texts of Jn 12,32 and Jn 12,26b complement each other. In Jn 12,32 the passion-resurrection of Jesus is the condition of access to Jesus, or identification with him, promised to the disciple in Jn 12,26b; and Jn 12,26b explains that it is only the follower of Jesus who will actually attain to the goal of access to Jesus, or identification with Jesus, opened up through the passion-resurrection of Jesus in Jn 12,32. However, once the follower of Jesus is identified with him on the condition of the passion-resurrection, then the miniature parable of the seed in Jn 12,24 also applies to him at least indirectly.[80] Thus we move from a direct Christological application of the parable to an indirect application of it to the disciple of Jesus. The disciple shares in the passion-resurrection of Jesus, or his "exaltation".

(ii) *Jn 12,20-22.* It is only in the light of the passion-resurrection of Jesus that the apparently insignificant scene of the Greeks (Jn 12,20-22), which triggers off the discourse in Jn 12,23-33, also takes on its full depth of meaning.[81] This episode links back with Jn 11,55. These Greeks form part of the pilgrimage to the Jerusalem temple for the feast of the passover:

11,55 ἀνέβησαν πολλοὶ εἰς Ἱεροσόλυμα..πρὸ τοῦ πάσχα.

12,20 τινες ἐκ τῶν ἀναβαινόντων..ἐν τῇ ἑορτῇ.

They approach Philip (προσῆλθον) with a simple request: "we want to see Jesus" (ἰδεῖν). They are asking for access to Jesus (comp. Jn 3,3.5).[82] But their request is apparently left in suspense, unanswered. The Greeks themselves disappear from the scene almost immediately and unexpectedly.[83] But the mediation of Philip and Andrew in turn comes to Jesus (ἔρχεται). The movement of the scene by a series of chain-reactions from the Greeks through Philip and Andrew ends with access to Jesus, or

---

[80] J. Ferraro sums up well the conclusions of our analysis. See, *op. cit.* (n. 70), 34.

[81] Most commentators read the episode of the Greeks (Jn 12,20-22) as closely linked with the following discourse (Jn 12,23-33). A. Wikenhauser is a notable exception. See, *op. cit.* 318-19; also, M. J. Lagrange, *op. cit.* 330.

[82] We find a curious alternation to the verb ἰδεῖν of Jn 3,3 in the verb εἰσελθεῖν of Jn 3,5, which is a parallel text (comp. Lk 9,9; 23,8; Acts 28,20; Rom 1,11). C. Traets comments on this use of ἰδεῖν in Jn 12,21. See, *Voir Jésus et le Père en lui selon l'évangile de saint Jean* (Rome, 1967), 15.

[83] We may compare the role of Nicodemus in ch. 3, who also disappears unexpectedly, if not immediately, from the scene.

precisely what the Greeks request. But no response is given by Jesus to the request, either to the Greeks themselves directly, or even indirectly through the disciples. The αὐτοῖς of Jn 12,23 is deliberately vague. However, the reply is implicitly positive.[84] In typical Johannine fashion Jesus does reply in a positive way (at least implicitly) to the request at a deeper level of meaning in the discourse which follows: once the Son of Man is glorified the Greeks will be able to "see" him. At this level of meaning the Greeks voice the longing of the whole pagan world for access to Jesus. The "irony" of Jn 12,19 invests these Greeks with a representative role.

(iii) *Old Testament Background: Isaiah 2,2-5.* This picture of the Greeks as representatives of the whole pagan world on pilgrimage to the Jerusalem temple has a special significance against the OT background to Jn 12,32. It is generally accepted that the use of ὑψόω derives ultimately from Is 52,13.[85] The double designation of the Servant there as "exalted" (ὑψόω) and "glorified" (δοξάζω) is significant in view of the use of the verb δοξάζω also in the immediate context of Jn 12,32 (cf. Jn 12,23.28(2x)). However, the term ὑψόω also has a significant link with the OT theme of the temple.[86] The eschatological pilgrimage of the nations to the Jerusalem temple is easily evoked by the text and context of Jn 12,32 as the following significant parallels will show:[87]

Is 2,2 ὁ οἶκος τοῦ Θεοῦ..	Jn 11,56 ἐν τῷ ἱερῷ .....
καὶ ὑψωθήσεται	12,32 κἀγὼ ἐὰν ὑψωθῶ .....[88]
3 καὶ ἥξουσιν ἐπ' αὐτὸ	
πάντα τὰ ἔθνη,	12,20 Ἕλληνές τινες .....[89]
καὶ πορεύσονται ἔθνη πολλὰ	12,32 πάντας ἑλκύσω πρὸς ἐμ.
... δεῦτε καὶ ἀναβῶμεν	12,20 τινες....ἀναβαινόντων .....
	11,55 ἀνέβησαν πολλοὶ
εἰς τὸν οἶκον τοῦ Θεοῦ	εἰς Ἱεροσόλυμα .....

---

[84] We cannot agree with M.-J. LAGRANGE who sees the reply of Jesus as implicitly negative. See, *op. cit.* 330.

[85] On the literary links between Jn 12,32 and Is 52,13, see, I. DE LA POTTERIE, *op. cit.* (n. 70) 469.

[86] The verb ὑψόω is used to designate the throne of Yahweh in the sanctuary (Jer 7,12), the adjective ὑψηλός to designate the throne of Yahweh in the temple (Is 6,1) and the temple itself (2 Chr 7,21; 3 Kgs 9,8). Compare "the high abode of thy holiness" (מזבל קדשך) in Is 63,15, with reference to the heavenly temple.

[87] No exegete (to our knowledge) has established these literary links.

[88] The use of ὑψόω to designate the eschatological temple in Is 2,2 is replaced by the use of the adjective ἔτοιμος in the parallel text of Mi 4,1. We also find this adjective used of the temple in 2 Chr 6,2. We have already established an important link between our text of Jn 14,2-3 and Is 2,2-3 and Mi 4,1-4. See, ch. IV, p. 130.

[89] As the representatives of the pagan world the Ἕλληνες of Jn 12,20 correspond to the LXX use of τὰ ἔθνη in Is 2,3.

Is 2,5 καὶ νῦν, ὁ οἶκος τοῦ Ιακωβ,
       δεῦτε πορευθῶμεν   Jn 12,35-36 περιπατέω (2x).[90]
       τῷ φωτὶ κυρίου.   12,35-36 φῶς.[91]

The verb ἕλκω[92] describes the power exercised by the "exalted" Jesus. It also has important roots in the OT prophetic literature of the restoration. Jer 38,3 (LXX) records the words:

LXX	Vulgate
ἀγάπησιν αἰωνίαν ἠγάπησά σε,	in caritate perpetua dilexi te,
διὰ τοῦτο εἵλκυσά σε εἰς οἰκτίρημα.	ideo attraxi te miserans.[93]

However, it is the wider perspective of the gathering of all the nations evoked by Is 2,2 which corresponds more exactly to the universal dimension of Jn 12,32 (πάντας). The theme of reunion is evoked by both Is 2,2 and Jer 38,3 (LXX). But the gathering of the people of God evoked by ἕλκω becomes a vehicle to express the more universal theme of the eschatological gathering of all the nations to the Jerusalem temple evoked by the term ὑψόω.

Thus the apparently insignificant scene of the Greeks wishing to see Jesus in Jn 12,20-22, also apparently without any link with the subsequent discourse on Jn 12,23-33, takes on a profound significance when we interpret the discourse by way of reply to the request of the Greeks for access to Jesus. At a deeper level of understanding the drawing of all men to himself by Jesus "lifted up" in his passion-resurrection reinterprets the pilgrimage of the whole pagan world represented by the Greeks in terms of the future activity of the glorified Jesus drawing all men, who become his disciples, into union with himself, once a way of access has been opened through his passion-resurrection. Here, too, we have foretold in equivalent Johannine terms the fulfilment through the passion-resurrection of Jesus of Isaiah's description of the "exaltation" of the Jerusalem temple as the goal of the future eschatological pilgrimage of the nations.

---

[90] The πορεύομαι of Is 2,5 designates "to journey" in the moral sense of walking according to God's commands. On this OT use of the term, see, ch. III, p. 77. I. DE LA POTTERIE explains that the Johannine equivalent of this is περιπατέω in the fourth gospel. See, *op. cit.* (n. 70) 476.

[91] This term is the thematic word of this section (Jn 12,35-36(5x)).

[92] The verb ἕλκω occurs rarely in the NT (cf. Jn 6,44; 12,32; 18,10; 21,6.11; Acts 16,19). Apart from the references which clearly signify a physical act (Acts 16,19; Jn 18,10) the other uses of the verb all occur in John. The verb seems to have a special significance for John.

[93] D. MOLLAT explains the action as a "drawing" by a revelation of love. See, "Ils regarderont Celui qu'ils ont transpercé. La conversion chez Saint Jean", *LumV* 47 (1960) 113.

(e) APPLICATION TO JN 14,2-3.

(i) *Similarities.* Our study of Jn 12,26b in its immediate context highlights the deep significance of the several points of contact with our text:

    (i) ὅπου εἰμὶ ἐγώ (12,26) = ὅπου εἰμὶ ἐγώ (14,3c).

    (ii) καὶ ὁ διάκονος ὁ ἐμός (12,26) = καὶ ὑμεῖς (14,3c).

    (iii) πρὸς ἐμαυτόν (12,32) = πρὸς ἐμαυτόν (14,3b).

    (iv) ἐὰν ὑψωθῶ (12,32) = ἐὰν πορευθῶ (14,3a).

We will now consider each of these in detail.

The goal of discipleship is described in identical terms: (ὅπου εἰμὶ ἐγώ) (Jn 12,26b; 14,3c). This goal is where Jesus abides permanently and perpetually. As such we have complete confirmation of our understanding of the phrase in Jn 14,3c as a description of the goal of discipleship.[94]

Moreover, the promise of the goal of identity with Jesus in Jn 12,26b has a universal application, but relative to the one who serves Jesus (ὁ διάκονος ὁ ἐμός), or equivalently every follower or disciple of Jesus. Here we have a clear basis in support of the extension of the promised future union with Jesus in our understanding of Jn 14,2-3 beyond the disciples directly and explicitly designated by the ὑμεῖς of Jn 14,3c to embrace the whole future community of the disciples of Jesus of whom the disciples at the supper are the representatives or type.[95] In the full range of its meaning with reference directly and explicitly to the disciples themselves, and implicitly and indirectly to every future disciple of Jesus, the ὑμεῖς of Jn 14,3c is identical in meaning with the ὁ διάκονος ὁ ἐμός of Jn 12,26b.

So, too, the καί in the phrase καὶ ὁ διάκονος ὁ ἐμὸς ἔσται of Jn 12,26 and in the phrase καὶ ὑμεῖς ἦτε of Jn 14,3c has exactly the same meaning, and underlines that every disciple of Jesus, or everyone who serves him in Jn 12,26 will also (καί) share with Jesus in the goal of identification with him as his disciple, and all future disciples of whom the disciples in Jn 14,3c are the type will also (καί) share with Jesus in this same goal.

At a deeper level of meaning the verb ὑψόω of Jn 12,32 corresponds to the verb πορεύομαι in Jn 14,3a. Both designate the spiritual movement of Jesus into union with his Father through his passion-resurrection. Thus the conditional phrase ἐὰν ὑψωθῶ of Jn 12,32 is the equivalent in Johannine terms of the ἐὰν πορευθῶ of Jn 14,3a. Both designate the passion-resurrection of Jesus as the necessary precondition of the future unifying activity of Jn 12,32 and Jn 14,3b.

---

[94] See, ch. V, p, 163.
[95] See, ch. V, pp. 173-175.

Moreover, it is only after this "exaltation" through his passion-resurrection is complete in Jn 12,32 that Jesus will draw all men "to himself" (πρὸς ἐμαυτόν), and after the corresponding departure is complete in Jn 14,3a that Jesus will take the disciples "to himself" (πρὸς ἐμαυτόν). There is an exact correspondence between the πρὸς ἐμαυτόν of the two texts. Both designate the risen Jesus as the goal, or centre of unity.

Finally, the deeper significance in the light of the passion-resurrection of the episode of the Greeks in Jn 12,20-22, as the fulfilment of the eschatological pilgrimage of the nations to the Jerusalem temple, also supports our understanding of Jn 14,2-3, which describes an eschatological pilgrimage to the temple, as the risen Jesus takes the universal community of believers into union with himself as the New Temple. So, too, our understanding of the "exaltation" of Jesus through his passion-resurrection in Jn 12,32 in fulfilment of the prophecy of the "exaltation" of the Jerusalem temple as the goal of the future eschatological pilgrimage of the nations lends support to our interpretation of Jn 14,2-3, where the risen Jesus as the New Temple becomes the eschatological goal of the universal community of believers.

(ii) *Differences.* However, there is an important difference between the passive recipients of the future unifying activity of the risen Jesus in Jn 14,3b and Jn 12,32. The πάντας of Jn 12,32 is explicitly universal, but not so the ὑμεῖς of Jn 14,3b. The "drawing" power of the risen Jesus extends to "all men". By the "exaltation" of Jesus through his passion-resurrection the possibility is open to all men of being "drawn" by the risen Jesus to himself. But the passive recipients of the future unifying activity of the risen Jesus in Jn 14,3b are only relatively universal. These are the disciples themselves directly and indirectly all future disciples whom they represent. In equivalent Johannine terms, they are those who actually respond by faith (comp. Jn 6,44-45).[96]

There is also an important difference between the future activity of the risen Jesus in Jn 14,3b and Jn 12,32. In Jn 14,3b it is explicitly linked with a whole process of "coming" in anticipation of an ever future "coming". In this sense, Jn 14,3b is complementary to Jn 12,32. The union with the risen Jesus in Jn 12,32 and Jn 12,26b will be realised with every intervention of the risen Jesus in anticipation of an ever future intervention at the Second Coming. However, there is no more precise time indication in Jn 14,2-3 as to when this union will be established.

---

[96] On the response of the disciples by faith in the fourth gospel, see, A. VANHOYE, "Notre foi, œuvre divine, d'après le quatrième évangile", *NRT* 86 (1964) 338-54, especially, 342.

Finally, the goal of identity with Jesus promised in Jn 12,26 (ὅπου εἰμὶ ἐγώ) and Jn 12,32 (πρὸς ἐμαυτόν) is already in some way established in Jn 14,2-3, as the disciples are taken in union with the risen Jesus (παραλήμψομαι). However, although this goal of access is already realised in union with the risen Jesus it is not yet fully realised. It is continually in the process of being realised, as the disciples are continually in the process of being taken in union with the risen Jesus (παραλήμψομαι) into ever deeper union with him. This is the eschatological pilgrimage to the temple already realised, and yet not fully realised but continually in the process of being so until the end of time.

2. Union with Jesus: Jn 17,24

(a) LINKS WITH JN 14,2-3. Again the text of Jn 17,24 corresponds in part verbally with our text:

14,3c   ἵνα ὅπου εἰμὶ ἐγὼ καὶ ὑμεῖς   ἦτε.

17,24bc   θέλω ἵνα ὅπου εἰμὶ ἐγὼ κἀκεῖνοι   ὦσιν μετ᾽ ἐμοῦ.[97]

Clearly, the promise of Jn 14,3c must correspond in some way to the object of Christ's prayer in Jn 17,24bc.[98]

Moreover, both of these texts form part of the large unified section of the farewell discourses (Jn 13,1-17,26).[99] The concluding prayer of Jn 17,1-26, which provides the immediate context of Jn 17,24, may be seen as the climax of the movement of these discourses.[100] It is closely linked with the immediately preceding discourses (Jn 13,31-16,33), which provide the immediate context of Jn 14,2-3. The ταῦτα ἐλάλησεν which introduces the prayer refers back to the discourses (Jn 13,31-16,33), and

---

[97] Apart from the addition of μετ᾽ ἐμοῦ in Jn 17,24c, there are the obvious differences required by a prayer addressed directly to the Father in Jn 17,24bc and a promise addressed directly to the disciples in Jn 14,3c. However, we have already explained that the μετ᾽ ἐμοῦ of Jn 17,24c is not an addition with respect to Jn 14,3c. It corresponds to the πρὸς ἐμαυτόν of Jn 14,3b. The one phrase explains the other. See, ch. I, p. 43.

[98] There is also a link between the δόξα of Jn 17,24d and the δοξάζω of Jn 13,31-32(2x). Moreover, the glory of Jesus as the object of vision is linked in the fourth gospel with the theme of the temple (cf. Jn 1,14; comp. also, Jn 12,41). We shall treat of the glory of the New Temple more at length in the following chapter.

[99] On the unity of the farewell discourses (Jn 13,1-17,26), see, ch. V, pp. 140-142.

[100] R. E. BROWN writes: "We now come to one of the most majestic moments in the fourth gospel, the climax of the Last Discourse where Jesus turns to his Father in prayer". See, op. cit. 744; also, C. H. DODD, op. cit. (n. 40), 419-20.

joins the prayer to them.[101] The ταῦτα εἰπών of Jn 18,1 in turn points to what follows as an illustration of what precedes (comp. Jn 20,20.22).[102] The text of Jn 17,24 is thus intimately linked in its immediate context of Jn 17,1-26 with the preceding discourses of Jn 13,31-16,33. As such it is the prayer of Jesus' "hour" (comp. Jn 13,31; 17,1).[103] Like the farewell discourses which precede it, the prayer of Jn 17,1-26 also clarifies in anticipation the meaning of the passion-resurrection of Jesus.[104] Both texts share the common perspective of the "hour" of Jesus.

(b) STRUCTURE OF JN 17,20-24.[105] We may express the structure of Jn 17,20-24 as follows:

17,20a		οὐ περὶ τούτων δὲ ἐρωτῶ μόνον,
b		ἀλλὰ καὶ περὶ τῶν πιστευόντων
c a		διὰ τοῦ λόγου αὐτῶν εἰς ἐμέ,
21a		ἵνα πάντες ἕν ὦσιν,
b		καθὼς σύ, πατήρ, ἐν ἐμοὶ
c		κἀγὼ ἐν σοί,
d		ἵνα καὶ αὐτοὶ ἐν ἡμῖν ἕν ὦσιν,
e b		ἵνα ὁ κόσμος πιστεύσῃ
f		ὅτι σύ με ἀπέστειλας.
22a		κἀγὼ τὴν δόξαν
b c		ἣν δέδωκάς μοι
c		δέδωκα αὐτοῖς,
d		ἵνα ὦσιν ἕν
e		καθὼς ἡμεῖς ἕν·
23a		ἐγὼ ἐν αὐτοῖς
b		καὶ σὺ ἐν ἐμοί,
c		ἵνα ὦσιν τετελειωμένοι εἰς ἕν,
d b		ἵνα γινώσκῃ ὁ κόσμος
e		ὅτι σύ με ἀπέστειλας
f		καὶ ἠγάπησας αὐτοὺς
g		καθὼς ἐμὲ ἠγάπησας.
24a		πατήρ, ὃ δέδωκάς μοι,
b a´		θέλω ἵνα ὅπου εἰμὶ ἐγὼ
c		κἀκεῖνοι ὦσιν μετ' ἐμοῦ,
d		ἵνα θεωρῶσιν τὴν δόξαν τὴν ἐμήν,
e		ἣν δέδωκάς μοι,
f		ὅτι ἠγάπησάς με
g		πρὸ καταβολῆς κόσμου.

---

[101] C.H. DODD underlines the link for us. See, op. cit. (n. 40) 417. The immediate and direct link from the prayer of Jn 17,1-26 is with the phrase "I have overcome the world" of Jn 16,33. The perfect νενίκηκα marks the abiding effect. It places the prayer within the supreme moment of fulfilment.

[102] See, ch. V, also, pp. 140-142.

[103] See, A. GEORGE, "L'heure de Jean XVII", RB 61 (1954) 394.

[104] A. VANHOYE refers to the prayer of Jn 17,1-26 as "La prière qui éclaire le sens de la Passion". See, "L'œuvre du Christ, don du Père (Jn 5,36 et 17,4)", RecSR 48 (1960) 387.

[105] See, E. MALATESTA, "The Literary Structure of John 17", Bib 52 (1971) 190-214.

This minor section of Jn 17,20-24 is composed of three long and majestic sentences (Jn 17,20-21; 17,22-23; 17,24), constructed in a concentric pattern (Jn 17,20abc(a); 17,21(b); 17,22abc(c); 17,22de-23(b'); 17,24(a')). The first strophe (Jn 17,20abc) and the last (Jn 17,24)[106] correspond to each other in that they introduce respectively and conclude the petitions (ἐρωτάω, Jn 17,20a: θέλω, Jn 17,24a).[107] This parallel will help us to explain the full range of the κἀκεῖνοι of Jn 17,24c. Moreover, there is a clear correspondence between the theme of "glory" in the third strophe (Jn 17,22abc) and in the last (Jn 17,24de) and between the theme of "love" in the fourth strophe (Jn 17,23g) and in the last (Jn 17,24f). So, too, the second strophe (Jn 17,21) and the fourth (Jn 17,22de-23) are parallel developments of the theme of unity. This parallel in turn will help us to explain what is implicit in the ὅπου εἰμὶ ἐγώ of Jn 17,24b.

(c) TEXT OF JN 17,24. The nominative pendens ὅ δέδωκάς μοι (Jn 17,24a), artfully placed between πατήρ and θέλω, becomes explicit in the κἀκεῖνοι (Jn 17,24c). Both phrases refer to the same extended object of the prayer of Jesus in Jn 17,20. This is supported by the parallel between the second and fourth strophes (Jn 17,21; 17,22de-23). Jesus prays, then, for all future believers, together with the disciples, who are the gift of the Father to Jesus (comp. Jn 6,37; 10,16).

The petition itself consists of an adverbial clause and principal clause which are arranged in parallelism, and in chiastic order as follows:

17,24   ὅπου – εἰμὶ – ἐγώ // κἀκεῖνοι – ὦσιν – μετ᾽ ἐμοῦ.

This chiastic structure underlines the parallel between ὅπου and μετ᾽ ἐμοῦ. Jesus petitions some kind of fellowship for all believers with himself (μετ᾽ ἐμοῦ) in the place where he himself abides permanently (ὅπου εἰμὶ ἐγώ).

(d) CONTEXT OF JN 17,24. The phrase ὅπου εἰμὶ ἐγώ of Jn 17,24b describes the permanent dwelling-place of Jesus. However, we must turn to the immediate context in order to determine more exactly the implications of the phrase. In this petition of Jn 17,24bc we have the definitive answer to the problem of the departure of Jesus in Jn 17,11ac (comp. Jn 17,13a).[108] Jesus is leaving the world on his way to the Father.

---

[106] The text of Jn 17,24 itself is so constructed that the first three lines lead up to the central line (Jn 17,24d), while the last three lines modify the second part of the central line. This division into seven lines, based upon the major grammatical components of the sentence, illustrates the exquisite delicacy of its composition. See, E. MALATESTA, op. cit. (n. 105) 208.

[107] The latter verb is stronger and more majestic than the former.

[108] This point is well made by R. BULTMANN. See, op. cit. 519.

The ἔρχομαι of Jn 17,11c.13a is a futuristic present.[109] The journey of Jesus is still future, and yet in some way already in the process of being realised.[110] There is a marked contrast between this situation of Jesus leaving the world and journeying to the Father (Jn 17,11ac), and the disciples remaining behind in the world (Jn 17,11b; comp. Jn 17,15a).[111] This ultimately explains why Jesus prays for the disciples in Jn 17,24. He prays that his disciples may rejoin him one day (unspecified) after his departure from this world in order to be with him in the eternal dwelling-place, or temple of his Father, in heaven.[112] For the moment this heavenly sphere is unattainable by the disciples (comp. Jn 13,33).

This heavenly sphere of divine existence is where the Father of Jesus dwells in contrast to the human sphere of existence in-the-world which Jesus is leaving, and where the disciples must continue to dwell (Jn 17,11b; comp. Jn 17,15a). The contrast is clearly marked in the first lines of the prayer (ἐπι τῆς γῆς, Jn 17,4a..παρὰ σεαυτῷ ... πρὸ τοῦ τὸν κόσμον εἶναι παρὰ σοί, Jn 17,5bc; comp. πρὸ καταβολῆς κόσμου, Jn 17,24g). The opening gesture of the prayer also designates heaven as the dwelling-place of the Father.[113] So Jesus prays for all future believers to be there with him in the eternal temple. This is where Jesus himself abides permanently.

But the implications of the phrase ὅπου εἰμὶ ἐγώ of Jn 17,24b may also be determined still further. The ἐγώ εἰμι of the phrase indicates the present of the divine mode of existence-in-God which transcends the human mode of existence-in-the-world, the eternal being-in-God as distinct from the temporal being-in-the-world.[114] This heavenly a-temporal mode of existence is specified further in the immediate context as an in-being of Jesus in the Father.

The theme of unity dominates the whole prayer. Jesus prays that his disciples (Jn 17,11g) and all believers may be one, after the model of the in-being of Jesus in the Father (καθώς, Jn 17,11g; 17,21b; 17,22de). The implication of the goal for which Jesus prays in Jn 17,24bc is that the

---

[109] See, *BDF, 323, (3)*.

[110] Hence, C. H. DODD correctly observes: "The prayer in some sort is the ascent of the Son to the Father". See, *op. cit.* (n. 40), 419.

[111] The central portion of the prayer (Jn 17,6-19) contemplates the disciples in their situation in the world after Christ's departure (Jn 17,11ab).

[112] D. MOLLAT sees this as the whole purpose of the Incarnation. See, *op. cit.* (n. 38) 324.

[113] J. McPOLIN expresses the idea well: "The Johannine Christ, man and divine Son, in a solemn attitude of prayer raises human eyes to "heaven" (v. 1), that "space" in which he as Incarnate Son experiences communion with his Father". See, *John. New Testament Message 6* (Dublin, 1979) 182.

[114] See, ch. I, p. 45.

disciples may share in this in-being of Jesus in the Father. When Jesus prays, then, that his disciples may be with him in the eternal dwelling-place, or temple of his Father, in heaven, he is implicitly (or indirectly) asking also that they may be in union with himself where he dwells perpetually in union with his Father.

However, there are also further developments of this theme of unity in the immediate context of Jn 17,24.[115] It is further defined in terms of a unity of mutual in-being. The second (Jn 17,21) and fourth (Jn 17,22d-23) strophes of the unified section of Jn 17,20-24 are parallel developments of the theme of unity. In typical Johannine style of step-parallelism John takes up again in Jn 17,22d-23 the theme of unity from Jn 17,21, and develops it still further (just as the mention of the theme of unity in Jn 17,21 takes up the previous mention of the same theme of Jn 17,11g). This parallelism between Jn 17,21.22d-23 may be illustrated as follows:

21a ἵνα πάντες ἓν ὦσιν,	22d ἵνα ὦσιν ἓν (ἵνα ὦσιν ἓν
b καθὼς σύ, πατήρ, ἐν ἐμοὶ	Α΄.e καθὼς ἡμεῖς ἕν· καθὼς ἡμεῖς)
Α.c κἀγὼ ἐν σοί,	(17,11g)
d ἵνα καὶ αὐτοὶ ἐν ἡμῖν	23a ἐγὼ ἐν αὐτοῖς καὶ σὺ ἐν ἐμοί,
Β. ἓν ὦσιν,	Β΄.b ἵνα ὦσιν τετελειωμένοι εἰς ἕν,
e ἵνα ὁ κόσμος πιστεύσῃ	c ἵνα γινώσκῃ ὁ κόσμος
C.f ὅτι σύ με ἀπέστειλας.	C΄.d ὅτι σύ με ἀπέστειλας
	e καὶ ἠγάπησας αὐτοὺς
	f καθὼς ἐμὲ ἠγάπησας.

The ἡμεῖς ἕν (Jn 17,22e; comp. 17,11g) resumes the σύ......ἐν ἐμοὶ κἀγὼ ἐν σοί (17,21bc), where the unity of the Father and Jesus has been explained in terms of a mutual in-being of the Father and Jesus (comp. Jn 10,38). So, also, the ἵνα......ἐν ἡμῖν ἓν ὦσιν (Jn 17,21d), or unity of believers in the Father and Jesus (they in us) is resumed by the ἐγω ἐν αὐτοῖς καὶ σὺ ἐν ἐμοί (17,23a) and completed with its complementary Johannine aspect of a unity of Jesus and the Father in the disciples (we in them). The ἐγώ of Jn 17,23a depends on the ἵνα of Jn 17,22d, and not on the καθώς of Jn 17,22e.[116] Because it is explicitly stated that the Father is

---

[115] On these parallel developments of this theme of unity in Jn 17,21.22b-23, see, J. F. RANDALL, "The Theme of Unity in John 17: 20-23", *ETL* 41 (1965) 388-89; also, E. MALATESTA, *op. cit.* (n. 105) 206-207; Panel A provides us with his schematic arrangement of the Prayer of Jesus.

[116] This is erroneously suggested by E. MALATESTA. See, *op. cit.* (n. 105), 206-7. The two constructions καθώς..καί of Jn 17,21bc.22e-23b are similar. But the καί in each construction has a different function. In the chiastic structure noted by Malatesta the ἐγώ (23a) does not depend on the καθώς in the second phrase, but depends on the ἵνα (22d); the ἡμεῖς ἕν (22e) omitted in the chiasm takes up again the σύ, πατήρ, ἐν ἐμοὶ κἀγὼ ἐν σοί.

in Jesus and that Jesus is in the disciples (Jn 17,23a), it can be inferred that the Father is in the disciples by being in Jesus.

Thus Jesus prays in Jn 17,24bc implicitly (or indirectly) that all future believers may be one in the Father and Jesus (they in us) (Jn 17,21d), and this same union is equivalently expressed in complementary Johannine terms of a reciprocal relationship in the union of the Father and Jesus in the believer (we in them) (Jn 17,23a).

(e) APPLICATION TO JN 14,2-3.

(i) *Similarities.* In Jn 17,24bc Jesus is praying to his Father for the fulfilment of the same goal, or destiny, which he promises to realise himself for his disciples in Jn 14,3c. Moreover, our understanding of κἀκεῖνοι in Jn 17,24c with reference to all future believers supports our extension of the meaning of the ὑμεῖς of Jn 14,3c beyond the disciples (directly and explicitly designated) to all future believers represented by them.[117]

So, too, the μετ᾽ ἐμοῦ of Jn 17,24c corresponds to the πρὸς ἐμαυτόν of Jn 14,3b. The presence of μετ᾽ἐμοῦ in Jn 17,24c is not really an addition with respect to Jn 14,2-3. Both phrases indicate some kind of fellowship with Jesus. The omission of μετ᾽ἐμοῦ in Jn 14,3c, or at least the fact that it was not deemed necessary by the evangelist, merely confirms our interpretation of our text. This aspect of fellowship with Jesus, or communion with him, in a common destiny is adequately contained without any μετ᾽ἐμοῦ in Jn 14,2-3, if our interpretation of πρὸς ἐμαυτόν is correct.

Also, our understanding of ὅπου εἰμὶ ἐγώ in Jn 17,24b with reference to the eternal temple of God/Father in heaven supports a similar understanding of the οἰκία τοῦ πατρός μου in Jn 14,2a, where the οἰκία τοῦ πατρός μου is qualified (at least indirectly) by the ὅπου εἰμὶ ἐγώ of Jn 14,3c as the place where Jesus is, or abides, perpetually and permanently.

The promise of being with Jesus where he is (Jn 14,3c) and the prayer for the same purpose (Jn 17,24bc), provide an answer to the problem of this departure of Jesus out of the world (negative aspect) to the Father (positive aspect). There is an exact correspondence between the perspective of the departure of Jesus out of the world (negative aspect) to the Father (positive aspect) in the text of Jn 14,2-3 (πορεύομαι, Jn 14,2b.3a; comp. ὑπάγω, Jn 13,33; 14,4.5) and the departure expressed in equivalent Johannine terms in the context of Jn 17,24 (ἔρχομαι, Jn 17,11c.13a). By this departure, as it were, Jesus is crossing the threshold of eternity.

---

[117] See, ch. V, pp. 173-175.

It is the same unity that is prayed for and promised implicitly in both texts (Jn 17,24bc; 14,3c). The implications of the phrase ὅπου εἰμὶ ἐγώ are identical as explained in the immediate context of both texts. We may express the parallels schematically as follows:

Jesus in the Father

14,10.11.20 ·   εγὼ ἐν τῷ πατρί (μου).   17,21   ἐγὼ ἐν σοί.

Disciples in Jesus

14,20   ὑμεῖς ἐν ἐμοί.   17,21   αὐτοὶ ἐν ἡμῖν ἓν ὦσιν.

The goal or destiny of the disciples is to share with Jesus in the unity of the Father, or to be in union with Jesus in the unity of the Father.

So, too, the complementary aspect of this same unity is expressed in equivalent Johannine terms in the immediate context of both texts. We may express these parallels schematically as follows:

14,10 ἐγὼ ἐν τῷ πατρὶ

    καὶ
ὁ πατὴρ ἐν ἐμοί.......
ὁ δὲ πατὴρ ὁ ἐν ἐμοὶ μένων.......

11 ἐγὼ ἐν τῷ πατρὶ   17,21 σύ, πατήρ, ἐν ἐμοὶ
    καὶ   καὶ
ὁ πατὴρ ἐν ἐμοί ·   ἐγὼ   ἐν σοί,

20 ἐγὼ ἐν τῷ πατρί μου   21 ἵνα καὶ αὐτοὶ ἐν
καὶ ὑμεῖς ἐν ἐμοὶ   ἡμῖν ἓν ὦσιν.....
κα(ὶ ἐγὼ) ἐν ὑμῖν.

23 μονὴν παρ' αὐτῷ ποιησόμεθα.   23 ἐγὼ ἐν αὐτοῖς,
                                 καὶ
                               σὺ ἐν ἐμοί.....

Thus we find confirmation of our understanding of the union of Jn 14,2-3 as the equivalent in reciprocal Johannine terms of the union described in Jn 14,23.[118]

(ii) *Differences.* However, there are also some important differences. The promise of Jn 14,3c is addressed directly (and explicitly) to the disciples only, but the prayer of Jn 14,24bc is for all believers (including the disciples).

Besides, what Jesus prays for in Jn 17,24bc as he crosses the threshold of eternity through his passion-resurrection is described in the process of fulfilment in Jn 14,3bc. It is certain that the prayer of Jn 17,24

---

[118] See, ch. V, pp. 163-166.

will be heard in view of the promise of Jn 14,3bc. In our understanding of Jn 14,2-3, then, everything that is prayed for in Jn 17,24bc is described in the process of fulfilment in the New Temple of the risen Jesus, or the τόπος prepared of Jn 14,2-3, in anticipation of the Second Coming. The prayer of Jn 17,24bc is perfectly complemented by the double perspective of realised and final eschatology in Jn 14,3bc.

No precise details are given of how, or when, the prayer of Jn 17,24bc will be answered.[119] Only the purpose of its fulfilment is designated in Jn 17,24d. In Jn 14,2-3, on the other hand, the promise is conditional on the preparation of a place and the return of Jesus to take the disciples to himself. Jesus must first depart to render the goal of the eternal temple in heaven accessible by the preparation of a place through his passion-resurrection before the prayer of Jn 17,24bc can be fulfilled (after the preparation) by Jesus "coming again" to take the disciples into union with himself. Moreover, the fulfilment of the prayer of Jn 17,24bc is not confined to any isolated intervention of the risen Jesus alone in Jn 14,3b, after the passion-resurrection is complete (ἐὰν πορευθῶ). It is the effect of every possible "coming" of the risen Jesus. In this sense, the promise of Jn 14,3bc is complementary to the prayer of Jn 17,24bc.

F. THE ASCENDING/DESCENDING MOVEMENT OF JN 14,2-3

We have already referred to the ascending/descending movement of our text.[120] Although there is nothing in the vocabulary of Jn 14,2-3 itself to indicate directly an ascending/descending movement, such a movement is at least implicit in the understanding of the text which we have gained so far at a second deeper level of meaning.[121] At this deeper level of meaning the πορεύομαι of Jn 14,2-3 is the equivalent in Johannine terms of the ὑψόω of Jn 12,32, meaning literally "to exalt" (comp. also 3,14; 8,28); and both verbs refer to the passion-resurrection of Jesus.[122] It follows that the goal of this journey in Jn 14,2-3 cannot at this level of understanding refer to the Jerusalem temple, but must indicate the heavenly temple of the Father's house. Hence, the movement of Jn 14,2-3 is (at least implicitly) an ascending/descending one.

Such an ascending/descending movement also pervades the whole discourse (Jn 13,31-14,31).[123] An attempt to discern the function which

---

[119] B. F. WESTCOTT comments well on Jn 17,24d: "The scene of this vision is not defined. Under one aspect it may be placed at the Lord's "Presence". But no one special application exhausts the meaning of the words. Comp. III, 18". See, op. cit. 247.

[120] See, ch. V, pp. 172-173.

[121] See, ch. V, pp. 172-173.

[122] See, ch. I, n. 29.

[123] See, ch. V, pp. 153-154.

this motif of ascent/descent has elsewhere in the fourth gospel may help us to clarify its significance in Jn 14,2-3. Two texts are particularly important (Jn 1,51; 3,13).[124]

(i) *JN 1,51.* The text is as follows:

> 1,51 ἀμὴν ἀμὴν, λέγω ὑμῖν,
> ὄψεσθε τὸν οὐρανὸν ἀνεῳγότα
> καὶ τοὺς ἀγγέλους τοῦ Θεοῦ ἀναβαίνοντας καὶ καταβαίνοντας
> ἐπὶ τὸν υἱὸν τοῦ ἀνθρώπου.

The pair of verbs ἀναβαίνω/καταβαίνω (ascend/descend) appears in John for the first time in Jn 1,51. Here most scholars see a reference to Gn 28,12 from which the participles, in just this precise order, are drawn.[125] A future vision of "heaven opened" (τὸν οὐρανὸν ἀνεῳγότα)[126] is promised to the disciples. This theme of the opening of the heavens and a subsequent revelation of the truth is frequent in apocalyptic literature.[127] The main point of Jn 1,51, then, is to assert that Jesus, the Son of Man, will be the place of heavenly revelation.[128] The "ascent/descent" of the angels between heaven and earth designates in figurative language a continual and unbroken exchange between the transcendent sphere of God and the sphere of men. The saying thus speaks of a close and continual intercourse between heaven and earth in Jesus, as the place of the revelation of heavenly things.

---

[124] We also have the "ascending/descending" pattern in Jn 6. There we find the verb ἀναβαίνω in 6,62 and the verb καταβαίνω in 6,33.38.41.42.50.51.58. However, Jn 1,51 and Jn 3,13 are the only two verses in the fourth gospel where the "ascending/descending" pattern occurs linked together in the same verse. The two cases are not entirely identical. In Jn 1,51 the angels, not the Son of Man, ascend and descend; in Jn 3,13 the "ascending/descending" pattern is used directly with reference to the Son of Man.

[125] W. MICHAELIS is a notable exception. See, "Joh. 1,51, Gen. 28,12 und das Menschensohn-Problem", *TLZ* 85 (1960) 578.

[126] In contrast with the perfect of the verb in John, we find the present in Mk 1,10, and the aorist in Mt 3,16 and Lk 3,21.

[127] Comp. Ap 4,1; 19,11; Test. Levi, 18,1-14; Test. Judah, 29,1-6. On this theme, see, F. LENTZEN-DEIS, "Das Motiv der 'Himmelsöffnung' in verschiedenen Gattungen der Umweltliteratur des N.T.", *Bib* 50 (1969) 315-27. The remarks of V. TAYLOR on Mk 1,10 are also pertinent. See, *The Gospel according to Mark* (London, 1966²) 160.

[128] Most scholars, despite differences in important details, correctly understand Jn 1,51 in this way. A full list of these authors with their views may be found in F.J. MOLONEY, *The Johannine Son of Man* (Rome, 1976) 30-32. S. PANCARO sums up our line of exegesis well: "The promise to Nathanael means that he will recognise Jesus as the new 'locus' of divine revelation (cf. Gen. 28,16f)". See, *The Law in the Fourth Gospel. The Torah and the Gospel. Moses and Jesus, Judaism and Christianity according to John* (Leiden, 1975) 304.

(ii) *JN 3,13*. The text is as follows:

3,13   καὶ οὐδεὶς ἀναβέβηκεν εἰς τὸν οὐρανὸν
εἰ μὴ ὁ ἐκ τοῦ οὐρανοῦ καταβάς,
ὁ υἱὸς τοῦ ἀνθρώπου.

Here we find once again the verbal pair "ascend/descend".[129] The text itself is elliptical. Some commentators attempt to understand it (and so complete its meaning) in the light of its immediate context. Jn 3,12 presents a contrast between "earthly things" (ἐπίγεια) and "heavenly things (ἐπουράνια)). It would seem that the ἐπίγεια refer to the "new generation" of Jn 3,3-8.[130] Nicodemus should have understood all about these ἐπίγεια. They were a part of Israel's heritage (cf. Wis 9,16-18; Jb 34,14; Ex 15,8; Pss 18,15; 51,10; Is 40,7; 44,3; 59,21; Ez 11,19-20; 36,26-27; Jl 2,28-29; comp. also IQS III, 13-IV, 26, especially IQS IV, 20-22). These things are ἐπίγεια, because they happen to men while still on earth.

The term ἐπουράνια is more difficult to explain. It occurs nowhere else in the fourth gospel. However, it would seem that it should be referred to the Johannine use of οὐρανός (heaven).[131] The use of the term οὐρανός in Jn 3,13(2x) recalls the use of this term ἐπουράνια in Jn 3,12. The term οὐρανός is closely linked with the person of Jesus himself. It indicates the source of his mission. But the phrase ἐκ τοῦ οὐρανοῦ καταβάς of Jn 3,13 does not affirm the heavenly origin of Jesus again merely as a fact. Jesus has just spoken of himself as revealer (Jn 3,11). His descent from heaven gives this revelation of Jesus a unique authority. Jn 3,13 is not a description of "heavenly things". It is a statement that Jesus reveals "heavenly things" with a unique authority. This same theme is taken up again later in the discourse (Jn 3,31-36).[132] In Jn 3,31 Jesus is he "who comes down from heaven" (ὁ ἄνωθεν ἐρχόμενος // ὁ ἐκ τοῦ οὐρανοῦ ἐρχόμενος). But he is also the revealer who "utters the words of God" in Jn 3,34. The authority of Jesus for this revelation is again his descent from heaven.

However, it is a mistake (in our view) to place the emphasis unduly on the heavenly descent of the Son of Man in our understanding of Jn

---

[129] We have already noted an important difference between the texts of Jn 1,51 and Jn 3,13. See, note, 124.

[130] On this line of interpretation, see J. F. MOLONEY, *op. cit.* (n. 128), 48, n. 39; also, I. DE LA POTTERIE, "Jesus et Nicodemus: de revelatione Jesus et vera fide in eum (Jo 3,11-21)", *VD* 47 (1969) 260-62.

[131] See, ch. I, p. 39.

[132] On the links between Jn 3,11-21 and Jn 3,31-36, see, J. F. MOLONEY, op. cit. (n. 128) 45-46.

3,13.[133] The movement of "ascent" is also essential to its meaning (ἀναβέβηκεν). The text is designedly elliptical. It cannot be adequately and completely explained, even with an ingenious paraphrase. It is true that the formula "no one ascends to heaven" or "who ascends to heaven" is a fixed formula in Sapiential literature (cf. Dt 30,12; Prv 30,4; I Bar 3,29; Wis 9,16-18; 4 Esd 4,8). The formula as such denies the possibility of man's ascent to heaven to learn the secrets of God. But the first part of Jn 3,13 does not say merely that "no one" (οὐδείς) has ascended to heaven. Jesus says: "no one....except the....." (οὐδείς... εἰ μὴ ὁ.....). This is a very different thing from a complete negation. Here we have an example of the "self-contained allusiveness" of the fourth gospel.[134] The "ascending/descending" pattern is again linked in Jn 3,13 with Jesus as the unique and authentic revealer of God. But the text also indicates, at least implicitly, that Jesus "has ascended" already (ἀναβέβηκεν — perfect of completed action). Hence, the theme of revelation is inseparably linked in this text with the "ascent" of the Son of Man, who alone has (in some sense) already "ascended" to heaven.

This "ascension" is explained as an "exaltation" in Jn 3,14 (ὑψόω) (2x). This verse is tightly linked with Jn 3,13 by co-ordinating καί, meaning "and so".[135] The Son of Man who is the unique revealer must be "lifted up" (ὑψόω). The δεῖ indicates that this "exaltation" is essential to God's plan.[136] The logical link between Jn 3,13 and Jn 3,14 is tight. It is because Jesus, the Son of Man, is the unique revealer of God that he must be "lifted up".

However, the four texts which mention "exaltation" (ὑψόω) in John all point to the cross (cf. Jn 3,14(2x); 8,28; 12,32.34).[137] The explanatory comment of Jn 12,33 puts this beyond doubt. So, too, does the interpretation of the crowd in Jn 12,34. The cross, then, is the high-point of revelation. But "exaltation" in John is something more than just a material "lifting up" of Jesus by his physical death on the cross. The verb ὑψόω has a double meaning'.[138] It designates a deep spiritual reality — the "exaltation" of Jesus to his Father by a movement into glory through

---

[133] We accept the shorter form of the text, without the addition ὁ ὢν ἐν τῷ οὐρανῷ. For a full discussion of the variants, see, I. DE LA POTTERIE, op. cit. (n. 130) 264.

[134] See, E. C. HOSKYNS, op. cit. 67.

[135] See, BDF, 442; also, G. GAETA, "Il dialogo con Nicodemo" (Studi Biblici 26) (Brescia, 1974) 78-79.

[136] The use of δεῖ here in Jn 3,14 suggests a link between this saying and passion predictions of the Synoptics (Mk 8,31; 9,31; 10,33, par.s).

[137] On the Johannine theme of "exaltation", see, W. THÜSING, Die Erhöhung und Verherrlichung Jesu im Johannesevangelium (Münster, ²1970).

[138] On the double meaning of this verb, see, D. W. WEAD, op. cit. (n. 43) 34-36.

the passion-resurrection-ascension. In the "exaltation" of Jesus there is no separation between the cross, the resurrection, the ascension, and the glory.[139] They are all facets of one and the same indivisible spiritual movement of Jesus into communion with his heavenly Father. This movement is described in John with a variety of verbs.[140] Among these verbs we find ὑψόω and πορεύομαι. At this deeper level of meaning the "exaltation" of the Son of Man in Jn 3,14 (ὑψόω) is identical with the journey of Jesus in Jn 14,2-3 (πορεύομαι). In fact, belief in the "heavenly things" (ἐπουράνια) of Jn 3,12 is only possible in John through this "exaltation" of Jesus by his journey to his Father through his glorifying passion-resurrection (cf. Jn 13,19; 14,29).

(iii) *JN 14,2-3*. It is hardly suprising, then, to find that the "ascending/descending" movement of Jn 14,2-3 is intimately linked in its immediate context with the theme of revelation. There Jesus is explicitly designated in Jn 14,6 as "the truth" (ἀλήθεια) in person (ἐγώ εἰμι), or the revelation of God; and response to him is indicated in terms of faith (πιστεύω, Jn 14,1(2x).10-11(3x).12.29). Besides, the whole subsequent development of the discourse unfolds in terms designated to evoke a theophany (δείκνυμι, Jn 14,8.9; ἐμφανίζω, Jn 14,21.22(2x)), and a response to it (γινώσκω, Jn 14,7(3x).9.20; ὁράω, Jn 14,7.9(2x); θεωρέω, Jn 14,19(2x)). So, too, the whole thrust of the dialogue which follows Jn 14,2-3 is to correct a popular Jewish misconception of the eschatological intervention as a theophany visible to all men by directing attention to a deeper spiritual understanding of it in the light of the passion-resurrection.[141] We will now explore the significance of this "ascending/descending" movement of Jn 14,2-3, when interpreted within this immediate context of the discourse as a whole (Jn 13,31-14,31), and in the light of the passion-resurrection of Jesus.

Jn 14,6 designates Jesus as "the way" (ὁδός) — the only way of access to the Father for all men as "the truth" (ἀλήθεια) and "the life" (ζωή). It should be noted that this idea of Jesus as "the way" gradually begins to dominate the subsequent development of the discourse. However, the idea of the Father as the goal is also expressed (πρὸς τὸν πατέρα). Hence, we find a significant correspondence between Jn 14,6 and Jn 14,2-3. We may express this schematically as follows:

---

[139] The movement is just one continuous action of ascent (comp. Jn 20,17). See, H. VAN DEN BUSSCHE, "L'attente de la grande révélation dans le quatrième évangile", *NRT* 75 (1953) 1009-1019.

[140] See, ch. I, n. 29.

[141] See, ch. V, pp. 154-157.

14,2-3: Goal:	Father's house (οἰκία) with many rooms (μοναί) where Jesus abides perpetually (ὅπου εἰμὶ ἐγώ)	14,6: Father (πρὸς τὸν πατέρα)
Way:	Journey of preparation (πορεύομαι ἑτοιμάσαι τόπον) ... return (πάλιν ἔρχομαι) to take the disciples (παραλήμψομαι).	Jesus (δι' ἐμοῦ) [142] as "the truth" (ἀλήθεια) and "the life" (ζωή).

Every comparison between Jn 14,6 and Jn 14,2-3 is subject to the absolute condition of the departure of Jesus to prepare a place for the disciples through his passion-resurrection (ἐὰν πορευθῶ καὶ ἑτοιμάσω τόπον ὑμῖν). At a deeper level of meaning, then, Jesus is "the way" to the Father as "the truth" (ἀλήθεια) and "the life" (ζωή) in his journey to the Father through his passion-resurrection (ascending movement of Jesus alone) (πορεύομαι). This is clearly in accord with Johannine perspectives elsewhere in the fourth gospel (comp. Jn 3,13-14; 8,28; [143] 12,32). As such the passion-resurrection of Jesus opens up the inner life of the Father in union with Jesus, that is, the profound import of the ὅπου εἰμὶ ἐγώ of Jn 14,3c (cf. Jn 14,10-11,20). When we interpret Jn 14,2-3 at this deeper level of meaning in the light of its immediate context, then, Jesus becomes the τόπος prepared through his passion-resurrection, or the New Temple, and at the same time and in the same way the supreme revelation of the inner life of the Father in union with Jesus. [144] As such he is the means by which men have access to the inner life of God, the manner also or the condition of their access (δι' ἐμοῦ).

After the journey of preparation (ἐὰν πορευθῶ) the risen Jesus (now the New Temple) becomes "the way" to the Father as "the truth" (ἀλήθεια) and "the life" (ζωή) by his return (πάλιν ἔρχομαι) (descending movement) and by taking the disciples to himself (παραλήμψομαι ὑμᾶς πρὸς ἐμαυτόν) (ascending movement). To the ascending movement of Jn 14,2-3 after the preparation by the passion-resurrection there is a

---

[142] The preposition should be understood in an instrumental sense to indicate that Jesus himself is the means of access to the Father. As such, it may be interpreted in a spatial sense to correspond to a local interpretation of Jn 14,2-3; and also in a spiritual sense to correspond to a deeper level of understanding. However, it may also be interpreted in a modal sense. See, *BDF*, 223 (3).

[143] W. BAUER relates Jn 8,28 to the passion in John. See, *op. cit.* 124. On this theme of revelation in John's passion, see, J. R. FORESTELL, *The Word of the Cross* (Rome, 1974); also, H. VAN DEN BUSSCHE, *op. cit.* (n. 139).

[144] J. M. REESE expresses this deeper import of the imagery of the "way". See, "Literary Structure of Jo 13:31-14,31; 16:5-6.16-33", *CBQ* 34 (1972) 325.

corresponding movement of ascent in Jn 14,6 (παραλήμψομαι ὑμᾶς πρὸς ἐμαυτόν//ἔρχεται πρὸς τὸν πατέρα). The action of the risen Jesus taking the disciples passively to the Father in Jn 14,2-3 corresponds to the action of the disciples themselves actively "coming" to the Father in Jn 14,6. In Jn 14,2-3, however, the ascending movement (παραλήμψομαι) is the effect of the descending movement of the ἔρχομαι. But such a descending movement is also implicit in Jn 14,6. As "the truth" Jesus is the revelation of the Father to men. In the perspective opened up by Jn 14,2-3 this implies a movement of descent, or an emanation of "the truth" (ἀλήθεια) from the Father (in heaven) to men (on earth).[145] When we interpret Jn 14,2-3 at this deeper level of meaning in the light of its immediate context, then, Jesus as the τόπος prepared, or the New Temple, becomes the source of a descending movement of revelation from God to men.

Besides, the whole immediate context suggests that Jn 14,2-3 should be interpreted in terms of faith. The parallel situation between the disciples and the Jews in Jn 13,33 already implies an inability of the disciples to "come" (ἔρχομαι) to the goal of Jesus' journey through lack of faith[146]. But this inability will be remedied after the departure of Jesus through his passion-resurrection, when he returns to take the disciples to himself in Jn 14,2-3. Besides, the chiastic structure of Jn 14,1b suggests that our text of Jn 14,2-3 should be interpreted of access to the Father through Jesus by faith.[147] The activity of the disciples significantly absent from Jn 14,2-3 would be thus adequately supplied by the faith-response of the disciples to the revelation emanating from the New Temple of the risen Jesus. This faith activity of the disciples would also provide the perfect complement to the activity of the risen Jesus taking the disciples passively into the inner life of the Father in the Son opened up by the passion-resurrection in "the truth" of his own person as the New Temple.

So, too, the ἔρχομαι of Jn 14,6 should be interpreted in its immediate context in terms of access to the Father through Jesus by faith. Such a role of Jesus as Mediator is formulated equivalently in Johannine terms of "knowledge" (γινώσκω, Jn 14,7-9(4x)) and "vision" (ὁράω, Jn 14,7-9(3x)). Moreover, the inclusion which brackets the whole immediate context of Jn 14,2-3 and Jn 14,6 points to faith as the dominant theme of this whole unified section of Jn 14,1-11 (πιστεύω, Jn 14,1(2x).10.11(3x)). When we interpret Jn 14,2-3 in the light of its immediate context, then, we find that men have access to the inner life of the Father by faith once

---

[145] I. DE LA POTTERIE highlights this ascending/descending movement of Jn 14,6. See, " 'Je suis la voie, la vérité et la vie' (Jn 14,6)", *NRT* 88 (1966) 938.

[146] See, ch. V, p. 149.

[147] See, ch. V, pp. 167-168.

it becomes accessible to them in the New Temple of the risen Jesus as "the truth" and "the life", or accessible to them in union with Jesus as the supreme revelation of the inner life of the Father. This access is by perfect faith, after the passion-resurrection of Jesus (comp. Jn 14,29).

However, in our understanding of Jn 14,2-3 the disciples will be given access to the Father in the New Temple of the risen Jesus, or the τόπος prepared (παραλήμψομαι). There is nothing in the text of Jn 14,2-3 to indicate when this movement of access begins, except that it is conditional on the passion-resurrection (ἐὰν πορευθῶ) and the effect of the "coming" of the risen Jesus (ἔρχομαι). However, there is some indication in the immediate context; and we also discover there an important complementary aspect to our understanding of Jn 14,2-3.

The ἔρχομαι of Jn 14,3b is taken up again in the ἔρχομαι of Jn 14,18 (descending movement). Here it designates a whole process of the "coming" of the risen Jesus inseparably linked with the inner revealing action of the Spirit of truth to which the disciples respond by perfect faith, and with an indwelling of Jesus (and the Father) in the believer — a process which is initiated by the immediate future intervention of the risen Jesus at the resurrection.[148] But this union of Jn 14,23 describes a reciprocal aspect of the same union described in Jn 14,2-3.[149] Once this union of Jn 14,23 is established in the believer by the inner revealing activity of the Spirit of truth, the goal of access to the Father promised in Jn 14,2-3 is attained at least initially, although the whole process of access described there will only be terminated in heaven at the end of time. It is this inner revealing action of the Spirit of truth which first establishes the link between Jesus (and the Father) and the believer in Jn 14,23, and thus sets the whole dynamic movement of Jn 14,2-3 (after the preparation) in motion.

In our understanding of Jn 14,2-3, then, when we interpret it within its immediate context clarified in the light of the passion-resurrection of Jesus the believer already possesses the eschatological reality of Jn 14,2-3 by faith under the action of the Spirit of truth in the New Temple of the risen Jesus. But the believer will also possess it ever more fully by an ever deepening faith under the same revealing action. This ever deepening action of the Spirit of truth described in the immediate context (comp. Jn 14,21.26) interprets perfectly in terms of an ever deepening faith the action of the risen Jesus in Jn 14,2-3 taking the disciples in(to) union with himself (πρὸς ἐμαυτόν) in the Father (ὅπου εἰμὶ ἐγώ). Thus the whole eschatological reality described in Jn 14,2-3 is interpreted in its immediate context in terms of the inner revealing action of the Spirit of truth in the heart of the believer. In response to this inner revealing action of the

---

[148] See, ch. V, pp. 154-157.
[149] See, ch. V, pp. 163-166.

Spirit of truth the believer already possesses this eschatological reality by faith, and possesses it ever more fully by an ever deepening faith, until it is possessed by him finally at death and by all believers together at the end of time.

CONCLUSION

We now have an interpretation of our text at the second level of meaning. The Father's house with the many rooms of the first member (Jn 14,2a) designates the heavenly temple as the inner spiritual "space" where Jesus abides permanently in union with his Father, and where there are also possibilities (enough and more than enough) for all believers to abide there spiritually in union with Jesus.

The second member (Jn 14,2a-3) indicates that Jesus is about to leave the disciples (and in some sense is already in the process of doing so) in order to make this eternal temple of the Father's house, with its many possibilities for others to dwell there, accessible to all future believers by providing the New Temple of his risen body through his passion-resurrection.

Afterwards, the risen Jesus (now the New Temple) will intervene in anticipation of his ever future eschatological intervention at the Second Coming (and in some sense is already in the process of continually doing so) in order to take all believers in union with himself (and so already occupying by their "spiritual positions" in the risen Jesus the μοναί of the Father's house prepared for them) into an ever deeper union with himself in the Father. Moreover, this journey of union is along the same way previously opened up by Jesus himself in his passion-resurrection.

Jesus is thus represented as one who will intervene continually (after his passion-resurrection) in order to take believers along the way of his passion-resurrection into the heavenly sanctuary of the Father's house. This future activity of the risen Jesus is a unifying activity which will continue throughout the whole eschatological period until the end of time. But believers once they are united to Jesus in the New Temple of his risen body will occupy, in anticipation of the Parousia, the μοναί of the Father's house prepared for them.

Moreover, we can now see how this profound spiritual meaning of our text may be further clarified in the light of its immediate context. It is the imminent future "coming" of Jesus at the resurrection, linked as it is with the inner revealing action of the Spirit of truth to which believers respond by perfect faith, which establishes the bond of unity between the risen Jesus (with the Father) and the believers; and thus sets in motion the whole dynamic process by which the risen Jesus takes believers in union with himself into ever deeper union, after the preparation of a place. So, too, the ever deepening faith of believers under the action of the Spirit of truth complements this action of the risen Jesus taking believers into ever deeper union with himself in the Father. It is by faith, under the action of the Spirit of truth, that believers possess the eschatological reality described in our text, and by an ever deepening faith under the ever deepening action of the same Spirit of truth that believers possess ever more fully this same eschatological reality.

At this deeper level of meaning the way is now open for a solution to the apparent contradictions in our understanding of Jn 14,2-3 at the first level of understanding. To this we shall turn our attention in the final chapter of our thesis. But first we will compare the perspectives opened up by our interpretation of Jn 14,2-3 at this second level of understanding with those of other Johannine texts.

CHAPTER VII

COMPLEMENTARY TEXTS

We will now compare the perspectives of Jn 14,2-3 with some other Johannine texts.[1] Our choice of texts will be dictated by John's treatment of the temple theme elsewhere in the gospel. Moreover, we will consider all of these texts as they occur in their gospel sequence. We can thus observe the gradual development of the temple theme in the fourth gospel. This study is necessarily restricted by limitations of space. Hence, we will concentrate primarily on the deeper meaning of these texts in the light of the passion-death of Jesus, or the second level of meaning. In this way, we hope to be able to confirm our interpretation of Jn 14,2-3 and at the same time (where possible) to complement it.

A. THE NEW TEMPLE OF THE TRUTH (JN 1,14)

Our comparison is with the following text of Jn 1,14:[2]

Jn 1,14a   Καὶ ὁ Λόγος σὰρξ ἐγένετο
     b   καὶ ἐσκήνωσεν ἐν ἡμῖν,
     c   καὶ ἐθεασάμεθα τὴν δόξαν αὐτοῦ,
     d   δόξαν ὡς μονογενοῦς παρὰ πατρός,
     e   πλήρης χάριτος καὶ ἀληθείας.

---

[1] We have already compared Jn 14,2-3 in some detail with several Johannine texts, e.g. Jn 1,51; 2,13-22; 7,33-34; 8,21-22; 8,35; 12,26b; 17,24. However, a consideration of Jn 2,13-22 is fundamental to our treatment of all the texts in this chapter. See, ch. VI, pp.185-190.

[2] Apart from the commentaries, we found the following studies helpful in our interpretation of Jn 1,14, M.-E. Boismard, *St. John's Prologue* (London, 1957); S. A. Panimolle, *Il dono della legge e la grazia della verità* (Roma, 1973); I. de la Potterie, *La vérité dans saint Jean* (Rome, 1977), 168-241; idem, *Exegesis Quarti Evangelii. Prologus S. Joannis* (Romae, 1974-75); C. K. Barrett, *The Prologue of St. John's Gospel* (London, 1971); M. F. Lacan, "Le prologue de saint Jean. Ses thèmes, sa structure, son mouvement", *LumV* 33 (1957) 91-110; D. Mollat, *L'évangile et les epîtres de saint Jean* (Paris, 1960); G. Traets, *Voir Jésus et le Père en lui selon l'évangile de saint Jean* (Rome, 1967) 101-106.

The temple theme is already implicit in Jn 1,14b. The verb σκηνόω evokes the OT noun σκηνή, which is the common term for the tabernacle, or desert-sanctuary.[3] Besides, there is a significant verbal link between this text and the immediate context of Jn 14,2-3 (cf. ἀλήθεια, 1,14e; 14,6a).

The Word of Jn 1,14a links back with the Word of Jn 1,1. This Word became flesh. It took on the weakness and transitoriness of the human condition (cf. Ps 56(55),4; Is 31,3; 40,5-8).[4] The Word which existed eternally, one-with-God (1,1) now becomes flesh, one-with-man (1,14a) — a new created reality.[5]

This Word is inseparably linked in the prologue with the dominant Johannine theme of revelation (cf. 1,4.5.18).[6] In Jn 1,14e it is full of "grace and truth". The phrase is best taken as a hendiadys, meaning "the gift of truth".[7] This Sanctuary of the Word made flesh contains the fulness of God's truth. Jesus in person is the Temple of the definitive revelation of God (comp. 1,14; 14,6). All this is perfectly intelligible against the OT background of the tabernacle as the place of the revelation of God to his people.

As such the Word made flesh is an object of vision (1,14c; comp. 1 Jn 1,1). The verb θεάομαι is well suited (in Johannine usage) to designate a whole range of vision, physical and spiritual.[8] We take the aorist of Jn 1,14c as "complexive".[9] The ἐθεασάμεθα of Jn 1,14c read in retrospect (after the passion-death of Jesus) may be taken to designate, not merely the physical vision by the eye-witnesses of the glory of God manifested in Jesus, but also the spiritual vision of the Word made flesh by these same eye-witnesses who saw this same glory manifested in the "signs" of the ministry (cf. 2,11;[10] 11,4.40); and who gradually attained to a deeper spiritual vision by perfect faith, when this same glory was manifested in the passion-death of Jesus (cf. 12,23.28; 13,31-32). The vision of the glory

---

[3] D. MOLLAT sums up the evidence of the OT concerning the background to the temple theme of Jn 1,14. See, op. cit. (n. 2) 69, ns. "e" and "f".

[4] "La 'chair' désigne l'homme dans sa condition de faiblesse et de mortalité. cf. 3,6; 17,2; Gn 6,3; Ps 65,5; Is 40,6. Voir Rm 7,54". See, BJ ad loc., n. "m".

[5] The verb γίνομαι with a complement always has a "sensus praegnans" in John. See, I. DE LA POTTERIE, op. cit. (n. 2) 892-895 for an extensive analysis of the Johannine use of this verb.

[6] This is succinctly expressed by R. BULTMANN: "the 'Logos doctrine' of the prologue gives expression to the idea of revelation which dominates the whole gospel". See, op. cit. 13, n. 1.

[7] On "grace and truth" as a hendiadys, see, S. PANIMOLLE, op. cit. (n. 2) 380-83.

[8] C. TRAETS explains this well. See, op. cit. (n. 2) 44; also, 104.

[9] The "complexive" aorist would seem to harmonise better with the definition of "glory" as that which is due to Jesus in his quality of an only Son.

[10] The reference to "glory" in Jn 2,11 is meant to recall the last previous reference to "glory" in Jn 1,14.

of Jesus which began for the eye-witnesses when the Word became flesh (1,14c), continued throughout the ministry (2,11; 11,4.40) and reached its culmination in the "hour" of Jesus.[11]

In the light of this same vision of perfect faith the profound import of the "truth" of Jn 1,14c is also opened up under the action of the Spirit of truth (cf. 14,17.26; 15,26; 16,13). The risen Jesus becomes effectively the New Temple of the truth for believers, or the place where the definitive revelation of God is in fact finally revealed to believers (cf. 8,28).

We have now confirmation of our understanding of Jn 14,2-3 within its immediate context.[12] The New Temple of Jn 14,2-3 becomes effectively for all believers the way of access to the Father as the truth in person (14,6) by means of the Spirit of truth (14,16-17.26). It is this same New Temple of the risen Jesus which is the object of vision by perfect faith in our understanding of the deeper import of the ἐθεασάμεθα of Jn 1,14c.

However, Jn 1,14 and Jn 14,2-3 are also complementary. Jn 1,14 presents the Incarnation as a single event in the work of salvation. However, our understanding of Jn 14,2-3 shows that there are several facets of this event which must be distinguished. The work of salvation is not complete with the descent of the Word at the Incarnation (1,14). Jesus must also ascend to the Father through his passion-death before he can return to take the disciples to be with him there. God becomes one with men in the temple of the flesh of Jesus (1,14) in order that men may become one with God in the New Temple of his glorified flesh (14,2-3).

The purpose of the Incarnation is achieved in our understanding of Jn 14,2-3. Moreover, it is continually in the process of being ever more fully realised as Jesus promises to take believers in union with himself after his passion-death into ever deeper union in the New Temple of his risen body. In this sense, the risen Jesus will be effectively a permanent Mediator between God and man.

---

[11] This precise handling of the theme of "glory" is regarded by W. GROSSOUW as an indication of Johannine originality. See, "La glorification du Christ dans le quatrième évangile", in *L'évangile de Jean* (Louvain, 1958) 133-145.

[12] For our argument in full, see, ch. VI, pp. 216-220.

B. THE NEW TEMPLE AS THE MEETING-PLACE BETWEEN GOD AND MAN (JN 1,51)

Our comparison is with the following text of Jn 1,51: [13]

Jn 1,51a ἀμὴν ἀμὴν λέγω ὑμῖν,
 b ὄψεσθε τὸν οὐρανὸν ἀνεῳγότα
 c καὶ τοὺς ἀγγέλους τοῦ θεοῦ ἀναβαίνοντας καὶ καταβαίνοντας
 d ἐπὶ τὸν υἱὸν τοῦ ἀνθρώπου.

The theme of the temple is again evoked indirectly by the OT resonance of Gn 28,12 in Jn 1,51. Besides, the term τόπος occurs repeatedly in the immediate context of Gn 28,12 (cf. 28,11(3x).16.17.19), and three times with a cultic significance to designate a "sanctuary" or "holy place" (cf. 28,16.17.19). This would provide an important literary link with the use of τόπος, meaning "temple" in our understanding of Jn 14,2-3. No exegete (to our knowledge) has discovered this possible link. So, too, the two-way intercommunication between heaven and earth is central to Jn 1,51 and Gn 28,12, and also recurs in our interpretation of Jn 14,2-3.[14]

The tertium comparationis between the vision of Jacob in Gn 28,12 and the promised future vision of the Son of Man in Jn 1,51 is the revelation of "a house of God and the gate of heaven".[15] In the symbolic vision of Jn 1,51 the disciples will see the Son of Man as a τόπος, that is a "sanctuary", or "holy place", where heaven will be opened up for an unbroken two-way intercommunication between God and man.

The object of the vision of Jn 1,51 is "heaven opened".[16] We have already seen that the imagery is drawn from apocalyptic literature.[17] It

---

[13] In our exegesis of this text of Jn 1,51 we are especially indebted to I. FRITSCH, "...videbitis angelos Dei ascendentes et descendentes super Filium hominis (Io. 1,51)", VD 37 (1959) 3-11. Besides, this text has been admirably treated by A. SERRA, Contributi dell'antica letteratura giudaica per l'esegesi di Giovanni 2,1-12 e 19,25-27 (Roma, 1977) 259-301; and by F.J. MOLONEY, The Johannine Son of Man (Rome, 1976) 23-41. So, too, we have already treated this text ourselves briefly. See, ch. VI, p. 213.

[14] There is also a highly significant link between the use of the verb μένω in the immediate context of Jn 1,51 (cf. 1,38-39(3x)) and the use of the noun μονή in Jn 14,2-3.

[15] It is not only Gn 28,12 which is important for an understanting of Jn 1,51. So, too, is the whole immediate context of the Bethel scene (Gn 28,10-22), where the vision of Gn 28,12 is interpreted for us by the reaction of Jacob: "How awesome is this place (ὁ τόπος). This is none other than the house of God (οἶκος Θεοῦ), and this is the gate of heaven (ἡ πύλη τοῦ οὐρανοῦ)" (Gn 28,17).

[16] The perfect marks the completed action as continually operative (contrast, Mt 3,16; Mk 1,10; comp. Acts 7,56; Ap 4,1).

[17] See, ch. VI, n. 127.

marks some kind of extraordinary contact between heaven and earth. It is also significantly linked with the revelation of heavenly things, and has eschatological connotations (cf. Is 64,1).[18]

The sudden awkward transition from the singular ὄψῃ in Jn 1,50 to the plural ὄψεσθε in Jn 1,51 opens up (in typical Johannine style) a wider perspective.[19] The disciples in this perspective take on their universal role in the fourth gospel as representatives of all future believers.[20] It is to them as such that the future vision of the Son of Man is promised in Jn 1,51.

The vague figure of the Son of Man is gradually identified in the fourth gospel with the person of Jesus.[21] This is done indirectly (cf. 3,13; 5,27; 6,27; 6,62; 6,63; 8,28; 9,35; 12,23.34(2x); 13,31). So, too, as the narrative develops the Son of Man is more clearly identified as an eschatological figure (cf. 5,27), whose role is described both in terms of final eschatology (cf. 5,28-29) and in typical Johannine terms of realised eschatology (cf. 5,22-24).[22]

Moreover, this eschatological figure of the Son of Man is designedly linked in the fourth gospel with the "exaltation" of Jesus and his final manifestation, or revelation, through his passion-death (cf. 3,14; 8,28; 12,32). The eschatological figure of the Son of Man on the cross becomes the place par excellence of heavenly revelation in the fourth gospel.[23] This is the object of the promised future vision of Jn 1,51, when interpreted in the light of the passion-death of Jesus.[24]

But the object of Jn 1,51 is specified as a sanctuary. In the light of the passion-death of Jesus this would correspond to the promised future "sign" in our interpretation of Jn 2,19-22 — the New Temple of the risen Jesus.[25]

Once again we find confirmation of our interpretation of Jn 14,2-3. The object of the promised future vision of Jn 1,51 is the same reality

---

[18] The ἀπ' ἄρτι before ὄψεσθε is certainly not original. Here the expression seems to have been imported into Jn 1,51 from Mt 26,64. If this is so, it may be an indication of a certain interpretation related in some way to the eschatological discourse of the Synoptics (cf. Mt 26,64; 24,40). Thus the eschatological interpretation of Jn 1,51 would find support.

[19] B. F. Westcott would thus seem to be correct when he writes of this verse: "The word is for Nathanael, but the blessing is for all believers". See, op. cit. 28.

[20] See, ch. V, pp. 173-175.

[21] F. J. Moloney aptly observes: "There is a concentration on the human figure of Jesus in the use of the title 'Son of Man'". See, op. cit. (n. 13) 213.

[22] On the eschatological figure of the Son of Man, see, J. J. Collins, The Apocalyptic Vision of the Book of Daniel (Missoula, 1977).

[23] See, ch. VI, n. 128.

[24] On this line of interpretation, see, R. E. Brown, cit. cit. 88; also, I. Fritsch, op. cit. (n. 13) 11.

[25] See, ch. VI, pp. 185-190.

designated in Jn 14,2-3: the New Temple of the risen Jesus as "a house of God and the gate of heaven", with an unbroken intercommunication there between heaven and earth. In Jn 14,2-3 this reality of the New Temple is already in the process of preparation through the passion-death of Jesus and after this process of preparation is complete the same reality, as the τόπος prepared, becomes "a house of God and the gate of heaven". It is "a house of God", his dwelling-place, or home; for Jesus as the τόπος prepared of Jn 14,2-3 becomes identified through the process of preparation with the "the Father's house" and with the "dwelling-places" prepared for the disciples there. So, too, it is "the gate of heaven"; for "the Father's house", with its "dwelling-places" for the disciples, is rendered accessible to them in this same τόπος prepared of the risen Jesus. The constant ascending/descending movement of Jn 14,2-3 is evidence of an unbroken intercommunication between heaven and earth.

Our interpretation of Jn 14,2-3 is also in turn complemented by Jn 1,51. The reality described in Jn 14,2-3 is promised as an object of vision in Jn 1,51. But this theme of "vision", which is central to Jn 1,51, is entirely absent from Jn 14,2-3.

C. THE NEW TEMPLE OF WORSHIP (JN 4,20-24)

Our comparison is with the following text of Jn 4,20-24: [26]

Jn 4,20a   οἱ πατέρες ἡμῶν ἐν τῷ ὄρει τούτῳ προσεκύνησαν·
       b   καὶ ὑμεῖς λέγετε ὅτι ἐν Ἰεροσολύμοις ἐστὶν ὁ τόπος ὅπου προσκυνεῖν δεῖ.
     21a   λέγει αὐτῇ ὁ Ἰησοῦς· πίστευέ μοι, γύναι, ὅτι ἔρχεται ὥρα,
       b   ὅτε οὔτε ἐν τῷ ὄρει τούτῳ οὔτε ἐν Ἰεροσολύμοις προσκυνήσετε τῷ πατρί.
     22a   ὑμεῖς προσκυνεῖτε ὃ οὐκ οἴδατε, ἡμεῖς προσκυνοῦμεν ὃ οἴδαμεν,
       b   ὅτι ἡ σωτηρία ἐκ τῶν Ἰουδαίων ἐστίν.
     23a   ἀλλὰ ἔρχεται ὥρα καὶ νῦν ἐστιν, ὅτε οἱ ἀληθινοὶ προσκυνηταὶ προσκυνήσουσιν τῷ πατρὶ ἐν πνεύματι καὶ ἀληθείᾳ·
       b   καὶ γὰρ ὁ πατὴρ τοιούτους ζητεῖ τοὺς προσκυνοῦντας αὐτόν.
     24   πνεῦμα ὁ θεός, καὶ τοὺς προσκυνοῦντας αὐτὸν ἐν πνεύματι καὶ ἀληθείᾳ δεῖ προσκυνεῖν.

---

[26] Apart from the commentaries, we have found the following studies helpful in our interpretation of Jn 4,20-24. J. BLIGH, "Jesus in Samaria", *HeyJ* 3 (1962) 329-346; F. M. BRAUN, "In spiritu et veritate", *RT* 52 (1952) 245-274; D. MOLLAT, "Le puits de Jacob (Jn 4,1-42)", *BVC* 6 (1954) 83-91; I. DE LA POTTERIE, *La vérité dans saint Jean* (Rome, 1977) 673-706. This last exegete provides an ample bibliography for a study of Jn 4,20-24 in his notes to pp. 673-74, especially, ns. 88.99.

The temple theme is explicit in Jn 4,20-24, where the temple vocabulary also bears a striking similarity with that of Jn 14,2-3 (τόπος, 4,20;[27] 14,2b.3a). Again, the use of the term "truth" (ἀλήθεια) also provides a highly significant verbal link with the immediate context of Jn 14,2-3 (cf. 14,6a; 4,23a.24). Besides, the theme of the Spirit explicit in Jn 4,20-24 (cf. 4,23a.24(2x)) is a dominant theme in the immediate context of Jn 14,2-3 (cf. 14,16-17.26).

The repetition of some key-terms clearly marks Jn 4,20-24 as a distinct unit in itself.[28] The implicit question of the woman (4,20b) is answered by Jesus with the announcement of the future arrival (4,21b)[29] of a new place of true worship "in spirit and truth" (4,23a.24), but which in some sense has already arrived with the coming of Jesus (4,23a).

The reply of Jesus (4,21-24) falls naturally into two further minor subdivisions (4,21-22; 4,23-24) structured in antithetical parallelism within a similar framework.[30] Here the thought develops in two stages. The "place" of worship is described in response to the words of the woman (4,20) negatively in the first member (4,21b) and positively in the second member (4,23a). Both members of the antithetical parallelism (4,21b; 4,23a) have an expansion (4,22; 4,23b; 4,24), which together with the verbal framework (4,21a.23a) do not in a sense pertain directly to the argument of Jn 4,20-24.

Thus we have a significant chiastic formation in the reply of Jesus about the place of worship:

	4,21b		4,23a
a	οὔτε ἐν τῷ ὄρει τούτῳ	b	ἀλλὰ..... προσκυνήσουσιν
	οὔτε ἐν Ἱεροσολύμοις		τῷ πατρὶ
b′	προσκυνήσετε τῷ πατρί.	a′	ἐν πνεύματι καὶ ἀληθείᾳ.

The place of worship is neither on this mountain nor in Jerusalem (4,21b).[31] This, however, must be complemented by the positive

---

[27] The τόπος of Jn 4,20b refers to the Jerusalem temple. See, *BJ* ad loc. n. "a".

[28] ἐν τῷ ὄρει τούτῳ (2x); ἐν Ἱεροσολύμοις (2x); ἐν πνεύματι καὶ ἀληθείᾳ (2x); ἔρχεται (2x); προσκυνέω (9x); προσκυνηταί.

[29] The ἔρχομαι of Jn 4,21 is a futuristic present. It refers to something still in the future, and something which is also at the same time in some way in the process of being realised. Hence, the further qualification of καὶ νῦν ἐστιν in Jn 4,23a. See, *BDF,* 323.

[30] For this more detailed structure of Jn 4,21-24, we are indebted to I. DE LA POTTERIE. See, *Exegesis IV Evangelii - Cap. III-IV* (Romae, 1968-69) 90. See, also S. PANIMOLLE, *op. cit.* (n. 2) 379-80.

[31] This contrast must be seen against the OT background of the law promulgated by Josiah (621 B.C.) to establish one central sanctuary (cf. Dt. 12,2-11). This was interpreted by the Jews with reference to the Jewish temple (2 Kgs 23,4.27), which under Solomon became the central shrine of the nation's public worship. On the other hand, it was interpreted by the Samaritans with reference to Mt. Gerizim.

implication of Jesus' reply, which identifies the τόπος of future worship with "in spirit and truth". The text of Jn 4,20-24 does not directly identify Jesus in person as the new "place" or "sanctuary" of worship. But it is entirely open to such a Christological interpretation (cf. 1,14c; 14,6a).[32]

The perspective of the "hour" of the passion-death of Jesus dominates Jn 4,20-24 (ὥρα, 4,21a.23a; comp. 12,23-29; 13,31-32; 17,1-5). The future temple of true worship, the τόπος, which has (in some sense) already arrived with Jesus (4,23a) still depends (in another sense) on this "hour" of the passion-death of Jesus, which has not yet arrived (4,21a.23a). In some sense, then, the promised future temple of true worship still awaits the arrival of the passion-death of Jesus.

In this same perspective of the "hour" the phrase "in spirit and truth" (4,23a.24) also takes on its deeper significance. The gift of the Spirit to believers depends entirely on the glorification of Jesus through his passion-death (cf. 7,39). Moreover, the Spirit is explicitly designated as "the spirit of truth" (cf. 14,17; 15,26; 16,13). As such the activity of the Spirit is centered entirely on Jesus who is "the truth" in person (cf. 1,14e; 14,6a; comp. 16,13). It is a revealing activity (cf. 14,26; 16,13). This worship "in spirit and truth", then, is a worship of believers in the risen Jesus which springs from the truth, or revelation of Jesus opened up to perfect faith under the action of the Spirit of truth.[33] At this level of meaning the text takes on a profound Christological import.

Again, we find confirmation of our understanding of Jn 14,2-3 within its immediate context. It is only after the preparation of a place by means of his passion-death that the risen Jesus becomes the New Temple, or the τόπος prepared, where "the truth" (ἀλήθεια) of Jn 14,6a is opened up fully and finally to believers under the action of the Spirit of truth (cf. 14,16-17.26). In this New Temple of the risen Jesus men can worship in "the truth".

So, too, our interpretation of Jn 14,2-3 is also complemented. The profound reality of the New Temple in Jn 14,2-3 may be expressed in equivalent Johannine terms as the New Place of worship. Jn 4,20-24 speaks repeatedly and explicitly of "worship". Jn 14,2-3, on the other hand, never refers to "worship". Neither does it contain a single term which refers directly to the cult. Here the vocabulary pertains rather to that of the family (οἰκία) and to personal relationships within that family (τοῦ πατρός μου ... πρὸς ἐμαυτόν ... ὅπου εἰμὶ ἐγώ).

---

[32] There is a growing tendency in recent criticism to identify the new place of worship with the person of Jesus himself. However, it should be noted that this is not explicit in the text.

[33] The preposition "in" of the phrase "in spirit and truth" may be interpreted both as locative and instrumental. It is by means of the Spirit's revealing action that the new worship is rendered possible. But the risen Jesus is also the milieu , or spiritual 'space' which constitutes the New Sanctuary of worship.

D. THE NEW TEMPLE AS THE SOURCE OF THE SPIRIT
(JN 7,37-39)

Our comparison is with the following text of Jn 7,37-39: [34]

Jn 7,37a Ἐν δὲ τῇ ἐσχάτῃ ἡμέρᾳ τῇ μεγάλῃ τῆς ἑορτῆς
   b εἰστήκει ὁ Ἰησοῦς καὶ ἔκραξεν λέγων·
   c ἐάν τις διψᾷ, ἐρχέσθω πρός με
   d καὶ πινέτω ὁ πιστεύων εἰς ἐμέ.

  38a καθὼς εἶπεν ἡ γραφή,
    b ποταμοὶ ἐκ τῆς κοιλίας αὐτοῦ ῥεύσουσιν ὕδατος ζῶντος.

  39a τοῦτο δέ εἶπεν περὶ τοῦ πνεύματος
    b οὗ ἔμελλον λαμβάνειν οἱ πιστεύοντες εἰς αὐτόν·
    c οὔπω γὰρ ἦν πνεῦμα,
    d ὅτι Ἰησοῦς οὐδέπω ἐδοξάσθη.

The imagery of "living water" in Jn 7,37-39 (cf. 7,38b) is significantly linked in the OT with the temple theme.[35] Besides, the immediate context of Jn 7,37-39 is evoked directly and explicitly in the immediate context of Jn 14,2-3 (cf. 13,33; comp. 7,33-36; 8,21-22).[36] So, too, the theme of the Spirit explicit in Jn 7,37-39 (cf. 7,39c) is also a dominant theme in the immediate context of Jn 14,2-3 (cf. 14,16-17.26).

In the OT the imagery of "living water" is a symbol of spiritual realities.[37] But it is also directly linked there with the temple (cf. Ps 36(35),8-10). Ezekiel refers explicitly to "living water" which issues from

---

[34] Apart from the commentaries, we have found the following works helpful in our study of Jn 7,37-39, M.-E. BOISMARD, "De son ventre couleront des fleuves d'eau (Jo. VII,38)", RB 65 (1958) 523-46; Idem, "Les citations targumiques du IVᵉ évangile", RB 66 (1959) 374-79; P. GRELOT, "De son ventre couleront des fleuves d'eau. La citation scripturaire de Jean, VII, 38", RB 66 (1959) 369-74: Idem, "Jean VII,38: eau du rocher ou source du temple?", RB 70 (1963) 43-51; A. FEUILLET, "Les fleuves d'eau vive de Jo. 7,38. Contribution a l'étude des rapports entre quatrième évangile et apocalypse", in Parole et Sacerdoce (Melanges J. Weber) (Tournai-Paris, 1962) 107-120; J. DANIÉLOU, "Joh 7,37 et Ezech. 47,1-11", StudEvang II (TU 89) 158-63.

[35] The OT background to Jn 7,37-39 has been treated briefly by I. DE LA POTTERIE. See, op. cit. (n. 26) 691f.

[36] See, ch. V, pp. 146-149.

[37] God himself is "the source of living water" (cf. Jer 2,13; 17,13). The image of "living water" is also a symbol of the messianic benefits characteristic of the eschatological age (cf. Ze 14,8; Ez 47,1; Jl 4,18; comp. Is 43,19-20; 49,10). Most often, however, the image is intimately linked with the theme of wisdom and law (cf. Sir 24,21.23-29; Prv 13,14; comp. Is 55,1). Moreover, the association of "water" and the "spirit" is not unknown in the OT (cf. Is 44,3). The metaphorical use of the verbs "to thirst" (7,37c) and "to drink" (7,37d) are also perfectly in harmony with the OT imagery (Is 55,1; comp. Pss 42(41),2; 63(62),1; Prv 9,1-6.18 (LXX); Sir 15,3).

the eschatological temple (cf. 47,1-12). The plural "rivers" (ποταμοί) in Jn 7,38b in contrast to the singular "river" (ποταμός) of Ezekiel (cf. 47,6.7.9(2x).12) may be designed to evoke other appropriate texts. In fact, many such texts may be found (cf. Ze 12,10; 13,1; 14,8; Jl 4,18). The OT link between the symbolism of "living water" and the temple is clearly beyond question.

So, too, there can be little doubt that Jn 7,37-39 was influenced by the liturgy of Tabernacles (cf. 7,2.14.37).[38] It is surely not without significance for an understanding of Jn 7,37-39 that the ascent of the nations to the eschatological temple for the feast of Tabernacles is also closely linked in the OT with the theme of the temple as the source of living water (cf. Ze 14,16-21; comp. Ze 14,8; also, Jl 4,18; 3,11-12).

Against this OT background Jesus extends his invitation to come to him in Jn 7,37-39. Explicitly, we have an invitation to come to Jesus (7,37c), and then implicitly to believe in him (7,37d). But Jn 7,37-39 is not just a simple invitation. The words are also a promise that Jesus himself will be for all who thirst a source of living water (7,38b),[39] where they may slake their unsatisfied desires with the benefits of salvation. Moreover, Jesus would also seem to claim (at least implicitly) that he is in person the eschatological temple, which replaces the material temple. But the meaning of Jn 7,37-39 is even more astounding for the reader who is aware of the redactional comment of Jn 7,39. For him Jesus would claim in addition to be the source of the gift of the Spirit, which is proper to the eschatological age.

However, this future gift of the Spirit is explicitly linked with the glorification of Jesus through his passion-death (7,39cd). The full import of Jn 7,37-39 only emerges in the light of the glorifying passion-death of Jesus by which Jesus himself becomes at one and the same time the New Temple in his risen body (2,21) and the source of the Spirit (14,16-17.26; 15,26; 16,7-15). In Jn 7,37-39 all men are invited to come by faith to the New Temple of the risen Jesus as the source of the Spirit.

Our understanding of Jn 14,2-3 within its immediate context is once again confirmed. There the risen Jesus by the journey of his glorifying passion-death becomes the τόπος prepared, or the New Temple. As such

---

[38] The Scripture citation of Jn 7,38 clearly alludes to the libation rite of the Water Gate on the Feast of Tabernacles. P. GRELOT sums up the different significations which the rite takes on in the Jewish tradition. See, "Jean, VII,38: eau du rocher ou source du temple?", RB 70 (1963) 46-47.49.

[39] We place the full stop in Jn 7,37d. For a full discussion of the various possibilities, see, R. E. BROWN, op. cit. 320-22. The arguments in favour of placing a full stop at the end of Jn 7,37d have been well summed up and outlined by C. H. DODD, The Interpretation of the Fourth Gospel (Cambridge, 1953) 349. See also H. RAHNER "Flumina de ventre Christi. Die patristische Auslegung von Joh. 7,37-38", Bib 22 (1941) 269-302; 367-403.

he also becomes the source of the Spirit (14,16-17.26; comp. 16,7-15), and
as the place of the definitive revelation of God (14,6a) the way of access
to the Father (14,6b) under the revealing action of the Spirit
(14,16-17.26).

The temporary inability of the disciples to follow Jesus on the
journey of his passion-death (cf. 13,36.37) disappears in Jn 14,2-3, when
the risen Jesus intervenes after the preparation to take the disciples into
union with himself in the New Temple. This same union is described in
reciprocal Johannine terms in Jn 14,23 as the effect of the inner revealing
action of the glorified Jesus (14,21) working through the Spirit in the
hearts of believers (14,16-17.26).

The dynamic movement of Jesus in Jn 14,2-3, who goes to prepare a
place and then returns to take the disciples with him to the heavenly
temple, stands out in stark contrast to the static figure of Jesus in Jn
7,37-39, who invites those who thirst to come and slake their unsatisfied
desires. In the promise of Jn 14,2-3 we see how believers will respond to
the invitation of Jn 7,37-39 to come to the New Temple of the risen Jesus
as the source of the Spirit, when the risen Jesus returns to take them into
union with himself as the New Temple. The prophecy of the "living
water" issuing from the eschatological temple (Ez 47,1-12), and the
eschatological pilgrimage of the nations to the temple (Ze 14,16-21), are
thus both fulfilled in a remarkable way in our understanding of Jn 14,2-3,
within its immediate context.

E. THE SANCTIFICATION OF THE NEW TEMPLE (JN 10,36)[40]

Our comparison is with the following text of Jn 10,36:

Jn 10,36a   ὃν ὁ πατὴρ ἡγίασεν
       b   καὶ ἀπέστειλεν εἰς τὸν κόσμον,
       c   ὑμεῖς λέγετε ὅτι βλασφημεῖς,
       d   ὅτι εἶπον· υἱὸς τοῦ θεοῦ εἰμι;

---

[40] Our caption derives from the use of the verb ἁγιάζω in Jn 10,36a and Jn 17,17a.
19ab, which are the two texts used directly in our argument. I. DE LA POTTERIE has studied
in considerable detail the several possible translations of this verb. We accept with him
that the meaning "to sanctify" comes closest to John's intention. See, "Consécration ou
sanctification du chrétien d'après Jean 17?", in Le Sacré. Études et recherches (Actes du
colloque de Rome, 4-9 janvier, 1974, aux soins de E. CASTELLI) (Aubier, 1974) 333-349.
See, also J. DELORME, "Sacerdoce du Christ et ministère (à propos de Jean 17).
Sémantique et théologie biblique", RecSR 62 (1974) 199-219.

The chronological setting of the feast of the Dedication[41] in the immediate context (10,22) would seem to suggest that the sanctification of Jesus in Jn 10,36 should be related in some way to the sanctification, or dedication of the temple.[42]

At first sight it would appear that the Father sanctifies Jesus in Jn 10,36 for his prophetic mission to the world. The verb ἁγιάζω means literally "to sanctify".[43] The normal biblical usage is "to set apart or to hand over to God" (cf. Nm 3,13; comp. Sir 33,12). There is clear LXX evidence for the use of the verb to designate sanctification for a prophetic role (cf. Jer 1,5; Sir 45,4). Indeed, the explicit allusion to Ps 82(81),6 in the immediate context would seem to confirm that Jesus is sanctified in Jn 10,36 for a prophetic role.[44]

However, Jn 10,36 is also open to interpretation with reference to a temple in line with LXX use of the verb ἁγιάζω. The verb is used to sanctify the tabernacle (Nm 7,1(2x); Ex 29,36.43; Lv 8,11), the temple of Solomon (I Kgs 8,64; 9,3; 2 Chr 7,7.16.20) and the second temple (I Mc 4,48). It is even used alternatively with the verb ἐγκαινίζω (which is related to the noun τὰ ἐγκαίνια) to designate the sanctification and dedication of the temple (cf. I Mc 4,36.54; comp. I Mc 4,48).[45] So, too, the verb ἁγιάζω may also have a sacrificial import (cf. Dt 15,19-21). However, "to sanctify" and "to sacrifice" are by no means synonymous.

Clearly, Jn 10,36 may be interpreted in line with LXX usage to indicate that the Father in some sense sanctified Jesus as a temple and at the same time as a sacrificial victim. However, such an interpretation is only possible in Johannine terms in the light of the passion-death of Jesus. Indeed, this deeper meaning would appear to be John's intention. The sanctification of Jesus is presented with direct reference to his claim to be the Son of God in Jn 10,36. But this precise claim to be the Son of God is explicitly designated by the Jews as their reason for demanding the death of Jesus (cf. 19,7).

---

[41] The feast of the Dedication of the temple (Jn 10,22) is one of a series of feasts in John (cf. Jn 2,13; 5,1; 6,4; 7,2; 11,55; cf. also Jn 12,1; 13,1). It recalls in particular the Maccabaean consecration of the temple (I Mc 4,41-61; cf. I Mc 1,54).

[42] J. MARSH explains John's use of the verb "to sanctify" in Jn 10,36 precisely in this way. See, op. cit. 407.

[43] "to hallow, or make sacred, esp. by burning a sacrifice". See, L.S. 9.

[44] The psalm is addressed to the rulers and judges of Israel, but Jesus applies it to the Jews in general. The reason why the judges could be called gods was because they were vehicles of the word of God (cf. Jn 10,35), and on that basis Jesus himself merits much more to be called "Son of God". He has been sanctified and sent into the world as the unique vehicle of the word of God (cf. Jn 1,14; 14,6).

[45] Thus ἁγιάζω and ἐγκαινίζω may be applied to one and the same ceremony, but it is a mistake to say that "the two are synonymous", as R. E. BROWN seems to indicate. See, op. cit. 404.

In this perspective of the "hour" of his passion-death the verb ἁγιάζω takes on a deep sacrificial import in Jn 17,19a (cf. 17,1; 13,1).[46] Here Jesus sanctifies himself as a sacrificial victim. He lays down his life in full submission to his Father's will and his death is a sacrifice (cf. 10,17-18).[47] This ἁγιάζω of Jn 17,19a is a futuristic present.[48] It designates a continuous action of Jesus sanctifying himself as a sacrificial victim throughout his whole life from the first moment of the Incarnation until his death on the cross.[49] The death of Jesus climaxes a life of submission to his Father's will (cf. 4,34; 6,38; 8,28-29). This life-long acceptance of Jesus is the inner core of the continual sacrifice of his life which finds its outward expression on the cross.[50] Jesus is sanctified as a victim of sacrifice from the first moment of his earthly life (comp. Heb 10,7).[51]

We understand the ἡγίασεν of Jn 10,36, then, as complexive.[52] It takes on its full range of meaning as such when read in retrospect (after the passion-death of Jesus). It designates the sanctification of Jesus by the Father as a victim of sacrifice from the first moment of his earthly life until the final consummation of this sacrifice on the cross.

In this, same perspective of the passion-death of Jesus the link between the sanctification of Jesus in Jn 10,36 and the feast of the Dedication in Jn 10,22 now becomes clear. The sanctification of Jesus by his Father as a sacrificial victim is at the same time the sanctification of Jesus as the New Temple, which emerges from the passion-death of Jesus (cf. 2,19-21). In his passion-death Jesus becomes the sacrificial victim of the dedication and the New Temple sanctified by this same sacrificial victim. In Jn 10,36, then, the Father already designates Jesus as the sacrificial victim by which the New Temple is to be sanctified.

---

[46] For the history of the origin of the sacrificial interpretation of Jn 17,17-19, see I. DE LA POTTERIE, op. cit. (n. 2) 758-60, with the accompanying notes. His acceptance of the sacrificial import of the phrase in Jn 17,19a, with an "indirect" allusion to the cross, is essentially the same as our sacrificial interpretation of the phrase at a second deeper level of understanding.

[47] On the sacrificial import of this text, see, ch. I, n. 30.

[48] See, *BDF*, 323, 2. J. REID explains well the import of the use of the verb in Jn 17,19a. See, "The Sanctification of Christ and His Disciples", *ExpT* 24 (1912-13) 460.

[49] Our interpretation has been well summed up by I. DE LA POTTERIE. See, op. cit. (n. 2) 761.

[50] ST. AUGUSTINE explains this inner core of sacrifice. See, *De Civitate Dei*, X, 6; *PL*. 41, 283; also, ST. THOMAS, *S. Theologica*, III, 48, 3. See, also F. BOURASSA, "Verum sacrificium", *ScEccl* 3 (1950) 146-182; also, idem, 4 (1951) 91-139.

[51] On this text, see, A. VANHOYE, "De 'aspectu' oblationis Christi secundum Epistolam ad Hebraeos", *VD* 37 (1959) 32.38.

[52] The verb may well be taken as "ingressive" aorist at a first level of meaning to mark the initial point of sanctification by the Father. However, at a second deeper level of understanding the verb embraces the whole process of sanctification globally.

Once again our interpretation of Jn 14,2-3 is confirmed. The journey of Jesus in Jn 14,2-3 is a sacrificial act (cf. 13,37-38; comp. 10,17-18).[53] Jesus himself is the sacrificial victim. So, too, it is by means of this same sacrificial act that the temple of the body of Jesus is transformed spiritually into the New Temple of his glorified body. This emergence of the New Temple of the risen Jesus by means of the sacrificial journey of Jesus to the Father through his passion-death in Jn 14,2-3 may be described in equivalent Johannine terms as the sanctification, or dedication, of the New Temple referred to in Jn 10,36.

But there is also a sense in which our interpretation of Jn 14,2-3 finds support in the missionary aspect of Jn 10,36. Jesus is sanctified as the New Temple in Jn 10,36 precisely for his mission to the world. Again, we find a movement towards men implicit in the ἔρχομαι of Jn 14,2-3 (comp. ἔρχομαι πρὸς ὑμᾶς, 14,28). Besides, this outward movement towards men is carefully linked in Jn 14,2-3 with the journey of Jesus to his Father through his passion-death, which provides the New Temple, and is totally dependent on it (ἐὰν πορευθῶ). This outward missionary movement of Jesus in Jn 14,2-3 constitutes the crowning achievement of the work of redemption. Thus there is an intrinsic element of expansion in the New Temple of the risen Jesus in Jn 14,2-3 — an outward movement of the risen Jesus to all believers. This link between the New Temple and mission highlights a significant aspect of the Christian fulfilment of the mystery of the New Temple.[54]

F. THE GOAL OF THE NEW TEMPLE (JN 11,47-53)

Our comparison is with the following text of Jn 11,47-53:

Jn 11,47a Συνήγαγον οὖν οἱ ἀρχιερεῖς καὶ οἱ φαρισαῖοι συνέδριον,
        b καὶ ἔλεγον· τί ποιοῦμεν,
        c ὅτι οὗτος ὁ ἄνθρωπος πολλὰ ποιεῖ σημεῖα;

    48a ἐὰν ἀφῶμεν αὐτὸν οὕτως, πάντες πιστεύσουσιν εἰς αὐτόν,
      b καὶ ἐλεύσονται οἱ Ῥωμαῖοι καὶ ἀροῦσιν ἡμῶν καὶ τὸν τόπον καὶ τὸ ἔθνος.

    49a εἷς δέ τις ἐξ αὐτῶν Καϊάφας, ἀρχιερεὺς ὢν τοῦ ἐνιαυτοῦ ἐκείνου, εἶπεν αὐτοῖς·
      b ὑμεῖς οὐκ οἴδατε οὐδέν, οὐδὲ λογίζεσθε

---

[53] See, n. 47.

[54] This significant aspect of the Christian fulfilment of the mystery of the New Temple has been well treated by A. VANHOYE. See, "La chiesa locale nel nuovo testamento", in *La chiesa locale* (Prospettive teologiche e pastorali) (LAS-Roma, 1976) 15-27, esp. 21-22.

50a ὅτι συμφέρει ὑμῖν ἵνα εἷς ἄνθρωπος ἀποθάνῃ ὑπὲρ τοῦ λαοῦ
  b καὶ μὴ ὅλον τὸ ἔθνος ἀπόληται.

51a τοῦτο δὲ ἀφ᾽ ἑαυτοῦ οὐκ εἶπεν,
  b ἀλλὰ ἀρχιερεὺς ὢν τοῦ ἐνιαυτοῦ ἐκείνου
  c ἐπροφήτευσεν ὅτι ἔμελλεν Ἰησοῦς ἀποθνῄσκειν ὑπὲρ τοῦ
     ἔθνους,

52a καὶ οὐχ ὑπὲρ τοῦ ἔθνους μόνον,
  b ἀλλ᾽ ἵνα καὶ τὰ τέκνα τοῦ θεοῦ τὰ διεσκορπισμένα συναγάγῃ
     εἰς ἕν.

53   ἀπ᾽ ἐκείνης οὖν τῆς ἡμέρας ἐβουλεύσαντο ἵνα ἀποκτείνωσιν
     αὐτόν.

The theme of the temple is directly evoked in Jn 11,48b by the use of the term τόπος, meaning "sanctuary" or "holy place" (comp. 4,20).[55] This term occurs again twice with the same meaning in our understanding of Jn 14,2-3. Besides, the theme of the reunification of the scattered children of God evoked by Jn 11,52b is closely linked in the OT with the theme of the temple (cf. 2 Mc 1,27-29; 2,17-18).

At first sight it would appear that Jn 11,47-53 may be explained adequately in political, or non-religious terms. Fundamental to this interpretation is an identical meaning for the terms ἔθνος and λαός.[56] The Sanhedrin would then express apprehension at the success of Jesus and the consequences of their own possible inactivity — the destruction of the temple and the Jewish state (11,47-48). The death of Jesus would be proposed by way of political expediency (11,49-52), and accepted (11,53).

However, the pericope takes on a much deeper meaning in the light of the passion-death of Jesus. A double meaning is possible for the two terms ἔθνος (11,48b.50b.51c; 52a) and λαός (11,50a).[57] The term ἔθνος may designate the Jewish nation, not as a political entity merely, but also as a religious entity, or the people of God as such.[58] The term λαός can also signify the Jewish nation, again not as a political entity merely, but also as a religious entity, or the people of God as such.[59]

---

[55] See, ch. VI, p. 185.

[56] These terms are in fact interpreted as synonyms by C. K. BARRETT. See, op. cit. 339; also by R. BULTMANN. See, op. cit. 410, n. 7.

[57] S. PANCARO fails to invest the term ἔθνος with a double meaning. He does so only for the term λαός. See, " 'People of God' in St. John's Gospel", NTS 16 (1970) 121-123.

[58] See, Gn 28,2; 48,4; Ex 23,2; Lv 19,16; 20,2; 21,1; Est 3,8.11; Ez 38,12; comp. Lk 7,5; 23,2; Acts 10,22; 24,2.10.17; 26,4; 28,19.

[59] We find the term λαός with reference to the Israelites 21x in the Pentateuch alone (cf. Gn 25,8; 49,53; Ex 30,33 etc). On the use of λαός in the LXX, see, I. DE LA POTTERIE, "L'origine et le sens primitif du mot 'Laïc'" in La vie selon l'Esprit. Condition du chrétien (Paris, 1965) 18. In the NT we find the term also to designate the Christian community of all believers (cf. Rom 9,24-26; 2 Cor 6,14f; Ti 2,14; I Pt 2,9-10; Ap 18,4).

Accordingly, if we interpret λαός as "the new people of God" in the sense of the Christian community of all believers, which in turn is not entirely identical with the OT people of God designated by ἔθνος, John is seen to be playing on a double meaning of both terms. He affirms in Jn 11,50-52 that Jesus will die for the new people of God, or the community of all believers (11,50a); but explains that part of the old people of God is included (11,50b); because Jesus dies for the Jewish nation as God's people too (11,51c), but not for the Jewish people as such only (11,52a). In Jn 11,50-53 Johannine irony reaches a fine point.

We can now see the fuller implications of the temple theme of Jn 11,47-53. Explicitly evoked by the τόπος of Jn 11,48b, it reappears implicitly in the OT echoes of Jn 11,52b. The total destruction of the Jerusalem temple is the negative effect of the death of Jesus in Jn 11,48b; the gathering together of the nations to the temple is the positive effect of this same death in Jn 11,52b. However, the destruction of this τόπος is inseparable elsewhere in John from the destruction of the temple of the body of Jesus and the emergence of the New Temple of his glorified body through his passion-death (cf. 2,19-21). To this τόπος the new people of God, or the new community of all believers, will be gathered by Jesus through his passion-death (comp. 12,32).

Our understanding of Jn 14,2-3 is clearly in line with these Johannine perspectives. Both texts describe the gathering of the new people of God to the New Temple by means of the passion-death of Jesus, explicit in Jn 14,3b and implicit in Jn 11,52b. In both texts this new people of God are the passive recipients of a unifying action, explicit in Jn 11,52b and implicit in Jn 14,3b. So, too, the gathering of the new community into unity, implicit in Jn 14,2-3 and explicit in Jn 11,52b, is entirely dependent in both texts on the intervention of the same unifying agent: Jesus himself.

So, too, our understanding of Jn 14,2-3 is complemented. Jn 11,48b designates the negative effect of the death of Jesus as the total destruction of the τόπος of the Jerusalem temple (comp. 2,19; 4,20-24). This is a significant complementary Johannine aspect of the emergence of the New Temple of the glorified body of Jesus as the positive effect of the passion-death of Jesus in our understanding of Jn 14,2-3.

Our understanding of the universality of the new community represented by the disciples in Jn 14,2-3 is complemented by Jn 11,47-53, where the OT people of God are not completely destroyed, but assumed into the wider and more universal reality of the new people of God, or the new community of believers.

G. THE GLORY OF THE NEW TEMPLE (JN 12,41) [60]

Our comparison is with the following text of Jn 12,41:

Jn 12,41a   ταῦτα εἶπεν Ἠσαΐας, ὅτι εἶδεν τὴν δόξαν αὐτοῦ,
    b   καὶ ἐλάλησεν περὶ αὐτοῦ.

The theme of the glory of Jesus is here linked with the temple through the OT background of Is 6,1, which is evoked implicitly by Jn 12,41.[61] However, this same theme of the glory of Jesus is again mentioned explicitly in Jn 17,24 (cf. 17,24d), which has a direct link with Jn 14,2-3.[62] It would appear, then, that the theme of glory may be related in some way with the promise of Jn 14,2-3. We will try to determine this more in detail.

In Jn 14,2-3 Jesus promises what he prays for in Jn 17,24abc — a permanent union of the disciples with himself in the Father.[63] The union is further directed in Jn 17,24 to a vision of the glory of Jesus (cf. 17,24d). This "glory" of Jn 17,24d is designated as belonging to Jesus ("the glory which is mine"). This is the eternal "glory" which Jesus had before the world began (cf. 17,5b). But it is also qualified as the "glory" which is "given" to Jesus by the Father (cf. 17,24e; comp. 17,22b).[64] The "glory"

---

[60] Apart from the commentaries, we have found the following studies helpful for our interpretation of Jn 12,41, I. DE LA POTTERIE, *La vérité dans saint Jean* (Rome, 1977), 191-200; A. M. RAMSEY, *The Glory of God and the Transfiguration of Christ* (London, 1949); B. BOTTE, *La gloire du Christ dans l'évangile de saint Jean* (Questions Liturgiques et Paroissiales 12) (1927) 65-76; J. SCHNEIDER, *Doxa. Eine bedeutungsgeschichtliche Studie* (Gütersloh, 1932) 115-128; H. KITTEL, *Die Herrlichkeit Gottes. Studien zu Geschichte und Wesen eines neutestamentlichen Begriffs* (BZNW 16) (Giessen 1934), 238-262; A. CHARUE, *Vie, lumière et gloire chez S. Jean* (Collationes Namurcenses 29) (1935) 65-67. 229-241; G. VON RAD - G. KITTEL "Doxa", *TWNT*, II (1935) 233-253 (cf. 233-237 by Kittel); J. DUPONT *Essais sur la Christologie de saint Jean* (Bruges, 1951) 235-96; W. GROSSOUW, "La glorification du Christ dans le quatrième évangile", in *L'évangile de Jean. Études et problèmes* (RechBib III) (Louvain, 1958) 131-45; W. THÜSING, *Die Erhöhung und Verherrlichung Jesu im Johannesevangelium* (Neutest. Abh. XXI, 1/2) (Münster/W., 1960); D. MOLLAT, "Gloire", *VThB*, 505-11; C. TRAETS, *Voir Jésus et le Père en lui selon l'évangile de Jean* (Rome, 1967) 89-106; F. MONTAGNINI, "La vocazione di Isaia", *BibOr* 6 (1964) 163-172; B. RENAUD, "La vocation d'Isaïe. Experience de la foi", *VieSp* 119 (1968) 129-45.

[61] This would seem to be the unanimous opinion of the commentators. I. DE LA POTTERIE sums up the position well. See, *op. cit.* (n. 60) 193; also 631, n. 71.

[62] For our treatment of Jn 17,24 more in detail, see, ch. VI, pp. 205-210.

[63] For the resemblances between Jn 17,24 and Jn 14,2-3, see, ch. VI, pp. 210-211.

[64] The glory which is "given" refers necessarily to the glory of the Word Incarnate. As B. F. WESTCOTT aptly observes: "The 'glory' of the Word, apart from the Incarnation, is not said in the language of the New Testament to be 'given'". See, *op. cit.* 248.

of Jn 17,24, then, refers to the heavenly and transcendent glory of God communicated to Jesus as the Word made flesh and which was manifested in him at the Incarnation (1,14cd)[65], throughout his ministry by "signs" (2,11; 11,4.40), only to reach its culmination in the passion-death (7,39; 12,16; comp. 12,23.29; 13,31-32),[66] when Jesus is "glorified" by entering again into the eternal and transcendent "glory" of God for which he prays in Jn 17,5.[67]

Jn 14,2-3 and Jn 17,24, then, both complement each other. The same union of believers with Jesus is conditional on the emergence of Jesus as the New Temple in Jn 14,2-3 and is further directed in Jn 17,24 to a vision of the glory of Jesus. The vision of the glory of Jesus in Jn 17,24de depends ultimately on the emergence of Jesus from his passion-death as the New Temple in Jn 14,2-3. Thus the vision of the glory of Jesus in Jn 17,24 becomes necessarily through the complementary text of Jn 14,2-3 a vision of the glory of the New Temple.

We find a similar perspective in Jn 12,41 (comp. 1,14). Here John affirms that the glory of Jesus was already seen (in some way) by Isaiah in his vision of the temple-glory of YY.[68] The ὅτι stresses some kind of causal nexus.[69] Isaiah, then, foretold Jewish blindness, because he saw the temple-glory of YY manifested in Jesus. The large semitic inclusion between Jn 12,41 and Jn 1,14c (δόξα) would lend support to this interpretation.[70]

However, the ταῦτα may also be taken to refer (at least indirectly) to Is 53,1 (cf. Jn 12,38; comp. Rom. 10,16). This text occurs in the context of the Fourth Servant Song (Is 52,13-53,12). It is also significantly linked within that context with the theme of glory (cf. Is 52,13). The manifestation of the temple-glory of YY in the glory of Jesus is thus

---

[65] W. GROSSOUW points out that the whole subsequent development of the Johannine theme of "glory" is contained in embryo in Jn 1,14. See, op. cit. (n. 60) 133.

[66] W. GROSSOUW explains the use of the verb δοξάζω in Jn 7,39 as "quasi technique". See, op. cit. (n. 60) 135.

[67] This is a point well made by A. M. RAMSEY: "it is in His human nature that the Son receives glory from the Father, and He asks that through the Passion and Resurrection the human nature may be exalted into the eternal glory of the Godhead". See, op. it. (n. 60) 85.

[68] The theme of glory is closely linked in general with the temple in the OT (cf. Ex 40,34-35; Nm 14,10; I Kgs 8,10-11; 2 Chr 7,1-3; 2 Mc 2,8; Ps 26(25),8; Ez 1,28f; 43,1f; Hag 1,8; 2,3.7; Sir 36,14 (LXX v. 13).

[69] GNT designates ὅτε as the reading of the majority of witnesses. However, there is also strong manuscript support for ὅτι. Besides, the ὅτι would appear, on the surface, to be somewhat less appropriate in the context than either ὅτε or ἐπεί, and so would be likely to provoke scribal alteration.

[70] On this semitic inclusion, see, H. VAN DEN BUSSCHE, "La structure de Jean I-XII" in L'évangile de Jean. Études et problèmes (RechBib III) (Bruges, 1958) 61-109, esp. 106-7.

linked in Jn 12,41 with Is 53,1, which evokes again (in typical Johannine style) the whole immediate context of the Song of the Suffering Servant (Is 52,13-53,12). In this way, the evangelist underlines a highly significant link between the temple-glory of Jesus in Jn 12,41 and the glorification of the Servant through suffering and death.

This profound import of Jn 12,41 is only intelligible in the light of the glorification of the New Temple by the passion-death of Jesus (cf. 2,19). The rejection of Jesus, then, was already foretold by Isaiah, because he saw in anticipation the temple-glory of YY manifested in the New Temple of the crucified Jesus.

Our interpretation of Jn 14,2-3 is again confirmed. Here Jesus provides the New Temple and is at the same time himself glorified by one and the same journey to prepare a place through his passion-death. Thus the temple-glory of Jesus which is the object of vision in Jn 12,41 is one with the New Temple of Jesus glorified by his passion-death in our understanding of Jn 14,2-3. The vocabulary is different. But the profound spiritual reality is the same.

So, too, Jn 14,2-3 is complemented by Jn 12,41. The same New Temple of the glorified Jesus in Jn 14,2-3 is presented as an object of vision in Jn 12,41. No such vision is mentioned in Jn 14,2-3.

However, we have seen that the union of believers with Jesus promised in Jn 14,2-3 is further directed in Jn 17,24 to a vision of the glory of Jesus, which thus becomes necessarily a vision of the glory of the New Temple. This perspective is also confirmed by Jn 12,41. Moreover, such a vision is in some way the goal of the whole work of salvation (cf. 1,14; comp. also 1,51).

H. THE "SIGN" OF THE NEW TEMPLE (JN 20,19-29)

Our comparison is with the following text of Jn 20,19-29:[71]

Jn 20,19a Οὔσης οὖν ὀψίας τῇ ἡμέρᾳ ἐκείνῃ τῇ μιᾷ σαββάτων,
       b καὶ τῶν θυρῶν κεκλεισμένων ὅπου ἦσαν οἱ μαθηταὶ
          διὰ τὸν φόβον τῶν Ἰουδαίων,
       c ἦλθεν ὁ Ἰησοῦς καὶ ἔστη εἰς τὸ μέσον,
       d καὶ λέγει αὐτοῖς· εἰρήνη ὑμῖν.

---

[71] Apart from the commentaries, we have found the following works helpful in our interpretation of Jn 20,19-29, D. MOLLAT, "L'apparition du Ressuscité et le don de l'Esprit - Jn 20,19-23", in *Fête de la Pentecôte* (AssSeign 30) 42-56; idem, *La révélation de l'Esprit-Saint chez saint Jean* (Rome, 1971); idem, "La foi pascale selon le chapitre 20 de l'évangile de saint Jean" (Essai de théologie biblique), in *Resurrexit, Actes du symposium international sur la résurrection de Jésus* (Rome, 1970) 316-339; X. LÉON-DUFOUR, *Resurrection and Message of Easter* (London, 1974); S. A. PANIMOLLE, *Il dono della legge e la grazia della verità* (Gv 1,17) (Roma, 1973) 234-38, n. 146.

20a καὶ τοῦτο εἰπὼν ἔδειξεν
       καὶ τὰς χεῖρας καὶ τὴν πλευρὰν αὐτοῖς.
  b ἐχάρησαν οὖν οἱ μαθηταὶ ἰδόντες τὸν Κύριον.
21a εἶπεν οὖν αὐτοῖς ὁ Ἰησοῦς πάλιν· εἰρήνη ὑμῖν.
  b καθὼς ἀπέσταλκέν με ὁ πατήρ, κἀγὼ πέμπω ὑμᾶς.
22a καὶ τοῦτο εἰπὼν ἐνεφύσησεν καὶ λέγει αὐτοῖς·
  b λάβετε πνεῦμα ἅγιον.
23a ἄν τινων ἀφῆτε τὰς ἁμαρτίας, ἀφέωνται αὐτοῖς·
  b ἄν τινων κρατῆτε, κεκράτηνται.
24a Θωμᾶς δὲ εἷς ἐκ τῶν δώδεκα, ὁ λεγόμενος Δίδυμος,
  b οὐκ ἦν μετ' αὐτῶν ὅτε ἦλθεν ὁ Ἰησοῦς.
25a ἔλεγον οὖν αὐτῷ οἱ ἄλλοι μαθηταί·
  b ἑωράκαμεν τὸν Κύριον.
  c ὁ δὲ εἶπεν αὐτοῖς· ἐὰν μὴ ἴδω
       ἐν ταῖς χερσὶν αὐτοῦ τὸν τύπον τῶν ἥλων
  d καὶ βάλω τὸν δάκτυλόν μου εἰς τὸν τόπον τῶν ἥλων
  e καὶ βάλω μου τὴν χεῖραν εἰς τὴν πλευρὰν αὐτοῦ,
  f οὐ μὴ πιστεύσω.
26a Καὶ μεθ' ἡμέρας ὀκτὼ πάλιν ἦσαν
       ἔσω οἱ μαθηταὶ αὐτοῦ, καὶ Θωμᾶς μετ' αὐτῶν.
  b ἔρχεται ὁ Ἰησοῦς τῶν θυρῶν κεκλεισμένων,
  c καὶ ἔστη εἰς τὸ μέσον καὶ εἶπεν· εἰρήνη ὑμῖν.
27a εἶτα λέγει τῷ Θωμᾷ· φέρε τὸν δάκτυλόν σου ὧδε
  b καὶ ἴδε τὰς χεῖράς μου,
  c καὶ φέρε τὴν χεῖρα σου καὶ βάλε εἰς τὴν πλευράν μου,
  d καὶ μὴ γίνου ἄπιστος ἀλλὰ πιστός.
28a ἀπεκρίθη Θωμᾶς καὶ εἶπεν αὐτῷ·
  b ὁ Κύριός μου καὶ ὁ Θεός μου.
29a λέγει αὐτῷ ὁ Ἰησοῦς· ὅτι ἑώρακάς με, πεπίστευκας;
  b μακάριοι οἱ μὴ ἰδόντες καὶ πιστεύσαντες.

The term "side" (πλευρά) repeated three times in Jn 20,19-29 (cf. 20,20a.25e.27c) has been interpreted in Jn 19,34[72] to identify the crucified Jesus with the New Temple as the source of the Spirit (comp. κοιλία, 7,38b).[73] This would seem to suggest a continuation in some sense of this same theme of the New Temple in Jn 20,19-29. Besides, there is an important literary link between the use of ἔρχομαι in Jn 20,19-29 (cf. 20,19c.24b.26b) and in Jn 14,2-3 (cf. 14,3b).[74]

---

[72] There are only four uses of the term in the fourth gospel (cf. Jn 19,34a; 20,20a. 25e. 27c).

[73] The important link between these three Johannine texts (Jn 7,37-39; 19,31-37; 20,19-29) has been rightly stressed by S. A. PANIMOLLE. See, op. cit. (n. 71) 237.

[74] This verb is never used in the Synoptics to describe the appearances of the risen Jesus.

The Johannine dramatic technique is clearly at work in Jn 20,19-29. The evangelist designedly withdraws Thomas from the gathering of the disciples in Jn 20,19-23 in order to climax the resurrection narrative and the whole gospel with a sublime expression of the faith of the primitive community on his lips in Jn 20,28.[75]

There is virtually unanimous agreement that the titles "Lord" and "God" on the lips of Thomas derive from the OT (comp. Ps 35(34),23). This profession of faith combines the terms used in the LXX to translate YHWH and ELOHIM. It makes clear that the crucified-risen Jesus may be addressed in the same language in which Israel addressed YY. The resurrection appearance is a visible "sign" for Thomas of the profound significance of the passion-death of Jesus. It evokes an act of perfect faith in the crucified-risen Jesus as God (Jn 20,28).[76]

In the light of this same perfect faith the profound symbolic import of Jn 20,19-29 also unfolds. The link with the passion-death of Jesus is firmly stressed by the symbolic gesture of the risen Jesus when "he showed his hands and his side" (20,20; comp. 19,34). The two facets of the one "hour" of the passion-resurrection of Jesus are thus closely linked.[77]

Moreover, this first symbolic gesture of the risen Jesus is also in turn closely linked with the subsequent gesture of the risen Jesus when he "breathed" the Spirit on his disciples (20,22). It is the same gift of the Spirit which is symbolised by the issue of "water" from the pierced "side" of the crucified Jesus in Jn 19,34.[78]

However, the pierced "side" on Calvary would seem to identify the crucified Jesus with the New Temple as the source of the Spirit. There is a significant verbal link between the "water" of Jn 19,34b and of Jn 7,37-39 (cf. 7,38b).[79] Besides, the OT background common to the Calvary scene (Jn 19,31-37) and Jn 7,37-39 also seems to suggest a close link between

---

[75] See, R. E. Brown, op. cit. 1015. 1031.

[76] C. K, Barrett remarks: "There can be no doubt that John intended this confession of faith to form the climax of the gospel ... it is his final Christological pronouncement". See, op. cit. 477.

[77] The apparition on Easter evening only resumes the revelation of the cross, clarifying it in a new and decisive way. It represents, beyond death, the other side of the same truth: the truth of "the hour" of Jesus (Jn 12,23; 13,1; 13,32; 17,1).

[78] This is also the profound import of Jn 19,30 for several exegetes who accept a double meaning for the phrase "he handed over the Spirit". Jesus breathes his last in death. However, he also hands over the Spirit at the moment of his glorifying death as promised in Jn 7,39. C. H. Dodd is a notable exception to an interpretation of Jn 19,30 in a double sense. See, op. cit. (n. 39) 428.

[79] Commentators have repeatedly underlined the link between Jn 7,37-39 and Jn 19,31-37. See, S. A. Panimolle, op. cit. (n. 71) 237, n. 146.

them.[80] Jn 19,37 evokes directly Zechariah 12,10b. But this text is in turn intimately linked with the OT texts evoked by way of background to Jn 7,37-39 (e.g. Ze 12,10a; 13,1; 14,8; comp. Ez 47,1-12). When John evokes directly Zechariah 12,10b in Jn 19,37 he also evokes (in typical Johannine style) the whole immediate context with it. But we have seen that these are the very texts which provide the OT background to our interpretation of Jn 7,37-39 with reference to the New Temple of the risen Jesus as the source of the Spirit (cf. Ze 12,10a; 13,1; 14,8). This would seem to suggest that John is continuing this same theme in Jn 19,31-37.[81]

The first scene of the risen Jesus in Jn 20,19-23 resumes this revelation of the cross, with its full symbolic import. In the response of faith by the disciples to the risen Jesus the "side" of Jesus takes on again the profound symbolic import of the Calvary scene. Thus it identifies the crucified-risen Jesus with the New Temple as the source of the Spirit. The future "sign" of the crucified-risen Jesus as the New Temple promised indirectly by way of response to the demand of the Jews in Jn 2,18 is now fulfilled.[82]

Thus the risen Jesus reveals himself to perfect faith in Jn 20,20a as the New Temple, which is the source of the Spirit (20,22). Moreover, the response of faith on the lips of Thomas makes it clear that one may address the risen Jesus revealed as the New Temple in the same language in which Israel addressed YY (20,28). As such the "sign" of the New Temple does not signify in the strict sense, or point beyond itself.[83] The risen Jesus is the "sign" of the New Temple, and is himself in his intimate union with his Father the reality signified (cf. 8,28; 10,30.38). Thus the "sign" itself and the reality signified are one.

Once again our interpretation of Jn 14,2-3 is confirmed. The "sign" of the New Temple in Jn 20,19-29 points to the same profound reality which emerges by means of the preparation of a place through the passion-resurrection of Jesus in Jn 14,2-3. So, too, our interpretation of Jn 14,2-3 within its immediate context with reference to the New Temple as the source of the Spirit (cf. 14,16-17.26) is also confirmed by Jn

---

[80] We have a link in the prophet Zechariah between the glance towards the pierced one (Ze 12,10b) and the cleansing spring of salvation (Ze 13,1; 12,10a; comp. Ze 14,8).

[81] Besides, the κοιλία of Jn 7,38b may be identified even more precisely as a reference to the temple. See, J. DANIÉLOU, op. cit. (n. 34) 161. As such the πλευρά of Jn 19,34a would correspond to the κοιλία of Jn 7,38b, and identify the pierced Jesus with the New Temple as the source of the Spirit.

[82] D. MOLLAT notes well this important link between the use of δείκνυμι in Jn 2,18 and Jn 20,20a. See, op. cit. (n. 71) "L'apparition du Ressuscité..." 46.

[83] There is no evidence to show that John himself calls anything that is not miraculous, or at least extraordinary, a "sign" in the strict sense of the term. On the various uses of the term "sign" in the fourth gospel, see, D. W. WEAD, The Literary Devices in John's Gospel (Basel, 1970) 12-28.

20,19-29, where the risen Jesus as the New Temple breathes the Spirit on his disciples (20,22).

Moreover, our interpretation of the "coming" of Jesus in Jn 14,2-3 with reference among other "comings" to the "coming" of the risen Jesus at the Easter apparitions is confirmed. The promise of Jn 14,2-3 that Jesus will "come again" is clearly fulfilled in the resurrection appearances, where the intervention of the risen Jesus is again designated with the verb ἔρχομαι (cf. 20,19c.24b.26b). This immediate future intervention of the risen Jesus explicitly referred to in the immediate context of Jn 14,2-3 (cf. 14,18) sets in motion the whole dynamic process of "coming" in Jn 14,2-3, but by no means exhausts all its possibilities.

CONCLUSION

We have now compared the perspectives opened up by our deeper understanding of Jn 14,2-3 with those of other Johannine texts. Here we find ample confirmation of our interpretation of our text in line with the Johannine perspectives of the fourth gospel. There is confirmation of our interpretation of the New Temple of Jn 14,2-3 within its immediate context with reference to the New Temple of the truth (14,6a) in Jn 1,14 and Jn 4,20-24; confirmation of our interpretation of the New Temple of Jn 14,2-3 as the Sanctuary of an unbroken intercommunication between heaven and earth, or the Meeting-Place between God and man, in Jn 1,51; confirmation of our interpretation of the New Temple of Jn 14,2-3 within its immediate context with reference to the New Temple as the Source of the Spirit (14,16-17.26) in Jn 7,37-39 and Jn 20,19-29, and in this latter text also confirmation of our interpretation of the coming of Jesus in Jn 14,2-3 with reference, among other comings of Jesus, to the resurrection appearances; confirmation of our interpretation of the preparation of a place in Jn 14,2-3 as a sacrificial act by which the temple of the body of Jesus is transformed spiritually into the New Temple in Jn 10,36, and here also confirmation of our interpretation of the coming of Jesus in Jn 14,2-3 as the missionary aspect of the New Temple; confirmation of our interpretation of the New Temple of Jn 14,2-3 as the goal of discipleship in Jn 11,47-53; and finally confirmation of our interpretation of the preparation of a place as the glorification of the New Temple through the glorifying passion-death of Jesus in Jn 12,41.

So, too, our interpretation of Jn 14,2-3 is considerably enriched and complemented by these other Johannine texts. The New Temple of Jn 14,2-3 is designated elsewhere in the gospel as an object of vision (cf. 1,14; 1,51; 17,24; 12,41). Indeed, the union of believers in the New Temple of Jn 14,2-3 is directed precisely to such a vision (17,24), which is in someway also the goal of the whole work of salvation (1,14). From these other Johannine texts we can also see that there is a significant complementary aspect to the emergence of the New Temple in our understanding of Jn 14,2-3, which is the destruction of the temple of the body of Jesus. This in turn is linked inseparably with the destruction of the Jerusalem temple (2,19; 4,20-24). Moreover, the universality of the new community represented by the disciples in Jn 14,2-3 is complemented by Jn 11,47-53, where the OT people of God form part of the new people of God, or the new community of believers. Finally, the profound reality of Jn 14,2-3 may be described in equivalent Johannine terms as the New Sanctuary of worship (4,20-24).

The perspective of the New Temple which emerges in our interpretation of Jn 14,2-3 clearly dominates the fourth gospel and the parting discourses. It is hardly surprising that the gospel ends with a final vision of the risen Jesus as the "sign" of the New Temple (20,19-29).

CHAPTER VIII

A UNITY OF TWO LEVELS

We have already stated that there should be no dichotomy between our two levels of understanding.[1] Here we hope to show briefly that this is so.

A. THE FATHER'S HOUSE WITH THE MANY ROOMS

1. The Father's House

The term οἰκία has two levels of meaning. At a first level it indicates in a material (or spatial) sense the building where God/Father of Jesus dwells: his temple. This temple is also the goal of Jesus' journey where (in some mysterious way) he already dwells permanently, and to which he promises to take the disciples to be with him later, after his journey to prepare a place for them is complete. Still, there is a certain ambivalence in the text at this level of understanding. It is by no means clear whether it is the Jerusalem temple or the heavenly temple which is intended.

However, the term οἰκία takes on a deeper spiritual meaning at a second level of understanding. It indicates a "family" or "household" — a corporate unity forged by intimate personal relationships. As such the οἰκία designates an inner spiritual "space" where Jesus himself already abides as Son in a close union with his Father to be shared by all believers in union with Jesus later. When it is thus shared believers themselves in union with Jesus in the Father constitute "the house", or "the family" of God (comp. Heb 3,6). It is now clearly the eternal temple which is the goal of this journey of Jesus through his passion-resurrection, and to which Jesus will take all believers later to be reunited with him there.

---

[1] See, Introduction, p. 26.

2. The Many Rooms

The term μονή also has two levels of meaning. At the first level it indicates in a material (or spatial) sense a "spatial area" within a house where one dwells: a room. The Father's house has "many" of these rooms. The image evoked, then, is one of a large spacious house with "many rooms" to provide ample accommodation for the disciples to dwell there, after the journey to prepare a place for them is complete. This Father's house, then, has many possibilities for others to dwell in it.

However, the term μονή has a still deeper meaning at a second level of understanding. It indicates a spiritual "abiding-space" or "dwelling-space" in the eternal temple. There is the possibility for many to "abide" or "dwell" spiritually there in the inner spiritual "space" of the eternal temple. Moreover, all believers will actually dwell there spiritually, or have their spiritual positions there, when Jesus returns to take them there.

Thus the ambivalence of the text open as it is to interpretation with reference to the Jerusalem temple and/or the heavenly temple disappears in favour of the latter meaning at the second level of understanding. Moreover, at this same level we discover the profound spiritual import of the image of the large house spacious enough to accommodate many people. It designates the spiritual area where Jesus himself abides as Son in close personal union with the Father and the possibilities there for the whole community of believers also to abide in it spiritually later in union with Jesus in the Father. In our understanding of Jn 14,2-3, the image of the dwelling capable of receiving a great number of persons designates God's universal plan of redemption, or more precisely the possibility of universal redemption.

B. THE WAY TO THE FATHER'S HOUSE

1. The Journey of Jesus

Again the term πορεύομαι has two levels of meaning. At a first level it indicates in a material (or spatial) sense a journey of Jesus, by a physical movement in space, which implies departure from the disciples (negative aspect) and access to the Father's house (positive aspect). By this journey, then, Jesus traverses the distance between the disciples and the Father's house. Moreover, this is an immediate future journey, and one which is (in some mysterious way) in the process of being realised.

However, the term πορεύομαι takes on a deeper spiritual meaning at a second level of understanding. It indicates a sacrificial movement of Jesus into communion with his Father through his passion-resurrection — an indivisible spiritual journey of ascent to the Father. This spiritual movement implies departure from the world of men (negative aspect) and access to the heavenly world of God/Father (positive aspect). By this journey, then, Jesus traverses the abyss which separates heaven and earth, God and man. Here the passion-resurrection of Jesus is conceived as an immediate future event, and one which is (in some mysterious way) in the process of being realised.

2. The Preparation of a Place

The purpose of this journey is "to prepare a place" for the disciples in the Father's house. The phrase has a double level of meaning. At the first level the term τόπος designates in a material (or spatial) sense some kind of physical "space", or spatial area, in the Father's house, where the disciples might dwell. In this sense, the purpose of Jesus' journey is to open up the possibility of dwelling in the Father's house for the disciples, or to render the Father's house accessible to them.

However, the term τόπος takes on a deeper spiritual meaning at a second level of understanding. At this level it refers to the "temple" or "sanctuary" of the body of Jesus. This physical temple is spiritualised by the sacrificial transformation of the passion-resurrection of Jesus. In this way, it becomes the spiritual reality of the New Temple of the risen body of Jesus. The purpose, then, of Jesus' journey at this second level is to provide this New Temple by preparing the temple of his own body through his passion-resurrection.

These two levels of meaning are in harmony. The τόπος which is open to interpretation with reference to any particular sanctuary, or temple, is now understood with reference to the temple of the body of Jesus. So, too, the manner of this journey of Jesus, open to interpretation with reference to any particular journey of Jesus, is now interpreted in a deep spiritual sense with reference to the passion-resurrection of Jesus. It is this same journey of Jesus through his passion-resurrection which provides the New Temple of the risen body of Jesus, and at the same time renders the eternal temple with many μοναί accessible to all believers. The New Temple of the risen body of Jesus thus becomes the spiritual "space" where all believers may occupy their μοναί in the eternal temple. The physical "space" prepared for the disciples in the Father's house in order that they may dwell there, or have their μοναί there, now becomes identified with the spiritual "space" of the New Temple of the risen Jesus.

C. THE RETURN OF JESUS FOR HIS DISCIPLES

1. Return

The phrase πάλιν ἔρχομαι also has two levels of meaning. At the first level it designates in a material (or spatial) sense a movement of Jesus who comes by a physical bodily descent in space from the Father's house to the disciples. The departure of Jesus is directed to this return, which in turn is absolutely conditional upon the previous departure. By this journey, then, Jesus must also traverse in a reverse movement the distance between the Father's house and the disciples. It is a salvific intervention from the Father's house in favour of the disciples. Moreover, it is an eschatological intervention which is (in some mysterious way) continually in the process of being realised.

But this phrase takes on a deeper spiritual meaning at a second level of understanding. At this level it refers to the salvific intervention of the risen Jesus by a descending movement from the Father to the disciples. By this reverse movement the risen Jesus spans the abyss between heaven and earth, God and man. As such it is a heavenly intervention of the risen Jesus in favour of the disciples. It designates a continual eschatological intervention of the risen Jesus in anticipation of his ever future Second Coming. The previous departure of Jesus to the Father through the passion-resurrection is directed to this subsequent eschatological intervention of the risen Jesus, which in turn is also conditional upon the passion-resurrection of Jesus. However, in itself this eschatological intervention is unspecified with reference to any particular intervention, imminent or remote, in anticipation of the ever future Second Coming.

Again the two levels of understanding are in harmony. The manner of this intervention of Jesus after the preparation of a place is interpreted at the second level of understanding in a deeper spiritual sense with reference to the continual process of the eschatological intervention of the risen Jesus in anticipation of his ever future Second Coming. Moreover, it is the eschatological intervention of the risen Jesus who has now become in his own person the New Temple through his passion-resurrection.

2. The Journey of the Disciples with Jesus

The term παραλήμψομαι also has two levels of meaning. At a first level it indicates in a material (or spatial) sense a journey of the disciples with Jesus, by a physical movement in space. It designates the effect of the intervention of Jesus in favour of his disciples. It implies a departure of the disciples with Jesus (negative aspect) and their journey of entrance with him into the Father's house (positive aspect). By this journey the disciples traverse the same distance along the same way already traversed by Jesus alone previously in his journey to the Father's house.

However, the term παραλήμψομαι takes on a deeper spiritual meaning at a second level of understanding. It indicates the effect of the heavenly intervention of the risen Jesus as an indivisible spiritual journey of ascent to the eternal temple of the Father's house by believers united spiritually with the risen Jesus. It implies a departure from the world of sin, or unbelief, by believers in union with Jesus (negative aspect) and access in union with Jesus to the eternal temple of God/Father (positive aspect). The removal of believers from the sphere of "sin", or unbelief, and entrance into union with the Father in Jesus are inseparably linked with one another as two different ways of expressing in complementary Johannine terms the effect of the sacrifice of the passion-resurrection of Jesus (comp. I Jn 3,14). By this spiritual journey in union with Jesus out of the sphere of "sin", or unbelief, into communion with the Father the disciples traverse the same distance along the same way already traversed by Jesus himself previously in his passion-resurrection.

The two levels are again in harmony. The manner of this journey of the disciples with Jesus, open as it is to interpretation with reference to any particular journey of the disciples with Jesus, is now interpreted in a deep spiritual sense with reference to the spiritual journey of believers intimately united with Jesus in his passion-resurrection. On this journey, then, at this deeper level of understanding believers already occupy the μοναί of the eternal temple rendered accessible to them in the New Temple of the risen Jesus.

D. THE GOAL OF THE DISCIPLES' JOURNEY

The phrase ὅπου εἰμὶ ἐγώ has two levels of meaning. At a first level it indicates in a material (or spatial) sense the Father's house as the place where Jesus himself dwells (or is) permanently. This is the goal of the journey of the disciples with Jesus. The πρὸς ἐμαυτόν further designates this same goal, and stresses the progressive and dynamic aspect of the movement of ascent by the disciples into fellowship with Jesus in the Father's house. After the Father's house has been rendered accessible, Jesus will take the disciples to be personally reunited with him there. Still there is something incongruous at this level of understanding about Jesus having to take the disciples to the distant goal of the Father's house in order to share in his fellowship, if the disciples already share this fellowship with Jesus as he takes them on their way to his Father's house.

However, the phrase ὅπου εἰμὶ ἐγώ takes on a deeper spiritual meaning at a second level of understanding. It indicates the eternal temple as the goal where Jesus dwells in close personal union with his Father. This is the goal of believers. But this same goal is already attained by believers who are already united spiritually with the risen Jesus as they occupy the μοναί of the eternal temple rendered accessible to them in the New Temple of the risen Jesus. For believers, then, the goal and the way to it are already one in union with the risen Jesus. The πρὸς ἐμαυτόν indicates the risen Jesus himself as this same goal of unity, and stresses the progressive and dynamic movement of believers into an ever deeper union with the risen Jesus in the Father. Although the goal of union with the risen Jesus in the Father is already attained, it is also in some sense not yet fully so.

Thus the incongruity of the text is clarified at this second level of understanding. The activity of the risen Jesus throughout the eschatological period is presented as a continual unifying action of taking the disciples in union with himself into ever deeper union with himself in the Father. Moreover, there is harmony between the two levels of understanding. The manner of dwelling in the eternal temple which is left entirely open in the phrase ὅπου εἰμὶ ἐγώ is specified at this second level in terms of a deep spiritual "in-being", or "indwelling", of Jesus in the Father and of the disciples with Jesus in the Father. The ὅπου εἰμὶ ἐγώ which designates the eternal temple is now interpreted at a second deeper level of the "in-being" of Jesus in the Father which believers already share as they occupy the μοναί of the eternal temple rendered accessible to them in the New Temple of the risen Jesus.

The second level merely provides a deep spiritual understanding of the manner of the journey of Jesus alone to the Father's house through his passion-resurrection, and the manner of the continual intervention of the risen Jesus in favour of believers as they journey along the same way in union with the risen Jesus later. It also provides a deep spiritual understanding of the manner in which the promised goal of dwelling with Jesus in the Father's house is realised in a close personal "in-being" of the disciples with Jesus in the Father — a deep spiritual at-one-ment of the disciples with Jesus.

E. THE PERFECT MEDIATOR

Yet another incongruity of our text is also clarified at this second level of understanding. Jesus is paradoxically at a distance from his Father to whom he must journey (πορεύομαι) and at the same time intimately united with him (ὅπου εἰμὶ ἐγώ). There are obviously two levels which must be distinguished in the situation of the historical Jesus, before the preparation of a place.[2] At one level he is with the Father perpetually and continually in the sphere of God (ὅπου εἰμὶ ἐγώ); at another level he shares the condition of men at a distance from his Father to whom he must still journey (πορεύομαι). But this chasm between heaven where Jesus is with the Father and the world where Jesus is with men and is still going to the Father must first be bridged, if union between God and man is to be made possible. The effect of the journey of Jesus to the Father through his passion-resurrection (πορεύομαι) in our interpretation of the text is precisely to render heaven accessible to men by providing the New Temple of the risen body of Jesus as the meeting-place of God and man. It is the earthly mission of Jesus to suppress this distance by bridging the gap between heaven and earth in the New Temple. Moreover, the παραλήμψομαι of our text designates a journey of the whole community of believers already occupying the μοναί of the heavenly temple in the New Temple of the risen Jesus. In this sense, the distance between heaven and earth is effectively and definitively bridged for all believers in the New Temple. The risen Jesus becomes through his passion-resurrection the perfect mediator between God and man, one-with-God and one-with-man.

As this perfect mediator the risen Jesus is an abiding spiritual reality continually present and effective throughout the whole eschatological period. This is the import of the present form of the verb ἔρχομαι, which in turn is conditional on the πορεύομαι, so that the journey of Jesus to the Father through his passion-resurrection (πορεύομαι) is continually effective in the continual eschatological intervention of the risen Jesus (ἔρχομαι). In this way, the earthly mission of Jesus accomplished by himself alone in his passion-resurrection (πορεύομαι) is always present and effective — a permanent and perpetual "now", after the passion-resurrection of Jesus is complete, in the New Temple of the risen Jesus.

Thus the purpose of the earthly mission of Jesus to bridge the gap between God and man by his passion-resurrection is effective in the New Temple of the risen Jesus, where God and believers are one. Moreover, it is continually effective in the continual eschatological intervention of the risen Jesus as he takes believers by a continual unifying action into union with the Father in the New Temple of his risen body. The risen Jesus as the perfect mediator in the New Temple of his risen body becomes the place of an unbroken exchange between

---

[2] Such a distinction is aptly made by C. H. Dodd: "John works, like most religious thinkers of his time, with a Weltanschauung which is, prima facie at least, dualistic. There are two planes of being, denominated τὰ ἄνω and τὰ κάτω". See, *The Interpretation of the Fourth Gospel* (Cambridge, 1960) 258.

heaven/Father and earth/believers. This is the abiding eschatological reality of Jn 14,2-3 ever present and effective as a result of the passion-resurrection of Jesus in the New Temple of the risen Jesus as the perfect mediator between God and man. One indivisible moment in the life of the historical Jesus is marked clearly and sharply distinct from what follows by means of the πορεύομαι of Jn 14,2-3, as the solitary figure of Jesus strides across the threshold of eternity and enters the heavenly temple through his passion-resurrection. But this moment is perpetually effective and present afterwards throughout the whole eschatological period which follows as the community of believers enters this same eternal temple along the same way in the New Temple of the risen Jesus, which is the effect of the passion-resurrection of Jesus. It is the risen Jesus as the New Temple who spans in his risen body the distance which separates heaven and earth, and becomes the perfect mediator of a perpetual exchange between heaven and earth.

However, it is by faith under the action of the Spirit of truth that the believer is first linked to the risen Jesus as the perfect mediator between God and man, or the New Temple in his risen body. Access to the Father through the risen Jesus begins under the action of the Spirit of truth. It is in this way that the indivisible spiritual journey of the disciples in union with Jesus out of the world of sin or unbelief (negative aspect) into communion with the Father (positive aspect) is set in motion. The believer retains his human condition in the world (comp. Jn 17,11.15), and yet in a deep spiritual sense he is not of this world (comp. Jn 17,14.16). Still in the world, the believer is translated by faith under the action of the Spirit of truth out of the world of unbelief, or in equivalent Johannine language out of the world of "sin" and of spiritual death (comp. Jn 5,25;[3] I Jn 3,14), dominated by the Prince of this world (comp. Jn 12,31; 14,30), and transported into communion with the Father in the heavenly sphere opened up to the believer in the New Temple of the risen Jesus as "the truth". Hence, there is a twofold effect of the sacrificial journey of Jesus to the Father through his passion-resurrection in Jn 14,2-3: a departure from the world of unbelief or sin (negative aspect), and union with the Father in the risen Jesus, or at-one-ment with God (positive aspect). In this sense, the sacrificial journey of Jesus to his Father through his passion-resurrection is clearly one of expiation for sin (negative aspect) and at-one-ment with God (positive aspect).

---

[3] The spiritual import of Jn 5,25 has been well explained by M.-E. BOISMARD. See, "L'évolution du thème eschatologique dans les traditions johanniques", *RB* 68 (1961) 517.

CONCLUSION

At the deeper level of understanding we find an adequate and final solution for all the deeper possibilities of our text. The second deeper level of understanding, the post-Paschal, is merely a deeper understanding of the first level, the pre-Paschal. We find development from one level of understanding to the next, but no contradiction.

It is the same goal of being with Jesus in the Father's house which is promised in Jn 14,2-3, but the goal itself and the manner of sharing it is specified more precisely as the eternal temple, where believers share with Jesus in his intimate mode of in-being in the Father. It is the same journey of Jesus, but the manner of the journey is understood in terms of the passion-resurrection of Jesus. It is the same preparation of a place, with the manner and object of preparation clarified. The passion-resurrection of Jesus renders the eternal temple of the Father's house, with its many possibilities for abiding there, accessible by providing the New Temple of the risen Jesus. It is the same eschatological intervention of Jesus, but the manner is specified more precisely with reference to every possible intervention of the risen Jesus (now the New Temple in his risen body) in anticipation of an ever future Second Coming. It is the same journey of the disciples being taken by Jesus along the same way first traced out by Jesus himself into the heavenly temple, with the μοναί there accessible to them after the preparation a place. However, the manner of this journey is specified more precisely as a journey of the disciples in union with the risen Jesus (and so already occupying the μοναί of the eternal temple prepared for them in the New Temple of the risen Jesus) into ever deeper union with him in the Father, along the way of his passion-resurrection. It is the same unifying activity of Jesus, but it is specified more exactly with reference to the whole unifying activity of the risen Jesus throughout the eschatological period after the passion- resurrection in anticipation of the Second Coming.

The ambivalence of our text also disappears at the second level of understanding. The Father's house with the many rooms is not the Jerusalem temple, but the eternal temple, with its many possibilities for others to dwell there. Also, the two apparent contradictions in the text are clarified. At this deeper level of understanding the goal of the Father's house with its many possibilities for others to dwell in it and the way to it are one in the New Temple of the risen Jesus, where believers already occupy the μοναί of the eternal temple prepared for them as Jesus takes them along the same way of his passion-resurrection (after it is completed) into ever deeper union with himself in the Father. So, too, we must distinguish two levels in the situation of the earthly Jesus before the preparation of a place, the human and the divine. The effect of the passion-resurrection of Jesus is to suppress the distance between these two planes in the risen Jesus by the sacrificial transformation of the body of Jesus into the New Temple. The earthly mission of Jesus is complete: the distance between heaven and earth is levelled out in the New Temple of the risen Jesus.

RECAPITULATION

By way of conclusion to Part II and to our thesis as a whole we now recapitulate briefly. Our study of some literary questions, the structural unity of the first farewell discourse (Jn 13,31-14,31) within the more general framework of the farewell discourses (Jn 13,1-17,26), and the structural unity of our text in its more immediate context of Jn 14,1-4, with our analysis of the deeper Johannine possibilities of the vocabulary of the text itself have all provided us with an interpretation of Jn 14,2-3 at a second deeper level of understanding in harmony with our first level of understanding, and in which the apparent contradictions of our first level of understanding are satisfactorily explained.

The OT echoes of Jn 14,2-3 now take on a profound significance. The vocabulary of our text with its OT exodus associations provides John with a vehicle well suited to express the unity of God's design of eschatological redemption as an entrance into the heavenly temple in a New Exodus first by Jesus himself through his passion-resurrection and later by the whole new people of God along the same way of the passion-resurrection in union with the risen Jesus. The OT connotations of our text also point to this New Exodus of Jesus and the new people of God as the fulfilment of the promised eschatological pilgrimage of the nations to the temple (cf. Is 2,2-3; Mi 4,1-4).

Moreover, our interpretation of Jn 14,2-3 is also another argument in favour of the liturgical influence at work in the fourth gospel. The text itself has a liturgical connotation. It seems to presuppose a cultic *Sitz im Leben*, like the solemn entrance of the High Priest once a year into the Holy of Holies on the Day of Atonement (cf. Lv 16,1ff; 23,26ff; Nm 29,7ff; comp. Heb 9,11). The journey of Jesus is a priestly activity. Jesus enters through his passion-resurrection into the heavenly temple of the Father's House by the sacrificial transformation of his body into the New Temple of his risen body in which believers have permanent and abiding at-one-ment with God. By this sacrificial entrance Jesus becomes at the same time the Great High Priest, one-with-God and one-with-the-community of believers. In our text of Jn 14,2-3 at the centre of the farewell discourses (Jn 13,1-17,26) a phrase which pertains to the family and to the intimate personal relationships within that family thus describes the continual realisation of the eschatological work of redemption with an implicit reference to the temple and to the liturgy.

Finally, we have shown that the perspectives opened up in our understanding of Jn 14,2-3 at a second deeper level of understanding are in harmony with those of other temple-texts of the fourth gospel (comp. Jn 1,14; 1,51; 4,20-24; 7,37-39; 10,36; 11,47-53; 12,41; 20,19-29). The temple theme has always been acknowledged as a leading theme of the fourth gospel. It would seem strange, to say the least, if no reference to the temple were to be found in the so-called farewell discourses (Jn 13,1-17,26). Our text of Jn 14,2-3 is the hinge on which the first farewell discourse pivots (Jn 13,31-14,31), and this same first farewell discourse in turn cannot be adequately explained without reference to the complementary developments of the second farewell discourse (Jn 15,1-16,33) and the priestly prayer (Jn 17,1-26). Hence, our interpretation of Jn 14,2-3 within the context of these farewell discourses clearly points to the temple as an important theme of yet another large section of the fourth gospel, which cannot be adequately explained without reference to it.

SELECT BIBLIOGRAPHY

Students of the fourth gospel are now privileged to have at their disposal the incomparable bibliographical tool prepared by Edward Malatesta, S.J., *St. John's Gospel 1920-1965. A Cumulative and Classified Bibliography of Books and Periodical Literature on the Fourth Gospel* (Analecta Biblica 32, Rome, 1967). This may be complemented and updated with the bibliography provided by James McPolin, S.J., "Studies in the Fourth Gospel — Some Contemporary Trends", in *Irish Biblical Studies*: Issue 2: January, 1980, 3-26. Ignace de la Potterie, S J., has also provided us with an exhaustive list of commentaries on the fourth gospel in his monumental work, *La vérité dans Saint Jean*, 2 vol. (Analecta Biblica 73-74, Rome, 1977). The following bibliography, therefore, does not pretend to duplicate the work of these scholars. It contains only those commentaries primarily used in the present study and other literature not contained in the above-mentioned studies; and also works found particularly helpful in the praparation of this work.

COMMENTARIES

AUGUSTINE, *In Joannis Evangelium tractatus* CXXIV, PL 35, 1379-1976; CCL 36.

BARRETT, C. K., *The Gospel according to St. John*, London, 1955, ²1978.

BAUER, W., *Das Johannesevangelium* (Handbuch zum Neuen Testament, 6), Leipzig, 1912, ³1933.

BERNARD, J. H., *A Critical and Exegetical Commentary on the Gospel according to St. John* (ICC), 2 vol., Edinburgh, 1928.

BOUYER, L., *Le quatrième évangile* (1ᵉ ed., Les livres de la Bible; 2ᵉ ed., Bible et vie chrétienne), Paris, 1938, ²1955.

BRAUN, F.-M., *Évangile selon saint Jean* (La Sainte Bible, éd. L. Pirot. X), Paris, 1935, ³1951.

BROWN, R. E., *The Gospel according to John*, 2 vol. (The Anchor Bible, 29 and 29a), New York, 1966, 1970.

BULTMANN, R., *Das Evangelium des Johannes* (Kritisch-exegetischer Kommentar über das Neue Testament, 2. Abteilung, 18. Aufl.), Göttingen, 1964. ET: *The Gospel of John. A Commentary* (Translated by G. R. Beasley-Murray), Philadelphia, 1971.

CYRIL OF ALEXANDRIA, *Commentarius in Joannis Evangelium*, ed. P. E. Pusey, 3 vol., Oxford, 1872; PG 73-74.

GODET, F., *Commentaire sur l'évangile de saint Jean*, 3 tom., Neuchâtel, 1864, ⁴1902-1903.

HOSKYNS, E. C., *The Fourth Gospel* (ed. by F. N. Davey), London, 1939, ²1947.

JOHN CHRYSOSTOM, *Homiliae LXXXVIII in Joannem*, PG 59, 23-482.

LAGRANGE, M.-J., *Évangile selon saint Jean* (Études bibliques), Paris, 1925, [8]1948.
LIGHTFOOT, R. H., *St. John's Gospel. A Commentary* (ed. by C. F. Evans), Oxford, 1956.
LOISY, A., *Le quatrième Évangile*, Paris, 1903, [2]1921.
MARSH, J., *The Gospel of St. John*, London, 1968.
MAC GREGOR, G. H. C., *The Gospel of John* (The Moffat New Testament Commentary), London, 1928, [2]1953.
MILLIGAN, W. M., MOULTON, WM. F., *Commentary on the Gospel of St. John*, Edinburgh, 1898.
MOLLAT, D., *L'Évangile selon saint Jean* (La Sainte Bible), Paris, 1953, [2]1960, [3]1973.
SCHNACKENBURG, R., *Das Johannesevangelium*, I. Teil (Einl. und Komm. zu K. I-4); II Teil (Komm. zu K. 5-12) (Herders Theol. Komm. zum N.T., IV, 1-2), Freiburg, 1965, 1971. ET: *The Gospel According to St. John*, Vol. I. (Translated by Kevin Smith), Herder and Herder, New York, 1968. Vol. II. (Translated by Cecily Hastings, Francis McDonagh, David Smith and Richard Foley), Burns and Oates, London, 1980. Vol. III (Translated by David Smith and G. A. Kon), Burns and Oates, London, 1982.
————, *Das Johannesevangelium. Ergänzende Auslegungen und Exkurse* (not translated), Herder, Freiburg, 1984.
STRACHAN, R. H., *The Fourth Gospel. Its Significance and Environment*, London, 1941, [3]1946.
THOMAS AQUINAS, *Super Evangelium S. Ioannis lectura*, ed. R. Cai, Taurini-Romae, [5]1952.
VAN DEN BUSSCHE, H., *Het vierde Evangelie*, 4 vol., Tielt - Den Haag. I: Het Boek der Tekens. Jo I-4, 1959, [2]1961; II; *Het Boek der Werken.* Jo 5-12, 1960, [2]1962; III: *Jezus' woorden bij het Afscheidsmaal.* Jo 13-17, 1955, [3]1960; IV: *Het Boek der Passie*, Jo 18-21, 1960. FT: *Jean. Commentaire de l'Évangile spirituel* (Bible et vie chrétienne), Desclée De Brouwer, 1967.
WESTCOTT, B. F., *The Gospel according to St. John*, London, 1881 (New edition prepared by A. Fox, London, 1958).
WIKENHAUSER, A., *Das Evangelium nach Johannes* (Das Regensburger Neue Testament), Regensburg, 1948, [3]1961.
ZAHN, T., *Das Evangelium des Johannes* (Kommentar zum Neuen Testament), Leipzig, 1908, [5-6]1921.

REFERENCE WORKS

ABBOTT, E. A., *Johannine Vocabulary* (Diatessarica, V), London, 1905.
————, *Johannine Grammar* (Diatessarica, VI), London, 1906.
ABEL, F.-M., *Grammaire du grec biblique suivie d'un choix de papyrus* (Études bibliques), Paris, 1927.
ALAND, K. (ed.), *Synopsis Quattuor Evangeliorum. Locis parallelis evangeliorum apocryphorum et patrum adhibitis*, Stuttgart, 1969.
ALAND, K.-BLACK, M.-MARTINI, C. M.-METZGER, B. M.-WIKGREN, A. (ed.), *The Greek New Testament* (United Bible Societies), Stuttgart, [2]1973.

BAUER, W., *Griechisch-Deutsches Wörterbuch zu den Schriften des Neuen Testaments und der übrigen urchristlichen Literatur*, Berlin, [5]1958. ET: Bauer, W. - Arndt, W. F. - Gingrich, F. W., *A Greek-English Lexicon of the New Testament and Other Early Christian Literature*, Chicago, 1957.

BLASS, FR., *Grammatik des neutestamentlichen Griechisch* (bearbeitet von A. Debrunner), Göttingen, [10]1959. ET: Blass, F. - DEBRUNNER, R. - FUNK, R. W., *A Greek Grammar of the New Testament and Other Early Christian Literature*, Chicago, 1969.

BROWN, F.-DRIVER, S. R. - BRIGGS, C. A. (eds), *A Hebrew and English Lexicon of the Old Testament with an Appendix Containing the Biblical Aramaic*, Oxford, 1907.

CHARLES, R. H., *The Apocrypha and Pseudepigrapha of the Old Testament*, 2 vol., Oxford, 1913.

DANBY, H. (ed.), *The Mishnah Translated from the Hebrew with Introduction and Brief Explanatory Notes*, Oxford, 1933.

DIEZ MACHO, A. (ed.), *Neophyti I. Targum Palestinense MS de la Biblioteca Vaticana* (Consejo Superior de investigaciones cientificas), Madrid, 1968.

EPSTEIN, I. (ed.), *The Talmud*, 35 vol., London, 1948-1952.

ETHERIDGE, J. W. (ed.), *The Targum of Onkelos and Jonathan Ben Uzziel on the Pentateuch, with the Fragments of the Jerusalem Targum: From the Chaldee*, 2 vol., London, 1862-1863.

GINSBURGER, M. (ed.), *Pseudo-Jonathan (Targum Jonathan ben Usiël zum Pentateuch). Nach der Londoner Handschrift (Brit. Mus. add 29031)*, Berlin, 1903.

HATCH, E. - REDPATH, M. A., *A Concordance to the Septuagint and Other Greek Versions of the Old Testament (Including the Apocryphal Books)*, Oxford, 1897.

HENNECKE, E. - SCHNEEMELCHER, W. - WILSON, R. McL. (eds), *New Testament Apocrypha*, 2 vol., London, 1965.

JASTROW, M., *Dictionary of Talmud Babli, Yerushalmi, Midrashic Literature and Targumim*, 2 vol., New York, 1950.

JOÜON, P., *Grammaire de l'Hébreu Biblique*, Rome, 1923.

KITTEL, R. (ed.), *Biblia Hebraica*, Stuttgart, [4]1949.

KITTEL, G. - FRIEDRICH, G. (ed.), *Theologisches Wörterbuch zum Neuen Testament*, 10 vol., Stuttgart, 1933-1973. ET: *Theological Dictionary of the New Testament*, 10 vol., Grand Rapids, Michigan, 1964-1976.

LAMPE, G. S. H., *A Patristic Greek Lexicon*, Oxford, 1961.

LEVI, J., *Neuhebräisches und Chaldäisches Wörterbuch über die Talmud und Midraschim*, 4 vol., Leipzig, 1876.

LIDDELL, H. G. - SCOTT, R., *A Greek-English Lexicon. A New Edition by H. J. Jones*, Oxford, 1958.

LISOWSKY, G., *Konkordanz zum Hebräischen Alten Testament*, Stuttgart, [2]1958.

LOHSE, E. (ed.), *Die Texte aus Qumran. Hebräisch und Deutsch*, München, [2]1971.

MANDELKERN, S. (ed.), *Veteris Testamenti Concordantiae Hebraicae atque Chaldaicae*, 2 vol., Jerusalem/Tel Aviv, [9]1971.

METZGER, B., *A Textual Commentary on the Greek New Testament* (United Bible Societies), London/New York, 1971.

MORGENTHALER, R., *Statistik des neutestamentlichen Wortschatzes*, Zürich, 1958.

MOULTON, J. H. - MILLIGAN, G., *The Vocabulary of the Greek Testament: Illustrated from the Papyri and Other Non-Literary Sources*, London, 1930.

MOULTON, W. F. - GEDEN, A. S., *A Concordance to the Greek Testament*, Edinburgh, 1897. ²1899. ³1926. ⁴1963, ⁵1978.

RAHLFS, A. (ed.), *Septuaginta*, Stuttgart, ⁸1965.

ROBERTSON, A. T., *A Grammar of the Greek New Testament in the Light of Historical Research*, New York, 1914.

SCHLEUSNER, J. F., *Novum Lexicon Graeco-Latinum in N.T.*, 4 vol., Lipsiac, 1819.

———, *Lexicon in LXX et Reliquos Interpretes Graecos ac Scriptores Apocryphos Veteris Testamenti*, Londini, 1829.

SCHWAB, M. (ed.), *Le Talmud de Jérusalem*, 11 vol., Paris, 1878-1890.

SCHWEIZER, E., *Ego eimi... Die religionsgeschichtliche Herkunft und theologische Bedeutung der johanneischen Bildreden* (FRLANT N. F., 38), Göttingen, 1939.

STRACK, H. L. - BILLERBECK, P., *Kommentar zum Neuen Testament aus Talmud und Midrash*, München, ²1956.

TISCHENDORF, C., *Novum Testamentum Graece*, 2 vol., (editio octava critica maior), Leipzig, 1869-1872.

VERMES, G., *The Dead Sea Scrolls in English*, Garmondsworth, 1968.

WALTON, B. (ed.), *Sanctissima Biblia Polyglotta*, 7 vol., London, 1657.

ZERWICK, M., *Graecitas biblica exemplis illustratur* (Scripta Pont. Inst. Bibl.), Romae, ⁵1966. ET: *Biblical Greek*, Rome, 1963.

ZORELL, FR., *Lexicon graecum Novi Testamenti*, Parisiis, ³1961.

OTHER WORKS QUOTED

AALEN, S., " 'Reign' and 'House'in the Kingdom of God in the Gospels", *NTS* 8 (1962) 215-240.

ALFRINK, B., "L'idée de résurrection d'après Da., XII, 1.2", *Bib* 40 (1959) 355-71.

AUDET, J.-P., " 'De son ventre couleront des fleuves d'eau'. La soif, l'eau et la parole", *RB* 66 (1959) 379-86.

BACON, W. B., "In my Father's House are many Mansions (Jn 14,2)", *ExpT* 43 (1931-32) 477-478.

BARRETT, C. K., "The Old Testament in the Fourth Gospel", *JTS* 48-49 (1947-1948) 155-169.

———, *The Prologue of St. John's Gospel*, London, 1971.

———, "The Place of Eschatology in the Fourth Gospel", *ExpT* 59 (1948) 302-5.

BARROIS, G. A., *Jesus Christ and the Temple* (St. Vladimer's Seminary Press). New York, 1980.

BEAUCAMP, E., *Man's Destiny in the Books of Wisdom*, New York, 1970.

BEAUCHAMP, P., "Le salut corporel des justes et la conclusion du livre de la Sagesse", *Bib* 45 (1964) 491-526.

BECKER, F., "Die Abschiedsreden Jesu im Johannesevangelium", *ZNW* 61 (1970) 215-246.

BEHLER, G.-M., *Les paroles d'adieux du Seigneur. S. Jean 13-17* (Lectio divina), Paris, 1960. ET: *The Last Discourse of Jesus*, Baltimore, 1966.

BERRY, T.S., "Critical Note on St. John XIV, 2", *Exp* (2nd series) 3 (1882) 397-400.

BLACK, M., *An Aramaic Approach to the Gospels and Acts*, Oxford, ³1967.

BLASS, F., *Evangelium secundum Ioannem cum variae lectionis delectu*, Leipzig, 1902.

BOISMARD, M.-E., "L'évolution du thème eschatologique dans les traditions johanniques", *RB* 68 (1961) 507-524.

————, La connaissance dans l'Alliance nouvelle, d'après la première lettre de saint Jean, *RB* 56 (1949) 365-91.

————, "Critique textuelle et citations patristiques", *RB* (1950) 388-91.

BOWEN, R., "The Fourth Gospel as Dramatic Material", *JBL* 49 (1930) 292-304.

BOYD, W.J.P., "The Ascension according to St. John. Chapters 14-17 not pre-Passion but post-Resurrection", *Theology* 70 (1967) 207-11.

BOYLE, J.L., "The Last Discourse (Jn 13,31-16,33) and Prayer (Jn 17): Some Observations on their Unity and Development", *Bib* 56 (1975) 210-22.

BRAUN, F.-M., *Jean le Théologien I: Jean le Théologien et son Évangile dans l'Église ancienne* (Études bibliques); II: *Les grandes traditions d'Israël et l'accord des Écritures selon le quatrième Évangile* (Études bibliques); III: Sa théologie, 1: Le mystère de Jésus-Christ; 2: Le Christ, notre Seigneur hier, aujourd'hui, demain (Études bibliques), Paris, 1959 (I). 1964 (II). 1966 (III).

————, "L'arrière-fond du quatrième évangile", *RechBibl* 111 (1958) 179-196.

————, "Quatre 'Signes' johanniques de l'unité chrétienne", *NTS* 9 (1963) 147-55.

BRÉCHET, R., "Du Christ à l'Église: le dynamisme de l'Incarnation dans l'évangile selon saint Jean". *DivThom* 56 (1953) 67-98.

BRUN, L., *"Jesus als Zeuge von irdischen und himmlischen Dingen. Jo. 3,12-13",* SymbOs 8 (1929) 55-77.

BULTMANN, R., "Die Eschatologie des Johannesevangeliums" in *Glauben und Verstehen* I, Tübingen, 1933. ²1954. ET: *Faith and Understanding* I (Edited by R.W. Funk from the 6th German ed. Translated by L.P. Smith), New York, 1969, 165-83.

BUSINK, Th.A., *Der Tempel von Jerusalem von Solomo bis Herodes. Eine archäologisch-historische Studie unter Berücksichtigung des westsemitischen Tempelbaus*, 2 Band: *Von Ezechiel bis Middot*, Leiden, 1980.

CAQUOT, A., "La prophétie de Nathan et ses échos lyriques", *VetTSup* 9, Leiden, 1962, 213-224.

CATHARINET, F.-M., "Note sur le verset de l'Évangile de Jean (20,17)", in *Memorial J. Chaine*, Lyon, 1950, 51-59.

CERFAUX, L., "La charité fraternelle et le retour du Christ (Jo., XIII, 33-38)", *ETL* 24 (1948) 321-22.

————, "Le thème littéraire parabolique dans l'évangile de saint Jean" (Mélanges A. Fridrischen), *ConiNT* XI, Lund, 1947, 15-25.

CHARLIER, C., "La présence dans l'absence (Jean 13,31-14,31)", *BVC* 2 (1953) 61-75.

CLAVIER, H., "L'ironie dans le quatrième évangile", *StudEvang* I (TU 73) 261-276.

CLEMENTS, R. E., *God and Temple. The Idea of the Divine Presence in Ancient Israel*, Oxford, 1965.

COLLINS, J. J., *The Apocalyptic Vision of the Book of Daniel* (Scholars Press), Missoula, 1977.

CONGAR, Y., *Le Mystère du temple* (Lectio divina 22) (2e édition corrigée), Paris, 1957. ET: *The Mystery of the Temple*, London, 1962.

CORSSEN, P., "Die Abschiedsreden Jesu im vierten Evangelium", *ZNW* 8 (1907) 125-42.

COURTENAY JAMES, J., "Mansiones Multae", *ExpT* 27 (1915-1916) 427-428.

CROSS, F. M. (Jr), *Studies and Texts, vol. III. Biblical Motifs — Origins and Transformations*, Cambridge, Massachusetts, 1966.

———, "Light on Tabernacle Terminology", *BA* 10 (1947) 65-68.

CROSS, M. - FREEDMAN, D. N., "The Song of Miriam", *JNES* 14 (1955) 237-50.

CULLMANN, O., *Urchristentum und Gottesdienst*, Zürich, 1950. FT: *Les Sacrements dans l'évangile johannique*, Paris, 1951. ET: *Early Christian Worship (SBT 10)*, London, 1953.

———, "L'opposition contre le temple de Jérusalem, motif commun de la théologie johannique et du monde ambient", *NTS* 5 (1959) 157-73.

———, "Der johanneische Gebrauch doppeldeutiger Ausdrücke als Schlüssel zum Verständnis des vierten Evangeliums", *TZ* 4 (1948) 360-72.

———, "Εἶδεν καὶ ἐπίστευσεν. La vie de Jésus, objet de la 'vue' et de la 'foi', d'après le quatrième évangile", in *Aux Sources de la Tradition Chrétienne* (Mélanges Goguel), Neuchâtel, 1950, 52-61.

DANIÉLOU, J., "Le symbolisme eschatologique de la fête des tabernacles", *Irénikon* 31 (1958) 19-40.

———, "Joh. 7,38 et Ezéch. 47, 1-11", *StudEvang II* (TU 89) 158-63.

D'ARAGON, J. L., "La notion johannique de l'unité", *ScEcc* 11 (1959) 111-119.

DA SPINETOLI, O., "Il ritorno di Gesù al Padre nella soteriologia giovannea", in *San Giovanni* (XVII Settimana Biblica), Brescia, 1964, 145-159.

DAVIES, W. D., *The Gospel and the Land. Early Christianity and Jewish Territorial Doctrine* (University of California Press), Berkley-Los Angeles-London, 1974.

DEEKS, D., "The Structure of the Fourth Gospel", *NTS* 15 (1969) 107-129.

DE BROUWER, A., "Il parlait du temple de son corps", *BVC* 20 (1957) 59-64.

DE GOEDT, M., "Un schème de révélation dans le quatrième évangile", *NTS* 8 (1962) 142-150.

DE JONGE, M., "Nicodemus and Jesus: Some Observations on Misunderstanding and Understanding in the Fourth Gospel", *BJRL* 53 (1971) 337-59.

DE LA POTTERIE, I., *La vérité dans saint Jean. Tome I: Le Christ et la vérité. L'Esprit et la vérité*; Tome II: *Le croyant et la vérité* (An Bib 73-74), Rome, 1977.

———, "'Je suis la voie, la vérité et la vie' (Jn 14,6)", *NRT* 88 (1966) 907-942.

———, "L'emploi dynamique de 'εἰς' dans saint Jean et ses incidences théologiques", *Bib* 43 (1962) 366-87.

———, "Οἶδα et γινώσκω. Les deux modes de la connaissance dans le quatrième évangile", *Bib* 40 (1959) 709-25.

———, "L'exaltation du Fils de l'homme (Jn 12, 31-36)", *Greg* 49 (1968) 460-78.

DE LA POTTERIE, I.-LYONNET, S., "*La Vie selon l'Esprit. Condition du chrétien*
(Unam sanctam 55), Paris, 1965. ET: *The Christian Lives by Faith*, New
York, 1970.

DE VAUX, R., *Les Institutions de l'Ancien Testament*, 2 vol., Paris, 1958-1960. ET:
Ancient Israel. Its Life and Institutions (translated by John McHugh), New
York.

———, "Le Lieu que Yahvé a choisi pour y établir son nom", in *Das Ferne und
Nahe Wort* (Festschrift L. Rost) (Beihefte zur ZAW 105), Berlin, 1967,
219-28.

———, "God's Presence and Absence in History: the Old Testament View",
Conc 10 (n. 5) (1969), 5-11.

DODD, C. H., *Historical Tradition in the Fourth Gospel*, Cambridge, 1963.

———, *The Interpretation of the Fourth Gospel*, Cambridge, 1960.

———, "A l'arrière-plan d'un discours johannique", *RHPR* 37 (1937) 5-17.

DUBARLE, A. M., "Le signe du temple", *RB* 48 (1939) 21-44.

DUPONT, J., *Essais sur la christologie de saint Jean*, Bruges, 1951.

DURAND, A., "Le discours de la cène (Saint Jean xiii,31-xvii,26)", *RecSR 1
(1910) 97-131. 513-39; also, RecSR* 2 (1911) 321-49. 521-45.

EDWARDS, R. A., *The Gospel according to St. John — its Criticism and
Interpretation*, London, 1954.

ENSLIN, M. S., "The Perfect Tense in the Fourth Gospel", *JBL* 55 (1936) 121-31.

ENZ, J., "The Book of Exodus as a Literary Type for the Gospel of John", *JBL*
76 (1957) 208-15.

FERRARO, J., *L'Ora di Cristo nel Quarto Vangelo. Analisi di Strutture Letterarie*
(Excerpta ex dissertatione ad Lauream in Facultate Theologica Pontificiae
Universitatis Gregorianae), Roma, 1970.

FEUILLET, A., "Le discours de Jésus sur la ruine du temple", *RB* 56 (1949)
61-92.

———, "Le Fils de l'Homme de Daniel et la tradition biblique (Le Fils de
l'Homme et la littérature de sagesse)", *RB* 60 (1953) 170-202. 321-46.

———, *Études Johanniques* (Museum Lessianum, Section Biblique 4), Bruges,
1962. ET: *Johannine Studies* (Translated by T. E. Crane), New York, 1964.

———, "Quatre 'Signes' johanniques de l'unité chrétienne", *NTS* 9 (1963) 147-153.

FISCHER, G., *Die himmlischen Wohnungen. Untersuchungen zu Joh. 14,2f.*
(Europäische Hochschulschriften, 23), Frankfurt-M.-Bern, 1975.

FORESTELL, J. T., *The Word of the Cross* (AnBib 57), Rome, 1974.

FORTNA, R., *The Gospel of Signs*, Cambridge, 1970.

FRAEYMAN, M., "La spiritualisation de l'idée du temple dans les épîtres
pauliniennes", *ETL* 23 (1947) 378-412.

FREED, E. D., "The Entry into Jerusalem in the Gospel of John", *JBL* 80 (1961)
329-38.

———, "The Son of Man in the Fourth Gospel", *JBL* 86 (1967) 402-09.

FRITSCH, I., " '..... videbitis ..... angelos ascendentes et descendentes .....' (Jo. I,
51)", *VD* 37 (1959) 1-11.

GÄCHTER, P., Der formale Aufbau der Abschiedsreden Jesu", *ZKT* 58 (1934)
155-207.

GÄRTNER, B., *The Temple and the Community in Qumran and the New Testament*,
Cambridge, 1965.

GELIN, A., "La prière du pèlerin du temple (Psaume 84)", *BVC* 9-12 (1955-1956) 88-92.

GELSTON, A., "A Note on II Samuel 7,10", *ZAW* 84 (1972) 92-94.

GEORGE, A., "'L'heure' de Jean XVII", *RB* 61 (1954) 392-97.

GIBLET, J., "Tu verras le ciel ouvert (Jean 1,51)", *BVC* 36 (1960) 26-30.

———, "Sanctifie-les dans la vérité (Jean 17,1-26)", *BVC* 19 (1957) 58-73.

GLASSON, T. F., *Moses in the Fourth Gospel* (Studies in Biblical Theology, 40), London, 1963.

GRELOT, P., *De la mort à la vie éternelle* (Lectio divina 67), Paris, 1971.

———, "Aujourd'hui tu seras avec moi dans le paradis" (Luc xxiii,43)", *RB* 74 (1967) 194-214.

———, "La légende d'Hénoch dans les apocryphes et dans la bible. Origine et signification", *RecSR* 46 (1958) 5-26. 181-210.

GROSSOUW, W., "La glorification du Christ dans le quatrième évangile", in *L'Évangile de Jean* (Études et problèmes) (RechBib III), Louvain, 1958, 133-145.

———, "A Note on John 13,1-3", *NovT* 8 (1966) 124-131.

GUILDING, A., *The Fourth Gospel and Jewish Worship. A Study of the Relation of St. John's Gospel to the Ancient Jewish Lectionary System,* Oxford, 1960.

GUNDRY, R. H., "'In my Father's House are many Μοναί' (John 14:2)", *ZNW* 58 (1967) 68-72.

HEISE, J., *Bleiben. Menein in den johanneischen Schriften* (Hermeneutische Untersuchungen zur Theologie), Tübingen, 1967.

HUMPHRIES, A. L., "A Note on πρὸς ἐμαυτόν (John XIV,3) and εἰς τὰ ἴδια (John I,11)", *ExpT* 53 (1941) 356.

JOÜON, P., "Les mots employés pour désigner 'Le Temple' dans l'Ancien Testament, le Nouveau Testament et Josèphe", *RecSR* 25 (1935) 329-43.

JUEL, D., *Messiah and Temple* (SBL Dissertation Series 31), Missoula, 1977.

KEET, C. L., *A Study of the Psalms of Ascents. A Critical and Exegetical Commentary upon Psalms CXX-CXXXIV,* London, 1969.

KLINZING, G., *Die Umdeutung des Kultus in der Qumrangemeinde und im Neuen Testament,* Göttingen, 1971.

KUNDSIN, K., "Die Wiederkunft Jesu in der Abschiedsreden des Johannesevangeliums", *ZNW* 33 (1934) 210-15.

KYSAR, R., *The Fourth Evangelist and His Gospel. An Examination of Contemporary Scholarship,* Minnesota, 1975.

LACAN, M.-F., "Le prologue de saint Jean. Ses thèmes, sa structure, son mouvements", *LumV* 33 (1957) 91-110.

LAURENTIN, R., "W^e' attah-kaí nun. Formule caractéristique des textes juridiques et liturgiques (à propos de Jean, 17,5)", *Bib* 45 (1964) 168-195. 413-32.

———, *Jésus au temple. Mystère de Pâques et foi de Marie en Lc. 2,48-50* (Études bibliques), Paris, 1966.

LE DÉAUT, R., "Targumic Literature and New Testament Interpretation", *BTB* 4 (1974) 243-89.

———, La Nuit Paschale (AnBib 22), Rome, 1963.

LE DÉAUT, R. - ROBERT, J., *Targum des Chroniques (Cod. Vat. Urb. Ebr. I),* 2 vol. (AnBib 51), Rome, 1971.

LÉGASSE, S., "Le retour du Christ d'après l'évangile de Jean, chapitre 14 et 16: une adaptation du motif de la Parousie", *BLE 81 (1980) 161-174*.

LENTZEN-DEIS, F., "Das Motiv der 'Himmelsöffnung' in verschiedenen Gattungen der Umweltliteratur des NT", Bib 50 (1968) 315-27.

LÉON, D. M., *Dios-Palabra*, Roma, 1967.

LÉON-DUFOUR, X., "Trois chiasmes johanniques", NTS 7 (1961) 249-55.

———, "Le signe du temple selon saint Jean", RecSR 39 (1951-1952) 155-175.

LEROY, H., "Das johanneische Missverständnis als literarische Form", BuL 9 (1968) 196-207.

———, *Rätsel und Missverständnis. Ein Beitrag zur Formgeschichte des Johannesevangeliums* (BBB 30), Bonn, 1968.

LIEBREICH, L.J., "The Songs of Ascents and the Priestly Blessing", JBL 74 (1955) 33-36.

LINDESKOG, G., "The Veil of the Temple", ConiNT 11 (1949) 132-37.

LOEWE, R., "Apologetic Motifs in the Targum to the Song of Songs", in *Studies and Texts, vol. III: Biblical Motifs — Origins and Transformations*, Cambridge-Massachusetts, 1966.

LOHFINK, G., *Die Himmelfahrt Jesu. Untersuchungen zu den Himmelfahrts-und Erhöhungstexten bei Lukas*, München, 1971.

MALATESTA, E., "The Literary Structure of John 17", *Bib 52 (1971) 190-214*.

MANNS, F., *La vérité vous fera libres. Étude exégétique de Jean 8, 31-59*, Jérusalem, 1976.

MARTIN, F., *Le livre d'Hénoch*, Paris, 1906.

MARTYN, J.L., *History and Theology in the Fourth Gospel*, New York, 1968.

McKELVEY, R.J., *The New Temple. The Church in the New Testament*, Oxford, 1969.

McNAMARA, M., *The New Testament and the Palestine Targum to the Pentateuch* (AnBib 27a), Rome, 1978.

———, "To Prepare a Resting Place for you". A Targumic Expression and John 14,2f.", MillSt 3 (1979) 100-108.

McPOLIN, J., *The "Name" of the Father and of the Son in the Johannine Writings* (Excerpt from a Doctrinal Dissertation presented in the Pontifical Biblical Institute), Rome, 1972.

———, "Studies in the Fourth Gospel — Some Contemporary Trends", IBS 2 (1980) 3-26.

MEAGHER, J.C., "John 1,14 and the New Temple", JBL 88 (1969) 57-68.

MEEKS, W.A., *The Prophet-King. Moses Traditions and the Johannine Christology* (NovTSup 14), Leiden, 1967.

———, "The Man from Heaven in Johannine Sectarianism", JBL 91 (1972) 44-72.

MICHAELIS, W., "Joh 1,51, Gen 28,12 und das Menschensohn-Problem", TLZ 85 (1960) 561-78.

MILGROM, J., "The Temple Scroll", BA 41 (n. 3) (1978) 105-120.

MILIK, J.T.-BLACK, M. (ed), *The Books of Enoch. Aramaic Fragments of Qumran Cave 4*, Oxford, 1976.

MOLLAT, D., "Gloire", VTB col. 412-419.

———, "Le sèmeion johannique", SacrPag II, 209-218.

———, "Ils regarderont celui qu'ils ont transpercé. La conversion chez saint Jean", LumV 47 (1960) 95-114.

MOLLAT, D., "Remarques sur le vocabulaire spatial du quatrième évangile", *StudEvang* I (TU 73) 322-28.

———, "L'apparition du Ressuscité et le don de l'Esprit: Jn. 20,19-23", *AssSeign* 30, 42-56.

MOLONEY, F. J., *The Johannine Son of Man* (Biblioteca di Scienze Religiose 14), Rome, 1976.

———, "The Johannine Son of Man", *Sal* 38 (1976) 71-86.

MOWINCKEL, S., *He That Cometh* (Translated by G. W. Anderson), Oxford, 1956.

MUNCK, J., "Discours d'adieu dans le nouveau testament et dans la littérature biblique" in *Aux Sources de la Tradition Chrétienne* (Mélanges M. Goguel), Neuchâtel, 1950, 155-70.

NICACCI, A., "L'unità letteraria di Gv. 13,1-38", *Euntes Docete* (Commentaria Urbaniana), 29 (n. 2) (1976) 291-323.

NICKELSBURG, G. W. E., *Resurrection, Immortality, and Eternal Life in Intertestamental Judaism* (Oxford University Press), Oxford, 1972.

ORBE, A., "Las Tres Moradas de la Casa Paterna de S. Ireneo a Gregorio de Elvira", in *Miscellanea J. A. de Aldama*, Granada, 1969, 69-92.

PANCARO, S., "'People of God' in St. John's Gospel", *NTS* 16 (1970) 114-129.

PANIMOLLE, S. A., *Il dono della legge e la grazia della verità*, Roma, 1973.

PASQUETTO, V., "*Incarnazione e Comunione con Dio*". *La venuta di Gesù nel mondo e il suo ritorno al luogo d'origine secondo il IV vangelo*, (Studia Theologica - Teresianum, 2), Roma, 1982.

PECORARA, G., "De verbo 'manere' apud Joannem", *DivThom* 40 (1937) 159-71.

PHILLIPS, G. L., "Faith and Vision in the Fourth Gospel", in *Studies in the Fourth Gospel*, London, 1957, 83-96.

PORTER, J., "The Interpretation of 2 Sam. VI and Psalm CXXXII", *JTS (1954) 161-173*.

PORSCH, F., *Pneuma und Wort. Ein exegetischer Beitrag zur Pneumatologie des Johannesevangeliums*, Frankfurt am Main, 1974.

RADERMAKERS, J., "Mission et apostolat dans l'évangile johannique", *StudEvang* II (TU 89), 100-121.

RAHNER, H., "Flumina de ventre Christi. Die patristische Auslegung von Joh. 7,37-38", *Bib* 22 (1941) 269-302, 367-403.

RAMSEY, A. M., *The Glory of God and the Transfiguration of Christ*, London, 1949.

RANDALL, J. F., "The Theme of Unity in John, 17,21-23", *ETL* 41 (1965) 373-94.

RASCO, E., "Christus granum frumenti (Jo 12,24)", *VD* 37 (1959) 12-25, 65-77.

REESE, J. M., "Literary Structure of Jn. 13,31-14,31; 16,5-6,16-33", *CBQ* 34 (1972) 321-331.

ROTH, C., "The Cleansing of the People and Zechariah, 14,21", *NovT* 4 (1960) 174-81.

RUCKSTUHL, E., *Die literarische Einheit des Johannesevangeliums*, Freiburg, 1951.

RUSSELL, D. S., *The Method and Message of Jewish Apocalyptic*, London, 1964.

SCHAEFER, O., "Der Sinn der Rede Jesu von den vielen Wohnungen in seines Vaters Hause und von dem Weg zu ihm (Joh. 14,1-2)", *ZNW* 32 (1933) 210-17.

SCHMIDT, M., *Prophet und Tempel*, Zürich, 1948.

SCHNACKENBURG, R., "Das Anliegen der Abschiedsreden in Joh. 14", in *Wort Gottes in der Zeit* (Festschrift für K. H. Schelke), Düsseldorf, 1973, 95-110.

SCHNEIDER, J., "Die Abschiedsreden Jesu. Ein Beitrag zur Frage der Komposition von Joh 13,31-17,26", in *Gott und die Götter* (Festgabe E. Fascher zum 60 Geburtstag), Berlin, 1958, 103-112.

SCHWARTZ, E., "Aporien im vierten Evangelium", in *Nachrichten von der königlichen Gesellschaft der Wissenschaften zu Göttingen*, 1907, 342-372; 1908, 115-188. 497-560.

SERRA, A. M., *Contributi dell'antica letteratura giudaica per l'esegesi di Giovanni. 2,1-12 e 19,27-29*, Roma, 1977.

SIDEBOTTOM, E. M., *The Christ of the Fourth Gospel in the Light of the First Century Thought*, London, 1961.

——, "The Ascent and Descent of the Son of Man in the Gospel of St. John", *ATR* 2 (1957) 115-22.

SIMOENS, Y., *La gloire d'aimer. Structures stylistiques et interprétatives dans le discours de la cène (Jn 13-17)* (AnBib 90), Rome, 1981.

SIMON, M., "Retour du Christ et reconstruction du temple dans la pensée chrétienne primitive", in *Aux Sources de la Tradition Chrétienne* (Goguel Festschrift), Paris, 1950, 247-57.

SIMONIS, A. J., *Die Hirtenrede im Johannes-Evangelium. Versuch einer Analyse von Johannes 10,1-18 nach Entstehung, Hintergrund und Inhalt* (AnBib 29), Roma, 1967.

SMITH, R. H., "Exodus Typology in the Fourth Gospel", *JBL* 81 (1962) 329-42.

SOFFER, A., "The House of God/Lord in the Septuagint of the Pentateuch", *JBL* 75 (1956) 144-45.

SPICQ, C., *Agapè dans le Nouveau Testament*, 3 vol., Paris, 1958.

——, "L'origine johannique de la conception du Christ-prêtre dans l'Épître aux Hébreux", in *Aux Sources de la Tradition Chrétienne*, (Mélanges offert a M. Maurice Goguel), Paris, 1950.

STAGG, F., "The Farewell Discourse: John 13-17", *Review and Expositor* 62 (1965) 459-72.

STAUFFER, E., "Valedictions and Farewell Speeches", in *New Testament Theology*, New York, 1955.

STÄHLIN, G., "Zum Problem der johanneischen Eschatologie", *ZNW* 33 (1934) 225-59.

TALBERT, C. H., "Artistry and Theology: An Analysis of the Architecture of Jn. 1,19-5,47", *CBQ* (1970) 341-66.

——, "The Myth of a Descending-Ascending Redeemer in Mediterranean Antiquity", *NTS* 22 (1976) 418-40.

THACKERAY, St.-J. - MARCUS, R., (eds), *Josephus* (with an English translation by St.-J. Thackeray and R. Marcus), vol. II-IX Jewish Antiquities (Loeb edition), London, 1926-65.

THÜSING, W., *Die Erhöhung und Verherrlichung Jesu im Johannesevangelium* (Neutestamentliche Abhandlungen, XXI/1-2), Münster, [2]1970.

——, *Herrlichkeit und Einheit: Eine Auslegung des hohepriesterlichen Gebets Jesu (Johannes 17)*, Düsseldorf, 1962.

TRAETS, C., *Voir Jésus et le Père en lui selon l'évangile de saint Jean*, Rome, 1967.

TUÑI-VANCELLS, J. O., *La verdad os hará libres, Jn. 8,32. Liberación y libertad del creyente en el cuarto evangelio*, Barcelona, 1973.

VAN DEN BUSSCHE, H., "Le signe du temple", *BVC* 20 (1957) 92-100.

——, "L'attente de la grande révélation dans le quatrième évangile", *NRT* 75 (1953) 1009-19.

——, *Le discours d'adieux de Jésus*, Tournai, 1959.

VANHOYE, A., "La chiesa locale nel nuovo testamento" in *La Chiesa Locale* (Biblioteca Scienze Religiose 16), Rome, 1976, 15-27.

——, "Longue marche ou accès tout proche? Le contexte biblique de Hébreux 3,7-4,11", *Bib* 49 (1968) 9-26.

——, "La chiesa come casa spirituale, secondo la prima lettera di S. Pietro", in *Bollettino della Diocesi di Verona*, 1975, 903-920.

——, "Par la tente plus grande et plus parfaite..... He 9,11", *Bib* 46 (1965) 1-27.

——, "L'œuvre du Christ, don du Père (Jn. 5,36 et 17,4), *RecSR* 48 (1960) 377-419 (for a resume of this article, cf. "Opera Jesu Donum Patris", *VD* 36 (1958) 83-92).

VERGOTE, A., "L'exaltation du Christ en croix selon le quatrième évangile", *ETL* 28 (1952) 5-23.

VOLZ, P., *Die Eschatologie der jüdischen Gemeinde im neutestamentlichen Zeitalter. Nach den Quellen der rabbinischen, apokalyptischen und apokryphen Literatur*, Tübingen, 1934.

WEAD, D. W., *The Literary Devices in John's Gospel*, Basel, 1970.

——, "The Johannine Double Meaning", *Restoration Quarterly* 13 (1970) 106-20.

WIDENGREN, G., "En la maison de mon Père sont demeures nombreuses", *Svensk Exegetisk Årsbok*, 37-38 (1972-73), 9-15.

WOLL, D. B., "The Departure of 'The Way': the First Farewell Discourse in the Gospel of John", *JBL* 99 (1980) 225-239.

INDEX OF SCRIPTURE REFERENCES

A. OLD TESTAMENT

B. NEW TESTAMENT

INDEX OF AUTHORS

TIPOGRAFIA POLIGLOTTA DELLA PONTIFICIA UNIVERSITÀ GREGORIANA
PIAZZA DELLA PILOTTA, 4 - ROMA